S0-EIH-379

Library of
Davidson College

THE
HIDDEN
HUMAN
IMAGE

THE HIDDEN HUMAN IMAGE

MAURICE FRIEDMAN

DELACORTE PRESS/NEW YORK

Copyright © 1974 by Maurice Friedman
All rights reserved.
No part of this book may be reproduced
in any form or by any means
without the prior written permission of the Publisher,
excepting brief quotes used in
connection with reviews written specifically
for inclusion in a magazine or newspaper.
Manufactured in the United States of America
First printing

Library of Congress Cataloging in Publication Data

Friedman, Maurice
The hidden human image.

Includes bibliographical references.
1. Man.   2. Civilization, Modern.   I. Title.
BD450.F74   128   74-10660
ISBN 0-440-03509-0

75-1011

*Acknowledgment is made to the following in whose pages
parts of this book first appeared.*

"The Changing Image of Human Nature: The Philosophical Aspect" in
The American Journal of Psychoanalysis, Vol. XXVI, No. 2 (1966);
"The Meeting of Religion and Literature" in *Main Currents in Modern
Thoughts*, Vol. XXVIII, No. 2 (November–December 1971); "Anxiety
in Our Culture" in *Humanitas*, Vol. 1, No. 1 (Spring 1965) pp. 35–47;
"Death and the Dialogue with the Absurd" in THE PHENOMENON
OF DEATH: FACES OF MORTALITY edited by Edith Wyschogrod,
Harper & Row, Publishers (1973); "The Crisis of Values and the
Image of Man" in *Humanitas*, Vol. IV, No. 3 (Winter 1969) pp. 261–
279; "The Transmoral Morality" in *Journal for the Scientific Study of
Religion*, Vol. 3, No. 2 (Spring 1964) pp. 174–180; "The Value of
Education and the Image of Man" in *Teachers College Record* (Novem-
ber 1968); "The Ivory Tower and the World: Our Contemporary
Image of Man" in *Liberation* (May 1962) 339 Lafayette Street, New
York, N.Y. 10012, $10 per year; "The Power of Violence and the
Power of Non-Violence" in GANDHI, INDIA AND THE WORLD
edited by Sibnarayan Ray, Hawthorne Press, Melbourne (1970);
"Martin Luther King: An American Gandhi and a Modern Job" in
NONVIOLENCE edited by G. Estey and Doris Hunter, Ginn and
Co. (1971).

*Grateful acknowledgment is made for permission
to reprint the following material.*

Passage #21 from THE WAY OF LIFE ACCORDING TO LAO-
TZU: Copyright © 1944 by Witter Bynner. Reprinted from THE
WAY OF LIFE ACCORDING TO LAO-TZU translated by Witter
Bynner by permission of The John Day Company, Inc., an Intext
publisher.

Lines from "Gerontion" and "The Waste Land" by T. S. Eliot: From
COLLECTED POEMS 1909–1962 published by Harcourt Brace
Jovanovich, Inc. and Faber and Faber Ltd.

Excerpt from I'VE BEEN TO THE MOUNTAIN TOP by Martin
Luther King, Jr. Reprinted by permission of Joan Daves. Copyright ©
1968 by the Estate of Dr. Martin Luther King, Jr.

"The Climate of War" by Kenneth Patchen: From Kenneth Patchen,
COLLECTED POEMS. Copyright 1942 by Kenneth Patchen. Reprinted by permission of New Directions Publishing Corporation.

"In A Dark Time" by Theodore Roethke: Copyright © 1960 by Beatrice
Roethke as Administratrix of the Estate of Theodore Roethke from
THE COLLECTED POEMS OF THEODORE ROETHKE. Reprinted
by permission of Doubleday & Company, Inc.

Lines from "Do not go gentle into that good night" and "Poem on His
Birthday" by Dylan Thomas: From Dylan Thomas, THE POEMS.
Copyright 1952 by Dylan Thomas. Reprinted by permission of New
Directions Publishing Corporation, J. M. Dent & Sons Ltd., and the
Trustees for the Copyrights of the late Dylan Thomas.

128
F911ん

ACKNOWLEDGMENTS

I wish to acknowledge the invaluable assistance of my typist Myrtle Keeny, of my friends Jen Good and Demaris Wehr who transcribed several tapes of my lectures, making them available to me as raw material, of David Hartsough who helped me find books and speeches by Martin Luther King, of my wife Eugenia and my friends Elie Wiesel, Jack Gibb, Ann Dreyfuss, Virginia Sattler, Frank Termini, Demaris Wehr, Betty Meador, and Miriam Carroll who read all or part of the manuscript and made helpful suggestions and criticisms, and above all, of my editor and friend Richard Huett who has gone far beyond any other editor of mine in vigorous and detailed critiques that have challenged me to bring many inchoate passages and sections into more meaningful and readable form. In his person and in his writings, Elie Wiesel has inspired much of this book, which I hope is worthy of him.

—Maurice Friedman
Del Mar, California
February, 1974

TO THE MEMORY OF MY FRIEND

ABRAHAM JOSHUA HESCHEL
(1905–1972)

The nineteenth century was the century of the death of God, the twentieth is that of the death of man.
—Erich Fromm

Today it is the humanity of man that is no longer self-evident. . . . Massive defamation of man may spell the doom of all of us. . . . The eclipse of humanity . . . is itself a dreadful punishment.
—Abraham J. Heschel, *Who Is Man?*

If the human race should perish by the nuclear bomb, this will be the punishment for Auschwitz, where, in the ashes, the hope of man was extinguished. . . . At Auschwitz, not only man died, but also the idea of man.
—Elie Wiesel, *One Generation After*

CONTENTS

PART

THE
"DEATH OF GOD"
AND THE
ECLIPSE OF
THE HUMAN

THE
HIDDEN HUMAN
IMAGE

One evening several of Rabbi Hayyim of Kosov's hasidim sat together in his House of Study and told one another stories about zaddikim, above all about the Baal Shem Tov. And because the telling and the listening were very sweet to them, they were at it even after midnight. Then one of them told still another story about the Baal Shem Tov. When he had ended, another sighed from the bottom of his heart. "Alas!" said he, half to himself. "Where could we find such a man today?"

At that instant, they heard steps coming down the wooden stair which led from the zaddik's room. The door opened and Rabbi Hayyim appeared on the threshold, in the short jacket he usually wore in the evening. "Fool," he said softly, "he is present in every generation, he, the Baal Shem Tov, only that in those days he was manifest while now he is hidden." He closed the door and went back up the stair. The hasidim sat together in silence.*

The question of the disciple was not, "Where could we find another founder of Hasidism today," but "Where could we find such a *man* today?" The answer of Rabbi Hayyim, similarly, was not the comforting knowledge of Isaiah's Immanuel, that God is with us, but that in every age "such a man" exists. In the eighteenth century this man was manifest in the Baal Shem Tov†

* Martin Buber, *Tales of the Hasidim: The Later Masters*, trans. by Olga Marx (New York: Schocken Books, 1961), "In Every Generation," p. 99.
† The Baal Shem Tov, literally the "Good Master of the Name of God," is the

while today he is hidden. Rabbi Hayyim goes further and says that the Baal Shem Tov himself is present in every age. The historical Baal Shem Tov thus becomes the image of the hidden, the imageless Baal Shem Tov of today. We cannot say that the historical Baal Shem, or the historical Christ, or the historical Buddha, *is* the image of man for today. Rather each of these manifest images points us to the unmanifest, hidden, imageless yet present, authentic man of today.

The human image, as I use the term, is not only an image of what man *is*, but also an image of authentic personal existence that helps him discover, in each age anew, what he may and can become, an image that helps him rediscover his humanity. "Image" in this context means not a static picture but a meaningful, personal direction, a response from within to what one meets in each new situation, standing one's ground and meeting the world with the attitude that is rooted in this ground. The human image embodies a way of responding. When one Hasidic rabbi asked the disciple of another, "What was most important to your teacher?" the disciple characterized his late master not by any particular interest or concern but by his wholehearted manner of response. "Most important to Rabbi Moshe," he said after reflection, "was whatever he happened to be doing at the moment." Because it is faithful response and not objective content that is central to the human image, each individual stands in a unique personal relation to his image of man even when it happens to be shared by a society as a whole—not some universal or archetypal Saint Francis, but the Saint Francis who emerges from his own meeting with this historical and legendary figure. One becomes oneself in dialogue with other selves and in response to one's image, one's images of man. Yet the more genuine the dialogue, the more unique the relationship and the more truly is the one who is becoming, becoming himself. The fruit of such response is not that bolstering of the ego that comes from comparing oneself

---

traditional name of Israel ben Eliezer (1700–1760), the founder of Hasidism—the popular communal mysticism of more than half of Eastern European Jewry during the eighteenth and nineteenth centuries.

favorably with another or modeling oneself on an ideal, but the
confirmation of one's unique personal existence, of the ground on
which one stands.

> Someone once told Rabbi Mendel that a certain person was
> greater than another whom he also mentioned by name. Rabbi
> Mendel replied: "If I am I because I am I, and you are you
> because you are you, then I am I, and you are you. But if I am I
> because you are you, and you are you because I am I, then I am
> not I, and you are not you."*

The human image does not mean some fully formed, conscious
model of what one should become—certainly not anything simply imposed on man by the culture, or any mere conformity with
society through identification with its goals. "When Rabbi Noah,
Rabbi Mordecai's son, assumed the succession after his father's
death, his disciples noticed that there were a number of ways in
which he conducted himself differently from his father, and
asked him about this. 'I do just as my father did,' he replied. 'He
did not imitate, and I do not imitate.'"† The paradox of the
image of man is that it is at once unique and universal, but
universal only through the unique. For each one of us, the human
image is made up of many images and half-formed images, and
it is itself constantly changing and evolving. In contrast to any
static ideal whatsoever, it always has to do only with the unique
response to the concrete moment, a response which cannot be
foreseen and cannot be repeated, objectified, or imitated.

> Rabbi Pinhas often cited the words: "A man's soul will teach
> him," and emphasized them by adding: "There is no man who is
> not incessantly being taught by his soul."
> One of his disciples asked: "If this is so, why don't men obey
> their souls?"
> "The soul teaches incessantly," Rabbi Pinhas explained, "but it
> never repeats."‡

---

* *Ibid.*, "Comparing One to Another," p. 283.
† *Ibid.*, "In His Father's Footsteps," p. 157.
‡ Martin Buber, *Tales of the Hasidim: The Early Masters*, trans. by Olga Marx
(New York: Schocken Books, 1961), "The Teaching of the Soul," p. 121.

The very concern with "self-expression," "creativity," and "originality" that characterizes our time bars the way to true creativity
because it mars the spontaneity and faithfulness of our response
to what calls us out.

> Rabbi Pinhas said: "When a man embarks on something great, in
> the spirit of truth, he need not be afraid that another may imitate
> him. But if he does not do it in the spirit of truth, but plans to do
> it in a way no one could imitate, then he drags the great down to
> the lowest level—and everyone can do the same."*

Every real confrontation with an image of man is of inestima-
ble value if we bring ourselves to it in sufficient seriousness and
depth. The value of our confrontations with particular images of
man can be greatly enhanced, moreover, by an understanding of
the *problematic* of the contemporary image of man, a problematic that I point to in the title of this book—*The Hidden Human
Image*. One may distinguish with some meaning between those
images of man that one makes one's own through ordinary life
encounters and those that are, in some sense, the product of a
search.

My own search for an image of man began, like that of most
thoughtful and conflicted young people, in my adolescence and
continued through high school and college, social consciousness
and intellectual concern, studies in labor economics, student activities, and the anguished decision, over a year and a half, to
become a conscientious objector in the Second World War. At
first this search was theoretical, idealistic, and eclectic. Later it
became more focused in concrete figures. One of my images of
man during my Harvard days was Lenin leaving *The State and
Revolution* unfinished because he was called to lead a revolution.
Later when I became a conscientious objector, it was Gandhi
with his practice of *satyagraha*. Then as I became a mystic, men
like Saint Francis, Ramakrishna, Jesus, the Buddha, and the Baal
Shem spoke to me. As my social action gave way to mysticism,

* *Ibid.*, "Originality," p. 135.

my admiration of the man of action was replaced by the ideal of the saint.*

My first piece of serious writing after three and a half years in camps and units for conscientious objectors was a master's thesis entitled "From Inquisitor to Saint: the Search for Faith in Ten Modern European Novels." Twenty years later I was still so deeply moved by one of the novels that I dealt with there— Bernanos' *Diary of a Country Priest*—that when I saw a movie of it I emerged in tears. Yet in that thesis I took Ivan from Dostoevsky's *The Brothers Karamazov* as an example of the divided man who uses any means to his end until, too late, he realizes his error, and his brother Alyosha, as one who starting from there, completes the journey to saintliness. Some years later the question struck me, What help is that to Ivan Karamazov? If they are really two different men, it does not do to make them into two stages of a single journey. Again I berated K., the hero of Franz Kafka's novel *The Castle*, because he did not follow the way of the Tao. But after some years I had to ask myself in all seriousness, Was there any possibility for him to do so? K. is a stranger to such an extent that he is not wanted, that he is in everybody's way, that he cannot obtain any immediate relationship to existence.

In time the exclusively mystical and the specifically saintly were replaced for me by the concern for the image of man in all its height, breadth, and depth. I could perhaps say of my own intellectual path what Martin Buber said of Hasidism when it transformed the mysteries of the Kabbala into the hallowing of the everyday: "Where the mystic vortex circled, now stretches the way of man."

My first explicit use of the "image of man" was in the course that I developed my second year at Sarah Lawrence College— "The Image of Man in Modern Literature." Although my bachelor's degree was in economics, my Master's in English, and my

* See Maurice Friedman, *Touchstones of Reality: Existential Trust and the Community of Peace* (New York: Dutton Paperbacks, 1974), Part I, "An Opening Way."

Ph.D. in the history of culture, I had come to Sarah Lawrence as a philosopher, with the admonition of a dean of a Midwestern university still ringing in my ears: "Integration is a bridge with no land on either side!" Sarah Lawrence, nonetheless, chose to hire me in both philosophy and literature and to place me accordingly in two different faculties—literature and social science. After four years I discovered that even at Sarah Lawrence it was not safe to be the only person in more than one faculty and that my colleagues in each faculty were busy putting both of my feet in the other faculty because I had only one in theirs. I therefore bade farewell to literature, forever, became 100 percent a member of the social sciences faculty (in which both philosophy and religion were included), and, after a one year's lapse, offered the identical course, now retitled, "The Image of Man in Modern Thought"! The then dean suggested to me that I would have to choose between "straight" courses and the mixed bags that I was offering. I really had no choice. "Integrative studies" have been my personal way, my philosophical growing point, my destiny.

It was not until 1963, eleven years after my original course in the "image of man," that I wrote the first of the two books that grew directly out of this concern—*Problematic Rebel: An Image of Modern Man.** *Problematic Rebel* is built upon the foundation of the alienation of modern man resulting from the absence of an image of man such as gave some direction to biblical, Greek, and Renaissance man. In its original form *Problematic Rebel* was an intensive study of Melville, Dostoevsky, and Kafka. Then an editor said to me, "Why don't you turn them inside out to bring out the issues?" I told him I would try, and, after a year, all sorts of significant connections emerged that I would not have dreamed of before but which were already implicit in the original. Types came into view such as the Modern Exile, two Types of Modern Rebel—the Modern Promethean and the Modern Job—and the Problematic of Modern Man. And in connection with the Modern Job it became necessary to bring Camus in as a supplement to Kafka. It was in this second form that I published the book.

* Maurice Friedman, *Problematic Rebel: An Image of Modern Man* (New York: Random House, 1963).

It was not until five years later, when I used *Problematic Rebel* in a graduate seminar on religion and literature, that I realized that I had to take a third step and restore the integrity of the literary interpretations by grouping together the material concerning each novelist while retaining the types of the second form as the subheads under which I treated each writer. These types were then brought together with still greater cogency in the "depth-image of modern man" at the end. Thus evolved the second, radically reorganized and somewhat expanded edition of *Problematic Rebel* with the new subtitle *Melville, Dostoievsky, Kafka, Camus.** My wrestling with the relation of form and content in these three versions of *Problematic Rebel* is paradigmatic, I believe, of the problem with which the true author in our day must be centrally concerned—how to help reveal the hidden human image *even while allowing it to retain its concealed depths*.

In 1967 the sequel to *Problematic Rebel* was published—*To Deny Our Nothingness: Contemporary Images of Man.†* This book is extensive rather than intensive, it deals with direction-giving images rather than describing at length those conditions that frustrate such a finding of direction; it considers a variety of "live options"; and it deals in almost equal measure with literature, philosophy, psychotherapy, and religious thought rather than predominantly with the interpretation of literature. Originally I intended to organize *To Deny Our Nothingness* according to the type of material it dealt with: the Image of Man in Contemporary Literature, the Image of Man in Contemporary Philosophy, etc. But here too a further integrative step became necessary—bringing not only different authors but also different kinds of material under a typology of contemporary images of man: the Modern Socialist, the Modern Vitalist, the Modern Mystic, the Modern "Saint," the Modern Gnostic, Psychological Man, the Modern Pragmatist, the Existentialist, and the Absurd Man.

* Maurice Friedman, *Problematic Rebel: Melville, Dostoievsky, Kafka, Camus,* 2nd ed. (Chicago: University of Chicago Press, Phoenix Books [paperback], 1970).
† Maurice Friedman, *To Deny Our Nothingness: Contemporary Images of Man* (New York: Delacorte Press, 1967; Delta Books [paperback], 1968).

"Through considering together both literary and nonliterary works," I suggest in *To Deny Our Nothingness*, "we can gain a deeper understanding of the image of man as the hidden ground in which literature, philosophy, psychotherapy, religion, and social thought all meet." The human image might well be called the matrix from which each of these fields emerges, which they continue to embody within them, and which continues to bind them together in essential ways no matter how stringently the disciplines pertaining to each particular field make it necessary to hold them apart. This ground or matrix must necessarily remain hidden. It can be pointed to through one or the other field or through the meeting between them, but it cannot be disclosed or made manifest since this would always mean translating one discipline or field into another and thereby destroying its integrity. We cannot translate literature into philosophy and thereby get the image of man; for literature and philosophy are *both* rooted in the image of man. Realizing this, we can at one and the same time take seriously the need for the human image to be revealed, the need for our remaining faithful to each of these various ways of knowing man in its own terms, and yet the need *not* to take seriously that ultimate overclaim that it alone contains all the important knowledge about its own field. For each field is simply a human and ultimately arbitrary marking off which shades into another field. These fields of knowledge are so many partial ways of trying to get a purchase on the multidimensional reality of the wholeness and concreteness of man.

The habit of thinking in terms of fields can lead to a strange distortion in which abstract categories are taken for reality itself —a Whiteheadian "fallacy of misplaced concreteness" if ever there was one. A former president of Swarthmore College once said to me, "I know this is a terrible question to ask a polymath, but is there anything in particular you really are interested in?" Instead of seeing me as someone centrally concerned about the problem and image of man and relating to a variety of materials in terms of this concern, he saw me as someone with bits of knowledge in several different fields but with no center!

The same qualification must be made concerning the typology of contemporary images of man developed in *To Deny Our Nothingness*. If it throws fresh light on the figures and works with which the book deals, it also represents a necessary bracketing of the more basic fact of the interrelation and overlapping of types. Many of these thinkers belong to more than one type. Each has a uniqueness that cannot be captured by any type. What is more, even where they may be criticized for insufficient concreteness or insufficient concern with direction, each type of image contributes an essential element to an adequate contemporary image of man.

> We cannot do without the awareness of the social dimension of reality of the Modern Socialist; the emphasis on creativity and life-energy of the Modern Vitalist; the search for presentness and timelessness of the Modern Mystic; the dedication to personal holiness of the Modern "Saint"; the Modern Gnostic's concern with overcoming the effects of the dehumanized social world through individuation and fulfillment of the self; the awareness of personal dynamics of the Psychological Man; the emphasis upon concrete, personal reality and authentic human existence of the Existentialist; and the unresolvable cacophonies of the Absurd Man that set limits to our search for authenticity yet do not preclude the immediate, day-by-day meaning that may be found in the Dialogue with the Absurd.*

In *The Hidden Human Image* I shall apply the conclusions of *The Worlds of Existentialism, Problematic Rebel*, and *To Deny Our Nothingness* to such fields as values, education, science, psychotherapy, religion and literature, and social change, and in so doing I shall point in ever new ways to the hidden ground in which these fields all meet. The hidden ground of the human image needs to be made manifest even while remaining hidden. The depth of the human, like the original meaning of person, or *persona*—the mask—finds its true meaning and wholeness in at once being revealed and concealed. Our basic attitudes may be totally masked; they can never be totally laid bare; but they *may*

* Friedman, *To Deny Our Nothingness*, p. 357.

express themselves without losing their depth—in our response to
the situations that evoke us, in our dialogue with each other. "To
be aware of a man," writes Martin Buber in *The Knowledge of
Man*, "means to perceive the dynamic centre which stamps his
every utterance, action, and attitude with the recognizable sign
of uniqueness."* When Rabbi Menahem Mendel of Vorki was
asked what constitutes a true Jew, he said: "Three things are
fitting for us: upright kneeling, silent screaming, motionless
dance." No one who has seen the movie *The Pawnbroker* can
forget the sight and sound of silent screaming.

A good example of the hidden human image is the myth. The
nature of every myth is that it at once hides and reveals, just as a
face hides and reveals. Once a myth is so fully delineated that it
no longer has hidden depth, it is not a myth. The term *mythmongering* that I coined in *To Deny Our Nothingness* means the
tendency of modern man to substitute a rich sense of secondary
meaning for that direct primary meaning which was accessible to
the people who had the myths themselves. A myth which could
be adopted or constructed because we need it would be one of
the lowest types of mythmongering. We need myths, but we
need real myths that arise from real situations. You cannot fabri-
cate a myth. That is why when I speak of the "Modern Job," for
example, I am carrying over the trust *and* the contending which
is at the heart of the biblical Job but not the biblical faith which,
in the direct and overpowering form in which biblical man again
and again knew it, is not a "live option" for modern man. Even
so, I am only *pointing* to the *Modern* Job. It cannot be delineated.

The need to lead forth the figure of the human hidden in the
granite block to the full freedom of Michelangelo's "David" or
the partially articulated figuration of "The Prisoners" does *not*
mean that we should aim at acquiring an image of man. The
image of man can never be a conscious end nor can it be a means
to an end. It enters into our deepest attitudes and emerges in our

* Martin Buber, *The Knowledge of Man*, ed., with an Introductory Essay,
by Maurice Friedman (New York: Harper Torchbooks, 1966), p. 80.

responses to new persons and new situations. Our care and our love are not for Being but for beings, not for the image of man but for men and women, for the creatures with whom we live and in relationship to whom we find such genuine humanity and such personal uniqueness as is open to us.

Religion, culture, and the community are three major and interrelated forms of the unconcealment of the hidden human image, the disclosure of man in men. But so are the lives of exemplary persons, such as Socrates and Martin Luther King, Jr., who show us in their lives and in their deaths what man can be, what *we* are called to become. What cannot be revealed in words taken by themselves can be made manifest in three-dimensional, embodied reality—in the unique responses of authentic men to their situations, of Abraham Lincoln to the Civil War, of the successor of the Baal Shem Tov to even the most everyday of tasks:

> Rabbi Leib, son of Sarah, the hidden zaddik who wandered over the earth, following the course of rivers, in order to redeem the souls of the living and the dead, said this: "I did not go to the maggid in order to hear Torah from him, but to see how he unlaces his felt shoes and laces them up again."*

The "hidden zaddik" guards "the hidden human image"; the Torah should not be "expounded" but at once concealed and revealed through the actions *and* the words of the true man:

> What does it amount to—that they expound the Torah! A man should see to it that all his actions are a Torah and that he himself becomes so entirely a Torah that one can learn from his habits and his motions and his motionless clinging to God, that he has become like Heaven itself, of which it is said: "There is no speech, there are no words, neither is there voice heard. Their line is gone out through all the earth, and their words to the end of the world."†

* Buber, *Tales of the Hasidim: The Early Masters*, p. 107.
† *Ibid.*, p. 169.

The injunction "not to say Torah but to be Torah" in no way
implies that depreciation of thought and words in favor of "feeling" that is so common today. After a disciple of the Holy Yehudi's had taken upon himself the discipline of silence and for
three years had spoken no words save those of the Torah and of
prayer, the Yehudi sent for him and said, "Young man, how is it
that I do not see a single word of yours in the world of truth?"
When the young man justified himself by speaking of "the vanity
of speech," the Yehudi replied: " 'He who only learns and prays
is murdering the word of his own soul. . . . Whatever you have to
say can be vanity or it can be truth. . . . Come to me after the
Evening Prayer and I shall teach you how to talk.' "* "Real
words are not vain, vain words are not real," said Lao-tzu in the
same spirit. Once a Hasid came to a zaddik with so long a list of
sins that he sent him to a younger rabbi who would have the
strength to handle them. The awesome penance that the latter
imposed upon the sinner was never again to say a single word of
prayer without full inner intention!

"The nineteenth century was the century of the death of God,"
Erich Fromm once remarked, "the twentieth that of the death of
man." In our day it is man himself who has become questionable
and problematic. " 'History,' said Emerson, 'is but the lengthened
shadow of a man,' who had not seen the silhouette of Sweeney
straddled against the sun." Even the murder of Sweeney is not
tragic: The singing of the nightingales "near the Convent of the
Sacred Heart" in South Boston carries with it no essentially
human meaning born of suffering and reconciliation as it did
when they "sang within the bloody wood/where Agamemnon
cried aloud/and let their liquid siftings fall/to stain his stiff
dishonoured shroud." (T. S. Eliot) This is the third, truly terrible
sense in which we must speak in our day of the "hidden human
image." Auschwitz, Hiroshima, Vietnam, the assassination of
Gandhi, of John F. Kennedy, of Martin Luther King—these have
meant in our age the destruction of existential trust and with it of

* Buber, *Tales of the Hasidim: The Later Masters*, "Silence and Speech," p.
228.

the human image. "Man is created in God's image," says the Talmud, "and every time you injure a man you injure the image of God." In our day as never before in human history, the human image has been injured to the point of eclipse, of obliteration, of possible total destruction.

In the eighteenth century Thomas Jefferson could confidently declare: "We hold these truths to be self-evident, that all men are created equal." Today it is not self-evident to anyone that all men are created equal because the *inequality* of men has been made a fact of history, and the existence of that fact makes it all too probable that other such "facts" will occur. It is in the teeth of that, if at all, that we must affirm the equality of men—in the teeth of the monstrous consequence with which the Nazis declared some races inferior to others, exterminating six million Jews and a million Gypsies, in the teeth of the atomic bomb being dropped by the United States not on Germany but on Japan, in the teeth of men's readiness to turn some human beings into cakes of soap and condemn others to a horrible, fast or slow, death by radiation.

A few years ago I conducted a weekend seminar at the lovely ranch home of a doctor and his wife in California. From there I went to lecture at a nearby state university and in the evening to a party at the home of the university extension professor who had arranged both the seminar and the lecture. At the party we were asked to divide into pairs and each of us to find out from his partner—and later tell the group—what he felt it meant to be alive. I made no serious effort to enter into the game, but the next morning when my host came to wake me up I looked up at him and said, "To be alive is to be in California!" Within a year from then three dear friends of mine living in California—three of the most remarkable people I have ever known—committed suicide. One of these was the hostess of that seminar weekend—a brilliant, talented, and beautiful woman with depths of feeling and sensitivity, a large and happy family, and the most well-ordered life of anyone I have met. Her husband sent word that he would like me to help him understand her suicide. I could not.

To me too it is only a terrible question that remains and will not admit of an answer.

I do know this: Suicide, like murder, is not just the destruction of the self, aggression against others, or even willfulness taking the place of true will. It is the destruction of the human image, the destruction of man. Even when it is an act of real freedom, as Ludwig Binswanger assures us of Ellen West and as the mother of a second of these three friends assured me of her daughter, it is still a maiming of the human image. It is not irrational, as that mother thinks, but the very heart of the matter that the part she finds hardest to bear is the thought of her lovely daughter so decomposed from a week under the hot sun near a southern California freeway that the body could not be identified except through the teeth. Of course, she remains in her mother's memory and in mine as the beautiful person that she was, just as the presence and the "dream" of Martin Luther King remain with us all. Yet the suicides and the murders—the mountains of tangled corpses in the extermination camps, the disintegrating living-dead of Hiroshima, the horribly disfigured, napalm-burned children of Vietnam—remain with us too—as a threat to the very humanity of the hidden image.

Is the hidden image in our day so "hidden" that it can no longer be revealed? This is the existential question that lies at the heart of *Problematic Rebel* and *To Deny Our Nothingness*. The "death of God," as I use the term in *Problematic Rebel*, is not the watchword of "secular theology," but the corollary of the alienation of modern man. Whether or not one holds with Sartre that God never existed at all or with Buber that God is in "eclipse" and that it is we, the "slayers of God," who dwell in darkness, the "death of God" means the awareness of a basic crisis in modern history—the crisis that comes when man no longer knows what it means to be human and becomes aware that he does not know this. The mistrust of man and mistrust of eternity are corollaries, and both are expressions of the existential mistrust that is the daily bread of the Modern Exile. At the foundation of our world lies the crisis of "confidence": The question at the heart of our

problematic is, Is it possible for modern man to trust in existence? Must we, too, like Melville's Captain Ahab, find behind
the mask "inscrutable malice," or wonder, like Ishmael, whether
reality is not actually empty and impersonal—"the heartless voids
and immensities of the universe that threaten us with annihilation?" And if we cannot trust, can we live without trust—that
existential trust that would enable us to reaffirm man, to reaffirm
the meaning of a word, the meaning of an action? A special
problem that has faced practically every sensitive writer, leader,
or activist of our day is how, in spite of what has happened, to
witness for man.

The situation from which both the Modern Rebel and the
Modern Exile start and which they try either to escape or to
affirm is that of the alienation of modern man. Some try to escape this alienation by destroying the transcendent reality that
crushes them, others by destroying themselves. Some arrive at
the dead end of isolation and inauthentic existence. All begin
with alienation and inner emptiness, the "death of God" and the
absence of an image of meaningful personal and social life. The
Modern Rebel-Exile carries his alienation with him in the contradictions and inner divisions of his own existence—the problematic of modern man.

The crisis of the person in the modern world removes the
ground for that unqualified rebellion which was still possible for
the romantic hero or the "Modern Promethean." The need of the
self for confirmation, the problematic of the calling and the call,
the tension between personal and social confirmation—all these
make impossible those simple contrasts between the self and the
other, the "autonomous individual" and the "mass society," with
which the problematic of the Modern Rebel has been obscured
and the real crisis of the person in our age ignored. The person in
the modern world exists as pure paradox: responding with a
calling of which he is never sure to a call which he can never
clearly hear. For us it cannot be a question of overthrowing the
"authoritarian" in favor of the "humanistic," but of again and
again discovering the human in the very heart of the bewildering

social hierarchy, personal meaning in the midst of the impersonal absurd.

The human image cannot by its very nature emerge from its hiddenness. Yet that eclipse which obscures and obstructs its double movement of concealing and revealing can in some measure be overcome—despite and even because of Auschwitz and Vietnam, John F. Kennedy and Martin Luther King, the "death of God" and the alienation of man, the Modern Promethean who deepens his exile by his all-or-nothing rebellion, and the Modern Vitalist, Psychological Man, and Gnostic who strive for authentic existence in ways that vitiate and distort it. Perhaps through the crisis itself, the human image may emerge from its hiddenness. Even if it is not given to us to see it emerge, through our faithful dialogue in and with the crisis we may discover a way of remaining true to the human image in the midst of its hiddenness— going through the alienation, exile, and problematic rebellion of modern man to a "Dialogue with the Absurd."

The Dialogue with the Absurd, as I use that term both in *Problematic Rebel* and *To Deny Our Nothingness,* implies that, even though the Absurd will not cease to be Absurd, it does have a meaning which it will yield to us if we go forth to meet it directly, as Dr. Rieux did in *The Plague.* In the Dialogue with the Absurd the hidden image of man remains hidden; yet in the darkness itself the features of a truly human face can be dimly discerned. There is no way for us to discern this hidden image except by moving through the heart of the eclipse of man. We must take unto ourselves the problematic of modern man and shape from it an image of meaningful human existence: an image that neither leaves out this problematic nor simply reflects it but wrestles with it, contends with it until it has found a way forward. Our foremost task is to mold the resistant clay of contradiction and absurdity into a figure of genuine humanity.

BEYOND
EXISTENTIALISM

In my book *The Worlds of Existentialism* I define existentialism
not as a single school of philosophy but as a temper, a mood, a
direction of movement, which unites a number of streams of
philosophy and culture which often diverge more than they con-
verge. This temper is a movement from the abstract to the concrete, from the general to the particular, from the static to the
dynamic, from the universal as the self-understood source of
truth to the event. This temper also includes an emphasis upon
becoming a person, upon making real existential decisions, upon
becoming "authentic." Beyond that, however, the existentialists
diverge. There are basic cleavages over such issues as whether to
emphasize phenomenological analysis of existence or pointing to
the unique, whether to see the existential subject or the dialogue
between persons as the self-understood basis for reality, knowledge, and value, whether to postulate the "death of God" as the
starting point of existentialism, like Sartre, or demand mutual
relationship with a God who is met and not defined, like Kierkegaard, Buber, and Marcel.*

Existentialism meets the image of man as it points to the

* Maurice Friedman, ed., *The Worlds of Existentialism: A Critical Reader*
(New York: Random House, 1964; Chicago: University of Chicago Press,
Phoenix Books [paperback], 1973).

unique, as it discovers authenticity and values in the concrete situation. The existentialist denies that there is such a thing as human nature that can be culled out of all the varieties of man. Therefore, he must be centrally concerned with the human image in a way that the traditional philosopher was not. It also means that he denies that there is a metaphysical realm of Being somewhere out there in contrast with which the realm of the phenomena is merely seeming, illusion, emptiness. That means for the most part that he is concerned not with "man" and his essence but with the *image* of man. When we speak of the image of man, we are speaking of something that needs to be revealed, something that is not simply there on the surface ready to be grasped by this or that category of objective science or psychology.

Most existentialism has been concerned in one way or another with the revelation, not of the hidden world of Being up there but of the things of this world. As Heidegger has so brilliantly shown, the word *phenomenon* comes from the Greek, meaning "to show forth." The things of this world do not conceal reality. On the contrary, they are constantly showing it forth. When existentialism is less centered on the "ism" and more on the "existential," it tends to be concerned not with phenomenological analyses of the human condition—not even "I-Thou" and "I-It" or man's two primal ontological acts of distancing and relating (Martin Buber)—but with pointing to the *unique*, to the "lived concrete," to history or to particular men. The unique is not merely the different; the unique is what is seen for its own sake and in our relationship to it. This is where existentialism comes closest to the image of man. The image of man retains the concern and spirit of existentialism *and* the concreteness of literature, as most existentialist philosophy does not. Phenomenological analysis of the human condition, helpful as that is—whether in the form of Kierkegaard's "sickness unto death" and "concept of dread," Heidegger's "existence toward death," Sartre's dialectic of "for itself" and "in itself," or Buber's "I-Thou" and "I-It"—can never be as truly existential as pointing to the unique, pointing to the concrete.

To go beyond existentialism means moving from a formal call for "authenticity" to a concrete image of man to which one can respond. Once at the beginning of a New School class, a woman said to me, "Dr. Friedman, I am troubled for fear that my existence is inauthentic." "It would never occur to *me* to ask myself that question!" I exclaimed. "Rather I ask, What is it about my life that led me to forget the pencil that I needed to mark the text in the subway in order to be able to lecture tonight?" I was struck by her taking this perfectly abstract and formal category of "authentic" and "inauthentic" as a whip with which to lash herself, instead of starting with the concrete particulars of her present situation. There is no such thing as authenticity in general. There is only the act of authenticating in each new situation.

By the same token, to go beyond existentialism means to move away from the emphasis upon anxiety and guilt, important as they are, to some sort of spontaneity and immediacy. Existential anxiety and existential guilt can play a role in calling us back to genuine existence. But not if we focus on them. Once at a seminar in California in 1961 I was talking about Buber's concept of existential guilt as a failure to go out from the self, as remaining with oneself, as injuring the common order of existence. I noticed that there was a lot of tension rising in the group. During the peanut-butter-and-jelly break a young physicist said to me, "Maury, we're just asking you to tell us that we aren't existentially guilty." "Forget existential guilt," I exclaimed, "and respond to anything, I don't care what, spontaneously!" It is perfectly possible to use the concept of existential guilt, like all existentialist categories, as just another way of being preoccupied with yourself and, as a result, not responding to anything at all. The awareness of existential guilt is only meaningful as a moment within a whole, a moment from which we must move on to that image of man that enables us to respond rather than freezing that moment into an analysis of existence or ourselves.

To go through and beyond existentialism to the hidden human image means to move from the self as a center of reality, knowledge, and value—as it is not only for Kierkegaard but even for those who explicitly affirm intersubjectivity, like Sartre, Heidegger, and Tillich—to those who say that all real living is meeting, or *Kommunikation*, or the I-Thou relationship—like Buber, Karl Jaspers, and Gabriel Marcel. The hidden human image is not visual but dialogical: It is only known in our response to it. Even if we all had Gandhi, Martin Luther King, or Che Guevara as our image of man, each of us would still have a wholly singular, quite unique image of man—the product of this dialogue.

This also means the need to move to the interhuman, to communes, and to community, away from *both* mass man and individualism. Even the notion of "doing my own thing" means nothing unless my own thing is called out of me in my direct, open relationship to other people and situations. Otherwise it is at most sterile rebellion and at least a mere claim for originality. It also means a need to move from "God is dead" theology to a focus on basic human attitudes, from questions of metaphysics and belief to concrete images of the "Dialogue with the Absurd" —the concrete and irreducible—and of that existential trust that enables us to go on existing and gives us resources to meet each new situation.

In psychotherapy the hidden image of man means the need to move from the existential analysis of psychopathology to unique situations and problems. Ludwig Binswanger devotes 240 pages to the analysis of the case of Ellen West in terms of such phenomenological categories as spatiality and temporality, the "world of the swamp and the tomb," "sickness unto death," and the "I-Thou" relationship. But she was not his patient. He never even met her. Carl Rogers in response wrote a very small piece called "The Loneliness of Contemporary Man" where he pointed out that there was no one in the hospital who understood or confirmed Ellen West. Binswanger says that love knows no answer as to whether she should have committed suicide or not. That is impressive. But as he goes on, he is so swept away by the "world design" that he has given her that he loses her very real tragedy and what enables us to see her as a Thou.

Many of the existentialists have contributed both to the revelation and the obscuring of the hidden image of man. Kierkegaard has wrested the "Single One" from the crowd, but he has also "suspended the ethical," cut the "Knight of Faith" loose from relationship to community, and in his lonely relationship with God obscured the face of the human that is found in the meeting between man and man. Friedrich Nietzsche has pointed to the dynamic of the unique way, to man as the valuing animal, to the concrete, the whole, and the honest. Yet in his whole philosophy of the "will to power," the "superman," and the "eternal return," he has failed to show a direction of movement for personal and social existence—an image of man. Dostoevsky in *The Brothers Karamazov* has given us the problematic and breadth of man and modern man as no one else. Yet he has tried to find in Alyosha and Zossima, his unproblematic, saintly figures, the answer to the problematic of modern man. What he has given us is simply two halves of a whole, the two faces of Job—the one the patient, suffering, trusting, humble face, the other the contending and rebelling one—without finding any image of man that brings them together. Martin Heidegger sees one's ownmost, resolute, nonrelational existence toward death as that guilt, or conscience, which calls one back to authenticity. Yet he is the very man who saw his philosophy as expressing the heart of Hitler's Nazism.

In the philosophy that succeeded his great work *Being and Time*, Heidegger has singled man out as "the shepherd of Being," as the existing being through whom Being is led into unconcealment and to the evoking of a new procession of images of the holy. In contrast to this philosophy, I set the Hasidic teaching that man is called upon "to be *humanly* holy, in the measure and manner of man." If the Hebrew Bible asks, "What is man" who is dwarfed by the heavens yet has dominion over the creatures (Psalm 8), it also points to the nonanthropomorphic reality of creation that exceeds the scope and comprehension of man and to the solicitude, not of man but of God "who causes it to rain on a land where no man is, to satisfy the desolate and waste land." (Job) It is not Being but man that is in need of unconcealment, for "the bowels of existence," in Nietzsche's words, "only speak to man as man." Man is not "the shepherd of Being" but the bearer of the truly human in the midst of the uniquely personal. "When I get to heaven," said Rabbi Susya shortly before his death, "they will not ask me, 'Why were you not Moses?' but 'Why were you not Susya?'"

"Being-there," wrote Heidegger in *The Introduction to Metaphysics* (1936) "signifies care of the ecstatically manifest being of the essence as such, not only of human being . . . Being-there is *itself* by virtue of its essential relation to being in general." Although Heidegger subordinates our human existence to that metaphysical-mystical "Being" which he regards as ultimate, he sees man as having the very special task that nothing else in existence has, of allowing, helping, and actualizing the unfolding and historical manifestation of this "Being." This is something that the "existent" cannot do of itself. So, if Heidegger emphatically rejects Sartre's definition of existentialism as "a humanism," he nonetheless arrogates to man a place even more important than that given him by traditional biblical religion. The essence of being human, to Heidegger, is precisely the need of Being for a place of disclosure: "The being-there of historical man is the breach through which the being embodied in the essence can open." As a result, "the question of how it stands with being proves to be the question of how it stands with our being-there in history, the question of whether we *stand* in history or merely stagger." Heidegger did not expect the modern "pastry cooks" of philosophy, "the tired latecomers with their supercilious wit," to understand this question, so he answered it himself: "From a metaphysical point of view, we *are staggering*. We . . . no longer know how it stands with being," and we do not know that we no longer know!

> The darkening of the world, the flight of the gods, the destruction of the earth, the transformation of men into a mass, the hatred and suspicion of everything free and creative, have assumed such

proportions throughout the earth that such childish categories as
pessimism and optimism have long since become absurd.*

At the very time and in the very book in which Heidegger set
forth this teaching of man's essence and task as the unconcealment of Being, he quoted at length and with approval his 1933
Rector's Address at Freiburg University in which he celebrated
the Nazi accession to power and turned the university in thought
as in deed into the "instrument of the new state which the people's chancellor Hitler will bring to a reality." As rector of the
University of Freiburg, Heidegger took a leading part in all the
S.A. activities that led to further persecution of the Jews and to
the exclusion of Jewish professors, including fellow disciples of
his own Jewish teacher Edmund Husserl. Showing a high contempt for "the works that are being peddled about nowadays as
the philosophy of National Socialism," Heidegger proffered his
own philosophy as "indispensable if the peril of world darkening
is to be forestalled and if our nation in the center of the Western
world is to take on its historical mission." Being as a word, harmony, truth, a showing-forth, had as its corollary, for Heidegger,
the thoroughly Nazi assertion that "the true is not for every man
but only for the strong." "Spirit," he quoted from his Rector's
Address, is not the empty cleverness or boundless dismember-
ment that have prevailed in the Western university up till now
but "is a fundamental, knowing resolve toward the essence of
being."† In another address to the German students of November, 1933, Heidegger stated: "The rules of your being are not
doctrines and 'ideas.' The Fuehrer himself and he alone is German reality and its law, today and henceforth."‡

There is an "integral relationship between Heidegger's Nazi
terminology and his . . . later thought about Being," I write in my
Conclusion to *The Worlds of Existentialism*. The great enemy of
the anonymity of *das Man* "lent his thought to a totalitarianism

* Martin Heidegger, *An Introduction to Metaphysics*, trans. by Ralph Man-
heim (New York: Doubleday Anchor Books, 1961), p. 31.
† *Ibid.*, pp. 40 f.
‡ Friedman, *The Worlds of Existentialism*, p. 530.

that swallowed up and destroyed the unique individual in a way more terrible than any other in history."* Thus Heidegger's very teaching of man's leading Being to its unconcealment contributed to the obliteration, the eclipse, the destruction of the human image. Heidegger's illumination of Being meant, in fact, a darkening of man! That this was possible stems in part from Heidegger's metaphysical ontology of Being with its consequent reduction of the concrete image of man and of the relationship and "word" between man and man to a secondary, "ontic" position, that is, of a mere phenomenological manifestation of Being in existence and not as something really real in itself.

We must avoid the a priori limitations of mutuality between man and man that are set by Kierkegaard, who said we should be chary of having to do with each other; by Heidegger, who says that ultimately it is the nonrelational call back to yourself that is most important; by Sartre, who defines all the real mutuality out of existence by my recognizing you as a subject only when I find you looking at me as an object. Love is the nearest Sartre comes to mutuality, for in love I want you as a free subject and not as an object; but I want you to be a freedom *subject to my freedom*. We must even go beyond Paul Tillich, who begins with a "centered self" yet a self that is somehow alienated from the "ground of being." Tillich's "courage to be," as I have suggested in *Touchstones of Reality*, does not go far enough in the direction of concrete existence. There must be a redemptive bringing of anxiety and guilt into the wholeness of our response. In contrast to Tillich's "courage to be" there has to be a courage to address and a courage to respond.

The reality to which the hidden human image points lies deeper than the articulations of belief and nonbelief. It lies in the life-attitudes that inform them. It does not have to do primarily with metaphysical essences or theological creeds but with that existential trust which enables us to stand our ground before what confronts us and to meet it in a way faithful to its otherness and to our uniqueness.

* *Ibid.*, pp. 525–535.

The hidden human image is more existential than existentialism itself. It is closer to the unique, to the lived concrete, to existence as we actually find it.

The meaning and necessity of the movement *through* and *beyond* existentialism to the hidden human image are expressed in all clarity in a statement that Martin Buber wrote about my book *Problematic Rebel*:

> *Problematic Rebel* is especially important because its theme is not expounded through the discussion of concepts but through representative figures of the narrative literature of two generations— that of Melville and Dostoevsky and that of Kafka and Camus. The theme is the revolt of man against an existence emptied of meaning, the existence after the so-called "death of God." This emptying of meaning is not to be overcome through the illusionary program of a free "creation of values," as we know it in Nietzsche and Sartre. One must withstand this meaninglessness, must suffer it to the end, must do battle with it undauntedly, until out of the contradiction experienced in conflict and suffering, meaning shines forth anew.

We must go beyond Nietzsche and Sartre, whose concreteness in the destruction of old values is matched by an equal vagueness in any movement forward to new ones. We must go beyond them to Camus, who worked through his early philosophy ("I want to live with only what I can know") to his later creations, in all of which he pointed to an image of man toward which the mere act of negation was at best only a first step. We live with absurdities, he said. We must recognize them and fight them. But we must do so as shortly as we can and move through and beyond them. Perhaps we must even go beyond Camus to Elie Wiesel, who twenty-five years later has forced us, as no one could have in the time of Camus, to face the legacy of the Nazi holocaust and its devastating effect on our humanity. Like Wiesel we have to go through the heart of the problematic rebellion to that rebellion which is the more open, the freer, the stronger, the more courageous. To do this we must move from "existentialism" to the hidden human image.

PART ■■

SCIENCE
AND
PSYCHOLOGY

SCIENCE AND
SCIENTISM

"The surest test if a man be sane," said Lao-tzu,

> Is if he accepts life whole, as it is,
> Without needing by measure or touch to understand
> The measureless untouchable source
> Of its substance. . . .*

The Psalmist asks, "What is man that Thou are mindful of him?"
Job asks, "What is man that you try him every moment?" Greek
philosophy too begins in wonder—the wonder of Heraclitus'
"You could not in your going find the ends of the soul, though
you travelled the whole way: so deep is its *logos*," the wonder of
Socrates' "An unexamined life is not worth living," and of Plato's
endless questioning concerning the progress of the soul to the
Good. Descartes traded Plato's wonder for doubt and his soul
for the "thinking thing" whose existence is "proved" by the supposed impossibility of the "knowing subject's" doubting the fact
that it doubts. The modern idolaters of science and of "scientism"
follow Freud in asserting that what science does not know, nothing else can possibly supply. Scientism entirely disavows the
knowledge claims of philosophy and religion; for it cannot be

* Witter Bynner, *The Way of Life According to Lao-tzu.*

admitted that our ignorant and superstitious ancestors could know what we do not.

Yet from the wisdom literature of all antiquities it is abundantly clear that our "ignorant and superstitious ancestors" *did* know something that we are more and more losing sight of: the wholeness and uniqueness of man. We know far, far more *about* man in parts and in sum than any previous culture. But what makes man man and what ways of *human* knowing are most appropriate to knowing the *human*—these we do not know. Scientism does not often become an overt cult, like "Scientology," yet even in its more respectable forms it has many of the marks of a religious cult: the dogmatic insistence that there is only *one* form of knowing appropriate to all "objects" alike and the blind faith that what "science" does not *now* know, it will know in the not-too-distant future, as if "Science" were not *man's* knowledge and his way of knowing but itself the knower—an omniscient, if only gradually self-revealing, god.

One of the misapprehensions of modern man is that those who still care about religion, ethics, and the aesthetic are being anthropomorphic in contrast to the objective scientist. Nothing could be more anthropomorphic than science, man's highest capacity for abstracting from the full-bodied reality of the given. Today science has the prestige theology had in the Middle Ages. Every last psychology and social science wants to call itself "scientific" and often in the process falls into scientism. The so-called "empiricism" of "scientism" reduces our concrete meetings with the world to abstract "data," the full-bodied person to a detached and disembodied observer, the interrelationship between scientists to a merely technical interchange of data-gathering instruments, the feedback of a giant system of computers. Scientism is one of the most sinister, if not always the most romantic, embodiments of the Modern Promethean.

The full scope of the Promethean tragedy is becoming manifest only in our day, in which the "fate" that bears down on the unlimited man comes no less surely from *within* his own expanding potentialities than it did of old from the fixed eternal order of the ancient Greeks. Modern nuclear science, writes the historian C. Vann Woodward, has "placed in human hands at one and the same time the Promethean fire as well as the divine prerogative of putting an end to the whole human drama." Contemporary man lives under the sign of the Promethean fire of science in an all-encompassing way that neither a Faust's romantic search for experience nor an Ahab's defiance of nature and the science which cooperates with it can in the least diminish. Yet in the face of the threat of annihilation by an atomic war that will neither be desired nor deliberately started by any nation, it is increasingly difficult to regard man as the heroic *subject* of this Promethean expansion. He seems, rather, to be the *object* of it—the terrified Frankenstein cowering before the monster that he himself has created. Not only to the common man but even to the atomic scientists themselves, mankind's nuclear power seems an alien and hostile fate that threatens human values and human survival. The nightmare aspect of *homo faber* is made manifest in our day in a way far more terrible than Emerson could have imagined when he wrote: "*Things* are in the saddle and ride mankind"!

Even apart from the danger of annihilation by the weapons he has created, the man of today is forced, when confronting science, to shed the heroic attitudinizing of the Modern Promethean. The belief that "knowledge is power" had as its corollary the belief that the objective reality of nature was confined to "clear ideas"—what we could grasp with our logical categories. Thus for eighteenth-century man the "primary qualities"—dimension, extension, motion—were objective while the "secondary qualities"—color, smell, sound, touch—were subjective attributes added by man. Despite the influx of evolutionism and vitalism, the scientists of the nineteenth century followed their predecessors in viewing the world as a Newtonian mechanism that conformed to universal natural laws. It has remained for twentieth-century science, with Einstein's "relativity," Heisenberg's "indeterminacy," and Bohr's "complementarity," to recognize in its relation to nature what Ishmael acknowledges concerning his whale: "I know him not and I never will." The modern scientist can no longer regard his equations as universal laws but only as pragmatic formulae which answer the particular question that he has put. So far from thinking that his scientific categories correspond to the reality of the universe, he recognizes that his images are mutually contradictory aspects of a reality he can never grasp as a whole. A physical "substratum" which must be pictured at one time as waves and at another as quantum units may yield mathematical equations, but it can no longer provide the comfort of an image of the world such as earlier ages enjoyed. In a world that he cannot image, man can no longer feel himself master or even at home. One may have a mathematical model of the "world," to be sure, but one cannot *live* in such a model. "Our life in the world," writes Martin Buber, "is bound to . . . the notorious discrepancy between the penetrating images of our perception . . . and a physically or at least mathematically comprehensible substratum underlying them . . . that nowhere and never is accessible to us in reality."

> The realm of modes of observation into which our relation to the world has disintegrated no longer offers a unity . . . with whose life our life could unite as a unity. . . . There is no longer an *image* of the world. . . . Man . . . still desires . . . to live in a world of which one can form an image—not merely imageable as a symbol but as a real world constituted in a certain way. For to live in an unrepresentable world entails a contradiction which can become hopeless if borne in untransparent immanence. But now the mode of being of the space-time world as a whole and that of each part of it have become unrepresentable—indeed, this mode runs diametrically opposed to everything that can be imaged as world, that is, it is no longer capable of being received in lived life as the world of this life. . . . And nonetheless—we must proceed from this unimageable, unrealizable, uncanny, unhome-like world.°

In the social sciences too at this stage it is the humility of the Modern Job that seems called for rather than the world-

---

° Martin Buber, *The Knowledge of Man*, ed. by Maurice Friedman (New York: Harper Torchbooks, 1966), "Man and His Image-Work," trans. by Maurice Friedman, pp. 153–156.

conquering gestures of the Modern Promethean. Today many anthropologists, economists, political scientists, sociologists, and historians are becoming less categorical in their science as they become more deeply and fully aware of their subject— man. Humility here means no obscurantism or romantic rebellion against science. It is, rather, the growing awareness by each science of its proper limits and the salutary fear of overstepping them.

This humility might seem well in accord with the logical positivism and linguistic analysis which increasingly dominate the intellectual scene in America and England, not only in philosophy but in the social sciences, psychology, and sociology as well. The desire not to deal with unanswerable metaphysical questions that go beyond the possibility of human knowledge is certainly consonant with the spirit of the Modern Job as is the desire to use language carefully and precisely. Yet this very shunning of metaphysical certainties has led to a new and narrower certainty which is a less grandiose but equally significant manifestation of the Either/Or of the Modern Promethean. This new faith often seems to claim the total allegiance of disciples who, in an act of voluntary submission, don the blinders of a one-sided language analysis to shut out of the realm of "true knowledge" the broad human plain of ethics, religion, literature, and social values. The distinction between the exact physical sciences and the human studies is increasingly obscured by the reduction of qualitative social values to quantitative and measurable social facts. Social and psychological research today consists in an overwhelming preponderance of behavioral studies which describe the social relations of human beings as empirical phenomena shorn clean of the dimension of social values. Human relations are increasingly observed from without and reduced to effects of causes, to the Q factor of the behaviorist psychologist, or to interrelated units of a deterministic structure in which the objective description of "values" replaces valuing and value-decision seen from within.

In many cases, to be sure, more human and holistic approaches have gained ground, as the growth of existential psychiatry and humanist psychology suggests. But far more significant is the triumphant advance of behaviorist psychology and operant conditioning psychotherapy. Even the multiple movements for "human potential" and group dynamics that are springing up all around us often bear the marks of a scientism in which techniques for "sensitivity" and "encounter" take the place of the spontaneity and wholeness of real human awareness and response. Even in philosophy, the one discipline above all others that ought by its very nature to remain the open arena for free interchange, the new faith of logical empiricism and linguistic analysis has all but excluded the concern with the wholeness and uniqueness of man.

Those who find their emotional security in the prevailing "logical empiricism" of our time seek a greater and greater certainty about an ever more restricted area of human significance. "Nothing, surely, but an anxious preference for the indubitableness of mathematical and analytical assertion and for the apparent sense-solidities and regularities with which natural scientists concern themselves," writes Kathleen Nott, "could account for the attempt to drive poetry and ethics out of the world of meaning into the void of metaphysics."*

The paradox of this powerful modern drive to reduce human knowledge to the "empirically verifiable" and human values to observations of how people *do* behave or to mere emotional assertions of preference ("This is what *I* like. I want you to like the same.") is that it combines an unprecedented and immensely valuable logical precision with an exclusivist dogma, antiphilosophical to its very core, as to what questions may and may not be taken seriously by philosophers. It is a dogma because it rests on assumptions that can only be accepted or rejected but are in no way themselves subject to meaningful proof. It is antiphilosophical because it insists that the game be played only according to its rules and refuses to recognize that the questions of what we may meaningfully know and how we know are *them-*

---

* Kathleen Nott, "The Misery of Philosophy," *Encounter*, Vol. VII, No. 4 (October, 1956).

selves philosophical questions of profound significance. The limits of meaningful human knowing cannot be set by mere assertion. The definition of philosophy, as Paul Tillich has said, is itself a philosophical question. It is exclusivist because, thinly disguising its intolerance as tolerance, it relegates all the fields of human values—aesthetics, ethics, social values, religion—to the realm of the subjective, the emotional, the poetic, the "unverifiable," in short, non-sense.

Many of the adherents of this new faith are not content to make a new and indisputably valuable contribution to modern philosophical and social thought. They wish to remake that thought in their own image, swallowing up these fields in a new synthesis in which the humanities, moral philosophy, social ethics, the history of philosophy are all pushed into the background as tolerated relics of an outworn, preanalytical age. They revive in modern dress the radical negation with which David Hume concluded his *Enquiry Concerning Human Understanding*:

> When we run over libraries, persuaded of these principles, what havoc must we make? If we take in our hand any volume . . . let us ask, *Does it contain any abstract reasoning concerning quantity or number?* No. *Does it contain any experimental reasoning concerning matter of fact and existence?* No. Commit it then to the flames: for it can contain nothing but sophistry and illusion.

In this same *Enquiry* Hume undermined the belief in the necessary nature of the link between cause and effect and with it the belief in causality as such. This relegation of causality to mere continuity and association bothered Hume himself so little that he was able to combine it with a thoroughgoing determinism, psychological as well as physical. Immanuel Kant, in contrast, found it necessary to construct a metaphysics of two worlds—the noumenal and the phenomenal—and an epistemology of two types of knowing—pure reason and practical reason—before he could regain his own philosophical equilibrium. The naiveté of Hume's contradictory positions paved the way for those empiricists who would forget about the reality of the knower as a

person while becoming tremendously concerned with the particulars of how we know. The sophistication of Kant's metaphysics
left an impossible dualism in which an unattainable "thing-in-
itself" informed the categories of our knowing—time and space,
order and unity, cause and effect—even while escaping from any
of our attempts to grasp it in our knowledge of the phenomenal
world.

The crude Either/Or at the heart of Hume's committing to the
flames all knowledge that does not fit his straitjacket is by no
means without parallel among his contemporary descendants. To
the behaviorist, said the noted psychologist B. F. Skinner, "there
is no difference between a man training for a race and a man
racing for a train." Skinner wishes to understand man *purely
from the outside,* and in so doing to reject once and for all the
openness of the humanistic approach in favor of the objective
certainties of social engineers who will manipulate society according to a "scientific" plan:

> The point at which the scientific method will take superiority over
> the humanistic will be the point at which it gives man the tech-
> niques for the *manipulation* and *control* of human *behavior.* . . .
> We are on the verge of a great change in *techniques of dealing
> with man* in every sphere, which *will result in a great change in
> our concept of man.* Hence if we must make a choice, we will
> abandon the humanistic tradition for the greater advantage which
> will come through the plodding and careful methods of science.*

From *Walden Two* (1945) to *Beyond Freedom and Dignity*
(1971), Skinner has remained consistent in regarding human nature itself as the proper subject of a science of behavior and
rejecting the "inner man" that was given to us by the Greeks, and
the unnecessary concepts of "dignity" or "worth" that accompany
the inner man. And again, we have the Modern Promethean
Either/Or: "When science begins to bear down on the question
of the individual, you must accept determinism or reject the
entire scientific worldview."

---

* B. F. Skinner, "The Image of Man," The New School Conference on
Methods in the Sciences and Social Sciences, 1954; italics mine.

But as Martin Gardner has pointed out in his iconoclastic book *In the Name of Science*, not all that is done in the name of science is properly called science. In the case of the behaviorist approach to psychology, this distinction between scientism and science has been lucidly spelled out by Amedeo Giorgi, a pioneer in the application of phenomenology to experimental psychology:

> Science becomes scientism when methods successful in one area are transferred uncritically to another domain where its legitimacy is at best questionable. Psychology turned to established and more prestigious sciences to imitate them. But the established sciences were physics, chemistry, biology—each of which was developed within an implicit ontology suitable for nature but not for the human person. The natural sciences were never *intended* to study man as a person. One need not leave the realm of science to study man adequately. We need only to broaden science itself.*

Giorgi summarizes the main features of the natural scientific approach that is uncritically carried over to psychology as "empirical, positivistic, reductionistic, quantitative, deterministic, verifiable and predictive." These characteristics have been helpful but their helpfulness is dependent upon their appropriateness to the subject studied. Giorgi follows Thomas Kuhn's *Structure of Scientific Revolutions* in recognizing the change of world view that underlies each new breakthrough in science. Like Kuhn, Giorgi "tries to account for the activity of science in terms of the processes of perception; whereas, psychologists try to account for the presence of perception in terms of the natural sciences." In the place of a prereflective or truly perceptual presence to the world, psychology substitutes a natural scientific reflective and conceptual apprehension of the world.

> Psychology in studying perception, mostly considers stimuli in terms of physics and speaks of the body in anatomical terms.

* Symposium on "Science and Scientism: The Human Sciences," Trinity College, May 15–16, 1970.

Library of

Davidson College

Psychology thus transforms our perceived world into the world of natural science and then tries to explain it in natural scientific terms and not in phenomenal or perceptual terms.*

In his book *Psychology as a Human Science* Giorgi states that instead of modeling itself on the natural sciences, the human sciences, including psychology, should have gone directly to the life-world, discovered its questions and methods from there, and only then tried to ascertain to what extent the human and the natural sciences have methods, concepts, and answers in common. The natural scientific approach applies an analytical process which breaks down the whole into its elements or parts, whereas the approach of the human sciences would understand the whole as part of a larger-structured context. The actual and the present would then become the point of departure for uncovering relationships, contexts, and meaning. Natural science considers man as *part of the world* but studies him without reference to his intentional relations *to* the world. The human sciences recognize that man is also one *for whom the world exists*. Natural science derives its theories and hypotheses from a vital level of integration below the human structural level and looks at the human in terms of pathological cases or traditional laboratory studies. The human sciences, being holistic, study man at his highest level of functioning, the unequivocally human, to which facts obtained at lower levels of function are only relevant if a human context is implicitly present.

This also implies that the human sciences are intersubjective not only as between scientist and scientist but also as between investigator and subject. Equal in their humanity, they must relate through a nonmanipulative structure based upon appeal and cooperation in which research designs will be open-ended, leaving the final closure to the subject himself. In contrast to the positivist, reductionistic, analytic, and quantitative approach of the natural sciences, the human sciences must be concerned with

---

* Amedeo Giorgi, "Psychology: A Human Science," *Social Research*, Vol. XXXVI, No. 3 (Autumn, 1969), p. 431.

meaning, qualitative differences, intentional relations, and investigating human phenomena in a human way. The meaning that the *subjects* bring to the situation thus becomes co-constitutive of the results.* This does not mean any attack on the "empirical" and the "real," but a broader, more indeterminate understanding of them and of the human image they imply:

> The only problem with empiricism and positivism is that these philosophies defined experience and the real too narrowly, and by means of certain *ideas* of experience and the real which brought closure too rapidly.†

Giorgi rightly recognizes in the *philosophy* with which B. F. Skinner approaches his psychological research a classic example of scientism. "Behaviorism, with an accent on the last syllable," Giorgi quotes Skinner, "is not the scientific study of behavior but a *philosophy* of science concerned with the subject matter and methods of psychology. If psychology is a science of . . . the behavior of organisms, human or otherwise, then it is part of biology, a natural science for which tested and highly successful methods are available."‡ Skinner is more concerned with carrying over the nineteenth-century conception of science as a particular method, Giorgi states, than with fidelity to the phenomenon under investigation. In *Beyond Freedom and Dignity* Skinner suggests that the fact that the unquestioned faith of popular culture in man's inner capacities, his mental and volitional life, is not to be found in modern physics or most of biology "may well explain why a science and a technology of behavior have been so long delayed." This is a perfect example of an uncritical carrying-over of the prestigious methods of more established sciences to psychology. Skinner justifies his elimination of the "supposed mediating states of the mind" in favor of

---

* Amedeo Giorgi, *Psychology as a Human Science. A Phenomenologically Based Approach* (New York: Harper & Row, 1970), pp. 176 f., 191 f., 198, 203–205.
† *Ibid.*, p. 205.
‡ B. F. Skinner, "Behaviorism at Fifty," in T. W. Wann, ed., *Behaviorism and Phenomenology* (Chicago: University of Chicago Press, 1964), p. 79.

the direct relation between behavior and environment as following "the path taken by physics and biology."* What Skinner
offers us is a less than heroic "Modern Promethean" who, in the
name of "scientific progress" in destroying the conception of autonomous man, sets himself, somewhat ludicrously, against the
whole of humanistic culture:

> We have moved forward by dispossessing autonomous man, but
> he has not departed gracefully. He is conducting a sort of rear-
> guard action in which, unfortunately, he can marshal formidable
> support. He is still an important figure in political science, law,
> religion, economics, anthropology, sociology, psychotherapy,
> philosophy, ethics, history, education, child care, linguistics,
> architecture, city planning, and family life. . . . The result is a
> tremendous weight of traditional "knowledge" which must be
> corrected or displaced by a scientific analysis.†

"Were it not for the unwarranted generalization that all control is wrong," writes Skinner, "we should deal with the social
environment as simply as we deal with the nonsocial." As Skinner
recognizes no distinction between natural science and human
science, so he recognizes no distinction between dealing with the
human and the nonhuman. His two-pronged attack on freedom
and dignity is based on a simplistic Either/Or. Either man has an
inner, autonomous center completely uninfluenced by what is
outside him or he is totally determined by the environment. A
variant of the same is his assertion that "any evidence that a
person's behavior may be attributed to external circumstances
seems to threaten his dignity of worth." He has no conception
of that "finite freedom" of which Paul Tillich speaks in which
man possesses freedom precisely in the midst of limitation and
conditioning. He misses entirely the understanding of dignity as
what one *is* and sees it simply as a matter of what one *does*: "We
recognize a person's dignity or worth when we give him credit
for what he has done." Not only does natural science take over

* B. F. Skinner, *Beyond Freedom and Dignity* (New York: Alfred A. Knopf,
1971), pp. 10, 14–15.
† *Ibid.*, p. 19.

one by one the functions of autonomous man as it better understands the role of the environment, but the very goal of science is "the destruction of mystery" through the fuller explanation of behavior.* Skinner is, indeed, paradigmatic of that analytical, reductive, and deriving look which, Martin Buber says, predominates today between man and man.

> This look is analytical, or rather pseudo-analytical, since it treats the whole being as put together and therefore able to be taken apart—not only the so-called unconscious which is accessible to relative objectification, but also the psychic stream itself, which can never, in fact, be grasped as an object. This look is a reductive one because it tries to contract the manifold person, who is nourished by the microcosmic richness of the possible, to some schematically surveyable and recurrent structures. And this look is a deriving one because it supposes it can grasp what man has become, or even is becoming, in genetic formulae, and it thinks that even the dynamic central principle of the individual in this becoming can be represented by a general concept. *An effort is being made today radically to destroy the mystery between man and man. The personal life, the ever near mystery, once the source of the stillest enthusiasms, is levelled down.*†

Buber is not, he explains, attacking "the analytical method of the human science, a method which is indispensable wherever it furthers knowledge of a phenomenon without impairing the essentially different knowledge of its uniqueness that transcends the valid circle of the method." Skinner not only impairs man's uniqueness. He dismisses it out of hand. Nor does he recognize that there is any valid knowledge that can transcend the circle of his method.

In contrast to Nicholas Berdyaev who insists that a compulsory good is not good, Skinner entirely dismisses character, personality, motivation, and intention in favor of the redesign of the environment through which we shall progress "toward a world in

---

* *Ibid.*, pp. 42, 44, 58.
† Buber, *The Knowledge of Man*, "Elements of the Interhuman," trans. by R. G. Smith, pp. 80 f.; italics mine.

which people may be automatically good." "The problem is to induce people not to be good but to behave well." By the same token, Skinner can recognize nothing in any moral injunction other than a purely extrinsic desire to escape the punishment that society or other people mete out for stealing, or killing. Since he sees *all* control as exerted by the environment and the task of mankind as designing better environments rather than better men, he necessarily dismisses as unreal any intrinsic morality, or unconditional imperative, hence any morality worth the name. He recognizes that his view cannot be proved yet claims that it is in the nature of scientific inquiry that evidence should shift in favor of the image of man as totally determined by genetic endowments and by environment. He attacks the "inner man" as an unnecessary hypostatization, but, without noticing it as it were, he does away at the same time with the whole man, the unique man, the person who can respond spontaneously as well as react to the control of the environment. Yet he claims that the technology he proposes is "ethically neutral" and that "there is nothing in a methodology which determines the values governing its use"! The human studies Skinner dismisses contemptuously and out of hand: "What, after all, have we to show for nonscientific or prescientific good judgment, or common sense, or the insights gained through personal experience? It is science or nothing...."*

The result of all this is a conscious change in the image of man and with it art and literature: "We shall not only have no reason to admire people who endure suffering, face danger, or struggle to be good, it is possible that we shall have little interest in pictures or books about them." Since "being good" will be a matter automatically taken care of by the controlled environment, Skinner need not concern himself with the difference between a real value decision as to what is good in this situation and "the things people call good." He combines crude cultural relativism with a slightly complexified pain-pleasure calculus in which individuals can be induced to identify their own good with

---

* Skinner, *Beyond Freedom and Dignity*, pp. 66–69, 82, 101, 113–115, 160.

that of others and with the survival of their culture. He asserts the necessity of intentional design of a culture and the control of human behavior as essential for the human species to develop and culture to progress; yet he has no criteria for what development or progress may mean, any more than he has any answer to the question he himself raises as to who is going to do the controlling and what will guide their control. Here too he says that what is essential is changing the environment rather than the men. He recognizes no *value* problem concerning the direction in which the environment might change. His only criteria are "Will it work?" and "Will it survive?" or perhaps be replaced by some other culture which "may make a greater contribution to the future." "The survival of a culture functions as a value"; yet cultures themselves embody values and can mix with other cultures, as he recognizes. Yet life, liberty, and the pursuit of happiness "have only a minor bearing on the survival of a culture," he asserts, and the literature of freedom and dignity is a positive threat to the self-understood value of exercising all available control, both of genetics and of the social environment.*

Not only is Skinner's behaviorism philosophy, it is bad philosophy, i.e., imprecise and unthought through. Although he himself speaks of reciprocal effect, he dogmatically asserts that "it is the environment which acts upon the perceiving person, not the perceiving person who acts upon the environment," thus excluding a priori the more likely possibility of a mutual interaction. He speculates wistfully that independent physiological evidence, if it existed, would confirm his interpretation. To say that the appeal to the mind explains nothing at all is to close the book as far as Skinner is concerned, since explanation is his self-understood *primum bonum*. "It is always the environment which builds the behavior with which problems are solved," he dogmatically asserts, "even when the problems are to be found in the private world inside the skin." His dogmatism flags for a second when he admits that "none of this has been investigated in a very produc-

* *Ibid.*, pp. 153, 163 f., 168, 173, 175, 180–183.

tive way," but it immediately returns reinforced by the self-righteous superiority of true faith: "But the inadequacy of our analysis is no reason to fall back on a miracle-working mind." Though his choice is the exact opposite of Captain Ahab, namely for science and against heroic man, Skinner has the same Modern Promethean Either/Or: In the traditional picture a person acts upon the world, says Skinner; in the "scientific" picture the world acts upon the person. This neither exhausts the alternatives nor has any logical cogency, but it is gratifying to the smug scientism of a mind that wants to see everything one way.*

Skinner looks forward with excitement to what man can make of man when the two processes of biological and cultural evolution are speeded up through design and control, and he imagines to himself "a world in which people live together without quarreling, maintain themselves by producing the food, shelter, and clothing they need, enjoy themselves and contribute to the enjoyment of others in art, music, literature, and games, consume only a reasonable part of the resources of the world and add as little as possible to its pollution, bear no more children than can be raised decently, . . . and come to know themselves accurately and, therefore, manage themselves effectively." But accuracy and effectiveness are no answer to the basic value question of who will set the guidelines for the designed social environment and by what criteria. Skinner asseverates that "it is not difficult to demonstrate a connection between the unlimited right of the individual to pursue happiness and the catastrophes threatened by unchecked breeding, the unrestrained affluence which exhausts resources and pollutes the environment, and the imminence of nuclear war."† But what will replace the individualism that he attacks? Skinner anticipates his Walden Two utopia; but the Nazis, the most thoroughgoing anti-individualist and totalitarian state in the history of mankind, have given us a preview of quite a different kind! Only the most highly organized collectivism with the fullest possible social engineering and design of the

* *Ibid.*, pp. 188, 192, 195, 211.
† *Ibid.*, pp. 215, 208, 214.

social and physical environment made possible that miracle of modern scientific ingenuity: the extermination of seven million people as if they had been insects!

The fact is that Skinner is a sawed-off dualist. He buys uncritically the dualism of inner and outer, and as the Modern Vitalist and the Modern Gnostic opt for the inner, he opts for the outer. As a result, he confuses freedom and solitariness, absolute freedom and personal wholeness: "Without the help of a verbal community," he writes, "all behavior would be unconscious. Consciousness is a social product. It is not only *not* the special field of autonomous man, it is not within range of a solitary man." That there might be a nonsolitary man who was nonetheless a person who could respond to what was outside of him from the ground of his own uniqueness does not even occur to Skinner as a possibility. "Man is not a moral animal in the sense of possessing a special trait or virtue; he has built a kind of social environment which induces him to behave in moral ways." He dismisses his critics—Joseph Wood Krutch, who speaks of the destruction of the image of man as the humanists of an earlier generation knew it, Floyd Matson, who speaks of the destruction of "a unique being, called Man," Abraham Maslow, who speaks of the attack on the very "being" of man, and C. S. Lewis, who speaks of the "abolition of man"—as merely so many rearguard actions in the retreat of those who wish to retain an autonomous inner man against an environmentally controlled outer man. The essence of man, the humanity of man, "man as Thou not It," or "as a person not a thing," really mean, translates Skinner, the "autonomous man—the inner man, the homunculus, the possessing demon, the man defended by the literature of freedom and dignity."* But man as Thou, to take one of his examples, does *not* mean inner or absolutely free man; it means man as person finding his personhood precisely in open, mutual relationships with other men and with the nonhuman world.

"Science," by which we should read Skinner's own scientism,

* *Ibid.*, pp. 192, 198, 200.

"does not dehumanize man," writes Skinner, "it de-homunculizes him, and it must do so if it is to prevent the abolition of the human species."

> To man *qua* man we readily say good riddance. Only by dispossessing him can we turn to the real causes of human behavior. Only then can we turn from the inferred to the observed, from the miraculous to the natural, from the inaccessible to the manipulable. *

Skinner clearly sees himself as leaving room for the uniqueness of every personal history even within the most regimented culture, as if uniqueness were no more than individuality and as such invulnerable to the atrophy that regimented cultures produce. But even this individuality he does not actually see as of value in itself: "The individual nevertheless remains merely a stage in a process which began long before he came into existence and will long outlast him."† All this, once again, is dogmatic faith and *not* science, not even modern physics and modern biology, as Skinner claims. In the end, Skinner's scientism extends far beyond Giorgi's definition to an act of faith that leaves forever unanswered and unanswerable the question of from whose point of view the individual is "merely a stage in a process." Who is the we that explains when Skinner's "science" is brought to bear? If man is only the object, who is the existential subject that does the knowing in this science? Even what Skinner writes of the investigator and controller is from without, as an object, rather than from within, as a subject, an experiencing person.

A formidable reply to Skinner from the realm of psychology itself is Isidor Chein's book *The Science of Behavior and the Image of Man*. At the heart of the issue of the nature of psychology, writes Chein, is the issue of the image of man. Chein contrasts two basic types of image—man as helpless, powerless reagent and man as active, responsible agent, and he opts for the

---

* *Ibid.*, pp. 200 f.
† *Ibid.*, p. 209.

latter as against the former. Man does not passively permit himself to be shaped by his environment; he injects himself into the causal process, shaping both what is around him and himself. "If Man is said to respond to his environment, the word 'response' is to be taken in the sense that it has in active dialogue rather than in the sense of an automatic consequence." This statement is similar to the distinction I make in *The Life of Dialogue* between "responding" and "reacting":

> When Buber speaks of the free man as free of causation, process, and defined being, he does not mean that the free man acts from within himself without connection with what has come to him from the outside. On the contrary, it is only the free man who really acts in response to concrete external events. It is only he who sees what is new and unique in each situation, whereas the unfree man sees only its resemblance to other things. But what comes to the free man from without is only the precondition for his action, it does not determine its nature. This is just as true of those social and psychological conditioning influences which he has internalized in the past as of immediate external events. To the former as to the latter, he responds freely from the depths as a whole and conscious person. The unfree person, on the other hand, is so defined by public opinion, social status, or his neurosis that he does not "respond" spontaneously and openly to what meets him but only "reacts." He does not see others as real persons, unique and of value in themselves, but in terms of their status, their usefulness, or their similarity to other individuals with whom he has had relationships in the past.*

In place of the image of responding, responsible man there dominates, not only among psychologists but among an astonishingly large number of those concerned with guidance, counseling, and psychotherapy, a "robotic image of man" resting "on the false assumption that . . . every determinant of behavior is either a body fact or an environment fact." In powerful reinforcement of our critique of scientism, Chein charges "that psychologists

---

* Maurice Friedman, *Martin Buber: The Life of Dialogue* (New York: Harper Torchbooks, 1960), pp. 67 f.

maintain the image of Man as a passive corporeal entity governed by a thermodynamic principle because of their philosophical precommitments and in flagrant disregard of contradictory information."*

Freedom to Chein rests on the simple premises that volitions—human desires and motivations—have behavioral consequences and are not themselves reducible to variables of physical environment or physiological process. Like the Gestalt psychologists, Chein holds that the unique aspects of a totality do not emerge from the combination of the components, "since the totality plays a role in determining what the components will be." The alternative to this image of man, declares Chein, is to reduce psychological science to a concern with "psychological trivia arbitrarily torn out of the context of their natural setting." This setting includes the fact that motivation implies a mission, a commitment to accomplish something. Strict behaviorists who avoid inner feeling and emotion as "mentalistic poison" pay the price of losing much of the human being and what makes him do what he does. Scientism is committed to a reductionism which goes beyond the parsimoniousness of science to a preselected set of primitive terms and propositions, usually drawn from physics, chemistry, or physiology, which are held to dogmatically in complete disrespect for the "unparsimoniousness of nature." In addition, the scientismist limits himself to clearly understandable verifiable forms even when they do not fit the case, thus betraying the scientific goal and purposes for the sake of maintaining the scientific form.†

In contrast to scientism, Chein puts forward a clinicalist image of man which coincides in every detail with the contrast which we have made between the attitude of the Modern Promethean and that of the Modern Job. The "clinicalist" is open to human context and human meaning as they are found in the concrete, the particular, and the unique, hence in the "image of man" as

---

* Isidor Chein, *The Science of Behavior and the Image of Man* (New York: Basic Books, 1972), pp. 6 f., 9, 17.
† *Ibid.*, pp. 20, 22, 26, 43, 268, 277, 309 f., 316.

opposed to "human nature" or the "construct of man." His desire
to comprehend every instance "in all of its particularity and
unique individuality" leads the clinicalist to be suspicious of any
fixed scheme of classification, consistent theory, or statistic evidence. "He rejects fiducial probabilities because the very concept
abandons the uniqueness of the particular case." "Evidence," to
him, is the phenomenal given itself, explained, when necessary,
in terms of "the subjective compellingness and fittingness of an
account in terms of temporal-situational context." Predictability
of nontrivial behavior is, to him, "*prima facie* evidence of con-
straints that distort normal behavior," and laboratory situations
he regards as "so abnormal that no generalizations from them are
warranted." He gains more from reading Dostoevsky, Mann,
Proust, and Shakespeare than all of the pages of the *Journal of
Experimental Psychology*; for "a good example of seeing human
behavior in its complexity may be worth more in developing
principles of grasping particularities than scores of statistically
significant generalizations about highly circumscribed behaviors
occurring under laboratory conditions."*

Chein concludes with a plea for an approach to science that
speaks from the very heart of the Modern Job:

> Let there be free competition of ideas, methodologies, and even
> of doctrinaire views. But let us also beware of permitting, if only
> by default, extremists to curtail the competition or to build walls
> that block channels of free communication. Let us be mature
> enough to recognize our interdependence and consequent respon-
> sibility, within our means, to provide to each the conditions that
> will optimize his potential and maximize his contribution.†

In his criticism of the scientismic approach to psychology,
Chein points out the obvious but nonetheless consistently overlooked fact that the behaviorist psychologist as active knower
and intervener cannot be included in his own image of man as
passive being, any more than the bold pioneer Freud could fit his

* *Ibid.*, pp. 310–313.
† *Ibid.*, pp. 317 f.

own picture of the ego as the passive servant of three masters—
id, superego, and external reality:

> The class *Man* includes the psychologist who adopts the image of
> Man as an impotent being; this psychologist, like everyone else,
> cannot live by this image. He may try to apply it to everyone else,
> but he cannot apply it to himself as a basis of action. He thus
> professes a faith in an order of law that applies to everyone else,
> but, implicitly at least, he reserves to himself a special order of
> law. He knows that he can intervene in events, but he claims that
> no one else can—and this in the name of science!*

This conception of scientific knowledge as involving the participation and intervention of the scientists is put forward with
all possible emphasis and detail by Michael Polanyi in his classic
book *Personal Knowledge*. This stress on the *personal participation* of the knower in all acts of understanding in no way makes
understanding subjective or arbitrary. Knowing, to Polanyi, like
the dialogical knowing of the I-Thou relationship, is a responsible act which is *objective* in the sense of establishing contact
with a hidden reality, a reality which cannot be known as it is "in
itself" but only in relationship.† This passionate contribution of
the personal knower is not an imperfection, Polanyi insists, but a
vital component of his knowledge. Such knowing, insofar as it is
not compulsive, is an act of commitment, a part of our calling
which includes the historical setting and culture in which we
have grown up but *from which* we go out to meet the other that
transcends that culture with universal aspirations shorn of the
uncritical illusions of an objectivity minus any participating subject.

This knowing is a knowing of reciprocal contact or mutuality
even in the companionship between the animal psychologist and
the rat on which he is experimenting, says Polanyi. Interpersonal
relations become ampler as we deal with higher animals until at
the interhuman level "mutuality prevails to such an extent . . .

---

* *Ibid.*, p. 17.
† See Friedman, *Martin Buber: The Life of Dialogue*, Chap. 19, "Buber's
Theory of Knowledge."

that the logical category of an observer facing an object placed on a lower logical level becomes altogether inapplicable." At this point mutuality in knowing brings about a qualitative shift from I-It knowledge to I-Thou knowing: "The I-It situation has been gradually transformed into an I-Thou relation," writes Polanyi, thus suggesting "the possibility of a continuous transition from statements of fact to affirmations of moral and civic commands." This I-Thou knowing is set, in turn, within the framework of the dialogue between the partners of science, a partnership which itself takes place within the common scientific world, a world built of mutual trust. "The bond of mutual trust" formed between two scientists, writes Polanyi, "is but one link in the vast network of confidence between thousands of scientists of different specialities through which—and through which alone—a consensus of science is established."*

Such a consensus of mutual trust and confidence would be impossible without the human image in the exact sense in which we have used it, including not only what man *is* but what he can and should become. For this becoming there is no greater source than the open dialogue of the scientist with great human beings. Human greatness can only be recognized, writes Polanyi, by submission to the "ontology of commitment" and "thus belongs to the family of things which exist only for those committed to them." Thus at the apex of the whole scientific enterprise stands the revelation of the human image.

> All manner of excellence that we accept for our guidance, and all obligations to which we grant jurisdiction over us, can be defined by our respect for human greatness. And from these objects of our respect we can pass on continuously to purely cognitive targets, such as facts, knowledge, proof, reality, science—all of which can likewise be said to exist only as binding on ourselves. . . .
>
> Thus, at the confluence of biology and philosophical self-accrediting, man stands rooted in his calling under a firmament

* Michael Polanyi, *Personal Knowledge: Towards a Post-Critical Philosophy* (New York: Harper Torchbooks, 1964), pp. xiii, 324, 346, 375.

of truth and greatness. Its teachings are the idiom of his intellectual standards. Its commands harness his powers to the exercise
of his responsibilities. It binds him to abiding purposes, and
grants him power and freedom to defend them.

And we can establish it now as a matter of logic that man has
no other power than this.*

If instead of listening and responding to these voices of his
calling, the scientist "examines what he respects in a detached
manner," trading in commitment for reductive analysis, he contributes to the eclipse of the human image.

> Then law is no more than what the courts will decide, art but an
> emollient of nerves, morality but a convention, tradition but an
> inertia, God but a psychological necessity. The man dominates a
> world in which he himself does not exist. For with his obligations
> he has lost his voice and his hope, and been left behind meaning-
> less to himself.†

It is important to recognize that what Polanyi is pointing to is not
the reestablishment of some metaphysical universal but that
mutual contact with otherness which I have called "touchstones
of reality"—touchstones which make no pretense to tell what
"reality" is in itself but do claim to have contact with real otherness and to bring to light knowledge which is itself a product of
this mutual contact. "An innate affinity for making contact with
reality," writes Polanyi, "moves our thoughts—under the guidance of useful clues and plausible rules—to increase ever further
our hold on reality." These touchstones of reality lay bare the
meaninglessness of that reductive scientism which tries to represent life in terms of physics and chemistry alone or to represent
mind in terms of a machine or of a neural model. "Lower levels
do not lack a bearing on higher levels; *they define the conditions
of their success and account for their failures, but they cannot
account for their success, for they cannot even define it.*"‡

A truly human science cannot leave out the image of man in

---

* *Ibid.*, p. 380.
† *Ibid.*
‡ *Ibid.*, pp. 403, 382. See Maurice Friedman, *Touchstones of Reality: Existen-*

his wholeness and uniqueness, and this wholeness and uniqueness arise precisely through personal involvement, decision, and
risk—through finding a meaningful direction of human existence,
a way of valuing that is at the same time a way of living. The
logical positivist's approach destroys the very essence of moral
and social philosophy because it obliterates the distinction between sheer objective description of what takes place when a
man values and his own inner decision in response to the question: "What ought I to do in this situation?" The logical positivist
tends to use his concern with logic and methodology as a means
of escaping from the inundations of actual experience into the
high plains of pure abstraction.

> These self-proclaimed empiricists accept as their data little be-
> sides thin scientific abstractions. In their hands empiricism is a
> technique of paying lip service to facts and carefully screening
> out practically all the facts which are critically relevant to moral
> philosophy. What it feels like actually to be confronted with a
> moral perplexity, to be torn between knowledge of duty and the
> drive of desire; what it is to hunger desperately for inward peace,
> for relief from chaotic passion, or from compulsion of vice; what
> it is to be poisoned by malice or hatred or envy and to know
> it.*

In the language of *Problematic Rebel*, the logical positivist is the
Modern Promethean who, turning from the conquest of nature to
that of man, seeks by simple fiat to override the problematic of
modern man, the problematic of man.

The most obvious fact about language, that it is a form of
communication, a medium of relationship between man and
man, seems to have been lost sight of by the logical analyst
through an insistence on abstract formulation and empirical verification coupled with a too narrow emphasis on analysis and use.
Of course, language bears a freight of socially objectified knowl-

tial *Trust and the Community of Peace* (New York: Dutton Paperbacks,
1974), Chap. 18, "A Meaning for Modern Man."
* Eliseo Vivas, *The Moral Life and the Ethical Life* (Chicago: University of
Chicago Press, 1950; Phoenix Books [paperback], 1970), p. 179.

edge. Of course, it is a useful tool for the accomplishment of set purposes. But it is infinitely more and other than this. In identifying meaning with the possibility of proof, the logical positivists have forgotten the true nature of knowledge and of language as primarily communication—as the "word" which results from the relation of two existing beings. When the symbolic character of knowledge as abstraction and social objectification is forgotten, the word ceases to point back toward the reality of direct, mutual knowing in relationship and instead becomes an obstruction to it. The objectified word then poses as reality itself. Words are taken to be entities independent of the dialogue between man and man and are understood as nominative designations for entirely objective empirical reality. This way of seeing words attempts to separate the object from the knowing subject, to reduce words to sheer denotation, and to relegate all "connotations" to subjective emotion or "poetic truth." It judges present knowing entirely by finished knowledge as if there were no present reality until that reality had become past and therefore capable of being dealt with in our thought categories. It abstracts the knowing subject from his existence as a person in relation to other persons and then attempts to establish an "objective" impersonal knowledge abstracted from even that knowing subject. The so-called objectivity of this approach turns out, on examination, to be nothing other than a forgetting of the part that the knower plays in all knowledge—of the fact that the object is the third-personal subject of a dialogue between persons who only know at all because they already exist within a context of social relations with other human beings.

The concern of the modern linguistic analyst for clarification of concepts is not new. It goes back to Confucius and Socrates. What makes designations problematic, however, is not, as the analysts think, the fact that there are no single, agreed-on definitions as to the way in which words are being used. "They are problematic," Martin Buber has said, "because they do not show a concrete context that can be controlled. Every abstraction must stand the test of being related to a concrete reality without which it has no meaning. This revision of designations entails a necessary destruction if the new generation is not to be the life-long slave of tradition." Our goal then is not agreement or unanimity. We clarify designations only in order that we may discuss them, and relate to each other in terms of them, whether in cooperation or opposition. Dialectic may lead to discovering basic agreement and disagreement if it takes place in genuine dialogue, but not if it becomes a dialectical exercise within the mind of a single thinker. Such *ratio* is one of the things that distinguishes man from the animal, but it is not the decisive factor, as Plato thinks. Nor is man understandable simply as the symbol-making animal, as Ernst Cassirer and Suzanne Langer hold. Basic to man as man is language, and language is, in the first instance, living speech between men.

Living speech presupposes the distancing which gives man the possibility of a world, as Martin Buber has pointed out in his philosophical anthropology, particularly *The Knowledge of Man*. It also presupposes the synthetic apperception whereby the world becomes one. But above all it presupposes, again as Buber has shown, that men become men in relating to each other. Language is, in the first instance, neither the unmediated cry of the animal nor the universal Platonic idea, but the mediate-immediate dialogue between two persons, each of whom recognizes himself as a self when he is speaking to the other person and the other person as a self even when he is speaking of himself to that person. Our common world is, therefore, as Heraclitus points out, a cosmos built upon *logos*—common speech-with-meaning. It is through this speech between man and man that we are confirmed as selves. It is through it too that we build up a world of language—of potential speech which again and again becomes actual in the spoken word. And it is through it, finally, that we build up a world of categories within which we think, communicate with one another, and develop our civilization. The true civilizing tool is not Prometheus' fire but Job's dialogue.

Yet language remains curiously ambiguous—being born, dying, going over from lived speech to conventional phrase, from

genuine dialogue to technical interchange, from interhuman contact to mass social manipulation. We must distinguish, therefore,
between the word as direct dialogue, the word as category pointing back to the immediacy of lived speech, and the word which
no longer points back but instead points out toward a world of
technical interaction. It is this last word which leads toward the
ultimate consummation of objectified, monological thought, the
electronic brain—an invention which fits Descartes' definition of
man as a "thinking thing" as no human being ever has.

Useful as precision and definition are for the exact sciences, the
true humanity and the very meaning of language depend upon
its being brought back to the fruitful disagreement of lived
speech between men whose meanings necessarily differ because
of the difference of their attitudes, their situations, their points of
view as persons. This fruitful disagreement can be much aided
by linguistic analysis as and to the extent that it sheds its unnecessary baggage: the illogical negativism of logical positivism.

The tremendous prestige of the scientific method has led many
to forget that science investigates man not as a whole but in
selective aspects and as part of the natural world. Scientific
method is man's most highly perfected development of the "I-It,"
or subject-object, way of knowing. Its methods of abstracting
from the concrete actuality and of largely ignoring the inevitable
difference beween observers reduce the I insofar as possible to
the abstract knowing subject and the It insofar as possible to the
passive and abstract object of thought. Just for these reasons
scientific method is not qualified to find the wholeness of man. It
can compare men with one another and man with animals, but
from such comparison and contrast there can only emerge an
expanding and contracting scale of similarities and differences
among objects in a world of objects, not the uniqueness of man
as man.

The relation of dialogue and the unique to science and to
man's personal wholeness comes into illuminating focus in
George Morgan's lucid and seminal book *The Human Predicament: Dissolution and Wholeness*. Science, says Morgan, who

was professor of applied mathematics at Brown University before he founded the Human Studies major there, is a road map
which substitutes a set of systematic and ordered concepts for
the actual "ploughed fields, ripe grain, vibrant poppies, sparkling
water, the smell of the earth" of the country through which the
road map passes. Only if we understand this limitation of scientific abstraction can we recognize that "awareness of inexhausti-
bility is of the utmost importance for human life, for it is the
complement of a sense of wonder." To apprehend with wonder
means to distinguish—as scientificists with their "prosaic mental-
ity" do not—between the concrete particular and the particular
as observed (and abstracted) by science. This also means that
we cannot pretend to understand the philosophy of a thinker if
we turn it into an object of our analysis, demanding at every step
that it prove itself to our satisfaction without meeting it with a
receptive understanding of its source.

In science as in philosophy, "the personal element is a necessary condition of apprehending." The attempt to understand
purely objectively necessarily entails the isolation or suppression
of one part of ourselves and the denial of those "essential human
apprehensions that are impossible without engagement of the
whole personality." Our modes of apprehension "span fundamentally diverse attitudes, approaches to the world, and kinds of
embodiment." They range from detachment to great emotional
involvement, from abstraction to concreteness. "What matters
most," says Morgan, "is that this span be acknowledged and
maintained, that the tensions be faced, not dissolved, that contrary movements of spirit be profoundly understood, cultivated,
and given their proper place within the wholeness of apprehension—in each activity, in the individual's life, and in the social
structure."

The prosaic mind uses, manipulates, and controls symbols, but
it fails to listen to them, to be really responsive to them. Yet only
through such responsiveness can we appreciate uniqueness, including the uniqueness of symbols. The same applies to values
and to education. Not only must our apprehension be whole, but

it must be integrated, in all its scope, with the whole of life. But that means freeing learning, including learning of the sciences, from the false alternative of "solid" specialism and "superficial" generalism. The real alternative is "between being ruled by methods, institutions, and standardized systems, and making personal responsible judgments; between seeking the security of boundaries and compartments, and taking the risk of going where it is important to go." As the poet Theodore Roethke puts it, we "learn by going where" we "have to go."

The wholeness of the person depends upon the human image. To reverse the ancient anthropomorphizing of the nonhuman world by dehumanizing man, writes Morgan, is to set analysis and reduction in the way of the fullness of man's being. Also inseparably linked with wholeness is freedom—the power of the self to be in the world with every part of the self acknowledged, accepted, and integrated into the whole. The cleavage between the rational and the emotional that so many people fall into is, for this reason, a fatal error: "The very doctrine . . . that in the search for knowledge one must expel emotion, that understanding can only be gained in detachment, is shaped under pressure of unrecognized emotions—not the least of which is fear of emotion and the consequent need to cling to the security of a sterile scheme."*

What takes place in the present is ordered through the abstracting function of science into the world of categories—of space and time, cause and effect. We usually think of these categories as reality itself, but they are actually merely the symbolic representation of what has become. Even our predictions of the future actually belong to the world of the past; for they are generalizations based on the assumptions of unity, continuity, cause and effect, and the resemblance of the future to the past. Nor does the partial success of these predictions show that we have real knowledge of the future; for we do not know this "future" until it is already past, that is, until it has been registered

* George Morgan, *The Human Predicament: Dissolution and Wholeness* (New York: Delta Books, 1970).

in the categories of our knowledge-world. Psychology, similarly, observes its phenomena after they have already taken their place in the categories of human knowing, and, insofar as it is scientific in the more limited sense of that term, it excludes the really direct and present knowing of the interhuman. Only as they recognize that to know man in his wholeness and uniqueness means to know him within the interhuman relationship will psychology and the social sciences establish their subject-object knowledge on its true foundation—the dialogical knowing from which it derives and to which it points.

Psychoanalysis began in the spirit of the Modern Promethean. To Freud, man's mind is an object of scientific study in exactly the same way as any nonhuman object. "It cannot be supported for a moment," writes Freud, that there can be some other way of regarding man aside from the scientific.

> For the spirit and the mind of man is a subject of investigation in exactly the same way, as any non-human entities. . . . The contribution of psycho-analysis to science consists precisely in having extended research to the region of the mind.*

Yet through the mind that studies mind, that is, through Freud himself, Feuerbach's dream of freeing man from the alienation of his creative freedom to an unreal transcendent seems finally realized and religion, conscience, and morality unmasked as mere products of the economy of the libido in the interaction of ego, superego, and id:

> Science . . . does well to distinguish carefully between illusion (the result of emotional demands of that kind) and knowledge. . . . It is inadmissible to declare that science is one field of intellectual activity, and that religion and philosophy are others . . . and . . . that they all have an equal claim to truth. The bare fact is that truth cannot be tolerant and cannot admit compromise or limitations, that scientific research looks on the whole field of human activity as its own, and must adopt an uncompromisingly critical

* Sigmund Freud, *New Introductory Lectures on Psycho-Analysis*, trans. by J. H. Sprott (New York: W. W. Norton, 1933), Chap. 7, "A Philosophy of Life," pp. 217 f.

attitude towards any other power that seeks to usurp any part of its province.*

Freud's identification of his own point of view with "truth" brings to mind Captain Ahab's Promethean cry, "Who's over me. Truth hath no confines!" It is for religion in particular that Freud reserves his Promethean attacks in the name of the scientific *Weltanschauung*, which he modestly claims for psychoanalysis as one that "limits itself to truth and rejects illusions."

> The final judgment of science on the religious *Weltanschauung*, then, runs as follows. While the different religions wrangle with one another as to which of them is in possession of the truth, in our view the truth of religion may be altogether disregarded. . . . Its doctrines carry with them the stamp of the times in which they originated, the ignorant childhood days of the human race. Its consolations deserve no trust. Experience teaches us that the world is not a nursery.†

Freud's arrogance leads him to dismiss not only religion but all the wisdom of earlier "prescientific" ages. Even odder than that reality should correspond to our wishes, as religion teaches, writes Freud, would be the notion that "our poor, ignorant, enslaved ancestors had succeeded in solving all these difficult riddles of the universe." Freud concludes *The Future of an Illusion* with the triumphant note of the Modern Promethean who has once and for all done away with any reality transcending man: "No, science is no illusion. But it would be an illusion to suppose that we could get anywhere else what it cannot give us."‡

Freud's severest critics among his followers, men like C. G. Jung and Erich Fromm, still cling to his Modern Prometheanism. Although Jung is above all a Modern Gnostic, as I have demonstrated at length in *To Deny Our Nothingness*, his pointing to psychic experience as the really real stands less under the aegis of the ancient Gnostic than it does of the Modern Promethean.

---

* *Ibid.*, pp. 218 f.
† *Ibid.*, pp. 229 f.
‡ Sigmund Freud, *The Future of an Illusion*, trans. by W. D. Robson-Scott (New York: Liveright Publishing Corp., 1949), pp. 58, 98.

Unlike the former and like the latter, he rejects any genuine transcendence in favor of the deified Self produced in the depths of the unconscious by the integration of the personality. "God" acts only "out of the unconscious of man," and the promise of the Holy Ghost means nothing other than that for modern man God becomes *wholly* man. Fromm, in *Man for Himself*, postulates a split between man and a cold, meaningless universe. If man acknowledges "his fundamental aloneness and solitude in a universe indifferent to his fate," he will recognize that *there is no meaning to life except the meaning man gives his life by the unfolding of his powers, by living productively*. Thus Fromm identifies himself with the familiar nineteenth-century theme of "alienation" whereby thinkers such as Feuerbach, Marx, and Nietzsche saw man's creativity and freedom as dependent upon his denial of any reality transcending him.* This motif is the Modern Promethean's Either/Or of dominating what faces him or being dominated by it.

Each of these three theorists of psychotherapy, in the name of science, goes beyond the proper limits of his science and establishes a negative metaphysics within which the Modern Promethean can keep alive his romantic, defiant Either/Or. Psychotherapy, however, is a science and not a metaphysics. It is not, of course, an objective laboratory science subject to experimental verification, but an interpersonal science of knowing within the special relationship of healer and patient.

Freud himself, and still more Jung and Fromm, would have been horrified had they been present at a public symposium on "Humanities versus Science" that I took part in at a Midwestern college not long ago. There a prominent psychologist informed me that my thought was still back in the seventeenth century since I could not accede to his distinctly seventeenth-century view of man as a machine (LaMettrie). On the basis of what biochemists have discovered about D.N.A. and R.N.A. and of what he himself had done by way of lopping off the heads of

* See Friedman, *To Deny Our Nothingness*, Chap. 9, "Carl Jung," and Chap. 13, "Erich Fromm and 'Self-Realization.'"

flatworms, he claimed that a proper injection of chemicals would eventually remove all need for education and that even now he could, through operant conditioning—electric shocks and the like —transform me at will into an Annapolis naval lieutenant! It is no accident that this same "scientist" does important research for the United States government on "persuasion," or, to give it its true name, "brainwashing."

Still less than modern physics can psychology dispose with absolute certainty of the reality with which it deals as if that reality were an entirely comprehensible and surveyable object of human knowledge. It must begin, rather, with the uniqueness of the person, with the concrete relation between experimenter and subject and between therapist and client, and with that bewildering intermixture of personal freedom and psychological compulsion to which I have pointed in *Problematic Rebel.* In psychotherapy, too, it is not the monological self-assertion of the Modern Promethean that is called for but the clear-sighted trust that is willing to confront each situation in its uniqueness, including, if necessary, even despair in the face of the ultimate absurdity which Freud and his followers sought to rationalize, namely, that the very "meaning" of madness may be its *absence* of meaning. "A dimension of terror is added to our existence," writes the psychiatrist Leslie H. Farber of the psychotherapist's work with schizophrenics, "as we learn to live with the insane possibility—which is, after all, one of the facts of madness—that meaning itself can be the mirage."*

Today the really creative worker in science, the social sciences, psychology, and psychotherapy is less characterized by the attitudinizings of the Modern Promethean than by the open and yet serious approach of the Modern Job. He stands at the boundaries of human knowledge, like Ishmael at the limits of his cetology, open to the wonder of the forever incomprehensible world that he encounters. "Dissect him how I may I go but skin deep." The

---

* Leslie H. Farber, *The Ways of the Will: Essays in the Psychology and Psychopathology of the Will* (New York: Harper Colophon Books, 1967), "The Therapeutic Despair," p. 177.

Modern Job accepts the challenge and the terror of real scientific advance while denying the pseudosecurity of scientism, which claims for science such knowledge and control that every "advance" is for the human good. It was the atomic scientists themselves who undertook to warn the world of a peril beyond its imaginings, just as it is some of our greatest chemists who have resisted the government's pressure to work on chemical warfare. The Modern Job does not fear technological or scientific advance per se or want to deny any part of its irreversible reality. But he remains concerned about the image of man that may give a human direction to these ever more amazing new potentialities. There is a powerful movement in the United Nations to attain common agreement about the common use of the resources of the sea rather than witnessing here too "a war of all against all."

THE
CHANGING IMAGE OF
HUMAN NATURE

If the divergent schools of contemporary philosophy are united in little else, they do at least join in rejecting the notion that man has some fixed, identifiable, universal essence. We look to contemporary philosophy, therefore, not so much for new definitions of human nature as for a new critical awareness of the issues that surround this term. This critical awareness is of particular significance for psychology and psychoanalytic theory, since both have often taken over quite uncritically many of the formulations of classic philosophy.

One of the classic problems of "human nature" is that of "free will" versus "determinism." Transposed into the realm of psychology, it becomes the much more fruitful problem of personal freedom and psychological compulsion. The reality of unconscious compulsion makes it impossible to assert the existence of full, conscious freedom. But it is equally impossible to reduce man to a purely deterministic system. Human existence—in the well man as in the ill—is a complex intermixture of personal freedom and psychological compulsion, a paradoxical phenomenon that can be understood only from within. As I have written in *Problematic Rebel.*

The problem of the relation of personal freedom to psychological compulsion cannot be solved by the attempt to reduce man to a

66

bundle of instinctual drives, unconscious complexes, the need for security or any other single factor. . . . Motivation is inextricably bound up with the wholeness of the person, with his direction of movement, with his struggles to authenticate himself. . . . No general theory of psychogenesis and no general knowledge of a person will tell us in advance what will be his actual mixture of spontaneity and compulsion in any particular situation.*

Another problem of human nature that psychoanalytic theory has inherited from classical philosophy is that of mind-body dualism. At first glance, most psychoanalysis would seem to be a denial of this dualism. In fact, however, the problem has only been transposed into the complex interrelationship between biological instinct and consciousness or, on a subtler plane, between the pleasure principle and the reality principle. Even the division between the conscious and the unconscious which is so central to psychoanalysis is in a certain sense a variant of the Cartesian mind-body dualism. Freud's "censor," Sartre points out, is in "bad faith" with itself; for it must know what it censors and then pretend not to know it. Thus psychoanalysis introduces into subjectivity the deepest structure of intersubjectivity. It leaves a dualism between the unconscious and consciousness which is bridged only by an autonomous consciousness which knows the drive to be repressed precisely *in order not to be* conscious of it.

A still more significant criticism of the psychoanalytic theory of the unconscious was hinted at in Martin Buber's seminars on the unconscious given in 1957 for the Washington (D.C.) School of Psychiatry. According to Buber, Freud and the whole psychoanalytic world have tended to assume that the unconscious is a sort of psychic deep freeze which contains ideas capable of being repressed and capable of being brought to consciousness through transference to the therapist or through encounter with the "shadow." This assumption overlooks the fact that if the unconscious is really unconscious, we may know its effects but can

---

* Maurice Friedman, *Problematic Rebel: Melville, Dostoievsky, Kafka, Camus*, 2nd ed. (Chicago: University of Chicago Press, Phoenix Books [paperback], 1970), pp. 470, 472.

never know it or its contents except as they are shaped and elaborated by the conscious. Buber suggests that the unconscious is the ground of personal wholeness before its elaboration into the physical and the psychic. Freud, he holds, and after him Jung, have made the simple logical error of assuming that the unconscious is psychic since they wished to deny that it is physical. They did not, Buber holds, see this third alternative and with it the possibility of bursting the bounds of psychologism by recognizing that the division of inner and outer that applies to the psyche and the physical need not apply to the unconscious. Here, in contrast, there might be direct meeting and direct communication (as in a handshake) between one unconscious and another.*

The basis for Buber's approach to the unconscious is his philosophical anthropology, according to which what gives man a world and an existence as a self over against other selves is the ability, unique to man, of executing two primary ontological movements—that of distancing and that of entering into relation. If, as Buber holds, only these constitute man as man, then the attempt of some psychological and psychoanalytical theories to deal with man in fundamentally biological terms, as if he were continuous with all other animals except for the modifications forced by civilization, is fundamentally in error. In error too is the individualism of the isolated consciousness which both Freud and Jung inherited from Descartes. Starting with "I think, therefore I am," Descartes was left with the insoluble problem of the knowledge of other minds. Edmund Husserl's phenomenology, Heidegger's ontology, and Sartre's existentialism have all transposed this problem by seeing the self as only existing in its transcendence toward a field of consciousness, or a world. The classical subject-object relation of knower and known is replaced here by the self and its world.

Immanuel Kant was the first philosopher to explicitly stake out

* Martin Buber, *A Believing Humanism: Gleanings*, trans. with an Introduction and Explanatory Comments by Maurice Friedman (New York: Simon & Schuster Paperbacks, 1969), "The Unconscious," Notes taken by Maurice Friedman, pp. 153–173.

philosophical anthropology as a branch of philosophy. Not only is the question, "What is man?" a part of the question, "What can I know?," but it is a very special part of this question with problems unique to itself. At the same time, as the view of man the knower changed, the view of what man is inevitably changed with it. Kant's great successor, Friedrich Hegel, removed Kant's dualism of the noumenal and the phenomenal into the concrete universal of the world-historical spirit. Among some of the radical neo-Hegelians, the continued cultivation of the philosophical soil they inherited was coupled with a rebellion against the idealist subject in favor of the whole human person (Kierkegaard and Nietzsche), against the historical spirit in favor of the concrete realities of social, economic, and political life (Feuerbach, Marx, and Nietzsche), against the isolated thinker in favor of the recognition of the origin of all thought and all philosophy in the dialogue of I and Thou (Feuerbach), or against metaphysics in favor of philosophical anthropology (Feuerbach and Nietzsche).*

An important advance in philosophical anthropology was the development of "phenomenology" by the German philosophers Wilhelm Dilthey and Edmund Husserl. Dilthey based his thought on the radical difference between the way of knowing proper to the *"Geisteswissenschaften"*—the human studies, such as philosophy, the social sciences, and psychology—and that proper to *"Naturwissenschaften"*—the natural sciences. In the former the knower cannot be merely a detached scientific observer but must also participate himself; for it is through his participation that he discovers both the typical and the unique in the aspects of human life that he is studying. At the same time he must suspend the foregone conclusions and the search for causality that mark the natural scientist in favor of an open attempt to discover what offers itself. Only through this open understanding (*das Verstehen*) can one value the unique that reveals itself in every human phenomenon.

* Cf. Karl Löwith, *From Hegel to Nietzsche: The Revolution in Nineteenth Century Thought*, trans. by David E. Greene (New York: Holt, Rinehart & Winston, 1964).

Husserl elaborated phenomenology into a full-fledged systematic philosophy. He went decisively beyond Descartes' *cogito* in his recognition that one cannot divorce the "I think" from what is thought, consciousness from intentionality. By the method of "parenthesizing," or phenomenological reduction, Husserl replaced the detached subject and independent object of older philosophy by a field of knowing in which the phenomena are accepted as pure phenomena without questioning their independent existence. From this he also obtained a "transcendental ego" which, as the subject of knowing, transcended all contents of knowing, including the psychophysical me. The exploration of the field of transcendental experience thus becomes equivalent to the phenomenological knowledge of the world.

Husserl's existential successors either emphasized the direct experiential quality of his thought as opposed to the idealist, like Maurice Merleau-Ponty, or broke with the transcendental ego altogether while retaining the method of phenomenology, like Jean-Paul Sartre, or transformed phenomenology from a method of knowledge into a "fundamental ontology," like Martin Heidegger. Both Sartre and Heidegger accept Husserl's motto "To the things themselves" as an obstacle to scientism's attempt to posit a substratum of independent but nonperceivable "matter" behind the phenomena. Only an existential analysis of the existent will yield any knowledge of being. For Heidegger this analysis is posited on his special use of *Dasein*—the person's "being there" in the world, thrown into a situation apart from which neither subject nor consciousness has any meaning. Heidegger and Sartre see the self as only existing in its transcendence toward a field of consciousness or a world. To exist is to be there, in the situation, and the situation includes, of course, the world of intersubjectivity in which we have to do with other men. Yet Heidegger and Sartre, as we have seen, still basically see the ontological as essentially discovered in the self, with the relations to others as an "ontic" dimension of the existence of the self.

Martin Buber, who stems from Feuerbach and Dilthey rather than from Husserl, sees the ontological as found in the *meeting* between man and man and between man and world, with the realization of the self the indispensable accompaniment and corollary of the dialogue. Buber has sharpened the social theory of the self to a distinction between direct, mutual interpersonal relations—"I-Thou," or "the interhuman"—and indirect, nonmutual interpersonal relations—"I-It." The American social psychologist and philosopher George Herbert Mead, the American psychiatrist Harry Stack Sullivan, and Erich Fromm all share with Buber what Paul Pfuetze calls "the social self," but they have not made the distinction Buber has between direct and indirect, mutual and nonmutual interpersonal relations. Nor is this distinction adequately grasped by Heidegger's *Mitsein* or Sartre's "world of intersubjectivity." Heidegger's "being-with" undoubtedly includes the I-Thou relationship in principle, but it gives very little attention to anything which could be recognized as such, and the ultimate relationship for him is explicitly with oneself. Sartre's intersubjectivity excludes free mutuality in principle in favor of a tormented interaction of subjectivity and objectivity in which one recognizes the other's freedom either as a threat and limitation to one's own or as something to be possessed and dominated for a time through sexual love.

Buber's view of man leads him to assert that the chasm between spirit and instincts is not an inherent structure of human nature, as Freud holds, but is a product of the sickness of modern man—the destruction of organic confidence and of organic community and the divorce between man and man.* It has also led Buber, and myself following him, to a more dialogical understanding of the task of the philosophical anthropologist than even Feuerbach and Dilthey. Philosophical anthropology goes beyond cultural anthropology in that it asks the question not just about men but about man: about man's wholeness and uniqueness, about what makes man man. As such, it necessarily transcends, even while making full use of, those sciences which deliberately

---

* Martin Buber, *Between Man and Man*, trans. by Ronald Gregor Smith, with an Introduction by Maurice Friedman (New York: Macmillan Paperbacks, 1965), pp. 196 f.

deal with man only as a part and not a whole—whether it be economic man, political man, sociological man, psychological man, or biological man. It can only touch on the problem of man, however, insofar as it recognizes that the philosophical anthropologist himself is a man and as such is *as subject* and not just as object a part of what he seeks to know. He must share in and not merely observe the problematic of modern man. He must reject all attempts to reduce this problematic to any single motive or complex of motives or to comprehend man simply on the analogy of biology or the behavior of animals. Only if the philosophical anthropologist is a problem to himself can he understand man as a problem to himself.

Only if he knows from within his own situation and in dialogue with the others with whom he has to do can he begin to approach that wholeness and uniqueness of man which slips through the net of every concept of man as object. To understand man one must be a participant who only afterward gains the distance from his subject matter that will enable him to formulate the insights he has attained. Otherwise, one inevitably sees man as a sum of parts some of which are labeled "objective" and hence oriented around the thing known, and some "subjective" and hence oriented around the knower.

Philosophical anthropology today begins on the far side of earlier notions of understanding man in terms of a universal and timeless "human nature." It looks away from essences of man in order to grasp man in his particularity and his complexity, his dynamic interrelatedness with other men, and the interplay within him of possibility, freedom, and personal direction. Existentialism similarly replaces the concept of "human nature" by the concept of the "human condition." Man is without a predetermined essence because he is free, but his freedom is a finite one, as Tillich points out. It must operate within the general human condition—the need to work, one's existence as a self in relation to other selves and to the nonhuman world, the awareness of solitude, of possibility, and of death. These represent radical changes in our view of man with far-reaching implications that have only begun to be spelled out. Yet the critical task of modern philosophy in relation to the concept of human nature cannot stop here.

If we wish to make a decisive break with the universal and essential "human nature" of earlier philosophy and attain a picture of man in his uniqueness and his wholeness, we must move from *concepts* about man, no matter how profound, to the *image* of man. It is this that I have tried to do in *Problematic Rebel* and *To Deny Our Nothingness* and in this third and last book on the image of man. The image of man is man's becoming in the truest sense of the word, that is, his becoming as a person and as a human being. In this becoming, what we call the "is" is not a static given. It is a dynamic, constantly changing material that is continually being shaped and given form not merely by inner and outer conditioning but by the directions that one takes as a person. Similarly, what we call the "ought" is not some abstract ideal but a constantly changing, flowing direction of movement that is at one and the same time a response to the present, a choice between possibilities in a given situation, and a line of advance into the future.

PSYCHOTHERAPY
AND THE
HUMAN IMAGE

There is perhaps no field of more interest for the hidden human image than psychotherapy. On the one hand, "depth psychology," or "depth analysis," undertakes to reveal, to bring to the light of day, much that is hidden, including in the case of some persons their hidden humanity. On the other hand, psychotherapy in its various schools of theory and practice has contributed its share to the eclipse of man, to the further hiding of the human image. This is in part because of the mechanistic approach that was taken toward science and even toward man. Psychiatry in the nineteenth century was a specific matter of curing symptoms. It had little to do with the wholeness of man. Psychoanalysis represented an important step in the direction of a concern for the whole man, but only a step. It arose under the aegis of "Science," and even, as we have seen, of scientism. In many branches of psychotherapy today, however, the movement is away from seeing it as an exact science toward seeing it as a humanistic task and a humanistic discipline.

Contemporary man's image of himself and of authentic human existence meets psychotherapy at the precise point at which this image enters into the process of his becoming. There is a growing recognition today of the importance of philosophy and the human studies for the full understanding of the methods and goals of psychotherapy. When the Washington School of Psychiatry brought Martin Buber from Jerusalem in 1957 to give the fourth William Alanson White Memorial Lectures, the title of the series was, "What Can Philosophical Anthropology Contribute to Psychiatry?" In his introduction to these lectures, Leslie H. Farber, M.D., the chairman of the faculty, pointed out that none of the sciences has asked the question about man in his *wholeness* that is the concern of philosophical anthropology.

> The medical and biological sciences were asking, What is man in his relation to nature—to natural history, the evolution of organisms, and the physical forces regulating his body? . . . And it was upon this natural basis that all the other sciences of man—anthropology, sociology, political science, and finally the new Freudian science of psychoanalysis—asked their question. . . . None of the sciences were asking the *whole* question, What is man? Nor were they asking the unique question, Who am I, in my uniquely human essence? . . . These are not smaller or more personal questions; they are larger and more comprehensive than the ones which science has been asking. They include . . . man's personal being—my personal experience and knowledge of myself —as well as my philosophical and scientific knowledge of what "*man* is."*

Especially helpful in Helen Merrell Lynd's *On Shame and the Search for Identity* are her clear insights into the implications of various personality theories for the image of man which a particular psychology or psychoanalytic theory assumes, and her recognition that such images are matters of basic assumption even more than of scientific evidence and methodology.

> It does make a difference whether the individual is considered as eager, curious, and trusting until specific experience in a given society and historical period lead him to be anxious, cautious,

---

* Leslie H. Farber, "Introduction" to Martin Buber, "The William Alanson White Memorial Lectures, Fourth Series," *Psychiatry*, Vol. XX, No. 2 (May, 1957), pp. 95 f. Buber's lectures are included in Martin Buber, *The Knowledge of Man*, ed. by Maurice Friedman (New York: Harper Torchbooks, 1966).

and aggressive, or whether he is regarded as born with hostility, aggression, and fear which specific experiences may modify only to a limited degree in the direction of trust, sympathy, and interest. *

The possibility of mutual relations "between persons as an enlargement, not a contradiction of individual freedom," is incompatible with personality theories "that see men primarily as need-satisfying objects, or in terms of their particular status or role relations to oneself" quite as much as with those theories centering in "release of tension, return to quiescence, and self-preservation." "Much depends," she writes, "upon whether one believes that isolation and alienation are inevitable in man's fate or that openness of communication between persons, mutual discovery, and love are actual possibilities."

"The aim of therapy is often that of helping the person to be better adjusted to existing circumstances," says Fromm in *Beyond the Chains of Illusion*. "Mental health is often considered to be nothing but this adjustment, or to put it differently, a state of mind in which one's individual unhappiness is reduced to the level of the general unhappiness. The real problem . . . need not even be touched in this type of psychoanalysis." "Psychologists and psychoanalysts," writes Helen Lynd, "have given more encouragement to the adjustment of individuals to the realities of a given society than to personal differentiation and deviation from them."

> They frequently fail to give explicit recognition to the distinction between normal or healthy in terms of what are the generally accepted norms of the society and in terms of what is humanly desirable. If the psychoanalyst . . . does not rigorously examine his own values in relation to those of society, he almost inevitably tends to accept tacitly the dominant values of the society as the norm of behavior, and to measure health and illness by these. Scientific objectivity, then, becomes indistinguishable from acceptance of social determinants. †

* Helen Merrell Lynd, *On Shame and the Search for Identity* (New York: Harcourt Brace, Harbrace Books [paperback], 1969), p. 142.
† *Ibid.*, p. 212.

Even if the psychoanalyst does rigorously reexamine his values, however, he is still likely to impose them under the mask of objectivity; for he is not going to lose his values through examining them. It is true, as Fromm says in *Man for Himself*, that it matters whether the therapist encourages his patient to adapt or strengthens him in his unwillingness to compromise his integrity. It is also true, as other therapists would point out, that the patient is sometimes so tied up in his neurotic rebellion against the culture that there is little else that he could do anyway. This makes his rebellion problematic but not necessarily illusory or unreal. In either case, the therapist cannot take the risk of encouraging the patient to oppose society and to undergo privation unless he has a sure enough sense of that person in his uniqueness. He must feel sure that the client has a ground on which to stand as a person and that he stands there in some real and creative relationship to the society that he is going to oppose. Otherwise the therapist cannot help encouraging a patient to adjust to this particular society and seeing his health and sickness in terms of that adjustment.

Another central problem is the relationship between therapist and client and its implications for both of their images of man. In *Beyond the Chains of Illusion* Erich Fromm tells how he began at first with the "strictly orthodox Freudian procedure of analyzing a patient while sitting behind him and listening to his associations." This procedure turned the patient into the object of a laboratory experiment, says Fromm. He was able to fit the patient's dreams into his theoretical expectations, but he was still talking *about* the patient rather than *to* him. Eventually, he found a new way: "Instead of being an observer, I had to become a participant; to be engaged with the patient; from center to center, rather than from periphery to periphery." That this means an even more radical departure from the traditional method than Sullivan's "participant observer" is suggested by Fromm's remark to me that he not only sees therapy as "healing through meeting" (a phrase of Martin Buber's and Hans Trüb's) but that he believes the therapist himself is healed in the process.

This stress on participation does not mean that Fromm is under any illusion about therapy being fully mutual. Even while he felt himself fully engaged, as he had never been before, and learned that he could understand his patient rather than interpret what he said, he discovered that he could at the same time remain fully objective—seeing the patient as he is, and not as Fromm might want him to be. "To be objective is only possible if one does not want anything for oneself, neither the patient's admiration, nor his submission, nor even his 'cure.' " The therapy takes place for the sake of the cure, but a genuine wish to help will protect the therapist from being hurt in his self-esteem when the patient does not improve or is elated about "his" achievement when he gets well.

Many psychotherapists today would join Fromm in taking issue with Freud's approach to psychotherapy. Looking on man in a purely "scientific" way similar to that which we bring to a nonhuman entity is not sufficient to understand man. It is necessary for the therapist to understand the person facing him from within through his own participation, through the fact that he himself is a person who must make basic decisions, that he confronts the other as a person and not merely as a scientific observer. C. G. Jung in *The Undiscovered Self* points out the difference between the psychotherapist when he is concerned with man in general, and therefore with statistical and scientific knowledge of man, and the same psychotherapist when he is concerned with the particular, unique individual before him and his concrete problems. The therapist, says Jung,

> is faced with the task of treating a sick person, who, especially in the case of psychic suffering, requires *individual understanding*. The more schematic the treatment is, the more resistances it— quite rightly—calls up in the patient, and the more the cure is jeopardized. . . . Today, over the whole field of medicine, it is recognized that the task of the doctor consists in treating the sick patient, not an abstract illness.*

* C. G. Jung, *The Undiscovered Self*, trans. by R. F. C. Hull (Boston: Little, Brown & Co., 1958), p. 12.

Freud found meaning in everything—in dreams, in slips of the tongue, in the psychopathology of everyday life. But it was only meaning as seen by the scientist from the outside, not the meaning of the personal life seen from within. Freud's one-time disciple, Carl G. Jung, offers the possibility of deep inner meaning beyond our ordinary imaginings. His goal is not merely curing sickness; it is "individuation" in which the four faculties— thought, sensation, feeling, and intuition—are united into a whole, integrated personality. Jung went much further than Freud did in the direction of a real mutuality between patient and therapist. He recognized before Freud that a therapist should be analyzed himself. He recognized that the therapist must risk himself, that he cannot hide behind his professional superiority. At the same time, Jung's "analytical psychology" is so focused on the patient's inwardness that the outer person tends to be seen as a mask or mere social role. There is also a danger of relating to the other not as a person but as an "anima" or an "animus" (the feminine and masculine aspects of the psyche). Jung holds that the aim of his therapy is to bring the patient back into relationship with the world freed from the "shadow" that has turned negative because it is repressed and is then projected onto the other. Only then, says Jung, can he have real relationships with others. Jung assumes that the person becomes whole first, and only then enters into a genuine relationship. One of the dangers of this assumption is that there is always a tendency for the other person to become the function of your becoming, as you of his. Another is the precarious nature of a "personal integration" attained apart from lived mutuality and the direction found in going out to meet what is not yourself.

The hidden human image has more to do with therapy itself than it does with our theories about therapy, important as the theories may be; for there is always the danger of the theory becoming a construct in which the therapist settles down. "Young therapists often regard the dreams of their patient as examinations," Fromm said to me. "They feel that they must be ready to give some theoretical interpretations, and as a result they do not really hear the dreams." When he was working with thirty of us in Washington, D.C., in a series of seminars on dreams and the unconscious, Martin Buber said that there are two kinds of relationship a therapist has to dreams—one in which he puts them into the categories of his school and the other in which he responds to them spontaneously and wholly in a "musical, floating relationship." "I am for the latter," Buber added. This musical relationship in which the therapist really hears the unique person and experiences his side of the relationship is crucial for all therapy, regardless of the school. No matter what school the therapist comes from and no matter what knowledge and experience he has, the basic question is still *when* his insights apply to this particular patient and when not. To answer this question he must use the categories of his school in a flexible, "musical" way in order again and again to try to arrive at this person's uniqueness. To do this the therapist must practice what Buber calls the act of "inclusion," experiencing the patient's side of the relationship as well as his own. Rollo May stresses the centrality of such inclusion for therapy and love in terms of what might be called a "field theory" of the emotions:

> Our feelings, like the artist's paints and brush, are ways of communicating and sharing something meaningful from us to the world. Our feelings not only take into consideration the other person but are in a real sense partially *formed by the feelings of the other person present*. We *feel* in a magnetic field. A sensitive person learns, often without being conscious of doing so, to pick up the feelings of the persons around him, as a violin string resonates to the vibration of every other musical string in the room. . . . Every successful lover knows this by "instinct." It is an essential—if not *the* essential—quality of the good therapist.*

Even the patient's "sickness" is part of his uniqueness; for even his sickness tells of the road he has not gone and has to go. If instead the therapist makes the patient into an object to himself, as well as to the therapist, he will have robbed him of part of his

* Rollo May, *Love and Will* (New York: W. W. Norton & Co., 1969), p. 91.

human potentiality and growth. This is not a question of a choice between the scientific generalization and the concrete individual, but of which direction is the primary one. Is the individual regarded as a collection of symptoms to be registered in the categories of a particular school or are the theories of the school regarded as primarily a means of returning again and again to the understanding of his unique person and his relationship with his therapist? An increasingly important trend in psychotherapy suggests that the basic direction of movement should be toward the concrete person and his uniqueness and not toward subsuming the patient's symptoms under theoretical categories or adjusting him to some socially derived view of the "ideal" man. This trend emphasizes the *image* of man as opposed to the *construct* of man. The image of man retains the understanding of man in his concrete uniqueness; it retains the wholeness of the person.

Sigmund Freud is one of the great Promethean explorers of our age who has pushed back the limits of human knowledge. No one in our age can have an image of man which has not been in some decisive way influenced by Freud. In the same year in which Martin Buber published his classic *Ich und Du* ("I and Thou")—1923—Freud published his famous book *Das Ich und das Es* (literally "The I and the It" but Latinized in English translation into *The Ego and the Id*). The person comes into being as person, Freud suggested, through libidinal "cathexes" in relation first to his mother and later his father. Through these psychobiological relations the whole psychic economy of id, ego, and superego arises. The superego, which even takes into itself some of the libidinal energy of the id, represents the introjected father figure, "conscience" being nothing other than the man-child's fear of castration by the father. There is certainly some justification in Ludwig Binswanger's complaint that Freud's genetic approach reduces human history to natural history and that this reduction is based upon "a complete taking apart of being-human as such and a natural-scientific-biological reconstruction of it." "The real battle," says Ludwig Binswanger of his argument with his lifelong friend Sigmund Freud, "is the battle over the image of man." "Only human existence is genuinely historical," writes Binswanger. Hence Freud misses that in man which is specifically human. Psychoanalysis has developed its entire critique and interpretation on the basis of Freud's *homo natura,* whose nature is driven instinctively and whose history is essentially formed by sexuality.

One of the decisive aspects of this "battle over the image of man" is the problem of the relation between psychological necessity and personal freedom. Kierkegaard once remarked that one cannot judge another person, for no one knows how much of his action is suffering—a compulsion he must bear—and how much is temptation—a matter about which he has some real choice. This is not a theoretical question of "free will" versus "determinism," but a concrete question of the resources of a particular person in a particular situation. Probably even he himself will not know afterward to what extent he was able to respond to the situation with the spontaneity of the whole person and to what extent his action was the product of fragmentary and conditioned responses. He will have lost the situation in its presentness, its concreteness, its need for decision, lost it, perhaps, in a cloud of refashioned and rationalized memory. Psychotherapy has contributed an enormous amount to the understanding of the importance of determining factors, but also, since it is therapy and concerned with healing, it aims at freedom, at freeing man for a real response in the present situation to what the therapist and the client can recognize as reality. This is the place where the meeting of therapy and the image of man becomes truly decisive.

Freud's one-sided naturalist distortion of the image of man focuses on what man has to be, says Binswanger, and leaves out what he may and should become, his own freedom in relation to the psychological given. "Even the neurotic is not only a neurotic and man in general is not only one compelled." Existence does not lay its own ground, Binswanger points out in his analysis of "The Case of Ilse," but it is still left with freedom in relation to that ground: "That Ilse got just that father and mother was her destiny, received as a heritage and as a task; how to bear up under this destiny was the problem of her existence. Hence, in her 'father complex' both destiny and freedom were at work." Even such phenomena as repression and resistance must be understood from the aspect of the mixture of necessity and freedom, writes Rollo May.

Through its awareness that "the battle is over the image of man," existential psychotherapy has made a decisive contribution to our understanding of the interrelationship of the image of man and psychotherapy. It has opened up genuine new directions of exploration, ranging from phenomenological analyses and the exploration of the world of the psychotic to a different understanding of the very meaning of such basic therapeutic terms as transference and healing. "Existential psychotherapy," says May in his introductory essay to *Existence*, "is based on the assumption that it is possible to have a science of man which does not fragmentize man and destroy his humanity at the same moment as it studies him." In contrast to the tendency to make technique an end in itself, "existential technique should have flexibility and versatility," writes May, "varying from patient to patient and from one phase to another in treatment with the same patient." This means the recognition that the patient's commitment, his basic decision about his life, precedes his knowledge of himself. In fact, he cannot even permit himself to get insight or knowledge until he is ready to take a decisive orientation to life and has made the preliminary decisions along the way.

A distinctive contribution of existential psychotherapy, Rollo May points out, is that it places time in the center of the psychological picture and in so doing replaces the Freudian emphasis on the past, the realm of natural history, with the concern of the future, that mode alone in which the self, personality, and, we would add, the image of man can be understood. In "Findings in a Case of Schizophrenic Depression," Eugene Minkowski demonstrates what happens to a man whose sense of the future is blocked. "Each day life began anew, like a solitary island in a gray sea of passing time." The normal synthetic view of time disintegrates, and life is lived "in a succession of similar days which follow one another with a boundless monotony and sadness." This blocking of the future and fragmentation of the present is reminiscent of Samuel Beckett's play *Waiting for Godot*. "The individual life impetus weakens, the synthesis of the human personality disintegrates; . . . there remains only the person face to face with a hostile universe."

Ludwig Binswanger places an analysis of temporality close to the center of his famous "Case of Ellen West." Ellen West was not Binswanger's own patient, but he had sufficient access to the records of her case to undertake an exhaustive analysis. Ellen West's existence is ruled by the past, encircled in a bare, empty present, and cut off from the future, writes Binswanger. Robbed of the authentic meaning of her life that only the future can give, Ellen West is driven to fill in time, to fill up the existential emptiness, through an insatiable animal greed that represents a desperate and always unsuccessful flight before the dread of nothingness. Binswanger also analyzes Ellen West in terms of a vertical axis of spatiality—the ethereal world, the terrestrial world, and the world of the tomb, or swamp. Binswanger shows how the loss of the ground on which to stand and work left her two conflicting worlds with the inevitable outcome of a dissipation of the ethereal world into empty possibility and the complete triumph of the world of the tomb.

Binswanger takes over from Heidegger the view of the self as capable of transcending itself and relating to the world and the world-design that results from his self-transcendence. Now the way is open, Binswanger claims, for scientifically exact investigations of the modifications in mental disease of the essential structure of being-in-the-world. The result of such investigations is the discovery of the patient's world-design and with it the possibility of understanding from within even those patients with whom the therapist can establish no "empathic" communication. This world-design "does not refer to anything psychic but to something which only makes possible the psychic fact," i.e., from existential realities and structures on which the psychological phenomena are based. Existential analysis attempts to understand words, actions, and attitudes "from basic modes of human existence prior to the separation of body, soul, and mind, and of consciousness and unconsciousness."

Binswanger sees Ellen West's suicide as both "arbitrary act" and "necessary event." "Who will say where in this case guilt begins and 'fate' ends?" One of the most interesting aspects of this case, indeed, is its setting aside the customary notions that suicide is necessarily bad and that, in the case of a mentally ill person, it is necessarily purely a product of the sickness. The existential emptying or impoverishment of Ellen's existence was "nothing but a metamorphosis of freedom into compulsion," writes Binswanger, but her suicide itself was the final desperate breakthrough of the free personality:

> That this existence can once again break through its congealing, that once more it is able to burst the prison of pastness, to exchange it for the world of an authentic present, and so once more to become authentically and wholly itself—this testifies to the power of freedom in general which, to some degree, makes itself felt even in the insidious form of schizophrenia.*

One may wonder at Binswanger's confidence in the positive nature of Ellen's suicide, especially given his own statement that "love knows no answer to the question of whether Ellen West's suicide had to take place of fateful necessity or whether she had the possibility of escaping it."

Binswanger adds to Heidegger's existence for the sake of oneself the dimension of love. Binswanger acknowledges his indebtedness to Martin Buber for this mode of "meeting," or "encounter," and passage after passage in his works bears witness to the importance of this influence. Binswanger sees clearly that the I-Thou relationship is an ontological reality and cannot be reduced to what takes place within each of the members of the relation-

* Ludwig Binswanger, "The Case of Ellen West" in Rollo May, Ernest Angel, Henri F. Ellenberger, eds., *Existence: A New Dimension in Psychiatry and Psychology* (New York: Basic Books, 1958; paperback, 1967), p. 311. The other quotations from Binswanger and most of those from Rollo May are also from *Existence*.

ship. At the same time Binswanger's "dual mode" of love is less inclusive and more in danger of becoming a sentimentalized unity than Buber's dialogue, which includes relations of conflict and opposition so long as they are personal and reciprocal and each affirms the other in his own being.

Binswanger analyzes the case of Ellen West in "I-Thou" terms. Ellen West's defiance and stubbornness exclude her from "the authentic I-Thou relationship of the being-with-one-another" and leave her to a world of interpersonal relations consisting of mere togetherness in which each seizes on the weak point of the other and tries to dominate him. Nonetheless, without a germ of true love, without that "readiness for Thou" which a number of life-long relations and attachments showed that Ellen possessed, Ellen would not have suffered so much as she did from the emptiness and poverty of her existence. "To him who is completely empty of love, existence can become a burden but not a hell," writes Binswanger. Correspondingly, Binswanger sees Ellen's suicide as a breaking through the single mode and a triumph, despite all, of the dual mode of existence with its knowledge of a relationship beyond the isolated self. Even the way we must look at Ellen's suicide, Binswanger suggests, is given us through the I-Thou relationship which lifts us above the judgmental perspective of the plural mode of existence. The "uniting of human existence with the common ground which I and Thou share" is prior to the dichotomy of freedom and necessity, guilt and destiny.

There is, however, an issue between Heidegger and Buber of which Binswanger does not seem adequately aware. "Heidegger's 'existence' is monological," writes Martin Buber in "What Is Man?" "Since self-being is there . . . *the* ultimate which it is able to reach, there is absolutely no starting-point for still understanding love and friendship as essential relations." To Buber, the self must be understood in dialogue with other selves, in the *between,* and never as an ontological entity understandable prior to its interhuman relations. We may doubt, therefore, whether Binswanger has succeeded in his attempted synthesis of Heidegger's ontology and Buber's dialogue. From the standpoint of the latter, it is not admissible to substitute an ontological analysis of dialogue for dialogue itself.

We may also question Binswanger's claim that the existential analyst can communicate even with those schizophrenic patients with whom he cannot enter into an empathic relationship. Phenomenological analysis can certainly help in understanding, but such understanding is not the same as direct communication between one person and another. "To analyze phenomenologically the given being-in-the-world" does not necessarily mean real dialogue or understanding the other as a Thou, nor does "the degree of potential and real agreement between my world and his world determine the degree of possible communication," as Binswanger asserts. Binswanger's analytic-synthetic "world-design" cannot capture the uniqueness and wholeness of a person, for these are only revealed in the dialogue between I and Thou.

Analysis of existence is not identical with existence: Concern with existence does not give ready-made phenomenological categories a privileged position over the categories of Freud or any other psychologist. "The temptation to use existential concepts in the service of intellectualizing tendencies is especially to be guarded against," Rollo May rightly points out, "since, because they refer to things that have to do with the center of personal reality, these concepts can the more seductively give the illusion of dealing with reality." "The configuration of self and world or self to self is not existential," Paul Goodman has remarked. "It is interpretation just in the Freudian sense. Real existential psychotherapy would try to do as far as possible without interpretations and stick to particular situations."

One writer on psychotherapy whose theories show marked evidence of growing out of and pointing back to particular situations is the Swiss psychotherapist Hans Trüb. The analyst must see the illness of the patient as an illness of his relations with the world, writes Trüb. The roots of the neurosis lie both in the patient's closing himself off from the world and in the pattern of society itself and its rejection and nonconfirmation of the patient.

Consequently, the analyst must change at some point from the consoler who takes the part of the patient against the world to the person who puts before the patient the claim of the world. This change is necessary to complete the second part of the cure—that establishment of real relationship with the world which can only take place in the world itself. "On the analyst falls the task of preparing the way for the resumption in direct meeting of the interrupted dialogical relationship between the individual and the community." The psychotherapist must test the patient's finding of himself by the criterion of whether his self-realization can be the starting point for a new personal meeting with the world. The patient must go forth whole in himself, but he must also recognize that it is not his own self but the world with which he must be concerned. This does not mean that the patient is simply integrated with or adjusted to the world. He does not cease to be a real person, responsible for himself, but at the same time he enters into responsible relationship with his community.*

Both Ludwig Binswanger and Hans Trüb adopt the language of "I and Thou" under the influence of Martin Buber, but the one uses it primarily in the service of phenomenological analysis of the patient's "world-design" (who in the case of Ellen West is not even his own patient), whereas the other uses it as a means of *pointing* to the existential situation of the patient and the concrete meeting between patient and therapist. Binswanger's existential analysis tends to lead to still another *construct of man* to set over against those given us by the older schools of psychotherapy. Only a psychotherapy which begins with the concrete existence of the person, with his wholeness and uniqueness, and with the healing that takes place through the meeting of the therapist and patient will point us toward the image of man. Existential psychotherapy is faced, in the last analysis, with the

---

* Maurice Friedman, ed., *The Worlds of Existentialism: A Critical Reader* (New York: Random House, 1964; University of Chicago Press, Phoenix Books [paperback], 1973), pp. 497–505. This is, unfortunately, the *only* selection of Trüb's writings that has been translated into English.

same issue that faces all the schools of psychotherapy: whether the *starting point* of therapy is to be found in the analytical category or the unique person—in the *construct of man* or the *image of man.*

The revelation of the human image—its coming forth from its hiding—is a revelation that takes place *between* the therapist and the client or *among* the members of the group. It cannot be equated with the image of man that each holds or comes to hold separately. Therefore, the coming into the light of the hidden human image is inseparable from the dialogue itself—a dialogue of mutual contact, trust, and shared humanity. In this sense "healing through meeting" is identical with the revelation of the hidden human image. This revelation is more than an individual finding an image of man. It is a *becoming* of man in relationship —a becoming human with such resources as the relationship affords, including the possibility of tragedy when such resources are lacking. It is not the diploma on the wall which assures the client that he has the right therapist. The "rightness" of the relationship depends upon mutual existential trust—and upon an existential grace that is not *in* the therapist or *in* the client but moves *between* the two. When these are not present, or not sufficiently so, then the ground of tragedy has been reached— whether or not the relationship ends in suicide, as with Ellen West. This touching of the tragic itself unfolds the hidden possibilities of the human as well as showing the real limitations in which we stand.

LITERATURE
AND
RELIGION

LITERATURE AND RELIGION: Meeting or Mismeeting?

The Bretons believe in the demonic book.

It has different names, one in each region. In that of Quimper it is called Ar Vif, that is, The Living.

It is a gigantic book. When it stands upright, it has the height of a man.

The pages are red, the letters are black.

But he who goes up to it and opens it sees nothing except red. The black signs only become visible when one has fought with the Vif and overpowered it.

For this book lives. And it will not let itself be questioned. Only he who conquers it tears from it its mystery.

He must labor with it hours at a time as with a headstrong horse, until covered with sweat he stands in front of it and reads this book that he has tamed.

It is a dangerous book. One fastens it up with a thick padlock and hangs it on a chain which is attached to the strongest beam. The beam must be warped.

He who has subdued the Vif knows the secret names of the demons and knows how to summon them all.

He does not walk like all the world. He hesitates at every step, for he fears to tread on a soul. He has experienced something.

I think that every real book is Ar Vif.

The real reader knows this, but far better still the real writer—for only the writing of a real book is actual danger, battle, and overpowering. Many a one loses his courage midway, and the work that he began in the reading of the signs of the mystery he completes in the vain

letters of his arbitrariness. There exists only a little reality of the spirit
in this book-rich world.*

Just before the publication of my book *To Deny Our Nothingness,* I lectured at a California state college on some of the contemporary images of man discussed in it, many of which are
illustrated through the interpretation of literature. The professor
of English who squired me around that day was unusually silent.
Finally at dinner, he looked at me and said, "Do you consider
literature to be merely an illustration of philosophy?" "No, I
don't," I replied. Then he explained to me, gently but firmly, that
the latest thing in literature was the New Criticism, or form
analysis, and that was quite enough for literature and that the
latest thing in philosophy was linguistic analysis and that was
quite enough for philosophy. "I understand that," I said, "but
don't you think there is room for someone like myself who knows
both philosophy and literature to go a step further and find
where the two meet?" "Well, it is rather messy!" he exclaimed.

There are times, indeed, when the meeting between literature
and philosophy, religion, or theology is "rather messy." But these
are for the most part special instances of the general mismeeting
between literature and the interpretation of literature. The most
frequent form that this mismeeting takes is that of reducing a
literary work to specific categories outside it. The great quarrels
among schools of literary interpretation are often quarrels about
how best we can reduce a great work of literature which should
speak to us as a whole into one or another separate aspects. This
is all too often common to all the contending schools, whether
that of the New Critics, the literary historians, the social analysts,
the psychological reductionists, the intellectual historians, the
theologians of literature, or the myth- and symbolmongers.

Whether in *Moby Dick,* for example, you say the harpoons are
phallic symbols, or falling into the whale's head a return to the
womb, or you deal with it as the "hero journey," or see the whole

---

* Martin Buber, *A Believing Humanism: Gleanings,* trans. with an Introduction and Explanatory Comments by Maurice Friedman (New York: Simon &
Schuster Paperbacks, 1969), "The Demonic Book," pp. 46 f.

thing in Jungian terms as a descending into the archetypal unconscious and working through to the individuation of the self,
what you tend to do is to reduce the actual novel to the set of
meanings that you have brought to it and prevent *its* saying what
it is. This also means reducing the dynamic moving event of
what takes place between you and the book to something which
can be put into a static category. Precisely the same thing happens if you approach literature looking for illustrations of a given
philosophy or theology. Once more you destroy the concreteness
of your encounter with the literature and make it subservient to
already fixed patterns of thought. When Queequeg's coffin comes
up at the end of *Moby Dick*, it is a resurrection symbol, just as in
Dostoevsky's novel *Crime and Punishment* there is a whole symbolism of Lazarus risen from the dead. Yet you dare not go
from the symbol to the meaning of the book unless that symbol
has become dramatically real in the book itself as it has not in
either *Moby Dick* or *Crime and Punishment*.

What is true of symbolmongering is also true of mythmongering. Both lie at the heart of the mismeeting between literature
and religion. The collector's urge of modern man leads him to
seek a universal myth in the myths of all peoples, whether it be
that of the flood, of creation, or of the dragon and the dragon-
slayer. These myths were man's first way of thinking—dramatic
events rather than discursive reasoning. We try instead to derive
a secondary meaning by identifying resemblances among myths.
We extract a perennial myth and feel we are very close to the
heart of reality when in fact we are freezing on the doorstep. No
myth catches us up as it did ancient man so that for that moment
all that is real and important is the heightened reality of the
mythic event. The mythmonger asks us to accept a rich sense of
everything having significant relation to everything else in place
of any immediate insight into any particular event or reality.

Both the symbolmonger and the mythmonger tend to see particular literary works as endlessly reproducing universal themes
and in so doing lose the very heart of religion, literature, and
myth. They find the meaning of literature in the static symbol or

concept and not in the concrete unique event and its dramatic,
dynamic unfolding in time. A similar distortion is introduced by
those who reduce a work to a single point of view—*Moby Dick*
as "Melville's quarrel with God" or *Billy Budd* as a Christ symbol
—or who identify the author's conscious intention with the intention that is implicit in the book. Dostoevsky wrote a letter to his
niece in which he said, "I want Prince Myshkin to be a Christ
figure, a really good man, a Don Quixote." But the intention that
becomes manifest in *The Idiot* is very different from this conscious intention; for Prince Myshkin is not in the least like Christ.
He does not say to the woman caught in adultery, "Go and sin no
more," but seeks instead to marry her and destroys both her and
himself in the process. When Dostoevsky wrote Book V of *The
Brothers Karamazov*—Ivan and the Grand Inquisitor—he described it in a letter as the real center of the book. But when he
wrote Book VI, he said the same thing. We cannot regard Ivan as
identical with the Grand Inquisitor. We have to take into account his thwarted relationship with Smerdyakov and the extent
to which he was a semiconscious accomplice in his father's murder. Neither can we take Father Zossima as the answer to the
questions so agonizingly raised by Ivan, despite Dostoevsky's
assertion that he is; for he is only the other half. Ivan has the
alienation, Father Zossima the closeness, to nature and the spirit,
and there is nothing that unites them. It is equally inadmissible
to reduce Kafka's novels to a single point of view, whether it be
nihilism, the insurance bureaucracy, the anticipation of the totalitarian state, waiting for grace, or God seen through the wrong
end of the telescope. In a religious play such as T. S. Eliot's
Murder in the Cathedral we have to recognize that the Thomas à
Becket whom Eliot presents in the first act as a complex modern
man, tempted by motives of pride to be lowest on earth in order
to be highest in heaven, cannot be dramatically squared with the
predestined martyr, the "Blessed Thomas," of the second act. The
dramatic effectiveness of the play is vitiated by an intention that
is not worked through.

The very effort of the more sophisticated to avoid the mismeet-

ings between religion and literature that we have discussed above
often leads to another, equally serious mismeeting, that is, the
attempt to preserve the separateness of theology and literature as
disciplines, languages, or modes of consciousness while searching
for a metatheory that underlies them or a formal meeting after
each has attained a reflective distance from the literature itself.
Whether this metatheory takes the form of a philosophy of symbolism, a phenomenology of linguistic comprehensions, a psychology of unconscious archetypes, or an ontology of the disclosure of the meaning of being, it has the same effect of relating
religion and literature in terms of concepts and world view rather
than in terms of the work itself. If religion and literature are
not already united in the piece of literature before us, no aesthetic or theory of symbolism will bring about their meeting.
What is more, to consign literature to separate, established disciplines means to approach it with fixed methods and to neglect
the all-important task of discovering new methods in relation to
each work.

Some seek to avoid all mismeetings by restricting the intercourse between religion and literature to an examination of literature for its explicitly religious contents. Comparing literary
expressions of doctrines, cults, and social groupings is valuable,
of course. But still more valuable is comparing the basic attitudes
toward reality reflected in literary images of man. This is so only
if religion is primarily understood neither as an objective philosophy nor as a subjective experience but as a lived reality
which is ontologically prior to its expression in creed, ritual, and
group. At the same time, it is inseparable from these expressions
and cannot be distilled out and objectified in itself. Religion at
this deepest level might be described as a basic *attitude* or relationship arising in the encounter with the whole reality directly
given to one in one's existence. From this standpoint, many
works of literature are as close to religious reality as any work of
theology, for both may be products of some genuine religious
encounter. This means taking seriously the full address of literature to the wholeness of man. The most fruitful approach to the

meeting of religion and literature, therefore, is not to treat literature as if it were covert theology but to discover in our meeting
with it that image of authentic human existence that is implicit in
the very style of most great literature.

In its very particularity, the image of man in literature gives us
the wholeness of man as more abstract disciplines cannot. Next
to the lives of actual men, literature comes closest to retaining
the concrete uniqueness of individual men while at the same time
enabling us to enter into a sufficiently close relationship with
these men so that they can speak to us as bearers of the human—
as exemplifications of what it does and can mean to be a man. It is
for this reason that I claim in *To Deny Our Nothingness* that
literature is the real homeland of the image of man. But I also
point out that it is the dialogue between author and character
and between character and reader that produces the image of
man.

> No novel can present an image of man if its author merely stands
> in objective relation to his character; none can present such an
> image if the author merely identifies with his character in a
> subjective way that destroys the aesthetic and personal distance
> between author and character. It is the dialogue between author
> and character that produces the image of man; this image is
> never a direct expression of the author's views, but a genuine
> product of this dialogue. Conversely, the image produced never
> takes on the fixed quality of a visual image, but retains the open,
> unfinished quality of living dialogue. The dialogue between au-
> thor and character also makes possible a dialogue between char-
> acter and reader—the personal response of the reader that is, in
> the end, the most important element of any character's becoming
> an image of man for him. He does not take over this character as
> an image through some sort of visual impression, but through a
> personal, even, in a sense, reciprocal relationship with him. *

The image of man, understood as a basic attitude toward reality, is a ground that is not identifiable in the first instance as

---

* Maurice Friedman, *To Deny Our Nothingness: Contemporary Images of
Man* (New York: Delacorte Press, 1967; Delta Books [paperback], 1968),
p. 27.

literature, theology, religion, or philosophy, though having implications for all of them. Religion and literature do not meet in the
once- or twice-remove of theology and literary criticism but in a
matrix deeper and older than both of them. If we go back behind
the time of the rise of a secular literature, generally seen as a
worldly distraction to be kept away from young girls and from
the religious, we find that originally literature was one of the
basic expressions of numinous awe or wonder, as in the Vedic
hymns and the Psalms. The Book of Job was not "the Bible as
living literature"; it was living literature that was later taken into
the Bible. When I first came to teach at Sarah Lawrence College,
I was struck by the fact that because the Book of Job was in the
Bible, my students regarded it as blind faith and were blocked
from understanding the actual text. They read it through the eyes
of what their ministers called "faith" but what was actually no
more than a mind-set, toward which their elders were positive
and they negative. We cannot recover those depths out of which
the Book of Job came unless we can come with that openness
and readiness to respond and even to be disturbed that very few
people bring to the reading of the text.

The meeting of religion and literature is not achieved by starting with the finished ideas of religion and then trying to find
literature to illustrate them. We must, rather, dig deeper into
both religion and literature in order that we may recover and
discover for ourselves that ground where they are one: those
basic human attitudes which arise in our response to ultimate life-
realities and to the daily life-situations that confront us. The
notion that so many people have today that meaning in literature
is to be found most directly in the novel of ideas or the drama of
ideas is exactly backward. On the contrary, we only reach the
level of abstraction and timeless ideas after hundreds of thousands of years of dealing with the more concrete in legend and in
myth. Even drama began as a religious celebration; only much
later did it acquire fixed roles and parts and become the detached drama of our stage. Religion and literature have a common matrix, and that matrix still informs their meeting, when it
takes place. Literature, indeed, is often far closer to original reli-

gious reality than any of its later objectifications in creed, doctrine, theology, and metaphysics.

To approach the meeting of literature and religion in terms of
the image of man means to understand literary interpretation as
essentially dialogical, as the English literary critic Walter Stein
has recognized in his book *Criticism as Dialogue*. Despite his
falling into such monological patterns of thinking as his exclusivist insistence that Christian radical humanism is the *only* adequate orientation open to the literary critic, his search for cosmic
order, his concern with "metaphysical" adequacy, and his confusion of "dialogue" and "dialectic," Stein recognizes in all explicit-
ness that "a proper seriousness" toward the literature that "confronts us *exacts*" the author's confrontation of works of literature
as "images of existence, a weighing of their ultimate 'adequacy to
reality.'" Dialogue means real meeting with otherness in contrast
to dialectic, which usually takes place as the unfolding of a single
consciousness through contrasting "points of view." Stein understands this too when he sees the task of the dialogical critic as
being set for him by the problematic but essential demand that
he reach out, through the most adequate confrontation and self-
exposure he can achieve, toward the visions of reality that confront him. What makes this dialogue a real meeting with otherness rather than a reading in of theological or metaphysical
assumptions is that "readiness to confront ultimate questions"
that enables the critic's judgment to emerge from his "innermost
grasp of, and response to, the work in its complex uniqueness; so
that it will be informed by his antecedently organized responses
to life, and at the same time be found irreducible to any terms
other than itself."

> The critic, if he is doing his job, cannot operate from the outside,
> with the help of a series of theological norms: if he does not sit
> down humbly in front of his poem or novel, prepared to receive it
> first of all on its own terms, and allow his response to develop
> from the centre of his personality, he will have nothing relevant
> to contribute.

In judging great literature, he is himself judged in his fundamental convictions.*

A still more radical dialogical approach to literature is that of
the American literary critic and philosopher of speech Walter J.
Ong. Ong recognizes, as more and more contemporary critics are
doing, that the chronological approach to literature of the traditional literary and intellectual historian must be complemented
by a synchronic approach which not only keeps in view the fact
that the literature of the past is read in and from the standpoint
of the present but also accepts the way in which contemporary
literature modifies our relationship to the literature of antiquity.†
Still more important, he sets the appreciation and interpretation
of literature within the dialectic of objective and aural correla-
tives, of literature as "a well wrought urn" and of the jinnee
within the urn that cannot be expelled. This jinnee is the personal voice that no amount of form criticism can permanently
banish, the voice of the I addressing the Thou that breaks
through even the thickest of masks and the most remote of objective forms to reestablish the reality of the word that is spoken
and the word that is heard. "A literary work can never get itself
entirely dissociated from this I-thou situation and the personal
involvement which it implies." "Poetry is often involved and mysterious, but by its very existence within our ken it is destined to
communicate." Indeed, drawing upon the two basic movements
of distancing and relating that Martin Buber describes in his
philosophical anthropology, Ong asserts that the greater the
remoteness between the voice of the writer which creates the
poem and those who hear or read it, the more evocative the work
becomes. "All communication," says Ong, "is an attempt to crash
through . . . the barriers which bar the ultimate compenetration of
the 'I' and the 'thou.' " Thus for Ong the voice in literature is
already a summons to faith in the sense of "trust in" rather than

* Walter Stein, *Criticism as Dialogue* (London and New York: Cambridge
University Press, 1969), pp. 12–16, 29, 31, 33 f., 42, 44.
† Walter J. Ong, S.J., *In the Human Grain: Further Explorations of Con-
temporary Culture* (New York: The Macmillan Co., 1967), pp. 37 f.

in the sense of "belief that." Faith in the possibility of communication is faith in someone with whom we can communicate.

> Our belief in a play or a poem is thus an invitation to the persons involved in composing it and presenting it to us either to say something worth our while or to betray our trust in them as persons. It involves a kind of openness to them and to their meaning at all levels, to what Professor Philip Wheelwright in *The Burning Fountain* styles "depth experience."*

This openness to meaning at all levels implies an openness to being changed by our encounter with literature. That faith to which Ong points is really existential and interhuman trust. This interhuman trust, this readiness to be open and respond without any prior commitment to assent, accounts for the possibility of an image of man coming alive for us in our meeting with literature, as Coleridge's "willing suspension of disbelief" could never do. It is only this personal involvement combined with obedient listening and faithful response to the voice of the other that addresses us in the novel, poem, or play that enables us to take literature out of the brackets of the purely aesthetic or the merely didactic so that our own image of man, or basic attitude, may enter into dialogue with the image of man, or basic attitude, underlying the work that confronts us. This brings to light a further religious dimension of our wrestling with literature than the one Ong referred to. If religion means bringing the whole of one's existence into dialogue with the "nameless Meeter," then literature as genuine personal dialogue must be an integral part of religious reality as we know it. Religion and literature, then, would not be thought of as different modes or languages, however much theology and literary criticism may be properly spoken of in that way, but as differing degrees of fullness of a single dialogical reality. If this means in one sense subsuming our dialogue with literature under our meeting with ultimate reality, it means in a still deeper sense that our meeting with ultimate reality takes

---

* Walter J. Ong, S.J., *The Barbarian Within: And Other Fugitive Essays and Studies* (New York: The Macmillan Co., 1962), pp. 52 f., 55, 62, 65 f.

place only within the very structures and events of our concrete daily existence, no unimportant part of which is our dialogue with literature.

A favorite phrase of youth that has been taken over by our culture is "doing one's thing," and "doing one's thing" is often defined in terms of what "turns one on" or "turns one off." Great literature, simply because it is great, is deeply threatening. Rather than opening ourselves to its address and responding from the depth, we often prefer to dismiss it as meaningless, irrelevant, or simply not conducive. But the life of dialogue, as Martin Buber points out in *I and Thou,* "teaches you to meet others and to hold your ground when you meet them." Applied to the dialogue with literature, this means the combination of faithfulness to literature in its concrete uniqueness and otherness, including the whole fullness of style and form, with response to that literature from the ground of one's own uniqueness. Reversing the emphasis, we can say that approaching the meeting of religion and literature in terms of the image of man implies not only bringing ourselves to the dialogue but the most faithful possible listening to the implicit intention, the underlying attitude, the point of view of the work of literature. Since every work of literature, even a poem, is a frozen speaking in which the voice must be liberated from the objective form, a really faithful listening will make it impossible to reduce the work to a single, directly expressed point of view. From this it follows that it is not the symbol, myth, or metaphor, still less the theological concept or metaphysical idea, but the tension of points of view that discloses the truly religious depth-dimension of a novel, play, or poem.

It is in the problem of point of view more than any other that the metaphysical dimension of Herman Melville's great novel *Moby Dick* is found. This metaphysical dimension is not the picture of what reality *is,* but of man's relation to that reality. The changing, ever-shifting point of view in *Moby Dick* corresponds with the ever-changing, ever-shifting attitude of man toward the reality that confronts him. *Moby Dick* is a gigantic

poem in which each stanza, each image, is of significance in
itself, and which at the same time moves along from image to
image and from chapter to chapter in such a way that the meaning of each particular image must be found within the dynamic,
dramatic progression of the whole. *Moby Dick* is a metaphysical
novel, but we must distinguish between the explicitly metaphysical passages which Melville so liberally strews throughout for
poetic and symbolic purposes and the implicit metaphysics which
we touch on only when we have gone through the dramatic
situation and the characters into the basic attitude toward existence that we glean from the interplay of symbolic suggestion,
action, and point of view. We can neither say that the evil associated with the White Whale is simply Melville's picture of the
universe and forget about "crazy Ahab," pitted "all mutilated"
against it, nor can we say that Moby Dick's "intangible malig-
nity" is merely a projection of Ahab's madness and forget about
the hostile reality confronting Ahab. It was necessary for Melville
to go imaginatively to the uttermost extreme with Captain Ahab
and not just stop short in his imagination with Ishmael and turn
back home.

> By going all the way with Ahab and at the same time turning
> back with Ishmael and by holding the tension of these two oppos-
> ing points of view within the form of *Moby Dick* itself, Melville
> creates an artistic meaning and balance great enough to contain
> his question, great enough, too, not to attempt an answer. Mel-
> ville's point of view comprehends both Ishmael's point of view
> and Ahab's without being identical with either, or being a moder-
> ate balance between them. . . . The greatness of *Moby Dick* does
> not lie in its providing us with an image of man, but in its
> refusing to do so—in the honesty, the intensity of concern, the
> breadth of scope.*

The most impressive and most positive example of the disclosure of a religious dimension of reality through point of view is

* Maurice Friedman, *Problematic Rebel: Melville, Dostoievsky, Kafka, Camus,*
2nd ed. (Chicago: University of Chicago Press, Phoenix Books [paperback],
1970), pp. 439 ff.

the work of Franz Kafka. Those who seek to understand and interpret Kafka through some allegorical key, whether religious, psychoanalytic, or sociological, miss the simple fact that, paradoxical as it is, Kafka's world is not a transparent one through which we can glimpse some other, more familiar reality. It is just what it is in its irreducible opaqueness and absurdity, the product of an altogether unique and concrete way of seeing human existence. "The only really difficult and insoluble problems are those which we cannot formulate," writes Kafka, "because they have the difficulties of life itself as their content."

Kafka rigorously presents his novels to us only through Joseph K.'s or K.'s perspective. Kafka's hero stands face to face with a reality which transcends him but which he sees only from his own point of view. As a result, we too are denied any overall, objective vantage point on K.'s relation to the world. Kafka gives up the position of the all-knowing metaphysician in favor of the limited knowledge which arises only in personal involvement—in facing and contending. Kafka's hero does not encounter some theological Transcendent; he confronts a world that cannot be removed into himself.

> Kafka offers us an image of modern man confronting a transcendent reality which can neither be dismissed as unreal nor rationalized as anything less than absurd. Kafka's hero is neither able to affirm meaning *despite* what confronts him as do Nietzsche's Zarathustra, Sartre's Orestes, and Camus' Sisyphus, nor to fix meaning *in* what confronts him, as do Plato's philosopher or Kierkegaard's "knight of faith." Unable to believe any longer in an objective absolute or order through which his personal destiny is determined or in a Biblical God who calls him, he nonetheless knows himself as a person face to face with a reality which transcends him. This reality demands from him response and punishes a failure to respond even while it offers neither confirmation nor meaning in return for response nor any guidance as to which response is "right" and which "wrong."*

* Ibid., p. 482.

ELIE WIESEL:
The Job of
Auschwitz

In contemporary literature the meeting of literature and religion
stands under the sign of that pervasive existential mistrust that
Martin Buber has described as the "eclipse of God." This literature must not be misunderstood as merely atheist, pessimistic, or
absurd, as is so often thought. Part of our existential and religious
hope lies in our confrontation with that contemporary literature
which in its depth asks us *the* religious questions of our time. In
our day the only way to the positive, perhaps, is not through the
negative certainly, but through the tension of the absurd, the
contradictions of modern existence, through the absence of a
modern image of meaningful personal and social existence and
the attempts to create such an image in response. Our image of
hope, therefore, is not the antithesis but the completion of our
image of despair. It is the image of a new courage, a new reli-
giousness which can only be reached by contending for meaning
within the Dialogue with the Absurd. It is a two-fold revelation
of the hidden human image—out of its original hiddenness and
out of the denigration and eclipse of the human image in our
day.

"How is life with God still possible in a time in which there is
an Auschwitz?" writes Martin Buber.

The estrangement has become too cruel, the hiddenness too deep. One can still "believe" in the God who allowed those things to happen, but can one still speak to Him? Can one still hear His word? . . . Dare we recommend to the survivors of Auschwitz, the Job of the gas chambers: "Give thanks unto the Lord, for He is good; for His mercy endureth forever"? . . . Do we stand overcome before the hidden face of God like the tragic hero of the Greeks before faceless fate? No, rather even now we contend, we too, with God. . . . We do not put up with earthly being; we struggle for its redemption, and struggling we appeal to the help of our Lord, who is again and still a hiding one.[*]

Auschwitz is here only a symbol for all of the extermination camps in which, as Buber said when he accepted the Peace Prize of the German Book Trade, "Millions of my people and fellow believers were exterminated in a systematic procedure the organized cruelty of which had no precedent in human history." Even when one speaks, as I often do, of Auschwitz and Hiroshima together, we have to realize that we cannot really compare 6 million deaths with 70,000 or 80,000 or even, as in the bombing of Dresden, 120,000. The figure staggers the imagination. People the world over have been moved by *The Diary of Anne Frank* because it enabled them to experience her part of the holocaust from within. But who can experience from within the death of 6 million or even a portion of that many?

This failure of the imagination was also experienced by the Jews of Europe themselves before they were deported. No one could really imagine, even in those rare cases where individuals came back and insisted that the deported were not being taken to work camps, as they had been told, but to extermination centers—no one could imagine something which so destroyed the very cement of social confidence beyond ordinary enmities, beyond anti-Semitism as it had been known, beyond anything conceivable, since society itself implies a certain minimal com-

---

[*] Martin Buber, *On Judaism*, ed. by Nahum Glatzer (New York: Schocken Books, 1967), pp. 224 f.

munication. No one could understand what had never had a precedent in history—that they were going to be turned into cakes of soap, such as I myself have seen on Mount Zion in Jerusalem, with the letters "R. J. F."—"Pure Jewish Fat"—on them. No one could understand because it had not happened, because actuality does not grow out of potentiality but the other way around, because only when it did happen did it become a very real possibility that can be repeated again and again in human history, despite the solemn pledge of all the nations at the United Nations that never again will a genocide be allowed to take place. The Modern Job begins with the scientific extermination of six million Jews and a million Gypsies, *and* with those who have had to continue living in the face of these unimaginable horrors.

The most impassioned complaint, the most stubborn and faithful Dialogue with the Absurd, the most moving embodiment of "the Job of the gas chambers" is found in the work of Elie Wiesel, as in the man himself for those of us who know him. His slim volumes form one unified outcry, one sustained protest, one sobbing and singing prayer.

In the first, *Night*, Wiesel tells the story of how he was deported with his family from his Hungarian-Jewish village when he was a child of twelve, how his mother and sister were metamorphosed into the smoke above the crematories, how he and his father suffered through Auschwitz, Buchenwald, and forced winter marches until finally, just before liberation, his father died. For Wiesel the "death of God" came all at once, without preparation—not as a stage in the history of culture but as a terrifying event that turned the pious Hasidic Jew into a Modern Job whose complaint against "the great injustice in the world" can never be silenced.

> Never shall I forget those flames which consumed my Faith forever. Never shall I forget that nocturnal silence which deprived me, for all eternity, of the desire to live. Never shall I forget those moments which murdered my God and my soul and turned my

dreams to dust. Never shall I forget these things, even if I am condemned to live as long as God Himself. Never.*

On a later day when he watched the hanging of a child with the sad face of an angel, he heard someone behind him groan, "Where is God? Where is He? Where can He be now?" and a voice within him answered: "Where? Here He is—He has been hanged here, on these gallows." When after the liberation of Buchenwald he looked at himself in a mirror, a corpse gazed back at him. "The look in his eyes, as they stared into mine, has never left me."

Wiesel's novels are continuous with the autobiography. In *Dawn* he places this same boy, now called Elisha, in the position of a Jewish terrorist, killing English soldiers in an effort to secure the independence of the Jewish state in Palestine. Elisha had wanted to study philosophy at the Sorbonne in order to redis-cover the image of man that had been destroyed for him by the extermination camps: "Where is God to be found? In suffering or in rebellion? When is a man most truly a man? When he submits or when he refuses? Where does suffering lead him? To purifica-tion or to bestiality?" Instead Elisha gives his future to the "Movement," the first group in his knowledge which changes the destiny of the Jew from that of victim to executioner. It is he himself who must execute the English hostage, Captain John Dawson, whom the Movement has sentenced to die as a reprisal for the hanging by the British of one of their number. He comes to realize, in taking upon himself an act so absolute as killing, that he is making his father, his mother, his teacher, his friends into murderers. He cannot rid himself of the impression that he has donned the field-gray uniform of the Nazi S.S. officer.

Elisha rediscovers the presence of God when he spends the last

---

* Elie Wiesel, *Night*, Foreword by François Mauriac, trans. from the French by Stella Rodway (New York: Avon Books [paperback], 1969), pp. 43 f. I have inserted into this chapter the section on Elie Wiesel in my *To Deny Our Nothingness: Contemporary Images of Man* (New York: Delacorte Press, 1967; Delta Books [paperback], 1968), Chap. 18, "The Dialogue with the Absurd," pp. 348–353.

hour with the hostage before shooting him. His victim-to-be is sorry for Elisha and troubled by him—an eighteen-year-old turned terrorist—while Elisha tries in vain to hate him as if the coming of the Messiah were dependent upon the Jews finally learning "to hate those who have humiliated and from time to time exterminated them." But when he kills John Dawson, he feels that he has killed himself, that he himself has become the night.*

In *The Accident* this same child of *Night*, somewhat older and now an Israeli correspondent at the United Nations, is almost killed by a taxi, and in the course of a long and painful recovery confronts the fact that he had seen the taxi, that he wanted to die, that he did not fight to stay alive even in the hospital but left the burden entirely on the doctor. Even "love" gives him no incentive for living in the present. He is one of the "spiritual cripples" whom the world does not dare to look in the eye, amputees who have lost not their legs or their eyes but their will and their taste for life. The sufferer is the pariah, the Modern Exile who must live apart from men because he tells them something about their common humanity that they cannot bear.

> Suffering pulls us farther away from other human beings. It builds a wall made of cries and contempt to separate us. Men cast aside the one who has known pure suffering, if they cannot make a god out of him; the one who tells them: I suffered not because I was God, nor because I was a saint trying to imitate Him, but only because I am a man, a man like you, with your weaknesses, your cowardice, your sins, your rebellion, and your ridiculous ambitions; such a man frightens men, because he makes them feel ashamed. . . . He poisons the air. He makes it unfit for breathing. He takes away from joy its spontaneity and its justification. He kills hope and the will to live.†

The accident occurs the day after he has entered into an agreement with his mistress Kathleen that he knows is meaningless—

---

* Elie Wiesel, *Dawn*, trans. by Frances Frenaye (New York: Avon Books [paperback], 1970).
† Elie Wiesel, *The Accident*, trans. by Annie Borchardt (New York: Avon Books [paperback], 1970), pp. 105 f.

an agreement to let her make him happy and forget the past.

In the last chapter of *The Accident*, Wiesel introduces the Hungarian painter Gyula who is at once foil and image of man and who provides the final judgment on the hero.

> Gyula was a living rock. A giant in every sense of the word. Tall, robust, gray and rebellious hair, mocking and burning eyes; he pushed aside everything around him: altars, ideas, mountains. Everything trembled, vibrated, at his touch, at the sight of him. . . . We encouraged each other to stick it out, not to make compromises, not to come to terms with life, not to accept easy victories.*

Gyula visits the hospital room repeatedly to do his portrait. He tries to tell Gyula his secret—that the accident was no accident, that on the deepest level he wanted to die—but Gyula will not listen. Yet when Gyula shows him the completed painting, he knows that he has guessed. The eyes are those of "a man who had seen God commit the most unforgivable crime: to kill without reason." Gyula confronts his friend's will to death with the silent offer of friendship—a proof that if God is dead, man is alive. Man's duty is to make suffering cease, not to increase it, Gyula tells him. This means a rejection of the lucidity that exchanges the light of hope for the clear darkness of the absurd.

> "Lucidity is fate's victory, not man's. It is an act of freedom that carries within itself the negation of freedom. Man must keep moving, searching, weighing, holding out his hand, offering himself, inventing himself." . . . "The dead, because they are no longer free, are no longer able to suffer. Only the living can. Kathleen is alive. I am alive. You must think of us. Not of them."†

Gyula poses the choice of life or death, but to Eliezer only lies can make happiness possible while the truth is on the side of death. Sensing his decision for death by the intensity with which he looks at the painting, Gyula puts a match to the canvas and

* *Ibid.*, pp. 110 f.
† *Ibid.*, p. 120.

burns it up. "No!" Eliezer exclaims in despair. "Don't do that! Gyula, don't do it!" For a long time after Gyula has closed the door behind him, he weeps. Gyula's angry act of friendship brings tears to the eyes of the man who cannot weep and brings him one step forward toward the Modern Job.

Next to Camus' *The Plague*, the clearest presentation in literature of the progression through the Modern Promethean to the Modern Job is Wiesel's novel *The Town Beyond the Wall*. The plot of the book is the return of Michael after the war to his native Hungarian city. Entering by means of the black market, the only organization that can get through the "Iron Curtain," he is arrested by the police and forced to say "prayers," i.e., to stand eight hours at a stretch before a wall without moving, eating, or drinking. The police hope to extract from him a confession as to who helped him get into the country—a confession that would condemn his friend Pedro to death or imprisonment—but they have reckoned without his tenacious loyalty to his friend and his capacity to endure by going inward to the sources of memory.

After the war and the extermination camps, Michael went to Paris and lived in utter solitude in order to seek his God, to track him down. Even in his determination not to give in so easily as Job, even in his insistence that he will be a match for God and will defy his inhuman Justice, he still remains within his dialogue with his God. "He took my childhood; I have a right to ask Him what He did with it." Michael combines the Modern Promethean and the Modern Job, and he shows the link between them: In our time man *has* to go through the first to reach the second, but he may not remain in the first. At the death of the "little prince" —a Jewish boy pampered by the Nazis in the concentration camps only to die under a truck in Paris—Michael's suffering leads him to the verge of madness.

> An immense wrath, savage and destructive, welled up suddenly in Michael. His eyes flashed. The little prince's death—this death— was too unjust, too absurd. He wanted to pit himself against the

angel as Jacob had: fell him with a blow, trample him. One gesture, just one, but a gesture in proportion to his misery.*

But Michael recognizes that greater than the mad revolt of the Modern Promethean is the tension of the Modern Job who refuses to go mad. "The man who chooses death is following an impulse of liberation from the self; so is the man who chooses madness. . . . To keep our balance then is the most difficult and absurd struggle in human existence." Madness is an easy, comfortable escape, a once-for-all act of free will that destroys freedom. Michael understands that madness represents a moral choice as well as a psychological compulsion. Michael's friend Pedro, "a living rock" like Gyula, warns him against the mad revolt which tempts him.

> "You frighten me," Pedro said. "You want to eliminate suffering by pushing it to the extreme: to madness. To say 'I suffer, therefore I am' is to become the enemy of man. What you must say is 'I suffer, therefore you are.' Camus wrote somewhere that to protest against a universe of unhappiness you had to create happiness. That's an arrow pointing the way: it leads to another human being. And not via absurdity."†

These, of all Pedro's words, are the ones that later come to Michael's aid.

In the prison cell—Michael's last "prayer"—Michael comes closest of all to madness, to "a door opening onto a forest, onto the liberty in which anything is permitted, anything is possible." Michael is obsessed by King Lear "who preferred suffering at the hands of men to flight into a trackless desert," who faced treason and cowardice directly and said, "I am here and nowhere else!" Yet he berates him for not going mad as a way of spitting in their faces, protesting against pain and injustice, rejecting their life and their sanity. Like Ivan Karamazov, Michael wants "to turn

* Elie Wiesel, *The Town Beyond the Wall*, trans. by Stephen Becker (New York: Avon Books [paperback], 1969), pp. 95 f.
† *Ibid.*, p. 127.

his ticket in"—not to reject God but his world. Madness is, indeed, the way of the Modern Promethean—Melville's Captain Ahab and Dostoevsky's Kirilov and Ivan. To resist it without glossing over *or* submitting to the suffering that gives rise to it is the way of the Modern Job. The Pedro whom Michael now imagines coming to speak with him in his cell points this latter way and shows it for the sober, courageous revolt that it is:

> "The only valuable protest, or attitude, is one rooted in the uncertain soil of humanity. Remaining human—in spite of all temptations and humiliations—is the only way to hold your own against the Other, whatever it may be. . . . To see liberty only in madness is wrong: liberation, yes; liberty, no."*

Michael finds the alternative to going mad in making himself responsible for his prison cellmate, a young boy who is completely silent and, until he responds to Michael's heartbreaking efforts, completely out of touch. In bringing Eliezer back into dialogue Michael brings himself back to humanity. Pedro has taught Michael and Michael teaches Eliezer the necessity of clinging to humanity. "It's in humanity itself that we find both our question and the strength to keep it within limits." To flee to a nirvana through a considered indifference or a sick apathy "is to oppose humanity in the most absurd, useless, and comfortable manner possible." Like Doctor Rieux in *The Plague*, Michael recognizes that "It's harder to remain human than to try to leap beyond humanity." The real heights and the real depths of humanity are found "at your own level, in simple and honest conversation, in glances heavy with existence." Man asks the question within himself ever more deeply, he feels ever more intimately the existence of an unknowable answer, and Michael brings both of these into the dialogue with Eliezer, into his Dialogue with the Absurd.

The Modern Job does not contend with an entirely alien Other, hostile and indifferent, such as Captain Ahab's White Whale or Caligula's absurd. Even the absurd reality over against

* *Ibid.*, p. 183.

us has a meaning—a meaning which can only be revealed in our trusting and contending. The dialogue, or duel, between man and his God does not end in nothingness: "As the liberation of the one was bound to the liberation of the other," says the legend at the end of the novel, "they renewed the ancient dialogue whose echoes come to us in the night, charged with hatred, with remorse, and most of all, with infinite yearning."

Malach, the Hebrew word that is usually translated "angel," actually means "messenger." *The Gates of the Forest* is the story of the lasting effect of two "messengers" on the life of Gregor, a young Jewish refugee. Gavriel, the nameless messenger to whom he gives his own Hebrew name, and the much more tangible Leib the Lion, accompany him—in person or in memory— through the spring when he hides from the Nazis in a cave in the forest, through summer when he plays the role of a feebleminded mute in the village where Maria, the former family servant, passes him off as her nephew, through autumn when he joins the partisans fighting under the leadership of his childhood friend, Leib the Lion, and through winter when he seeks a way forward in postwar New York where he has gone with his wife Clara, once the girl friend of Leib.

Gavriel tells Gregor that the Messiah has already come, that he is among men, that nonetheless the horror has taken place, and that all that is left is to learn to laugh in the face of the horror—a terrible, mad laugh that defies the absurd. It is the laugh of a man poised midway between the Modern Promethean and the Modern Job and holding the tension of both. The message which this messenger brings Gregor is that of the "final solution," the unsuspected extermination of the Jews. His father will not come back. No one will come back. His family has left without hope of return.

When the Hungarian soldiers come with dogs, Gavriel gives himself up to prevent their discovering Gregor. Before going, he tells Gregor of how he discovered the Messiah in a simple beadle who at night wept for the destruction of the Temple, for the exile of Israel and that of the Shekinah. When the Nazis came, Gavriel went to Moshe the Silent and demanded that he do his duty and disobey God for the sake of saving from annihilation the people of the witness, the martyr people, the people of the covenant. But the "Messiah" laid down his arms without resisting and let himself be taken prisoner and executed. "I tell you, Gregor," says Gavriel, "that hope is no longer possible nor permitted: . . . the Messiah has come and the world has remained what it was: an immense butchery." When Gregor goes to live with Maria in her village and impersonates a deaf-mute, he is forced to play Judas at the school play and is almost killed in the frenzy of the crowd. "Miraculously" casting off his dumbness and speaking with the voice of a prophet, he forces the people, including the priest, to beg Judas' pardon—for it is *he*, not Jesus, who is the crucified one. Yet Gregor resists his desire for vengeance. When he announces that he is not the son of Maria's sister Illeana but a Jew, a smile not of victory but of pity illuminates his face.

Escaping to the forest, he makes contact with a band of Jewish partisans and rediscovers his childhood friend Leib the Lion. When they were boys, Leib had taught him to fight the gang of children that descended on them on their way to school with cries of "dirty Jews!" and "Christ-killers!" on their lips. The mythic proportions that Leib took on then in Gregor's eyes are now realized in fact in his role as leader of the Jewish partisans, a latter-day Bar Kochba. Gregor informs Leib of what has been known for a long time already in Washington, London, and Stockholm but which no one had taken the trouble to radio to the Jews of Transylvania—that the deported Jews were not being taken to factories or labor camps but to extermination centers. The shocked and almost unbelieving Leib orders an attempt to liberate Gavriel from prison to ascertain the truth of Gregor's report and is captured himself in the process. It falls on Gregor to inform the other partisans that their leader is taken and to discover through their dismay and grief the image of man that he represented for them:

> Every one of his words and gestures enriched their hope by giving to it simplicity and humility: we shall prevail, for inasmuch as it

has any meaning, victory is within the domain of man and of that which elevates rather than denies him.*

Gregor makes the Promethean laughter of Gavriel and the Jobian courage of Leib his own, and they sustain him and give him strength until that distant day in postwar New York when he is confronted by a Hasidic rabbi who recognizes both his suffering and his pride. When Gregor admits that what he wants is that the rebbe cease to pray and that he howl instead, the rebbe, with a movement of revolt, says to him, slowly, accentuating every word and stopping after every phrase: "Who has told you that force comes from a cry and not from prayer, from anger and not from compassion? . . . The man who sings is the brother of him who goes to his death fighting." The dancing, the singing, the joy of the Hasid is *in spite of* the fact that all reason for dancing, singing, and joy has been taken from him.

> "He's guilty; do you think I don't know it? That I have no eyes to see, no ears to hear? That my heart doesn't revolt? That I have no desire to beat my head against the wall and shout like a madman, to give rein to my sorrow and disappointment? Yes, he is guilty. He has become an ally of evil, of death, of murder, but the problem is still not solved."†

The revolt of the Modern Promethean is unmasked by the rebbe as only a romantic gesture. It still leaves the question of what to do, of how to live, of the direction from which salvation and hope must come.

Unable to bear any longer the way his wife Clara betrays him by remaining faithful to her first lover, the dead Leib, Gregor has resolved to leave her. Now, after joining a *minyan* in reciting the *kaddish*—the prayer for the dead—he knows that he will return to Clara to take up again the battle of winning her back to the present, to life. It does not matter whether or not the Messiah comes, Gregor realizes, or the fact that he is too late. If we will

---

* Elie Wiesel, *The Gates of the Forest*, trans. by Frances Frenaye (New York: Avon Books [paperback], 1969), p. 161.
† *Ibid.*, p. 196.

be sincere, humble, and strong, the Messiah will come—every day, a thousand times a day—for he is not a single man but all men. When Clara learns to sing again and Gregor to weep, it will be he that sings and weeps in them.

Gregor's last *kaddish* is for Leib the Lion, his old comrade in battle, who, while alive, incarnated in himself what is immortal in man. This prayer for the dead is also a prayer for life—a prayer that the dead Leib will allow Gregor and Clara to live, but also that, despite their loyalty to the past, Eliezer, the "I" of *The Accident*, Michael, Gregor, and Elie Wiesel himself will be able to live for the living and not for the dead. It is a prayer for all of us—for we are all the inheritors of Auschwitz and Hiroshima—that we work our way through to the trust and contending of the Job of Auschwitz who meets the living present, including the absurd, with the courage that these "messengers on high" have bequeathed.

The original title of Wiesel's book *Chants des Morts* ("Songs of the Dead") might well be the title of all his books. But so also might be the English title, *Legends of Our Time*. Elie Wiesel, as anyone knows who has ever heard him speak, belongs to the oldest profession in the world, that of the storyteller—the man who preserves the awesome life of the tribe in the form of myths and legends—dramatic events—rather than of connected historical accounts. The art of story-telling was an oral one for countless millennia before it became a written one as well. Wiesel retains this oral quality not only in his speaking but also in his writing. In a series of poignant and powerful writings, he has woven together words and silence into tales of unexampled beauty and terror. In each successive work he has wrested an image of humanity from his Dialogue with the Absurd—his contending with the Nazi holocaust and the monstrous shadow which it cast on his life. The Job of Auschwitz "will always take the side of man confronted with the Absolute." God's presence, or his absence, at Treblinka or Maidanek "poses a problem which will forever remain insoluble." Nor does it matter that "loss of faith for some equaled discovery of God for others." Both stood within the

Modern Job's Dialogue with the Absurd: "Both answered the same need to take a stand, the same impulse to rebel. In both cases it was an accusation."

"My generation has been robbed of everything, even of our cemeteries," says Wiesel in *Legends of Our Time*.* Where there are no cemeteries, the dead refuse to stay dead, and the living must give them proper burial through creating a structure within which mourning can take place. The whole of Wiesel's writing is just such a work of mourning, of witnessing to the living dead: "The act of writing is for me often nothing more than the secret or conscious desire to carve words on a tombstone: to the memory of a town forever vanished, to the memory of a childhood in exile, to the memory of all those I loved and who, before I could tell them I loved them, went away." These include his playmates, his teachers, Moshe the Madman, the beadle, and his family—all from his town of Sighet. But they also include men whom he knew in the extermination camps, such as the man who went laughing to his death after he had fasted on Yom Kippur as a Job of Auschwitz must fast: "Not out of obedience, but out of defiance."

"Man defines himself by what disturbs him and not by what reassures him." Elie Wiesel lets himself be disturbed, and he disturbs us by insisting, in the face of *all* who turn away from it, on "the guilt we share." Witnessing the trial of Eichmann, Wiesel conducts a worldwide trial: of the indigenous populations of Hungary and Poland whose eagerness to become *Judenrein* alone made it possible for "the cattle trains with their suffocating human cargo" to "roll swiftly into the night"; of "the whole outside world, which looked on in a kind of paralysis and passively allowed" the murder of six million Jews, a number that could never have been reached had Roosevelt, Churchill, and the pope let loose an avalanche of angry protestations; of the American Jewish community which did not use its political and financial powers to move heaven and earth to save five to ten thousand

* Elie Wiesel, *Legends of Our Time* (New York: Avon Books [paperback], 1970).

Jews from murder each day; of Chaim Weizmann who put off for two weeks the messenger of the holocaust who had told him that "every passing day meant the lives of at least ten thousand Jews" ("How did Brand not go stark raving mad?" Wiesel asks.); of Gideon Hausner, Ben-Gurion, and the Israelis who tried Eichmann without crying out "in a voice loud enough to be heard by three generations: We never attempted the impossible—we never even exhausted the possible." From this trial, Wiesel concludes that "with the advent of the Nazi regime in Germany, humanity became witness to what Martin Buber would call an eclipse of God." It was above all, in fact, in the name of the "Job of Auschwitz," that Buber called this an age of the "eclipse of God."

It is Auschwitz that will engender Hiroshima and perhaps that extinction of the human race by nuclear warfare that "will be the punishment for Auschwitz, where, in the ashes, the hope of man was extinguished." At the time of the holocaust, those outside did not speak out. "One need only glimpse through the newspapers of the period to become disgusted with the human adventure on this earth." Nor were the inmates of the camps ignorant of this. Their seemingly weak "acceptance" of their death became, in consequence, "an act of lucidity, a protest" not only against their torturers, but also against the rest of humanity that had abandoned, excluded, and rejected them. "It is as though every country—and not only Germany—had decided to see the Jew as a kind of subhuman species" whose disappearance did not weigh on the conscience since the concept of brotherhood did not apply to him.

The most masterful expression of Wiesel's fight for the hidden image of man is his haunting and compelling novel of the Six Day War, *A Beggar in Jerusalem*. In *A Beggar in Jerusalem* the holocaust and the threat of extermination that seemed to hover over the people of the state of Israel on the eve of the Six Day War fuse into one reality. "They were alone," writes Wiesel, "as earlier in Europe in the time of *Night*." Perhaps it was the overwhelming feeling that Wiesel himself was the first to articulate—that we could not allow this extermination to happen twice in one lifetime—that gives this book a different time sense from all his other novels. In all of them there are flashbacks and the easy—and enormously painful—intermingling of what has been and what is. But only in *A Beggar* are all the ages present simultaneously. One of the circle of "beggars" who sit before the Wall during the long and story-laden nights after the Six Day War tells of when he came up to the man Jesus as he hung on the cross and said to him, "They will kill millions of your people in your name," at which Jesus wept so bitterly that the man who stood beneath him wept too. In *A Beggar*, as in *One Generation After*, there appears the bitter irony that alive, Jesus, the Jew, is the enemy of mankind; whereas once he is safely dead he becomes their God. "We have been crucified six million times," Wiesel seems to say, "and no amount of worship of the crucified ones will stay the hand of the next slayer who comes looking for a victim."

The plot of *A Beggar*, insofar as there is one, is the story of two men, David and Katriel, the one present throughout, the other both present and absent. We come to feel that David and Katriel are one person even before David is recognized by Katriel's wife Malka, whom he has never met before yet who is his wife. Nor is it clear to David which one of them, himself or Katriel, is "the beggar of Jerusalem"—the man who will come and tell you your own story in such a way that you will recognize in it your life and death.

Commenting on those Jews who wished, before the Six Day War, to define themselves simply as men and only accidentally as Jews, Wiesel neatly reverses the formula and suggests that in our day "one cannot be a man without assuming the condition of the Jew." "The Jew is the most exposed person in the world today," wrote Martin Buber in 1933. The inhumanity which has been unleashed upon the Jew since then so threatens the humanity of all men that only in sharing that exposure can any man today become man. Today we must all suffer with the "Modern Exile" or lose our birthright as men. When David recognizes himself as the permanently exiled stranger in a story of Katriel's, he speaks for every hero of Wiesel's novels and for Wiesel too:

Disguised as a stranger, I might have been living beside women
who were mistaking me for someone else. The real me remained
below, in the kingdom of the night, prisoner of the dead. . . . I
was nothing more than an echo of voices long since extinguished.
. . . I thought I was living my own life. I was only inventing
it.*

This state of exile is also the state of God today, *A Beggar in
Jerusalem* suggests. The Messiah does not dwell above in glory,
but below in the suffering and exposure of men. God too has
need of a witness: "In the beginning was the Word; the Word is
the history of man; and man is the history of God." The Shekinah, the indwelling Glory of God, remains in Jerusalem yet follows all Jews everywhere into exile. The Shekinah dwells in the
contradiction, and the greatest and most tormenting contradiction of all is to kill for the sake of God men who are created in
the image of God: "He who kills kills God. Each murder is a
suicide of which the Eternal is eternally the victim." This contradiction is similar to the question that haunts Elie Wiesel
throughout each of his novels: How is it possible to live for the
living without betraying the dead?

The answer to this question lies in bringing forth from its
concealment the hidden human image. If man is created in the
image of God, then the only way that that image can be transmitted is through transmitting the image of man. It is for this
that a whole people set out to march for a third time, and with
the living marched the dead: "Israel conquered because its
army, its people included six million additional names." Only
Elie Wiesel in our generation has been capable of uniting the
holocaust and the emergence and survival of the state of Israel
without denying the mystery or reality of either or turning one
into historical cause and the other into historical effect. In this
sense, all of Elie's other books were preparations for *A Beggar in
Jerusalem*; for only here do the living fight *with* the dead and

---

* Elie Wiesel, *A Beggar in Jerusalem*, trans. by Lily Edelman and Elie Wiesel
(New York: Random House, 1970), pp. 132 f. I have slightly altered the
translation for the sake of faithfulness to the French original.

not against them, only here is it possible for David to stay with
Malka despite their loyalty to Katriel. By its dedication, "For
Marion," and by the unification of past and present in the figures
of Katriel, Malka, and David, *A Beggar in Jerusalem* convinced
me that Elie too was now ready to live in the present, without
turning his back on the reality of the past.

In what he himself says will be his final book on the holocaust,
*One Generation After,** Wiesel repeatedly asserts that in the holocaust man betrayed his image and that whether or not the murder of a million children makes any historical sense, it denies and
condemns man. The Job of Auschwitz hears above all the command to witness to what has happened, recalling and telling
every detail, writing down his testimony moments before dying
in agony, surviving in order to be able to tell—to howl against
the wall of death that crushed a whole people. It is only this—
and the hope that someone might listen to this recounting—that
enables the Job of Auschwitz to continue at all. Nothing so
concisely sums up Elie Wiesel's mission as a person and as a writer
as his own sentence, "I do not demand of the raconteur that he
play the role of master but that he fulfill his duty as messenger
and as witness." What it means to "hold fast to one's integrity" in
this calling of messenger and witness Wiesel has shown us in every
one of his novels and stories and in *Night* and *The Jews of
Silence.*

Wiesel's identification with the state of Israel does not entail a
hatred for Israel's enemies. The victorious Jew "is no longer a
victim, but he will never become a torturer" or seek to break the
will of the vanquished. The state of Israel in no way cancels out
the extermination of six million Jews. It may nonetheless be
permitted to the Job of Auschwitz—the survivor who trusts *and*
contends and holds fast to the integrity of *man* in so doing—to
see in Israel "a victory over the absurd and the inhuman." "I
belong to a generation," writes Elie Wiesel, "that has not known
many such victories." This victory is not incompatible with the

* Elie Wiesel, *One Generation After,* trans. by Lily Edelman and Elie Wiesel
(New York: Random House, 1970).

continued exile of the Shekinah, the mark of an unredeemed
world, as the last chapter of *A Beggar in Jerusalem* makes clear.
David looks at Malka, *his* wife and not Katriel's, touches her and
loves loving her; yet something in him shrivels and rebels, and
he is compelled to walk so as to punish his body for keeping time
imprisoned and punish his spirit for having resisted. If the madmen that dwell in David's soul (the madmen who have reap-
peared constantly in Elie Wiesel's novels) come close to being
appeased in Jerusalem, the one city where time welcomes the
weary exile instead of expelling him, the key to peace is still in
Katriel, and it is perhaps David who is dead and Katriel the
survivor. David is the beggar of Jerusalem who knows how to
wait but who will also have to decide, to retrace his steps, to find
the forgotten road back that no one walks with impunity.

> A victor, he? Victory does not prevent suffering from having
> existed, nor death from having taken its toll. How can one work
> for the living without by that very act betraying those who are
> absent? . . . Of course, the mystery of good is no less disturbing
> than the mystery of evil. But one does not cancel out the other.
> Man alone is capable of uniting them by remembering.*

Even Wiesel's concern with "the Jews of silence"—the Jews of
the Soviet Union the discrimination against whom Wiesel has
done more than any other person in the world to make known—
stands under the sign of the Modern Job. *Simhat-Torah*, the day of
the rejoicing in the giving of the Torah, "will henceforth be associated with the Jews of silence," Wiesel testifies after going to Moscow for a second time to see the thousands of young Jews,
deprived of their heritage, publicly affirming and celebrating
their existence as Jews. "For those who participate in their dancing, each moment becomes privileged: a victory over silence."
From these Soviet Jews Wiesel learned that those who make of
their Judaism a song are of equal value with those who make of
it a prayer. "The staunchest Hasid could learn from the most
assimilated Jewish student in Moscow how to rejoice and how to

---

* Wiesel, *A Beggar in Jerusalem*, p. 210.

transform his song into an act of belief and defiance." Out of a situation of constraint these young Jews made an act of choice, out of what should break and humiliate them they drew their force of resistance.

In *One Generation After*, Wiesel tells a young German of the New Left that he confuses the lack of discipline with independence, feeling the need to challenge the regime—whatever it may be—and reject authority—whatever its source. He is, in short, the Modern Promethean. Wiesel wants him to be angry at being born "into the midst of a fanaticized and stubborn people that repudiated its Führer only after his military defeats and not for his crimes." If he does not despise his guilty fathers, he will become inhuman himself and unworthy of redemption. Wiesel demands that he face up to the reality of the past or become guilty of the holocaust himself. "I shall not hate you," Wiesel declares in an echo of Camus' "Letter to a Nazi Friend" that he quotes from at the head of this essay, but "I shall denounce, unmask and fight you with all my power."

In "To a Young Jew of Today" God himself is brought to trial as he was by Job and two and a half millennia later by the Hasidic rebbe Levi Yitzhak of Berditshev. "If God is an answer, it must be the wrong answer." There is no answer: "the agony of the believer equals the bewilderment of the non-believer." All there is, is a question which man must live and formulate and in so doing challenge God. This challenge is permissible, indeed required. "He who says no to God is not necessarily a renegade. . . . One can say anything as long as it is for man, not against him, as long as one remains inside the covenant." Here contending means faithfulness; to betray the present means to destroy the past, whereas to fulfill oneself means choosing to be a link "between the primary silence of creation and the silence that weighed on Treblinka."

The task of the Job of Auschwitz is contending for meaning within the Dialogue with the Absurd. If he rakes over the ashes of the holocaust, it is because "to be a Jew today . . . means to testify," to bear witness with fervent, if saddened, joy to the

Israel that is and to bear witness with "restrained, harnessed anger, free of sterile bitterness" to the world of the six million Jews that is no longer. "For the contemporary Jewish writer, there can be no theme more human, no project more universal."

"Was it not a mistake to testify, and by that very act, affirm their faith in man and word?" asks Wiesel, and replies for himself and the Job of Auschwitz, "I know of at least one who often feels like answering yes." This note of doubt and bitterness also belongs to the Job of Auschwitz as it did to the original Job. He would be a dishonest rebel if he did not sometimes say with Wiesel: "Nothing has been learned; Auschwitz has not even served as warning. For more detailed information, consult your daily newspaper." The storyteller is left with a sense of guilt and impotence. Writing itself is called in question; for by its uniqueness the holocaust defies literature. The storyteller who sees himself essentially as a witness realizes in anguish that he cannot "approach this universe of darkness without turning into a pedlar of night and agony." The messenger unable to deliver his message knows that "no image is sufficiently demented, no cry sufficiently blasphemous to illustrate the plight of a single victim, resigned or rebellious." And yet the story had to be told for the sake of our children. "We needed to face the dead again and again, in order . . . to seek among them, beyond all contradiction and absurdity, a symbol, a beginning of promise."

It is precisely this tension between the powerful urge to keep silent and the equally powerful call to witness that forms the heart of Wiesel's novel *The Oath*. Set in two time periods before and after the holocaust, *The Oath* only gradually reveals itself as the most terrifying of Wiesel's works in its suggestion of the possibility of the permanent eclipse of the hidden human image. It is, by the same token, a powerful comment on the holocaust itself— not just as a sickness of the Nazis or of modern man but of humanity. In the first instance, this is European, Christian humanity, but in the end it is the human as such that is tainted by senseless hatred and ultimate stupidity.

The Oath is structured around a dialogue between an old man

with a terrible secret protected by a solemn communal vow and
a young man contemplating suicide who just thereby tempts him
to break his vow. On a deeper level still, it is the hidden image
of Moshe the Madman, a recurrent figure through each of Wiesel's
works, and the story of Kolvillàg, a "small town, somewhere
between the Dnieper and the Carpathians." The story of Kolvillàg is an awesome embodiment of Rabbi Nachman of Brat-
zlav's parable of a town that contains all the towns of the world.
In this town is a street that contains all the streets of the world,
and in this street a house that contains all the houses of the
world, and in this house a room that contains all the rooms of
the world, and in this room a man who contains all the people
in the world, and this man laughs—with the laughter of madness!

The Oath begins and ends with visions of apocalyptic terror
and of the dread beast of the Apocalypse. The beast at work was
"alternately savage and attentive, radiant and hideous, . . . reducing to shreds whoever saw it at close range," turning the
town into "a desecrated, pillaged cemetery," crushing all its inhabitants into a twisted and tortured monster with a hundred
eyes and a thousand mouths all of which were spitting terror.
Witness to this ultimate destruction, the narrator has not been
silent by choice. Rather silence has been his master, drawing "its
strength and secret from a savagely demented universe doomed
by its wretched and deadly past."

If, despite this, the old man reveals all to the youth, it is
because of a residue of responsibility which forms the final stage
of every encounter even in the era of the eclipse of the human.
"Whoever says 'I' creates the 'you.' Such is the trap of every conscience. The 'I' signifies both solitude and rejection of solitude."
The narrator admonishes the youth not to oppose evil to evil,
committing one more injustice by killing himself. " 'I am not
telling you not to despair of man, but not to offer death one
more victim, one more victory.' " Every death is absurd, useless,
ugly. Whether life has a meaning or not, what counts is not to
make a gift of it to death. "It is not by legitimizing suffering—
and what is death if not the paroxysm of suffering—that one can

disarm it." To defeat evil one must help one's fellowman; to triumph over death one must begin by saving one's brother.

The name of the old man is Azriel, but he is also called by some Katriel. Like Wiesel's own teacher, whom he portrays in "The Wandering Jew" in *Legends of Our Time*, Azriel is a mysterious figure, someone equally at ease quoting from the Talmud or Mao Tse-tung, master of seven ancient tongues and a dozen living ones, "haughty with the powerful, humble with the deprived," and above all a *Na-venadnik*, one whose destiny is never to put down roots in any one place. Azriel's chronicler father and his mad teacher Moshe, by making him the repository of their tragic truths, doomed him to be a survivor, a messenger, and a perpetual exile—revealing and attaching himself to no one, watching over the inhabitants of the secret world inside him. In his daydreams it is not he but his village that is roaming the roads in search of help and redemption: He is but a link, the hyphen between countless communities.

There is nothing paradoxical in this; for Azriel's message is the message of silence—of events too monstrous to be told, too bewildering to be imagined. It is the silence of the holocaust, the burden of which the youth of today have inherited without its mystery. The Exterminating Angel has turned all men into victims, not least those who attempt to use its services. The culmination of fanaticism and stupidity affects equally victims and executioners. "Whoever kills, kills himself; whoever preaches murder will be murdered. One may not accept any meaning imposed on death by the living. Just as every murder is a suicide, every suicide is a murder." To kill the other, like the sin of Cain, is to murder the brother in oneself. To kill oneself is to murder oneself in one's brother.

A central motif in *The Oath*, as in *The Gates of the Forest*, is messianism—the inverted messianism of a cursed century. Man clamors for the Messiah, but he is fascinated by death. The Christian Messiah expires on the cross, leaving others to bear his shame. But the Jewish Messiah survives all generations, perhaps ashamed to reveal himself or ashamed for a world in which men claim to be brothers and are nothing but wild, solitary beasts. "In these days exile is becoming ever harsher. To have hope in God is to have hope against God." "What is the Messiah," said Moshe to Azriel, "if not man transcending his solitude in order to make his fellow-man less solitary?" "Every truth that shuts you in, that does not lead to others, is inhuman." In defying Moshe's vow of silence, Azriel is allowing Moshe, the hidden image of the human, to speak through him to the young man. Conversely, in forcing Azriel to reinvent a meaning to his quest, the young man is unwittingly helping Azriel even as Azriel is helping him. "May God save you not from suffering but from indifference to suffering," Moshe had said to Azriel, and it is out of gratitude to the young man for saving him from this indifference that Azriel breaks his oath.

Moshe is a great Kabbalist with miraculous powers who channels his fervor into prayer, study—and madness. Moshe takes as his only disciple Azriel, the son of Shmuel—the chronicler responsible in his generation for the Book of Kolvillàg. Both—Shmuel and Moshe—are trying to attain the same messianic goal, the one through memory of the past, the other through imagination of the future. The Messiah, Moshe tells Azriel, will not come to save men from death but from boredom, mediocrity, the commonplaces of routine. Yet when Moshe is married to a homely girl by a maneuver of the community, he brings his understanding of the messianic into his tender and confirming relationship with his wife Leah:

> He knew that nothing justifies the pain man causes another. Any messiah in whose name men are tortured can only be a false messiah. It is by diminishing evil, present and real evil, experienced evil, that one builds the city of the sun. It is by helping the person who looks at you with tears in his eyes, needing help, needing you or at least your presence, that you may attain perfection.*

---

* Elie Wiesel, *The Oath*, trans. from the French by Marion Wiesel (New York: Random House, 1973), p. 138.

When the Jews of Kolvillàg are threatened with a pogrom triggered by the disappearance of a Christian hoodlum who tor-
ments birds and children alike, Moshe takes it upon himself to
save the community by meeting the prefect's demand for a Jewish name on which to pin the supposed murder. Beaten into
unconsciousness by the sadistic sergeant to whom he "confesses,"
Moshe takes on the role of a Modern Job. "Nothing justifies
suffering," he thinks, but "nobody is required to explain it, only
to fight it." One cannot confer a meaning on death.

> "To turn death into a philosophy is not Jewish. To turn it into a
> theology is anti-Jewish. Whoever praises death ends up either
> serving or totally ignoring it. . . . We . . . consider death the
> primary defect and injustice inherent in creation. To die for God
> is to die against God. For us, man's ultimate confrontation is
> only with God."*

"What is essential," Moshe tells the boy Azriel, "is to live to the
limit. Let your words be shouts or silence but . . . nothing in
between. Let your desire be absolute and your wait as well. . . .
Whoever walks in the night, moves against night."

Moshe's desire to be a martyr for the sake of Israel is not
granted, for once stirred up, the senseless hatred will not stop
until everything is destroyed. Through the intervention of the
friendly prefect, Moshe is allowed to summon the whole of the
Jewish community to an extraordinary session where he sweeps
everyone up into his own rebellion against the traditional Jewish
task of pleasing God by becoming the illustrations of their own
tales of martyrdom. Jewish memory, it was held, robbed the
executioner of his final victory by preventing his attempts to
erase the evidence of his cruelty, haunting his conscience, and
warning humanity present and future of his crimes. Murdered,
plundered, humiliated, oppressed, expelled from society and history, forbidden the right to laugh or sing or even cry, the surviving Jews turned their ordeal into "a legend destined for men of
good will." "The more they hate us, the more we shout our love

---

* *Ibid.*, p. 189.

of man." But now, says Moshe the Madman, the time has come to put an end to this Jewish role of being mankind's memory and heart. "Now we shall adopt a new way: silence." By refusing to testify anymore, we can break the link between suffering and the history of suffering, thereby forestalling future abominations. With all the mystic power till now held in check, Moshe leads the whole community to take an oath that whoever may survive the massacre and humiliation which await the Jews of Kolvillàg will go to their graves without speaking of it, and he seals this oath by placing the entire people of Israel under the sign of the *Herem*—the dread word of excommunication and damnation!

What rules in Kolvillàg just before the attack is fear, fear "ready to rob you of vision and life and of your very desire to go on living." "Heralding disaster, fear becomes disaster." Fear operates in the besieged community of Kolvillàg exactly as the plague in Camus' Oran:

> Fear is absorbed and communicated like poison or leprosy. Once contaminated by fear, you too become a carrier. And you transmit it the way primary experience is transmitted: involuntarily, unwittingly, almost clandestinely; from eye to eye, from mouth to mouth.*

A father describes a pogrom to his daughter as worse than hell; for in hell there is no blind cruelty, no gratuitous savagery, no desecration, no trampled innocence. A pogrom is "insanity unleashed, demons at liberty, the basest instincts, the most vile laughter." Even the Hasidic rebbe says, "We were wrong . . . to try, wrong to hope. . . . A Jew must not expect anything from Christians, man must not expect anything from man."

At this point in his narrative, Azriel shares from the Book of Kolvillàg some of the records of earlier pogroms from the twelfth century onward. One of these is the story of Zemakh, a vignette which unforgettably portrays the hidden human image revealed in response to the very eclipse of the human. Zemakh the beadle, who cleaned, tended the hearth, carried messages and packages,

* *Ibid.*, p. 251.

Zemakh the man who never in his life said no, defies unto death
Lupu, the monster squire. When Lupu demands that Zemakh tell
him that he is a man endowed with many talents and indescrib-
able virtues, Zemakh responds, "Whoever feels compassion for a
man without pity will in the end be ruthless with a man of
compassion. . . . I shall not lie to please you." "To glorify the
executioner is the basest of slaveries," says Zemakh the rebel. "To
make him into a god the worst of perversions." Zemakh was "one
of those Just Men whose hidden qualities are revealed only at the
hour when body and soul no longer obey the same call."

When the attack comes it is "primitive and absolute hate," an
apocalyptic vision of "horsemen and beasts" which announces
"the explosion and end of the world." This terrifying inhuman
night does not stop at destroying the Jews but spreads to all, the
killers and the killed. "It is a night of punishment, of supreme
ultimate stupidity," Moshe says to the prefect who tries in vain to
save him. "They kill themselves by killing, they dig their own
graves by murdering us, they annihilate the world by destroying
our homes." What follows is a babel of mutual murder that spares
no one. "The killers were killing each other, senselessly, with
swords, hatchets and clubs. Brothers and sisters striking one another, friends and accomplices strangling one another." Here the
two voices of Elie Wiesel—the memory of Shmuel and the silence
of Moshe—are united in an unbearable vision of a "Second Coming": "Suddenly I understood with every fiber of my being why I
was shuddering at this vision of horror: I had just glimpsed the
future." The narrative, which dooms the youth to survival while
allowing Azriel to return to Kolvillàg to die in his stead, Azriel
concludes in the name of his mad friend Moshe, the "last prophet
and first messiah of a mankind that is no more."

Elie Wiesel did not become great, like Lincoln, through his
unique response at the time of the historical event. During his
years in the extermination camps, he was only a boy. Nor does he
suggest in *Night* that he was more admirable than any of the
other citizens of the "kingdom of night." He became great, rather,
in a lifetime of living with the most terrible event in human

history. In his living and writing, in his lectures and tales, he has
responded ever more deeply and faithfully to the holocaust and
has become, through this responding, the conscience of mankind.

The most sublime and impassioned protest of this Job of
Auschwitz, the most remarkable fusion of religion and literature
in his works, is neither novel, play, nor essay but the cantata *Ani
Maamin*, which in November 1973 was performed at Carnegie
Hall to music composed for it by the great French composer
Darius Milhaud in honor of the hundredth anniversary of the Hebrew Union College–Jewish Institute of Religion. It is the
haunting and powerful plaint of Abraham, Isaac, and Jacob, the
traditional intercessors for Israel, who, in the face of the holocaust, turn to God and then away from God to Israel to share the
fate of the exterminated millions and the tormented survivors.
Maimonides' statement of perfect faith that, though the Messiah
tarry, he will come, is not here the affirmation of those pious Jews
who went to their deaths in the gas chambers singing these
words as a hymn. It is Wiesel's and our affirmation *despite* God
and *despite* man, an affirmation that is as much contending as
trust.* It is the Dialogue with the Absurd embodied and voiced
by the man who, more than any other living human being, has become in his own person the "Job of Auschwitz." This Job of
Auschwitz is not the person who was exterminated, but, as Buber
stated when he coined the phrase, that *survivor* of the holocaust
who does not put up with faceless fate but struggles for redemption *with* and *against* our "cruel and kind Lord" whose revelation
in our times is only a deepening of his hiddenness.

Elie Wiesel's story-telling witness points to the only redemption
that we can hope for. We cannot bring the human image shining
and beautiful out of the holocaust, out of Hiroshima and Naga-
saki, out of Vietnam, out of Biafra and Bangladesh. The only
thing we can do is to face the eclipse of the human image sufficiently honestly and courageously, that in affirming the human,

* Elie Wiesel, *Ani Maamin: A Song Lost and Found Again*, music for the
Cantata composed by Darius Milhaud, trans. from the French by Marion
Wiesel (New York: Random House, 1973).

insofar as we can, we do not lose sight of what has all but obscured it—that monstrous inhumanity which we can never affirm. If we try to affirm the human less honestly than that, we shall not be affirming it at all—and the human image will only be more fully and terribly eclipsed. "The era of the moon opens at the very moment that, reluctantly, the age of Auschwitz comes to a close," writes Wiesel, and the concentration-camp man seals off his memory and steps down from the witness stand. Elie Wiesel—the messenger, the witness, the Job of Auschwitz—may carry on his Dialogue with the Absurd from now on in quite other legends and tales or someday even in silence. But in that silence—for generations to come—there will reverberate the awesome and somber fervor of his Books of Job, each one of which sears flaming light into the darkest recesses of our souls.

"LA CONDITION HUMAINE"

OUR AGE OF
ANXIETY

Whether or not we follow W. H. Auden in dubbing the present time as "the age of anxiety," no one would deny that there are a great many evidences of anxiety in our culture, manifestations that are all the more striking given the fact that we have attained a level of technological advance and a standard of living never before known to mankind. The hydrogen bomb, the cold war, racial conflict, the growing pressure on young children to compete for grades so they may have a chance to enter college, down to the anxiety of parents about toilet training and the right balance of discipline and permissiveness—all these are too well known to need elaboration.

Yet these manifestations of anxiety raise the question of whether we should regard anxiety as a product of our culture or our culture as an elaborate mechanism for the warding off of a basic human anxiety, or both. Here we shall part company according to our approach. If we are Freudians, we shall see anxiety as the repression of childhood fears, on the one hand, and as the individual's discontent with civilization, on the other, but in either case a product of guilt connected with the Oedipus complex or the too harsh repression of libidinal instincts. If we are Sullivanians, we shall see anxiety in terms of the dissociation between our images of ourselves and our actual interpersonal performances, necessitated by the fear of the disapproval of significant others. If we are Jungians, we shall see anxiety as the repression of the "shadow" self, those frightening elements of the self which turn negative and "evil" when we fail to integrate them with the rest of our personality. If we take a sociopsychological approach, we shall see anxiety in terms of competition, "keeping up with the Joneses," "what makes Sammy run." Or we shall talk of the anxiety created as well as allayed by the patterns of social conformity, such as the "Organization Man" and the "other-directed" person.

In contrast to these approaches are those which see anxiety as basically human and culture as either a manifestation or avoidance of this anxiety. For Kierkegaard anxiety begins with the leap from innocence to experience, the fear and trembling which the "single one" experiences in his unique relationship with God, the dread of the man who has fallen into demonic shut-in-ness, the despair of wishing to be or not to be oneself. For Martin Heidegger anxiety is the primordial phenomenon, which the "They" of culture, ambiguity, gossip, idle talk, cover over and conceal, and by the same token it is that which calls one back to one's "thrownness" and with it one's authentic existence.

> Anxiety throws Dasein back upon that which it is anxious about, its authentic potentiality-for-Being-in-the-world. Anxiety individualizes Dasein for its ownmost Being-in-the-world, which as something that understands, projects itself essentially upon possibilities. . . . Anxiety brings Dasein face to face with its BEING-FREE-FOR the authenticity of its Being, and for this authenticity as a possibility which it always is. . . . That kind of Being-in-the-world which is tranquillized and familiar is a mode of Dasein's uncanniness, not the reverse. FROM AN EXISTENTIAL-ONTOLOGICAL POINT OF VIEW, THE "NOT-AT-HOME" MUST BE CONCEIVED AS THE MORE PRIMORDIAL PHENOMENON.*

Paul Tillich also takes an ontological approach to anxiety and sees, beneath the layers of individual neuroticism, on the one

* Martin Heidegger, *Being and Time*, trans. by John Macquarrie and Edward Robinson (New York: Harper & Row, 1962), pp. 232, 234.

hand, and our specific culture, on the other, the general human anxiety before fate and death, before emptiness and meaning-lessness, and before guilt and self-condemnation. Tillich holds that to exist is to exist face-to-face with nonbeing, by which he means what is changing and passing away—all the negative in existence. The neurotic, according to Tillich, is not the man who is anxious but the man who is not anxious, that is, the man who through his fear of facing the anxiety of nonbeing cuts himself off from being as well and cruelly curtails the possibilities of his own existence.

All of these approaches have enough truth in them to add to our understanding of anxiety, yet none of them can answer the question whether anxiety is a product of our culture or whether culture is a means of warding off a basic human anxiety. To answer this question we need a new approach that does not choose between the psychological, sociological, and ontological but unites them within a larger framework, the historical. Anx-iety in our culture at its basic level means the special role our culture plays in reflecting, concealing, and creating anxiety about authentic existence, an anxiety that derives in turn from the absence of a modern image of man.

Martin Buber begins his little classic "The Way of Man" by re-counting the story of a gendarme who asked a Hasidic rabbi why God, who presumably knows everything, said to Adam, "Where art thou?" "In every era, God calls to every man, 'Where are you in the world?'" replied the rabbi. "'So many years and days of those allotted to you have passed, and how far have you gotten in your world?' God says something like this: 'You have lived forty-six years. How far along are you?'" Forty-six years was the age of the gendarme, and the effect of hearing his age mentioned thus was to awaken in him a heart-searching which destroys man's system of hideouts and leads him to render ac-counts so that he may find the unique direction purposed for him in his creation.*

* Martin Buber, *Hasidism and Modern Man*, ed. and trans. with an Introduc-tion by Maurice Friedman (New York: Harper Torchbooks, 1966), Book IV, "The Way of Man according to the Teachings of the Hasidim," pp. 130–135.

When I was forty-six years of age, I received from my Harvard class a printed book in which each of my classmates described "how far along" he was in his world, twenty-five years after graduation. When I read from my classmate Cabot that he is head of the million-dollar Cabot industries, that it helped to have the right grandfather, and that he is busy every night of the week on the board of one or another important organization or university, I did not envy classmate Cabot his millions. But I did have to ask myself just what I had done in the quarter of a century since I graduated from Harvard to justify that feeling of superiority to the Harvard "club man" that, as an undergraduate socialist, I took for granted.

I can remind myself, to be sure, that Buber is not talking about success and power. On the contrary, he writes: "Whatever success and enjoyment he may achieve, whatever power he may attain and whatever deeds he may do, life will remain way-less, so long as he does not face the Voice." I can remind myself too, following Buber's philosophy of dialogue, that "heart-searching" does not mean anything comparative but is the unique demand that is made on me as the person I am in the unique situation in which I find myself. Yet I cannot so easily as that divorce my anxiety about whether my existence is authentic and whether I am answering the true call of my vocation, from the anxiety concerning my place in my culture, my age, my status, my social position, my accomplishments or lack of them. It is not just that both anxieties coexist in me, as they must, I suppose, in a child of this culture, and most especially the child of immigrants. They become confusedly intermingled through the very conception of being a certain age and of being so far along in the world.

In my book *Problematic Rebel* I try to find the historical link that joins the basic anthropological, or ontological, reality of human existence, on the one hand, and the special alienation experienced by the men of our culture, on the other. I call this historical link "the death of God and the alienation of modern man," and I see arising from this alienation the Modern Exile and the "problematic of modern man." The former includes various types of isolation and alienation, the latter focuses on the intermixture of personal freedom and psychological compulsion, the effect of the absence of the father on the inner division of the son, the crisis of motives and the problematic of guilt, and the paradox of being a person who, in an era of the "death of God," must still hear and respond to the call that makes him a person.

The "death of God" is not just a question of the relativization of "values" and the absence of universally accepted mores. It is the absence of an image of meaningful human existence, the absence of the ground that enabled Greek, biblical, and Renaissance man to move with some sureness even in the midst of tragedy. The "death of God" is an anthropological-historical anxiety that is still more basic than the *Angst*—or dread—with which Kierkegaard's "knight of faith" is tried and the anxiety that makes Heidegger's man turn from the "They" to the possibilities of his own authentic existence toward death. Indeed, I should go so far as to say that the *Angst* of Kierkegaard and Heidegger are secondary products of this more basic anxiety. Both Kierkegaard and Heidegger reject society and culture for the lonely relation of the "single one" to God or the self to its own authentic existence. Both posit a dualism between the "crowd" or the "They" and the individual. Both reflect the loss of faith in the universal order and in the society that purports to be founded on it.

The "death of God" means the alienation of modern man, as Albert Camus has tirelessly pointed out in his discussion of the "absurd." The ultimate terror, to Herman Melville in *Moby Dick* similarly, is the blank indifference of an absolute that excludes man: "Is it by its indefiniteness," Ishmael asks, that whiteness "shadows forth the heartless voids and immensities of the universe, and thus stabs us from behind with the thought of annihilation, when beholding the white depths of the milky way?" While Ahab has a more terrible aloneness and isolation from other men than Ishmael, his exile is less profound than that of Ishmael, who cannot come up against, much less hate, the indifferent evil that oppresses him. An exactly analogous situation has occurred in

142 THE HIDDEN HUMAN IMAGE

our times with the scientific extermination of whole populations.
Speaking of the Nazis who murdered six million Jews, Martin
Buber said, "They have . . . so transposed themselves into a
sphere of monstrous inhumanity inaccessible to my power of
conception, that not even hatred, much less an overcoming of
hatred, was able to arise in me."*

Ishmael's impression as he stood at the helm of his ship "that
whatever swift, rushing thing I stood on was not so much bound
to any haven ahead as rushing from all havens astern" suggests a
modern man's sense of the earth hurtling through the empty
space of the heavens on its meaningless progress to extinction.
The "heartless immensity" forces us to realize our own limited-
ness, our own mortality. When a man loses his limits, he has lost
that condition that makes human existence possible. But it is not
the infinity of time and space alone that threatens modern man.
It is his increasing inability to stand before this infinite. He less
and less sees himself as a self with a ground on which to stand,
and at the same time he less and less trusts that existence outside
himself to which he must relate. As a result he cannot accept
Pascal's dictum that man is neither all nor nothing. He feels
compelled, instead, to the Either/Or of the Modern Promethean,
the rebel who believes that he must destroy the other that confronts him or he will be destroyed himself.

In Dostoevsky's "Underground Man" the anxiety of the Modern Exile is manifested in a different constellation, that of isolation from other men, inner emptiness, and inauthenticity. The
Underground Man, Raskolnikov, Svidrigailov, Kirilov, Stavrogin,
and Ivan Karamazov, are all essentially isolated from other men,
and their attempts to break out of this isolation, such as Raskolnikov's murder of the pawnbroker woman and Stavrogin's de-
bauchery, leave them more isolated still. It is interesting to
compare the different kinds of anxiety that are manifested in

* Martin Buber, *A Believing Humanism: Gleanings,* trans. with an Introduction
and Explanatory Comments by Maurice Friedman (New York: Simon &
Schuster Paperbacks, 1969), "Genuine Dialogue and the Possibilities of
Peace," p. 195.

Dostoevsky's suicides. The Underground Man has spoiled his life in his funk-hole because of his anxiety before any "real life," as he puts it—his desire to protect himself in his grandiloquent world of fantasy from the dirt and degradation that he considers his inevitable portion in reality. Svidrigailov kills himself out of inner emptiness, isolation, and guilt connected with a child he has raped whose image he cannot get out of his mind. Kirilov kills himself in an effort to liberate mankind from the fear of death and to make his own will absolute in the place of God's. Yet his actual suicide is a pure concentrate of fear and frozen horror which transmutes him from a man into a jerking, grotesque monster. It is his anxiety before his own fear of death coupled with his terror before the infinite Other that he can neither accept nor disregard that manifest themselves here. Stavrogin's suicide is the last act in an inauthentic existence. It is anxiety before boredom and inner emptiness, dissociation and vacuity, fixated guilt (he has committed the same crime as Svidrigailov), and the inability to bring himself wholly into any one act or relationship.

Even Dostoevsky's supposedly Christlike character Prince Myshkin ends in a suicide, or more literally, "selficide," through his passive identification with the sufferings of the demonic and tormented. Myshkin's attraction to suffering is a desperate release of the inner tension which he cannot bear. Even the element of compassion in it touches one of the deepest sources of anxiety in our culture: It is the hopeless attempt of the man who is unconfirmed himself to supply an absolute confirmation to others. Myshkin's anxiety leads directly to a self-destruction beyond all mere self-denial, the portion of the man who walks the lonely path of fear and trembling without the grace received from others that enables him to be human.

Franz Kafka's whole work is a profound demonstration of anxiety in our culture. In it is reflected Kafka's own anxiety about his choice between the imprisonment of marriage, on the one hand, and the progressive exile of the bachelor, on the other. Kafka chooses the latter way for himself and his heroes, and they all end with only enough space to bury them. Kafka's heroes move from self-sufficiency to ever more anxious isolation and exile. From beneath their compulsive mastery of their surroundings ever fresh anxiety inevitably breaks forth. Their metamorphosis turns someone who stands on a very narrow plot of ground into someone who has no ground at all. The self is torn out of the social role and the accustomed routine that it has built up for itself.

Absence of confirmation is also a central source of anxiety in Kafka. Had the "hunger artist" found some way open to a direct, meaningful existence, he would not have needed to seek the indirect confirmation of his art. In Kafka's novel *The Castle*, K. needs to be confirmed in his vocation as "land-surveyor" before he can practice it. To receive it he must make contact with the Castle, which he cannot do; yet without this confirmation from the Castle, he cannot remain in the Village.

All of this leads to "the problematic of modern man": the complex intermixture of personal freedom and psychological compulsion that brings deep anxiety not only to the sick person but to any modern man who is aware of the discontinuities of a personal existence in which one sometimes acts relatively wholly and spontaneously but very often more as a conditioned reflex or partial compulsion and not infrequently in such a way that one cannot tell which of these two is predominant and how they relate. The relation between anxiety and compulsion that threatens the sense of being a person must be coupled with the equally important relationship between anxiety and will. The mental illness of modern man is not just individual neurosis but the result of his uprooting from the community in which he formerly lived. It is only an aspect of his existence as an exile, his own exile and that of modern man.

This anxiety also applies to the modern man who goes through that crisis of motives in which he can no longer take at face value either other people's motives or his own. This means a mutual mistrust in which people cease to confirm one another, but it also means a mistrust and fragmentation of the self in which each person is incapable of confirming himself. In Camus' novel *The Fall* it is the anxiety before the shattered image of the man of goodwill that leads Jean-Baptiste Clamence to abandon any attempt at real existence. An even deeper anxiety leads Joseph K. in *The Trial* to try to handle his case as a business deal, to forget it almost entirely, and then to abandon his position at the bank in favor of futile efforts to circumvent a judgment which he can never comprehend.

How can we live in the face of the anxiety in our culture? Must we choose between accepting those cultural forms that help us to repress this anxiety—only to see it break out afresh in ever new areas—and being so aware of anxiety that it is reflexively intensified and reduplicated? Not necessarily. It is also possible to revolt against our modern exile rather than deny or underscore it. But here too the way in which we revolt against it makes an enormous difference as to whether this revolt will result in new anxiety which is greater than we need to bear or in a holding our own before anxiety which allows us some margin for a human and even meaningful existence. The Modern Promethean represents a romantic revolt which can only in the end make man subject to the very anxiety he is trying to escape, whereas the Modern Job represents a sober, unprogrammatic revolt that accepts the anxiety of our culture yet gains real ground in the face of it. By neither accepting nor cutting off from the anxiety of our culture but fighting with it and receiving from it, we may attain the meaning it has to give us.

DEATH AND
THE DIALOGUE
WITH THE ABSURD

> And if the Wine you drink, the Lip you press,
> End in the Nothing all Things end in—Yes—
> Then fancy while Thou art, Thou are but what
> Thou shalt be—Nothing—Thou shalt not be less.
> —*The Rubáiyát of Omar Khayyám*

> When you are dead and your body cremated and
> your ashes scattered, where are you?
> —ZEN MONDO

Man is the only creature who knows that he will die and who makes of this knowledge a foundation for his life and even for his *joie de vivre*.

For the *Upanishads* the knowledge of death leads to the choice of the good over the pleasant; for the Buddha it leads to overcoming the craving for existence and to the eight-fold path to nirvana; for Greek tragedy it leads to reconciliation with *moira*, the qualitative order that includes man, even when, as with Oedipus, one dare not count his lot as gain until the last breath is drawn without pain. For Lao-tzu death is no threat to life, since both are a part of the flowing of the Tao. For Psalm 90 the knowledge that all flesh is as the grass which grows up in the morning and withers in the evening leads to a desire, not to escape from

146

the mutable to the immutable, as with Plato, but to "number our days so that we may get us a heart of wisdom." For Ecclesiastes the fact of death merges with the passing of all things in time and grows to an impassioned cry to remember your Creator in the days of your youth before desire fails, the grasshopper drags itself along, the silver cord is loosed, the golden bowl broken at the cistern, and all the daughters of song laid low.

Only in the Book of Job does the human condition of death lead to outright rebellion: "Consider that my days are as a breath." "My sons will come to grief, and I will know it not." "Thou wilt seek me, and I shall not be." "It is all one, I despise my life. Therefore, I say, He mocks at the calamity of the guilt-less. If it be not He, who then is it?"

Martin Buber planned to have a chapter on death in his philo-sophical anthropology, *The Knowledge of Man*, but then decided against it because, as he told me, we do not know death in itself as we know the concrete realities of our existence. This is true, but what we do know is the anticipation of death, the imagining of death—one's own and others, and the attitude one brings to this somber and unavoidable future. Buber himself in his early mystical work *Daniel* saw death not just as the movement of past to future but of future to past and the two so intertwined that death permeated life at every moment:

> How could I become death's if I had not already now suffered it? My existence . . . was the bed in which two streams, coming from opposite directions, flowed to and in and over each other. There was not only in me a force that moved from the point of birth to the point of death or beyond; there was also a counterforce from death to birth, and each moment that I experienced as a living man had grown out of the mixture of the two. . . . A force bore me toward dying, and its flight I called time; but in my face blew a strange wind, and I did not know what name to give its flight. . . . Coming-to-be and passing-away . . . lay side by side in endless embrace, and each of my moments was their bed. It was foolish to wish to limit death to any particular moments of ceasing to be or of transformation; it was an ever-present might and the mother

of being. Life engendered being, death received and bore it; life scattered its fullness, death preserved what it wished to retain. *

My own conscious relationship to death began, as I remember, when I was five years old and could not sleep because of the sudden realization that I would die. I cried until my elder sister came up and comforted me with the statement that I would not die for a very long time. That this did not remove the problem for me was evident from the preoccupation with death that I had during my teens, sometimes expressing itself paradoxically in the idea of suicide which would free me from the tyranny of the body—or, as I thought more likely, hand me over to it. At Harvard I often thought of Lucretius, who committed suicide on the basis of reasoning that what would come after death would not be so bad as what we have now. This always seemed to me specious since I had no way of knowing that the "I" would exist at all after death to be subject to *any* experience, good or bad. When I was in high school, I once said to my girl friend that my whole goal in life was to live long enough to develop a philosophy that would enable me to accept death. Since I have come to know the tales of the Hasidim, I have often been struck by the resemblance between my statement and the Hasidic tale "The Meaning":

> When Rabbi Bunam lay dying his wife burst into tears.
> He said: "What are you crying for? My whole life was only that I might learn how to die."†

During my years of immersion in mysticism when I was in the camps and units for conscientious objectors during the Second World War, I seemed to have developed the philosophy I sought —the belief that consciousness is universal and eternal, that there is no individual self, and that the real self cannot die. But this

* Martin Buber, *Daniel: Dialogues on Realization*, trans. with an Introductory Essay by Maurice Friedman (New York: McGraw-Hill Paperbacks, 1965), pp. 130 f.
† Martin Buber, *Tales of the Hasidim: The Later Masters*, trans. by Olga Marx (New York: Schocken Books, 1961), p. 268.

belief did not stand the test of time or of encounters that made me feel that I had gone through a sort of death while still alive.*
Once I would have fully accepted the words of comfort that Rabbi Nahum of Tchernobil gave to several disciples who came weeping to him complaining that they had fallen prey to darkness and depression and could not lift up their heads either in teachings or in prayer:

> "My dear sons," Rabbi Nahum said to them, "do not be distressed at this seeming death which has come upon you. . . . Just as on New Year's Day life ceases on all the stars and they sink into a deep sleep . . . from which they awake with a new power of shining, so those men who truly desire to come close to God, must pass through the state of cessation of spiritual life, and 'the falling is for the sake of rising.'"†

Now I must rebel with Job and Ivan Karamazov and complain because "nights of weariness and months of emptiness" mean the passing away in absurdity of our all too mortal life.

Man's attitude toward death has always been bound up in the closest way with his posture vis-à-vis nature, time, and community. Although he is aware of the seasons, modern man hardly lives in the time of nature. His time is abstract, calendrical, and conventional, and his relations to nature are more and more detached—whether nature be the object to be exploited, the scene to rhapsodize over, the terrain for a holiday from the city, or the great Earth Goddess that was only recently celebrated every year to ward off the threat of pollution and ecological imbalance. As a result, it is hardly possible for modern man to see his own death as a part of the natural rhythms and cycles of nature, to be accepted with the wisdom of nature itself.

The awareness of past and future is an inextricable part of all living in the present. Man in the age of Jesus already needed to be told to live in the present and not sell it short for the sake of

---

* See Maurice Friedman, *Touchstones of Reality: Existential Trust and the Community of Peace* (New York: Dutton Paperbacks, 1974), Chaps. 3–5.
† Martin Buber, *Tales of the Hasidim: The Early Masters*, trans. by Olga Marx (New York: Schocken Books, 1961), "Words of Comfort," p. 173.

the imagined tomorrow. But only for modern man has presentness been thoroughly emptied of meaning. Only modern man's
relation to the present has become so technicized—so much the
effect of a past cause or the means to a future end—that Pascal's
dictum that we must be forever unhappy knowing no real present is plain to all who pause for a moment in the unending rush.
"The world is too much with us; late and soon, / Getting and
spending, we lay waste our powers," wrote Wordsworth. The death
of T. S. Eliot's Sweeney is no tragedy because he has never
known any meaningful life, and Eliot's Gerontion says, "Think at
last / We have not reached conclusion, when I / Stiffen in a rented
house." Time is a meaningless voyage whose haul will not bear
examination, wrote Eliot in *The Four Quartets*.

Like K. in Kafka's novel *The Castle*, modern man's attempt to
find a foothold in present reality cannot succeed because he is
always using the present as a means to some future end. This
functional relation to time is caused in turn—and reinforced—by
that sense of isolation, rootlessness, and exile which makes modern man feel, in moments of awareness, that he knows no real
life. He is cut off from the nourishing stream of community; the
prospect of his own death takes on an overwhelming importance
that robs life itself of meaning. This theme of isolation is endlessly repeated in modern literature: Hardy's Jude the Obscure,
dying, deserted by everyone, with Job's curse on his lips; Camus'
"Stranger," aware of that slow wind blowing from the future that
destroys all the false ideas of human brotherhood and solidarity
that men put forward in the "unreal years" before death; Kafka's
K., attaining a freedom greater than anyone has ever had—and
equally meaningless; Sartre's Matthieu, unable to belong to any
person or group because he cannot commit himself or cherish
any value beyond his own freedom.

Certainly, even in the best of communities, death is an individual affair. Even in traditional religions, the journey of the soul
to some Hades or Sheol must be facilitated by the community
through *rites de passage*. Death *is* that uttermost solitude of
which every other abandonment is only a foretaste, as Martin

Buber suggests, and time *is* a torrent carrying us irreversibly and inexorably toward "the starkest of all human perspectives"—one's own death. But our obsession with our own deaths, our focus upon them, is in no small part caused by our exile and isolation in the present. This same obsession leads us to use our cults of youth, of having "experiences," of realizing our potentials, as ways of not looking at the facts of old age and death. Our culture gives us no support in hearing Hopkins' "leaden echo" of old age in which we give up all the "girl-graces" of youth in favor of that vision in which every future is cut off except death. Yet this fear of time, old age, and death is woven into every moment of our existence, so that we have no real present and no real mutual presence for one another.

That which should be the very height of mutual presence—sex and love—has become the opposite. In *Love and Will* Rollo May has vividly shown how our culture uses sex as a way of not facing age or death, of pretending, with Mehitabel, that "there's life in the old gal yet," and that as long as we can go through some more or less adequate sexual functioning (itself endangered by our hurried relationship to time), we are still alive and not threatened by death!

Death is the Absurd precisely as Camus has defined it in *The Myth of Sisyphus*. It cuts us off from meaningful relationship to past and future *and* from meaningful relationship to each other. It is one thing to recognize with "Everyman" that no one else will go for you or that, like Jesus, "You gotta walk that lonesome valley, you gotta walk it by yourself." It is another to carry around one's general expectation and one's specific fears about death as an invisible barrier that gets in the way of any directness of relationship and of any present immediacy. How many of us can really say, with the Song of Songs, "For love is stronger than death," or with Martin Buber that "a great relationship throws a bridge across the abyss of dread of the universe," the abyss of death?

Death has always been the foremost advocate for the absurdity of life. "This too shall pass away." "All things change, all things perish, all things pass away." "Behold all flesh is as the grass and all the goodliness of man is as the flower of grass." "Vanity of vanities, all is vanity." It is death, as Bergson points out, that makes it necessary to supplement nature by habit and myth so that the depressing contingency which sunders present means and future end can be overlooked. But there is much in our day that has *heightened* the absurdity of death that modern man must confront to the point where it is qualitatively different.

The assassinations in our day of John F. Kennedy, Martin Luther King, and so many others have brought to the surface that terror and violence that seethes beneath the seemingly most successful civilization in the world's history. Hiroshima, with its sudden death and long years of slow death by radiation, has created, as Robert Jay Lifton has shown, a "death-culture" in which even those who live are weighed down by the conviction that they too will be stricken, as well as by the "survivor guilt" of those who seem senselessly spared from a common doom. The atomic bomb survivors—*hibakusha*—"seem not only to have experienced the atomic disaster, but to have imbibed and incorporated it into their beings, including all of its elements of horror, evil, and particularly of death." Their own identities merge not only with dead relatives but with the anonymous dead. "With both Hiroshima and Nazi concentration camp survivors," writes Lifton, *"the grotesqueness surrounding the death imprint . . .* conveyed the psychological sense that death was not only everywhere, but was bizarre, unnatural, indecent, absurd." Even the seeming recovery of the atomic bomb victim became "a lifelong sense of vulnerability to the same grotesque death": His *jarring awareness of the fact of death* and his own mortality issued into a "vast breakdown of faith in the larger human matrix, and in the general structure of existence."* This death anxiety was not just concerned with dying itself, stresses Lifton, "but with *premature death and unfulfilled life.*"

---

* Robert Jay Lifton, *Death in Life: Survivors of Hiroshima* (New York: Random House, 1967), pp. 201, 480 f.

The *hibakusha* and the Nazi concentration camp survivor witnessed mass death that was awesome in its randomness, in its inclusion of small children quite new to life, and young adults at their prime, as well as old people who had in any case not much longer to live. The anxiety-laden imprint retained by both groups of survivors was of death that has *no reasonable relationship to life span or life cycle, of profoundly inappropriate death.**

The grotesqueness and absurdity of the death imprint is exacerbated for the survivor of both types by the unconscious self-accusation "I am responsible for his death," which easily goes over into "I killed him," which in the concentration camp experience was sometimes literally true, from taking the other's food that he needed to keep alive, to jostling people out of line when the selection for death was so random as odd and even to selecting who lived and died when one held the awesome and fearful position of *kapo*. None could be totally unaffected by a pervasive "either-you-or-me" atmosphere, and it is this kind of death guilt which survivors of Nazi camps and Hiroshima refer to when they speak of their "living hell." Thus the original death imprint is complicated by a sense of continuous encounter with death, and death guilt is reinforced by group patterns within a "guilty community," and further reawakened, for the *hibakusha*, with every flexing of nuclear muscles—whether in words or testing—anywhere in the world.

Nor is this death guilt and death taint limited to the survivor alone. *We all share it.* "If only man knows that he will die," writes Lifton, "*only man could invent grotesquely absurd death. Only man through his technology, could render the meaningful totally meaningless.*" There is no longer any war-linked chivalry and glory nor even a distinction between victimizer and victim, "only the sharing in species annihilation." "In every age man faces a pervasive theme which defies his engagement and yet must be engaged," writes Lifton in a remarkable anticipation of the "Dia-

* *Ibid.*, p. 487.

logue with the Absurd." In our day "it is unlimited technological violence and *absurd death.*"*

Hiroshima is not an isolated example: The Soviet Union's starvation of three million Kulaks in the vain effort to put through their communizing of agriculture in the 1930s, the bombing of civilian populations during the Second World War, the starvation of the children of Biafra, and the continuing devastation in Indochina of millions of people by napalm, burning, bombing, disease, starvation, and outright murder—all these are illustrations of the readiness of dictatorships and democracies alike in our day to create vast death-cultures as instruments of national policy.

More than illustration—prototype—is the Nazi death camp in which six million Jews and one million gypsies were exterminated. "Auschwitz" not only stands for death and death-culture, but for a systematic dehumanization such as the world had never known, a scientific undermining of the very foundations of social existence. In the world of Camus' *Plague* social and natural evil are one. In the world of Auschwitz social mistrust and existential mistrust are interwoven into the greatest assault on man as man that human history has known.

If we add to this the ever-present threat of a nuclear holocaust that might destroy all life on the planet and the predictions of the ecologists that the conditions for human life may disappear within forty, thirty, or even twenty years, we cannot avoid the conclusion that, however much death has challenged human meaning in the past, death for modern man is preeminently an encounter with the Absurd.

In face of this situation, some men revolt. One type of revolt against death in its aspect of the Absurd is the "Modern Promethean." The Modern Promethean rebels against the very order of existence or against the absence of any order, and he does so in terms of the Either/Or of destroying what is over against him or being destroyed himself. This heroic approach toward death is a familiar one—from Browning's "Invictus" ("I would not face

---

* *Ibid.*, pp. 490 f., 540 f.; italics mine.

death blindfold.") to Dylan Thomas' "Do not go gentle into that goodnight. / Rage, rage against the dying of the light." Camus' Sisyphus rejects the possibility of suicide *despite* the absurdity of man's relation to the irrational silence of the universe. Sisyphus' struggle to the heights with his everlasting rock is "enough to fill a man's heart," says the early Camus. This heroic stance takes on greater depth with a character like Tarrou the journalist in Camus' novel *The Plague*—Tarrou who has chosen to be victim rather than executioner, who has vowed never to assist in the murder of another even for the sake of the political party that represents the victims, Tarrou who perseveres in his revolt to the end in an awesome struggle against his own death.

Franz Rosenzweig, the Jewish existentialist, begins his *magnum opus, The Star of Redemption,** by an attack on that "Philosophy of the All" which seeks to gloss over the fact that every creature awaits "the day of its journey into darkness with fear and trembling." Martin Heidegger makes the fact of individual death the cornerstone of his existentialist philosophy. Human existence, or *Dasein*—being-there—is, to Heidegger, *zum Tode sein*—being-toward-death; for it is only the resolute anticipation of one's unutterably unique and nonrelational death which individualizes *Dasein* down to its own potentiality and frees it from the power of *das Man*—the "They" of ambiguity, curiosity, and idle talk.

Jean-Paul Sartre rejects this cornerstone of Heidegger's philosophy on the ground that it is precisely in death that the person is abandoned to the *en-soi*, the objective in-itself, without any appeal left to that subjective personal becoming, or *pour soi*, that during one's lifetime constantly transcends the facticity of what one is. But there is not only our anticipation of being turned into a thing, the revulsion against which filled even the martyr's death of Celia in T. S. Eliot's *Cocktail Party*. There is also our relationship to our own death, including that fact of finitude that gives

* Franz Rosenzweig, *The Star of Redemption*, trans. by William Hallo, with an Introduction by Nahum Glatzer (New York: Holt, Rinehart & Winston, 1971; New York: Schocken Books [paperback], 1972).

concrete meaning to our existence—the precondition, says Tillich
in *Courage to Be*, of any enjoyment of positive being. The threat
of "nonbeing," of contingency and death, is the given of our
existence. But we have freedom in our relationship to that given.

Why then does Martin Buber (with special reference, I suspect,
to his emphasis on death) speak of Martin Heidegger's philosophy as a "nightmare"? What Heidegger has left out, as Buber has
argued in "What Is Man?,"* is the ultimate reality of the interhuman—the realm between man and man. Similarly the French
Catholic existentialist Gabriel Marcel has maintained, in dialogue
with Tillich and in explicit critique of Heidegger, that the death
of the person who is my *Thou* is more real and more important to
me than my own death.

Granting that our anticipation of our death is a present reality
that enters into every moment of our existence—and in this sense
granting Heidegger's case over Sartre's—I would nonetheless
hold that Heidegger seems at times to forget that what is given
to us, hence what is *existentially* of importance, is not the actual
future moment of death but the *present* moment of anticipation.
Putting it another way, Heidegger takes the half-truth of separation that the knowledge of our unique and individual death imparts to each of us and makes it into the specious whole truth of
our existence being "ultimately non-relational." If the present
moment of anticipation of death often gets in the way of our
open presence to others, as I have suggested, it also constitutes
the basis for genuine mutual presentness as opposed to any form
of symbiotic clinging or ecstatic "unity." At its fullness this
awareness of death in the present is far from being ultimately
nonrelational. On the contrary, it is an integral part of the life of
dialogue. It is the distancing that makes real the relating, the
moving apart that makes real the moving together. In this sense,
I maintain—against both Heidegger and Camus' Meursault—
that love *is* stronger than death. The anticipated reality of death

* Martin Buber, *Between Man and Man*, trans. by Ronald Gregor Smith with
an Introduction by Maurice Friedman (New York: Macmillan Paperbacks,
1965).

is present in love and gives it its special poignancy without—
when the love is real—destroying it.

Equally important, our existence is limitation and finitude even
without our resolute anticipation of our individual death, as Sartre points out. Nor is its unique potentiality so bound up with
this anticipation as Heidegger holds. Our uniqueness is much
more importantly connected with what calls us out in each hour
and with such reality as we find in responding or failing to respond to that call. Our awareness of our death enters into both
the situation and the response, but it does not dominate it. On
the contrary, only when we are not *focusing* on the future negation of life by death do we have any presentness and immediacy.

We can understand the problematic of the Modern Promethean
revolt against death better if we look at it in its somewhat less
heroic and more clearly desperate form—suicide. If man is indeed the only creature that can commit suicide—which is not just
the death of the body but the destruction of the self—man is also
the only creature of which we know that has a "self" in any fully
meaningful sense of that term. What is more, that self comes into
being in the meeting with other selves. That self-preoccupation
that makes suicide the only philosophical question of importance,
as Camus claims in *The Myth of Sisyphus*, is mostly laid to one
side in our actual lives, in which what is central is our response to
what is not ourselves, whereas our self-realization is *a by-product*
of our meeting with other persons and beings in situations that
include us rather than we them.

Leslie H. Farber has cogently asserted in *The Ways of the Will*
that suicide, or "the life of suicide," is at its most basic a "willfulness" which refuses to accept the give-and-take of life, the fact
that we are only on one side of the dialogue. Ippolit Terentyev
wants to commit suicide in Dostoevsky's novel *The Idiot* because
he had no freedom in his own creation but wants to assert his freedom in his destruction. In the character of Kirilov in Dostoevsky's
novel *The Possessed*, this posture is elevated to that of the "man-
god" who proposes to liberate all mankind from the fear of death
through his own suicide. Stavrogin's suicide is also a Modern

Promethean assertion of willfulness in the face of his inability to discover the genuine will that plays its part in the dialogue of being and being, without trying to control and manipulate existence itself. Meursault is really a willful suicide of this sort in Camus' novel *The Stranger*, and Camus' Caligula, who makes of death the logical conclusion of the absurdity of a world in which men are unhappy and die, is, as Camus himself says, "a superior suicide." But the man who most clearly combines the heroic attitudinizing of the Modern Promethean with the "life of suicide" is Captain Ahab of Melville's *Moby Dick*—the man who identifies himself with a Truth which has no confines, the man who sees his path as laid on iron rails, the man who feels he must destroy the White Whale or be destroyed himself, and who destroys his ship, his crew, and himself in the process. "O lonely death on lonely life," Ahab cries out at the end. "O now I feel my topmost greatness in my topmost grief!"

Ignoring the absurd, underlining it, heroically revolting against it, or willfully defying it through "the life of suicide" do not exhaust the alternatives of the response of modern man to death. There is also that stance which I have designated in both *Problematic Rebel* and *To Deny Our Nothingness* as the "Dialogue with the Absurd"—a dialogue in which meaning is found in immediacy without any pretense at an overall, comprehensive meaning that would make the Absurd anything less or other than Absurd.

The first aspect of this stance is the recognition and acceptance of death. Death, Freud points out, is a debt we owe to nature. This does not mean the aesthetic, decadent welcoming of death of Swinburne's "Garden of Proserpine":

> From too much love of living,
> From hope and fear set free,
> We thank with brief thanksgiving
> Whatever gods may be
> That no life lives forever,
> That dead men rise up never,
> That even the weariest river
> Winds somewhere safe to sea.

To a poem such as this, one can properly apply the strictures of Nietzsche's Zarathustra against the "preachers of death" who want to get beyond life in one "weary death-leap." Nor is this stance that of T. S. Eliot's Thomas à Becket, eager for martyrdom as part of a divine plan that will give him his place in the heavenly hierarchy. It is perhaps that of Jesus in the Garden of Gethsemane saying, "Father, if it be Thy will may this cup be taken from me. Nonetheless, Thy will be done, not mine." It is the stance of the twentieth-century American poet Theodore Roethke, who spent many of his later years in mental hospitals, picking himself up again after each blow that knocked his breath out and disoriented his mind:

> In a dark time, the eye begins to see,
> I meet my shadow in the deepening shade;
> I hear my echo in the echoing wood—
> A lord of nature weeping to a tree.
> I live between the heron and the wren,
> Beasts of the hill and serpents of the den.
>
> What's madness but nobility of soul
> At odds with circumstance? The day's on fire!
> I know the purity of pure despair,
> My shadow pinned against a sweating wall.
> That place among the rocks—is it a cave,
> Or winding path? The edge is what I have.
>
> A steady storm of correspondences!
> A night flowing with birds, a ragged moon,
> And in broad day the midnight come again!
> A man goes far to find out what he is—
> Death of the self in a long, tearless night,
> All natural shapes blazing unnatural light.
>
> Dark, dark my light, and darker my desire.
> My soul, like some heat-maddened summer fly,
> Keeps buzzing at the sill. Which I is *I*?
> A fallen man, I climb out of my fear.
> The mind enters itself, and God the mind,
> And one is One, free in the tearing wind.

There is no slightest admixture of acquiescence or surrender in this stance of the "Modern Job" vis-à-vis absurd death. "If there is a God," says Camus' atheist healer Dr. Rieux in *The Plague*, "I should think as he sits above in silence, he would want us to fight the order of death." If "the plague" teaches that there is more to admire than despise in men, it is because of the courage to address and respond, not *in spite of* death and the absurd, but precisely *to* and including them. In *The Gates of the Forest* and *A Beggar in Jerusalem*, as we have seen, Elie Wiesel shows us how a man who has lived through Auschwitz and Buchenwald can once again, finally, live in the present—bringing with him into that present all of the dead for whom he mourns. This is an unromantic posture, a fight for life without heroics, but it is also the only true courage—the only courage that is equal to life itself. It is this courage that I find in Dylan Thomas' poem on his thirty-fifth birthday:

> Oh, let me midlife mourn by the shrined
>   And druid herons' vows
> The voyage to ruin I must run,
>   Dawn ships clouted aground,
> Yet, though I cry with tumbledown tongue,
>   Count my blessings aloud:
>
> Four elements and five
> Senses, and man a spirit in love
>   Tangling through this spun slime
> To his nimbus bell cool kingdom come
> .   .   .   .
>   And this last blessing most,
>
>   That the closer I move
> To death, one man through his sundered hulks,
>   The louder the sun blooms
> And the tusked, ramshackling sea exults;
>   And every wave of the way
> And gale I tackle, the whole world then,
>   With more triumphant faith

Than ever was since the world was said,
Spins its morning of praise,

. . . .

And my shining men no more alone
As I sail out to die.

The memory of death and the anticipation of death is often a
calling to account, as in Kafka's novel *The Trial* and Tolstoy's
The Death of Ivan Ilyich. "This door is meant for you, and now I
am going to close it," says the doorkeeper to the dying man in
Kafka's "Parable of the Law." We are called to account for the
uniqueness of our lives and of the lives of all those with whom
we have been intertwined—not in some Last Judgment or moral-
istic, idealistic, superego standard, but in the simple perspective
of that moment when life and death are simultaneously present.
"Why is man afraid of dying?" asked the Hasidic rabbi of Ger,
and answered, "What man fears is the moment he will survey from
the other world everything he has experienced on this earth."

Franz Rosenzweig begins *The Star of Redemption* with the
reality of the fear of death and ends it with the phrase, "Into
Life." During those weeks when I believed, as my doctors did,
that I had cancer, I learned that death is not of the future at all,
nor of the past: It is an inescapable reality of the present. It is
inescapable because it colors our existence at its far horizons. Yet
all we ever know is the present, and all we know in that present
is life itself.

When we live with the death of one who was close to us, we
know that the mystery of his having existed as a person and
being with us no longer cannot be plumbed. It is part of the
paradox of personal existence itself, which has no secure or continuous duration in time yet does really exist again and again in
moments of present reality. We tend most of the time to think of
death as an objective event that we can understand through our
categories. But when we truly walk in the valley of the shadow,
the imminence of death tells us something that we have really
known all along: that life is the only reality that is given to us,

that this reality—and not some continuing entity or identity of a personal nature—is all that we actually know. We do not know life without our individual selves, but neither do we know our selves without life. We know death, to be sure, but we know it as death-in-life. Life is the reality in which we share while we are alive.

To say that we once did not exist and again shall not exist is not to make our existence itself nothing, as the quatrain from Omar Khayyám suggests; for this would be to equate reality with immutability. When you are dead and your body cremated and the ashes scattered, where are *you*? This is a question that cannot be answered in objective terms; for it is I myself that ask it of myself and am impelled to respond. I cannot think away my own present existence any more than I can deny "the undeniable clamor of the last annunciation, the bone's prayer to death its god." All I can do is hold the tension of these two existential realities and live in that tension. "In order really to live," said Rabbi Yitzhak, the zaddik of Vorki, "a man must give himself to death. But when he has done so, he discovers that he is not to die—but to live."

PART V

SEX,
LOVE, AND
WOMEN'S
LIBERATION

SEX AND LOVE

The paradox of the hidden human image with which we started is that it needs to be revealed yet must also remain, in its depth-dimension, concealed. This paradox is complemented and complicated by a second paradox—that many of the contemporary attempts to reveal it only serve to conceal it further, or sometimes reveal surface facets at the expense of causing the depth-image of man to draw ever deeper into hiding. In no case is this more so and in no area is the contemporary crisis of values more painfully and vividly embodied than in that of sex and love. One part of the natural hiddenness of man which can and should be naturally revealed is sex—or more exactly, sexual relationship, love, and marriage. Yet a large part of the obscuring of man in our day comes through precisely this area of his existence.

In the 1920s T. S. Eliot already expressed this dilemma with great forcefulness in his classic poem *The Waste Land.* The modern Waste Land is a sterile place. It has been violated because of the misuse of sex—because sex has nothing to do with real human emotions or depth and still less with genuine relationship between people. In his early poetry Eliot splits mankind, in almost Freudian fashion, into Sweeney, an embodiment of pure "id," and Prufrock, a man entirely dominated by "superego." Sweeney is hardly human, while Prufrock has lost touch with his vital forces almost entirely. Prufrock cannot summon up passion, for in the moment of giving himself to another, he is afraid that a chilling response from the other will suddenly make his action seem inappropriate, leaving him ludicrous and exposed. Hence, he is cut off equally from the lust of Sweeney and from the personal relationship of which Sweeney is incapable. Together Prufrock and Sweeney make up the world of *The Waste Land*— consciousness without life and lust without love. Both preclude any relationship between men. This absence of meeting between men is distilled in the figure of "Gerontion," the old man finishing out his meaningless existence with "thoughts of a dry brain in a dry season."

> I have lost my passion: why should I need to keep it
> Since what is kept must be adulterated?
> I have lost my sight, smell, hearing, taste and touch:
> How should I use them for your closer contact?

I cannot use my passion in any pure way, for my meaningless existence adulterates it as I use it. I have lost my five senses, the means whereby I came near your heart, but I could not have any real contact with you even if I had not lost them. All that is left to me is the decadence of pure sensation.

In *The Waste Land* Eliot uses the ancient myth of the land cursed by sterility because of the rape of the virgins at the shrine to portray the sterility of modern life, the rape of lust without love. The waste land is not only the world of the animal lust of Sweeney but also of the frustrated and trivialized passion of Prufrock. Above all, the modern violation of sex means isolation: "I have heard the key / Turn in the door once and turn once only / We think of the key, each in his prison / Thinking of the key, each confirms a prison." Only sympathy, Eliot implies, can begin to overcome the isolation of modern man, and with it control, discipline, direction, bringing oneself into the focus of a single intent. Yet this possibility seems to be open only for the exceptional individual. At the end of the poem the waste land is as sterile as before.*

Sex, which should be the crown of human relationships, becomes the opposite—the mark of its inauthenticity. Sex touches on the *problematic* of the hidden human image as few things do. One reason for this is that people are inclined to distrust themselves, and they are inclined to mistrust each other. This mistrust arises in part because of the popular Freudian view of man as a two-layer being whose instincts are likely at any moment to take over control from the rational mind. That ancient dualism in which the body and sex are regarded as evil has been modernized in no less puritanical form by Freud, who tells us that our conscious thoughts *and* feelings are rationalizations for the drive toward fulfillment of libidinal urges which we cannot admit directly to ourselves. How this affects the relationship of men and women is vividly illustrated by Germaine Greer in her colorful book *The Female Eunuch*:

> As long as man is at odds with his own sexuality and as long as he keeps woman as a solely sexual creature, he will hate her, at least some of the time. . . . Shakespeare was right in equating the strength of the lust drive and the intensity of the disgust that followed it. †

This is not to imply that Freud has not revealed something of the hidden human image in his stress on the dominant role of sex in human motivation. If we cannot join Freud in making the conscious mind so much the superstructure determined by and reflecting our unconscious motivations, we can certainly assert that what Martin Buber called "the world of It" and "the world of Thou" are nowhere so completely intermingled as in sex and love. That would be no problem if the It were transformed by

* For a full-scale interpretation of T. S. Eliot's *The Waste Land*, see Maurice Friedman, *To Deny Our Nothingness: Contemporary Images of Man* (New York: Delacorte Press, 1967; Delta Books [paperback], 1968), Chap. 2, "Images of Inauthenticity," pp. 31–38.
† Germaine Greer, *The Female Eunuch* (New York: McGraw-Hill Book Co., 1971), p. 250.

and taken up into the Thou. Often, in fact, we do not know which is in the service of which. Even if we could rid ourselves of the tenacious notion that sex is something innately evil, we would still have the problem of when it is a revealing of the human image and when an obscuring. More terrible still, how often does what seems to be a beautiful and gracious revealing turn out to be a hideous obscuring!

Although it may no longer be true to say that Freud dominates the psychiatric thought of our time, it is certainly true that he dominates its approach to sex. While many people might quarrel with the central role that Freud ascribes to libidinal sexuality in the human psychic economy, few look at sex itself in basically other terms than that of Freud—namely, as an irrational, instinctual, and largely unconscious drive that must be understood in the first instance in terms of the biological needs of the individual organism and only secondarily and derivatively in terms of interpersonal relations. The significance of Jean-Paul Sartre's approach to sex lies in the fact that, without any attempt to minimize its significance, he lifts it out of the Freudian categories to which we are accustomed and places it squarely within his own existentialist thought, with its emphasis upon the relation of the subject to himself and to others. This means, in the first instance, that Sartre rejects the Freudian unconscious which magically acts as its own censor in such a way that it knows what it must keep itself from knowing. Sartre puts forward instead the self which, in the middle of all facticity, inescapably remains responsible for itself, for the person which it becomes through its own project, and for the image of man which it chooses for itself and for all men.

This approach of Sartre's deals a death blow to the favorite concept of romantic love—the passion which overwhelms one and by which one has no choice but to let oneself be carried along. Man, to Sartre, is responsible for his passion. Sartre's existentialist "will never agree that a sweeping passion is a ravaging torrent which fatally leads a man to certain acts and is, therefore, an excuse." This does not mean that Sartre has retrogressed to some naive rationalism that ignores the dark, swirling forces in man's being that have been uncovered by the romantics and by depth psychology. It means, rather, that human existence can never be reduced for him to a psychological state, a pure content of feeling, minus the attitude which the subject has to that state or feeling. The pederast who admits that he has sexual relations with young boys but denies that he is a pederast is in bad faith, says Sartre; yet his friend, who hopes to liberate him by getting him to admit that he is a pederast, is equally in bad faith, since he wants him to call himself a pederast as one calls this table a table.

To understand Sartre's approach to sex we must understand his approach to intersubjectivity—the relation between subject and subject. "The Other *looks* at me and as such he holds the secret of my being, he knows what I am. Thus the profound meaning of my being is outside of me, imprisoned in an absence." The Other steals my being from me, and I recover myself only through absorbing him. Nonetheless, I exist by means of the Other's freedom; for I need his look in order to be. Therefore, I have no security in making him into an object. I must instead try to get hold of his freedom and reduce it to being a freedom subject to my freedom. This to Sartre, as to Proust before him, is the essence of love. "The lover does not desire to possess the beloved as one possesses a thing; he . . . wants to possess a freedom as freedom." I want to ensnare the Other's freedom within his facticity, to possess his body through his consciousness being identified with his body. But "desire is itself doomed to failure"! Pleasure is the death and failure of desire, says Sartre, for it produces a reflective consciousness which destroys the immediacy of pleasure and makes one forget the Other's incarnation. The very attempt to seize the Other's body, pull it toward me, grab hold of it, bite it, makes me aware of my own body as no longer flesh but a synthetic instrument, and thus destroys my incarnation as well.

What this approach to sex means in concrete situations of human life, Sartre has abundantly illustrated in his novels, plays, and

stories. In *No Exit* it is the hopeless situation of a man and two
women, one of them a Lesbian, shut together in a room where no
one can possess the other without interference by the third,
which occasions, in part, the conclusion "Hell is other people."
But even in less contrived situations, even when only two are
present, as in the scenes in *The Age of Reason* in which Matthieu is alone with Marcelle, his mistress, or with Ivich, the self-
centered young student, the sexual relations between two people
are abundant illustration of the thesis "Hell is other people." Not
only sexual desire must inevitably fail but love as well. The plot
of *The Age of Reason* turns on Matthieu's inability to experience
Marcelle's side of the relationship, to imagine that she might
want a child and not an abortion when she becomes pregnant
after seven years in which he has spent four nights with her
regularly every week.

Martin Buber would certainly agree with Sartre that sex is
human and not animal and that it cannot be divorced from our
relations to others. He is like Sartre too in his essentially positive
attitude toward sex. Sex is an "urge," or passion, which only
becomes evil when we leave it undirected and allow an undirected possibility to turn into an undirected reality. What counts
here is not the expression, repression, or sublimation of sexual
desire but the response with one's whole being that diverts our
powerful desires from the casual to the essential. We are not to
turn away from what attracts our hearts but to find mutual contact with it by making our relationship to it real. We are not necessarily torn between a cruel id and a cruel superego. Where some
degree of trust and relationship exists, we may bring our passions
into unification of a personal wholeness which is itself a by-product of the ever-renewed act of entering into dialogue. Buber calls
this becoming a whole, this shaping of the chaos of matter into the
cosmos of personal existence, "a cruelly hazardous enterprise." It
is, nonetheless, an enterprise that man can and must undertake.
Man is not for Buber what he is for Sartre—"a useless passion."

It would not be possible from Buber's standpoint to treat sexuality in abstraction from human relationships and, specifically,

from the interplay and interaction between the I-Thou and the I-It. On the other hand, we must recognize, perhaps even more strongly than Buber himself did, that nowhere is the relationship between these two attitudes so intermingled and confused as precisely in this sphere. Although we need not define bad faith as essentially one's relation to oneself, as Sartre does, we must certainly agree that in this sphere of sexuality, deception, illusion, and bad faith of every kind appear. Here, more than anywhere, monologue loves to mask itself as dialogue—not only because we are all of us "seeming" persons who seek confirmation from the other by trying to appear what we are not, but also because we do not wish to recognize the extent to which we are treating the other as an It and are letting him do the same to us. Real love, as Buber has pointed out, is not *in* the person but *between* I and Thou. Yet in all the much-discussed erotic philosophy of the age, it is not love between I and Thou that is represented but the precious experience of the I that enjoys the feelings that the other produces in him without giving himself to the other. Love of this sort, love without dialogue, without genuine outgoing to the other, Buber calls Lucifer. "Lame-winged beneath the rule of the lame-winged" Eros, the souls of lovers "cower where they are, each in his den, instead of soaring out each to the beloved partner."

The kingdom of the lame-winged Eros is a world of mirrors and mirrorings.

> Many years I have wandered through the land of men, and have not yet reached an end of studying the varieties of the "erotic man" (as the vassal of the broken-winged one at times describes himself). There a lover stamps around and is in love only with his passion. There one is wearing his differentiated feelings like medal-ribbons. There one is enjoying the adventures of his own fascinating effect. There one is gazing enraptured at the spectacle of his own supposed surrender. There one is collecting excitement. There one is displaying his "power." There one is preening himself with borrowed vitality. There one is delighting to exist simultaneously as himself and as an idol very unlike himself.

There one is warming himself at the blaze of what has fallen to
his lot. There one is experimenting. And so on and on—all the
manifold monologists with their mirrors, in the apartment of the
most intimate dialogue!*

"They are all beating the air," Buber concludes. One only receives the world in the other when one turns to him and opens
oneself to him. Only if I accept his otherness and live in the face
of it, only if he and I say to each other, "It is Thou," does Present
Being dwell between us. The true Eros of dialogue means a
knowing of the beloved in the biblical sense of mutual relationship. True lovers have a bipolar experience, a contemporaneity at
rest. They receive the common event from both sides at once
"and thus for the first time understand in a bodily way what an
event is." The lover feels the inclination of the head on the neck
of his beloved as an answer to the word of his own silence
without losing the feeling of his own self. He does not assimilate
the beloved into his own soul or attempt to possess her freedom.
He vows her faithfully to himself and turns to her in her otherness, her self-reality, with all the power of intention of his own
heart.

This is not Sartre's otherness of the object nor even of the alien
subject that makes me into an object or of the other whose freedom I make subject to my freedom. It is the otherness of the
other who lives with me as Thou, who faces me as partner, who
affirms me and contends with me, but vows me faithfully to
being as I him. Not the ancient Hindu teaching of identity in
which "Husband is not dear because of husband but because of
the Self in the husband" is the basis for authentic relationship
between the sexes, but the full acceptance of otherness. Uncur-
tailed personal existence first appears when wife says to husband
or husband to wife, not "I am you," but "I accept you as you
are." In avoiding sex and marriage as temptation to finitude,
Kierkegaard sidestepped the possibility of authentic existence.

* Martin Buber, *Between Man and Man*, trans. by Ronald Gregor Smith, with
an Introduction by Maurice Friedman (New York: Macmillan Paperbacks,
1965), "Dialogue," pp. 28 f.

What is exemplary in marriage is the fact that in it one must mean
one's partner in his real otherness because one affirms him as the
particular person he is. There is scarcely a substitute for marriage, indeed, for teaching us the "vital acknowledgement of
many-faced otherness"—that the other has not only a different
mind, way of thinking or feeling, conviction or attitude, "but has
also a different perception of the world, a different recognition
and order of meaning, a different touch from the regions of
existence, a different faith, a different soil." Through its crises
and the overcoming of these crises that arise out of the organic
depths, marriage enables us to affirm and withstand the otherness.*

Buber carries "inclusion," or experiencing of the other side of
the relationship, into the sexual act itself. He defines "imagining
the real" in *The Knowledge of Man* as a bold swinging into the
other which demands the intensest action of my being and which
enables me to imagine quite concretely what the other is feeling,
willing, thinking—to make her present in her wholeness and
uniqueness. In love this takes place not as some Emersonian
meeting of soul and soul but with the whole body-soul person,
and includes an experiencing of the other's reaction to the sexual
act far more radical than Sartre's incarnation of the other's freedom:

> A man caresses a woman, who lets herself be caressed. Then let
> us assume that he feels the contact from two sides—with the
> palm of his hand still, and also with the woman's skin. The
> twofold nature of the gesture, as one that takes place between
> two persons, thrills through the depth of enjoyment in his heart
> and stirs it. If he does not deafen his heart he will have—not to
> renounce the enjoyment—to love.
>
> I do not in the least mean that the man who has had such an
> experience would from then on have this two-sided sensation in
> every such meeting—that would perhaps destroy his instinct. But
> the one extreme experience makes the other person present to
> him for all time. A transfusion has taken place after which a

* *Ibid.*, "The Question to the Single One," pp. 61 f.

mere elaboration of subjectivity is never again possible or toler-
able to him. *

Erich Fromm follows Buber in emphasizing love as responsibility, but he tends to overvalue will and commitment so much
that he leaves no proper room for the erotic. "Every man is
Adam, every woman Eve," writes Fromm in *The Art of Loving*,
implying that if one commits oneself to the other, one can love
any person. This would hardly be compatible with Buber's emphasis on affirming the other as the particular person she is, for in
matters of sexual love this affirmation cannot be made with
everyone, any more than every sexual attraction can be the
ground for an enduring relationship. The Viennese logotherapist
Viktor Frankl comes much closer to Buber when he writes:

> There is not the least thing to be objected to in the sexual drive as
> long as it is included in the personal realm: as soon and as long
> as the sexuality is *personalized*, personalized through us to grasp
> another man in his being, in his suchness, in his uniqueness and
> particularity, but not only in his being and his suchness but also
> in his value, in what he shall become, and that means to affirm
> him. Love may be defined now as: being able to say Thou to
> someone—and beyond that to be able to say Yes to him; personal
> love must now join the sexual drive to the spiritual person, it
> must personalize it. *Only an I that means a Thou can integrate
> the It.*†

In his widely read book *Love and Will*,‡ Rollo May, in contrast
to both Sartre and Buber, shows us sex precisely in the fusion of I-
It and I-Thou: "To be human means to exist on the boundary
between the anonymous and the personal." The "normal" person
in our society finds, amid a plethora of sex, that very sterility
which Eliot's *Waste Land* foresaw. If the Victorian was guilty for
experiencing sex, we are guilty if we don't. The removal of all

* *Ibid.*, "Education," pp. 96 f.
† Viktor E. Frankl, *Das Menschenbild der Seelenheilkunde: Kritik des Dyna-
mischen Psychologismus* (Stuttgart: Hippokrates Verlag, 1959), p. 91; my
translation.
‡ Rollo May, *Love and Will* (New York: W. W. Norton & Co., 1969).

limits has only increased inner conflict; for "the sexual freedom to which we were devoted fell short of being fully human." The same can be said of the relatively greater education in sexual facts and techniques of our contemporaries compared to the generations that preceded us. Our bookish approach to "ideal marriage" has boomeranged, and the emphasis upon technique in sex has given us a mechanistic attitude toward lovemaking that has left us all the more alienated, lonely, and depersonalized. By a curious inversion people become more wary of the sharing of tenderness than of physical nakedness and sexual intimacy!

The reasons that May advances for the obsession with sex in our culture are a depressing commentary both on our lack of love and on the emptiness of our lives. In "desperate endeavor to escape feelings of emptiness and the threat of apathy, partners pant and quiver hoping to find an answering quiver in someone else's body." This search for a responding and longing in the other through which to prove their own feelings alive is called love, but it has nothing to do with it. Nor is there any real love present in that compulsion to demonstrate one's potency that leads one to treat the most intimate and personal of all acts "as a performance to be judged by exterior requirements." The ironic result of viewing oneself as a machine to be turned on, adjusted, and steered, is the loss of feeling for oneself and one's partner to the point where "the lover who is most efficient will also be the one who is impotent." Another cause of impotence is that compulsively hurried relationship to time that we have already noted in our discussion of death. In the age of "short-order sex" sex itself gets shortchanged. "The fact that many people tend not to give themselves *time* to know each other in love affairs is a general symptom of the malaise of our day," says May. Carried far enough this leads to actual impotence—the body's statement that it has been left behind in the compulsive rush to carry out an idea of what we are supposed to want. We *fly* to sex in order to avoid passion, pushed by an anxiety that cannot even know in the moment of intercourse itself any real presentness. Sex in our society, says May, is a technique for a gigantic repression of true passion. Or, as we have seen in our discussion of death, our obsession with sex results from our repression of death. "Sex is the easiest way to prove our vitality, to demonstrate we are still 'young,' attractive, and virile, to prove we are not dead yet."

Passion, then, is not identical with sex but is a separate force deeper than it. It may be expressed through sex, but it also may be pushed under by it. What gives the special depth-dimension to passion, according to May, is the "daimonic," which he defines not as something evil but as any force capable of taking over the whole personality. In the daimonic there is an affirmation of one's self that gives one the power to put one's self into the relationship. Without such self-assertion, one is unable to participate in a genuine relationship. And a genuine relationship is a reciprocal one in which each acts upon the other. Although May says that this relationship "always skates on the edge of the exploitation of the partner," the give-and-take, the experiencing of the other side of the relationship, prevents it from going over that edge while retaining the vitality of the relationship. It is only when love and will come together that we attain the truly personal, and the personal is never something I possess alone but only in a person-to-person relationship. The "human being has to make the creature with whom he has sexual relations in some way personal, even if only in fantasy, or else suffer depersonalization himself." The need for sex is not so powerful as the need for relationship, intimacy, acceptance, and affirmation. Therefore, exploitation, seduction, and the domination of another's freedom cannot, both Freud and Sartre to the contrary, be the last word in sex and love. In attitude as well as in physical fact sex means that posture of the ultimate baring of one's self. This mutual baring is not *despite* but *with* and *through* the fact that we are creatures destined to die. "Love is not only enriched by our sense of mortality," writes May, "but constituted by it."

Even our feelings are not private but part of the dialogue that takes place in love. They "are ways of communicating and sharing something meaningful from us to the world." "Our feelings not only take into consideration the other person," writes May, "but are in a real sense partially *formed by the feelings of the other persons present.*" Every successful lover knows by instinct to pick up the magnetic field of the feelings of the person he is with. Even the wish is not simply individual, as Freud thought, but is a reality *between*: "the wish in interpersonal relationships requires mutuality."

To open oneself to another in love means to be confronted with a vastly widened world including regions of which we never dreamed. This experience produces a vertigo in which we may genuinely wonder whether we are "capable of giving ourselves to our beloved and still preserving what center of autonomy we have." Sartre would answer no; for he has made real giving to the other and self-preservation opposites. May, using Tillich's language of the "centered self" which transcends itself, goes beyond Sartre. "Contrary to the usual assumption, we all begin life not as individuals, but as 'we.'" Only because this is so, can love push us toward a new dimension of consciousness in which we transcend our isolation.

What this does not tell us is whether there will be the resources in any particular situation "to meet others and hold our ground when we meet them." Still less can we say with confidence of ourselves what May says in a commentary on a traditional people, namely that "The community gives a humanly trustworthy, interpersonal world in which one can struggle against the negative forces." On the contrary, it may be just the absence of this "humanly trustworthy, interpersonal world" that leads to that "crisis of confidence" which sets the stage for the modern split between libidinal passion and superego which Freud took to be the nature of man. "The unaffectedness of wishing is stifled by mistrust," writes Buber. "The divorce between spirit and instincts is here, as often, the consequence of the divorce between man and man."

The special form of the divorce between man and man in our day, says the psychoanalyst Leslie H. Farber, is the "disordered will," that willfulness that wants to handle both sides of the dialogue. If this willfulness expresses itself in the "life of suicide," as we have seen, it is found even more regularly in the contemporary approach to sex. Indeed, Farber goes so far as to state as his conviction "that over the last fifty years sex has, for the most part, lost its viability as a human experience." The emphasis here is on the word *human*. Sexual activity itself has not decreased, but the human possibilities of sex are becoming ever more elusive, and the couplings that take place are "poultices after the fact" which "further extend the degradation of sex that has resulted from its ever-increasing bondage to the modern will." Sex has been emancipated, to be sure, but its "emancipation" is really an abstraction from all of life—except the will—and its exaltation as the very measure of existence. As a result, what sex once brought man—the possibility of that mutual knowing and being known within which he regains *his own* body through knowing the body of the loved one—is lost in favor of an empty *knowing about* in which both bodies again escape him. Farber traces this decline in a series of steps: man viewing nature as a variety of energies to be harnessed and utilized, a machine to be kept healthy so it might lead to never-ending progress and prosperity; coming to regard the human body as just such a machine; the decision that the dominant energy of the human machine is sex; the claim of the erotic life as the exclusive province of sexology and psychoanalysis; and the abstraction and isolation of sex into the function of the sexual organs.*

The true *reductio ad absurdum* of this historical process is Dr. William H. Masters' study of the female orgasm in an actual laboratory situation, excluding all subjects that could not produce orgasms at will, relying principally on automanipulation, or masturbation, and recording the results with color movies. Whatever else may have been discovered in this way, Farber suggests, nothing could be discovered about the human relationship between persons in sexual love. We might go further and say that here the paradox has reached its point of greatest tension: the

---

* Leslie H. Farber, *The Ways of the Will: Essays in the Psychology and Psychopathology of the Will* (New York: Harper Colophon Books, 1967), p. 55.

uttermost hiding and eclipse of the human image brought about
by what claims to be the farthest outpost of the revelation of
man! While many Women's Liberationists have lined up behind
Masters and Johnson, as if the clitoral orgasm were the very bas-
tion of feminine freedom, and have characterized Farber as a
"male chauvinist," Germaine Greer has rejected this emphasis on
the very same grounds as Farber: that it reduces human sexuality
to something partial and mechanical rather than whole and personal. She sees in Masters and Johnson a basically authoritarian
attempt to tame sex, "the blueprint for standard, low-agitation,
cool-out monogamy. If women are to avoid this last reduction of
their humanity, they must hold out not just for orgasm but for
ecstasy." Only the domination of "the performance ethic" can
explain women's finding the clitoris "the only site of their pleasure" instead of its "acting as a kind of sexual overdrive in a more
general response." This stress on the clitoral orgasm is but part of
a larger picture in which "Sex for many has become a sorry
business, a mechanical release involving neither discovery nor
triumph, stressing human isolation more dishearteningly than
ever before." Greer, like Rollo May, sees the modern ideal of sex
as really being mechanized sex, "laboriously and inhumanly com-
puterized," just as "the male sexual idea of virility without lan-
guor or amorousness" is a profoundly desolating illustration of
how the expression of the release in mechanical terms leads to
seeking it mechanically. "Sex becomes masturbation in the va-
gina." That is sex for the man. But the overstress on the man's
massaging of the clitoris to produce orgasm is no less masturbation for the woman.

Though we cannot return to the unawareness of the past, neither can we remain standing in the pseudoclinical situation of the
present, in which frigidity is seen as something *in* the woman,
impotence as something *in* the man. Both frigidity and impotence as well as male and female orgasms are essential aspects of
an interhuman betweenness in which *both man and woman must
work together on the sexual,* as on the financial and other problems of the relationship. I do not mean that both should deal

together with *her* problem of frigidity and/or *his* problem of impotence. I mean that the problems themselves do not belong to and cannot be simply located in one partner in the relationship; for they are a function of the relationship itself.

When and if the mutual trust that upholds the relationship is broken, especially if the separation is traumatic, it is inevitable in most cases that sexual "hang-ups" will be relegated by each partner to the other. Each protects himself from his former closeness by turning the other into a caricature of a person—an object possessing such and such characteristics. Actually, he does not know what the other might be in another relationship. I am not denying that some relationships are too difficult to work out. But I am saying that precisely when we know exactly what is wrong with our former partner and wonder why we wasted ten years of our lives with such a person, precisely when we seem to have reached an objective and secure ground, is the point when we have ceased to make him or her present to us as a person and are protecting ourselves from feeling any concern—from living in and with that person.

When I was thirteen, my young brother-in-law replaced my almost total ignorance of sex with the philosophy of the "man of action"—a philosophy which I did not put into practice for many years to come, if at all, but which left me, nonetheless, with the idea that sex was a Good Thing, regardless of whom one made love to or what one's relation was to one's partner. Later I came to recognize this same relationship not only in the college-boy boastings of "laying a girl" or "having a piece," but even in the morality of a society that claimed all premarital or extramarital sexuality to be wrong in abstraction from both the particular relationship and the concrete situation. When this morality was unmasked as the hypocritical double standard that it is, it was replaced for a great many by a no less immoral approval of sex as a "natural" act, again in abstraction from the actual relationship and the actual situation. Sex has been sought in our society as an "experience," a sensation somehow supposed to be of value in itself. Only this power of abstraction could lead so many to spend so much of their strength and effort trying to prove their "potency" with ever-fresh partners or trying to extend the variety and scope of their experience by the exchange of partners. The mark of success in our society, the distinguished American psychiatrist Harry Stack Sullivan once said, is what you can do with your genitals to someone else's genitals. I would go even further and say that most men and women in our society are ridden by a deep anxiety concerning their sexual adequacy, that no amount of actual sexual "conquest" or "experience" can ever really allay that anxiety, and that even those with the most self-satisfying sexual prowess live with dread of that day when their powers begin to fail. This day comes all the sooner, in fact, because of this anxiety, because of the compulsive need to allay it by sexual activity, and because of the dread of its someday proving the master. People are afraid of fumbling and faltering in sexual relations; for they do not wish to appear un*master*-ly. Their harsh self-judgment is, of course, accompanied by an equally harsh judgment of others; for if things do not work out according to the ideal of the sex books, then the blame must be placed on *his* "impotence" or *her* "frigidity." Some people manage to place all the blame on their partners, some take all the blame to themselves, and most go back and forth between blaming their partners and blaming themselves. Few take seriously the extent to which "good sexual functioning" is itself a function of good relationship or the fact that even good relationship, including all the anxieties and worries and fatigues of real life, is not on call to produce good sex at stated periods!

We are flooded with false images—caricatures—of manliness and femininity—from the John Wayne type of "he-man" to any of a number of sexy, voluptuous, clinging, or dream-girl-soft women. We fear in our sexual relationships themselves that consideration—failure to press our case to the very verge of exploitation—will be considered weakness or a lack of vitality. It takes courage to falter, to hesitate, to show bewilderment, confusion, and self-doubt. Naturally, we are vulnerable here as in perhaps no other sphere of our lives, and our most personal confirmation is at stake. "Love is being psychically wide-open to another," says Shulamith Firestone.

> It is a situation of total emotional vulnerability. Therefore it must be not only the incorporation of the other, but an *exchange* of selves. Anything short of mutual exchange will hurt one or the other party.*

Yet without the mutual revelation of weakness, of humanness, of hope and doubt, faith and despair, of the very ground in which each of us is rooted and of the strengths and foibles of our unique stances, there can be no revelation of the hidden human image in sexual love. And when the human image remains hidden, it does not flower in the darkness. It withers and atrophies and all the masks and pretenses of our smiling faces cannot dispel the growing stink of putrefaction that arises from the depths. Only when we cease to be concerned with our own images as masculine or feminine and trust ourselves to the *between* itself—allowing ourselves to be changed by the other, by the relationship—will the human image be revealed.

---

* Shulamith Firestone, *The Dialectic of Sex: The Case for Feminist Revolution* (New York: Bantam Books [paperback], 1971), pp. 128 f.

WOMEN'S LIBERATION AND THE FIGHT FOR THE HUMAN

> Faced with the slow death of self, the American woman must begin to take her life seriously.
>
> —Betty Friedan, *The Feminine Mystique*

Some years ago I was invited to participate in a two-hour TV "Under Discussion" program on "The American Male under Attack." Although I can claim no special knowledge on this subject, I was amazed by my fellow panelists' avoidance of what seemed the obvious problems in favoring one or another type of simplification. To my right were the simplifiers of "men are men and women are women," leading inexorably to the kitchen for women and the supermasculine he-man of *True* magazine for the men (with a bunny girl thrown in to console them for the failure of American women to accept their subordinate role). To my left were the feminists, the career women, who seemed to want to establish the independence of women to have a career without any consideration of the problem that every woman faces who wants both marriage and a career.

When we were off the air, the conditioned-reflex-psychiatrist-male-chauvinist told Betty Friedan and Marya Mannes that his wife was about to get a Ph.D. in sociology, but he stopped her. I

then told them of my wife who had begun with a career of college teaching and later a nursery school career and then had freely decided she wanted to put aside a career to have a family. I thought they would be pleased at this because I assumed that what they wanted was that women have free choice as to what to do with their lives including what combination of marriage and/or career they wished for. This is, for example, exactly how Florence Bryant defines the Women's Liberation Movement: "To me women's liberation means the freedom to choose what you want to do with your life and then to be able to implement that choice without having to feel guilty because you prefer to have a career or because you prefer to stay home and keep house."*
Instead of this, they both looked disapproving, as if every woman lost to a career was lost to mankind, no matter how good a wife and mother she was. Since then, in fact, my wife has enjoyed still a third career—teaching poetry to adults in a Quaker community and study center unmarred by the taint of credits and grades. But even if she had not, as long as the choice was really her own and she was doing what she really wanted to do, I fail to see how her decision could represent a blow to the dignity and equality of women. Germaine Greer has made a penetrating critique of just this aspect of Betty Friedan's position:

> Her whole case rests upon the frustration suffered by the educated woman who falls for the Freudian notion that physiology is destiny. For Mrs. Friedan sexuality seems to mean motherhood, an argument which other feminist groups also seem to be misled by, so that in rejecting the normative sex role of women they are forced to stress nonsexual aspects of a woman's destiny at the expense of her libido, a mistake which will have serious consequences. She represents the cream of American middle-class womanhood, and what she wants for them is equality of opportunity within the status quo, free admission to the world of the ulcer and the coronary.†

* Florence V. Bryant, "A Liberated Woman Looks at Woman's Liberation," *Trends*, Vol. III, No. 2 (October, 1970), p. 14.
† Germaine Greer, *The Female Eunuch* (New York: McGraw-Hill Book Co., 1971), p. 294.

When James Thurber drew his famous cartoons of "The Battle of the Sexes" for *The New Yorker* in the 1940s, the subject seemed both comic and real as the little kneeling figures advanced in droves on each other. I particularly enjoyed "The Unicorn in the Garden" (perhaps because I saw my sister-in-law dance the unicorn with the Charles Weidman dance company). When the husband wakes one morning and sees a beautiful unicorn in the garden, he calls his wife, who calls the authorities to come take him away. When they arrive, he says, "Why no, I saw no unicorn in the garden. It must be my wife's imagination," at which point they take her away! I even took part in a small drama of this sort once where I helped a wife arrange a meeting with her husband and a psychiatrist because she thought her husband had gone off the deep end. When she told the psychiatrist about her spirit boyfriends who dictated poems to her, he decided that *she* was "crackers," and this gave the husband the decided upper hand in the relationship.

Such amusing stories cover over a conflict of disturbing and sometimes even sinister nature. It was not surprising to me that the subject of men versus women produced a good deal of anxiety in my fellow participants on the TV panel. What was surprising was that it was precisely the real anxiety about being a man and being a woman—about being a man or a woman in this culture in this historical situation—that was consistently evaded. When I suggested that no small part of this anxiety arose out of the unsureness both men and women have about their "sexual role" in our culture, an unsureness having less to do with sexual adequacy per se than with general fears concerning one's stance as a man or woman in interhuman relationships, my suggestion fell into a total vacuum, much as if *they* were professors from an ivory tower and not I! Instead of looking at this anxiety in its intersubjective reality and its deep anthropological, historical, and cultural interconnections, they were content to isolate it into one sex or the other—into the tired old questions of women's rights or of what a man has the right to expect of a woman.

I am convinced that there could be few areas more fruitful for the study of interaction of anthropological, historical, and cultural anxiety than this one of the anxiety of men and women in relation to each other in this society. I am equally convinced, however, that none of the approaches that are usually taken to this problem are fruitful. By this I mean not merely the lowbrow approaches of my panel colleagues but also the highbrow approaches of Freud, Sullivan, Riesman, Kierkegaard, Heidegger, and Tillich. A male must be a man, not just a human being, and a female a woman. But they must also be men and women of our culture, and they must be both of these as human beings, not just animals. I cannot sidestep the anxiety of being a boy, a lover, a father, through being a "thinking thing," a universal mind, or an "authentic self." Nor can I sidestep the anxiety of what it means to be an authentic human being by developing myself into a caricature of masculinity. But both of these anxieties focus at the point in history in which our culture finds itself. This is the point at which a father cannot pass on to his son an image of what it means to be a man and a human being and a mother cannot pass on to her daughter an image of what it means to be a woman and a human being. Neither father nor mother has or embodies such an image.

We live in a culture in which men do not feel they are up to their duty as men and women do not feel they are up to their duty as women. Yet neither men nor women know what it means to be men or women in particular, much less what it means to be human through being a man or a woman. The tendency, as a result, is that each has so much guilt that he or she projects it on the other partner in the love relationship. It may be true, as Kate Millett suggests, that society places the guilt of sexuality overwhelmingly on the female, but within an enduring relationship between a man and a woman, guilt is like a hot potato that each tries to hand over to the other! Some aspects of the Women's Liberation Movement have taken on this Either/Or quality of blaming men for their conscious or unconscious male chauvinism rather than seeing it as a joint problem in which each must help the other to a more human relationship for both. "Those miserable women who blame the men who *let them down* for their misery and isolation," writes Germaine Greer, "enact every day the initial mistake of sacrificing their personal responsibility for themselves."

There is an argument for the separatism of women, as there is for that of the blacks. If you have independence and dignity, you also have the ground from which to move into real dialogue with the other and not have to choose between sterile submission and sterile rebellion. But the real thrust behind Women's Liberation, it seems to me, is the confusion and distortion that prevail in a province that should be that of the highest flowering of the human—the confusion about what it means to be a woman in relationship to man in this particular historical situation. Somehow it tends to become a mere social role and, what is more, an imposed social role in which women are subject to the tyranny of both men's and women's notions of what it means to be "feminine." "The universal sway of the feminine stereotype is the single most important factor in male and female woman-hatred," writes Germaine Greer. The battle for women's liberation is a battle for the wholeness of the human being, a battle for woman's right to be a person. The hidden image of the human must be revealed in order that woman as woman may become woman as person.

No one ever suggests that a career and fatherhood are incompatible, but if a woman wants a career she is told to choose between career and motherhood, since most of the responsibility in the family structure is placed upon the woman and neither men nor society in general are willing to provide women with the structural means of handling both roles. For many, woman's choices are more restricted still: Either she must marry and raise a family or face life with no identity at all, an "unwanted spinster." I shall never forget the way in which a senior donnee of mine at Sarah Lawrence College, a poetess gifted at portraying life with a light and humorous touch, told me in conference: "This morning my mother said to me, 'Twenty-two and so unmarried!'" Three months later when she graduated she had acquired the husband that her mother demanded.

Society imposes upon woman the role of passive consumer, an emotional nonintellectual who neither thinks nor acts beyond the confines of her home; and the media—TV, radio, the movies— reinforce this image. The interior colonization of women is sturdier even than segregation, says Kate Millett. It is, in fact, the most pervasive form of ideology, the most fundamental concept of power. Both sexes are socialized to basic patriarchal policies with regard to status, role, and temperament. The rights of women to divorce protection, citizenship, vote, and property have not affected their continued chattel status in name, residence, sex, domestic service, and economic dependence. All this is reinforced by the impact of popular Freudianism. Freud made sexual fulfillment the panacea for the social unrest of women. His theory of "penis envy" shifts to woman the blame for her own suffering for aspiring to a biologically impossible state. By the same token, Freud interprets women's expression of hostility to men or their attempts to transcend "woman's role" as a desire to castrate the male. Even in the academic world, women must seek survival or advancement from the approval of males who hold power.*

Basic to the cultural divisions of roles has been woman's reproductive role. It is this which society will not allow to be threatened, as a result of which all the freedoms which woman may obtain will be empty without freedom in relation to her own reproductive life. "The real question is not, 'How can we justify abortion?' but, 'How can we justify compulsory childbearing?' " At the same time, women are taught not to share love and sex but to use them for their profit. While verbally women are taught the finest values, the gut message that gets through is the all-importance of economic ascendancy and status acquisition reached by whatever means. In this sense a former prostitute could fairly say, "From the time a girl is old enough to go to school, she begins her education in the basic principles of hustling." But by the same token, women are taught that they are

* Kate Millett, *Sexual Politics* (Garden City, N.Y.: Doubleday & Co., 1970), pp. 25 f., 28 f., 31–35, 54, 58, 179, 189, 196.

only of value when they are young: "Men may mature, but women just obsolesce."

> Think what it is like to have most of your life ahead and be told you are obsolete! Think what it is like to feel attraction, desire, affection toward others . . . to be, in other words, still a living woman, and to be told every day that you are not a woman but a tired object that should disappear.*

There is another, equally essential, and corollary aspect of this battle, however, and that is the realm of the "between." Equality and dignity cannot be won by women themselves nor even by changing the attitude of any number of individual men. It must be won in the dynamic of lived and living relationship—in the concrete situations in which men and women meet and confirm one another as man or woman *and* as person, holding the tension between these two so that, if they can never be simply identified, neither can they ever be separated. If modern man in general knows anxiety, alienation, and exile, it is certain that modern woman knows it in still fuller measure—since she faces the simultaneous breakup of traditional values and of such traditional images of woman as might have satisfied her mother, grandmother, or great-grandmother. If the black man is invisible *as man* and person through his very visibility as black, woman is invisible as person and human being through her very visibility as woman. D. H. Lawrence gave eloquent expression to this situation:

> Man is willing to accept woman as an equal, as a man in skirts, as an angel, a devil, a baby-face, a machine, an instrument, a bosom, a womb, a pair of legs, a servant, an encyclopedia, an ideal or an obscenity; the only thing he won't accept her as is a human being, a real human being of the female sex.†

The invisibility of woman is less obvious than that of the black because of the great respect, veneration, and Mother's Day idol-

---

* Robin Morgan, ed., *Sisterhood Is Powerful: An Anthology of Writings from the Women's Liberation Movement* (New York: Vintage Books, 1970), pp. 45, 94, 181, 246, 278, 290 f., 172, 174 f.
† Quoted in Morgan, *Sisterhood Is Powerful*, p. 564.

ization woman enjoys in our culture, not to mention her unquestionable power to seduce, manipulate, control, and dominate men through her feminine charms and "wiles." But the seduction and manipulation work both ways: Women have been taught to be devious and indirect because it is unladylike or unfeminine to be "too" outspoken, direct, demanding, angry, aggressive, or just plain enraged. Not only does woman take a large measure of the image of what she should be from the predominant male culture, but "the battle between the sexes" has resulted in a long-standing and deep-seated *mutual* resentment and *mutual* mistrust. The very prince in *Rigoletto* who sings "La Donn' è mobile" is the one who so cruelly deceives the faithful Gilda; whereas Carmen in her famous "Habanera" says that love, so far from being mutual, feeds on rejection and disdain, which she promptly acts out by turning from Don José to the Toreador.

Our basic understanding of the "woman problem," therefore, must be that it is an integral part of the hidden human image in all of the senses in which we have used that term. *"The status quo is untenable,"* writes Mattie Humphrey, *"not because we are unequal to men or to white people, but because we have no adequate models of humanity in these polarized groups,"* and she complains with justice against "the forced polarization of Americans by age, color, income" which "serves to maintain our attitudinal hang-ups."* The psychiatrist Natalie Shainess points out the absence of an image of the human in the true sense—not as a description of what is, but as a meaningful direction for "what woman might be if she had full opportunity to develop and use her resources. Often what has been assumed to be pathologic, is the very thing that is healthiest in her; or if not that, has formed the core of her self and her humanness."† Marya Mannes similarly sees the pervasive anxiety in modern woman as

* Mattie L. Humphrey, "The Black Woman's Survival Kit," *Trends*, Vol. III, No. 2 (October, 1970), pp. 22, 24.
† Natalie Shainess, M.D., "A Psychiatrist's View: Images of Woman—Past and Present, Overt and Obscured," in Morgan, *Sisterhood Is Powerful*, pp. 231 f.

the result of the shutting out of the *human* image by the imposed *social* image:

> What I call the destructive anxieties are not the growth of wom-
> en's minds and powers, but quite the contrary: the pressures of
> society and the mass media to make women conform to the
> classic and traditional image in men's eyes. They must be not
> only the perfect wife, mother, and home-maker, but the ever-
> young, ever-slim, ever-alluring object of their desires. Every
> woman is deluged daily with urges to attain this impossible state.
> . . . The real demon is success—the anxieties engendered by this
> quest are relentless, degrading, corroding. What is worse, there is
> no end to this escalation of desire. . . . The legitimate anxiety—
> am I being true to myself as a human being?—is submerged in
> trivia and self-deception.[*]

The hiddenness of the human image is not just *in* women. It is *between* women and men. If men in our society must ask them-selves whether they are really capable of loving women or whether their sexuality is not just another expression of their hostility or their need for conquest, men and women together must recognize, as Kate Millett puts it, that "Our highly repres-sive and Puritan tradition has almost hopelessly confused sexual-ity with sadism, cruelty, and that which is in general inhumane and antisocial." Instead of a genuine image of woman, men and women alike are confronted at every turn in our culture by the reigning female fetish, a totally sexless, interminably smiling idol or doll whose lines are those of the castrated female. The passive sexual role assigned to women by our culture is itself a denial of female sexuality in favor of "femininity," or sexlessness. Women intellectuals are no less "female eunuchs": They are repressed, servile, and disenfranchised of their bodies. Both the feminine and the pseudomasculine roles represent castrations. "Most women who have arrived at positions of power in a men's world have done so by adopting masculine methods which are

[*] Marya Mannes, "The Roots of Anxiety in Modern Woman," *Journal of Neuropsychiatry*, Vol. V (1964), p. 412, quoted in Morgan, *Sisterhood Is Powerful*, p. 244.

not incompatible with the masquerade of femininity," writes
Germaine Greer. "They still exploit the sado-masochistic hookup of the sexes," in which "we have only the choice of being
hammer or anvil."* Even when men are directly the cause of
women's exile, it is inseparably tied up with the exile of the
men:

> The husband, after all, is trying to protect and bolster his frail
> ego, not drive his wife insane or force her suicide. He wants in
> the home to be able to hide from his own inner doubts, his own
> sense of shame, failure, and meaninglessness. He wants to shed
> the endless humiliation of endless days parading as a man in the
> male world, pretending a power, control, and understanding he
> does not have.
>   All he asks of his wife, aside from hours of menial work, is
> that she not see him as he sees himself. That she not challenge
> him, but admire and desire him, soothe and distract him.†

Sometimes the Women's Liberation Movement recognizes this
element of the "between" and sometimes not. In her Introduction to *Sisterhood Is Powerful* Robin Morgan makes a number of
clear and startling statements about the movement. "To deny
that you are oppressed is to collaborate in your repression."
"Women's liberation is the first radical movement to base its
politics—in fact, create its politics—out of concrete personal experiences." "It is also the first movement that has the potential of
cutting across all class, race, age, economic, and geographical
barriers—since women in every group must play the same role . . .
wife, mother, sexual object, baby producer, 'supplementary income statistic,' helpmate, nurturer, hostess." She goes further and
announces that "the women's movement has set itself the task of
analyzing divisions (race, class, age, hetero- and homosexuality)
that keep us apart from each other, and is working very concretely to break down these divisions." And although she recognizes that women from working-class backgrounds have been

* Greer, *The Female Eunuch*, pp. 52, 59 f., 69, 86, 108.
† Beverly Jones, "The Dynamics of Marriage and Motherhood," in Morgan,
Sisterhood Is Powerful, p. 52.

alienated from what seemed to be a middle-class women's movement, she claims that the movement *is* diverse in origins and that "most arrived via social mobility from the lower class anyway."*

One cannot legislate the removal of sexual differences arising from the culture just by recognizing that they are the product of the culture and not merely of biological inheritance, as Kate Millett does in *Sexual Politics*. Male and female, she says, are seen in our society as two distinct cultures, and this division and cataloguing reduce the human person to half of its potential in its struggle to fulfill "feminine" or "masculine" role expectations. This patriarchal system has probably exercised the most pervasive and insidious control of any other, innocently, wordlessly, installing itself as nature. To agree with this fully, as I do, is not to agree that one can so easily get back to "nature" minus culture or that we know anything about the human person and society in a state of nature. The problem is no less real if it is borne by culture rather than by inheritance, though this may change our attitude toward it and give us some hope of changing it. One cannot will to see women as pure person or pure human being minus their variegated but nonetheless unmistakable feminine appearance and social role. All we can do, here as elsewhere, is to hold the tension between the person and the social role, recognizing the necessity of both and proclaiming the freedom of every person to choose his own social role or roles and not have it imposed on him by others. We cannot live without social roles, and in our culture the differentiation of men and women, though hardly a simple matter, is nonetheless pervasive and insidiously corrupting. Most men still feel that women *expect* them to be dominant—in bed if nowhere else—and that most women are ready to express a not-too-well-disguised contempt for them if they are not. Women do not have the monopoly on kindness and consideration that some advocates of women's rights imagine when they picture men as educated to harsh competitiveness and women to gentle tenderness.

* Morgan, *Sisterhood Is Powerful*, pp. xvii f., xxv, xxvii.

Even if this problem were removed by mutual education in trust and respect and the right of everyone to become himself in relation to others, there would still remain irreducible givens and difficult problems. Men and women are not only different, as the French celebrate with their famous phrase *vive la différence!*, they are also unique. That means they are equal in dignity but not factually or functionally. More serious, our culture lacks any clear images of what it means to be a masculine and what it means to be a feminine human being. To establish ourselves as the sexual beings and persons we choose to be, we need to take great and sometimes dreadful risks. Moreover, there is a residual element in sex itself that places a demand on the partners which can only be satisfied if, *in that relationship and in that situation*, the man succeeds in evoking the feminine in the woman and the woman in evoking the masculine in the man. The human image only comes to revelation *between* persons and not *in* woman or man taken separately. Hence the unsureness about what it means to be a woman in our culture is complemented by an equal unsureness about what it means to be a man.

Do I mean by all this that women suffer no disadvantages compared to men? Not at all. If women have won the franchise in most Western countries, equal pay for equal work and equal opportunity for getting work are anything but a reality in most so-called democracies, and their supposed equality in the Soviet Union is more a matter of social role and function in the collective than of equal dignity and worth *as women*. Churches, governments, law firms, businesses still perpetuate in greater or smaller measure the myth of male dominance, and the jokes and laughter of men at women's movements betray not only anxiety but a desire not to face the issue squarely for fear of losing cherished prerogatives. If the Orthodox Jew prays consciously, "Thank God, I was not born a woman," most men pray it unconsciously! What John Stuart Mill wrote about the damage to boys that arises from reinforcing them from earliest days in their notion of superiority over the other sex is just as applicable today,

Kate Millett points out. "When the feeling of being raised above the whole of the other sex is combined with personal authority over one individual among them," writes Mill, this becomes to men whose strongest points of character are not conscience and affection, "a regularly constituted Academy or Gymnasium for training them in arrogance and overbearingness."* The images of woman as tender, receptive, healing, and helping; as wife, mother, homemaker, and housecleaner; as witch, bitch, shrew, and nag; as the eternal temptress, the courtesan, and the bunny girl—all do their part in making each woman invisible to many men and even to many women as the unique person she is.

For all this, I do not believe that men really do feel superior to women in our culture. They *need* to feel superior and to dominate, but that very need is a great dependence on the confirmation of women, which often gives the woman the whip hand or at the very least a far stronger role than is generally imagined. At a weekend seminar and encounter session that I co-led, a man who was known for his lonely life and his disdainful rejection of ordinary sociality insisted on the interdependence of men, whereas another man, who was married with a family and who seemed by all appearances sociable and happy, insisted on the self-sufficiency of man. The latter man was the successful one as far as the world goes, the "self-made man." But his wife, later, said to me, "He is only able to speak that way because of the support that I give him"—a support of which he was blissfully unaware until it was suddenly taken from him!

Both men and women must be liberated from the notion that only men have opinions to express and that it is unladylike for a woman to enter into a discussion or hold forth with an opinion or argument. What is more, the unique qualities of women's minds must be brought to flower in situations of mutual confirmation and appreciation which our present competitive business society hardly leaves room for and cannot envisage. The same

* John Stuart Mill, *The Subjection of Women* (1869), reprinted in *Three Essays by J. S. Mill*, World's Classics Series (London: Oxford University Press, 1966), pp. 523 f., quoted in Millett, *Sexual Politics*, p. 103.

applies to all of women's other talents and abilities. When I was an undergraduate at Harvard, some of the most distinguished of my professors would refuse to go to Radcliffe to give a lecture, on the principle that it was beneath their dignity to teach women. I gave thirteen years of my life to teaching at Sarah Lawrence, a progressive woman's college which at that time had no men. I did not think I was wasting my time educating women, nor did I judge women's intelligence by some quantitative scale that would put them in comparison with men. I came to recognize among the young women I taught a great variety of types of intelligence—logical, intuitive, emotional, sensory— which could not possibly be captured in any quantitative intelligence quotient and which not seldom got to the heart of the matter as young men their age did not. My own wife has a mind which is second to few men that I have met; yet it is in no sense a "masculine" mind. At the same time I must confess to the fear I often had in my years at Sarah Lawrence that the Sarah Lawrence girl was in some ways the conspicuous consumption of her family, to begin with, and later of the junior executive whom she might marry and whose cocktail parties she might grace with all the education and culture that she had taken so seriously during her college years. This is a caricature, of course, by no means applying to all or perhaps very much to any. Yet it was confirmed to some extent when, a few years after I had left Sarah Lawrence, I spent the night in the house of the parents of a then Sarah Lawrence freshman who was obviously the "ideal" Sarah Lawrence type—gifted in drama and music, intelligent and intellectually curious, eager to take in New York City—but somehow, with all that, her accomplishments seemed less a true blow for women's liberation than an extension of her father's having "made it," less obvious than dressing his wife in diamonds and furs but still conspicuous consumption.

The highly personalized education at Sarah Lawrence is unavailable to the vast majority of women, even of the well-to-do and middle-class families, to say nothing of the great numbers who are denied the possibility of college altogether and do not

get a high-school education of any value. It is of this majority
that the scientist Isaac Asimov can say, in reference to the traditional picture of woman as not intelligent in "masculine" subjects:

> Women cooperate since they must and through generation after
> generation carefully have taught themselves the ladylike art of
> being stupid. . . . The reward for all this is the privilege of being
> thought cute and of having a man patronizingly reward them
> with such nonsense services as the removal of a hat in the eleva-
> tor, the offer of an arm at the curb, the holding of a door, and
> the kissing of a hand.
>
> All this in exchange for abandoning the intellectual role that is
> the highest and proudest mark of a human being and for being
> condemned to a life-time of degrading service.*

In Kafka's novel *The Castle*, K. is the stranger whereas his
mistress Frieda is a thoroughgoing social conformist, rooted in
the life of the Village. But there is another person in the Village
who is no less of an exile than K. himself, although one with
considerably more dignity and self-sufficiency. This is Amalia,
who tore up the note and threw it in the face of the messenger
when she received an insulting order from a high Castle official
to present herself at the Castle Inn for exactly two hours in the
early morning so that he could satisfy the lust that the sight of
her had aroused in him. As a result of this action Amalia's whole
family become pariahs, and it is largely because of K.'s associations with this pariah family, with whom he hopes to make
common cause in reaching the Castle, that Frieda finally leaves
him. Any woman who like Amalia says that she will pay her own
way, open the door for herself, put on her own coat, and take
her chances getting across the street rather than enter into that
unspoken exchange in return for which she must proffer her
favors to a man, risks exile in the same ruthless way. How many
women secretaries today can afford to come on as thoroughgoing
independents without losing their jobs? How many women

* Isaac Asimov, "You've Come a Long Way, Baby—But Look Where You're
Going Tomorrow," *Trends*, Vol. III, No. 2 (October, 1970), pp. 25 f.

teachers can talk back to men superintendents as "man to man" without losing their jobs? How many young women in middle-class society can dispense with all the flirtation and subtle flattery that men expect without losing dates and eventually even mates? Already in the nineteenth-century novel there existed incomparable portraits of woman as Modern Exile, such as Flaubert's *Madame Bovary*, Tolstoy's *Anna Karenina*, and Henry James' *Portrait of a Lady*, and we can mention Djuna Barnes' *Nightwood* as one among many such portraits in the twentieth century.

Perhaps the classic expression of woman as Exile is the statement by the former Sarah Lawrence girl, Yoko Ono, "Woman is the nigger of the world." "Women are increasingly losing contact with their inner selves—their sentience—" says Natalie Shainess, "and as a result, become further alienated from meaningful living." If no woman is more of an exile than the Lesbian, upon whom society heaps the most severe contempt and ridicule, the radical Lesbian is right in pointing out that all women are struggling to liberate their minds from sick sexual roles. But the sexual is only one of myriad manifestations of women's exile. The society's image of woman has been so internalized by women themselves that they have tended to justify it, taking on the passive role that is expected of them, being afraid to speak out, feeling that if they are not married they will not have an identity, feeling the obligation to remain young if they are to retain their hold as women, buying a career at the price of feeling "less of a woman." By the time most women are in high school, they begin to do worse on intellectual tasks and in productivity and accomplishment in general, thus giving justification after the fact to the characterization that they are inconsistent, emotionally unstable, lacking in a strong conscience, weaker, intuitive rather than intelligent.* In her focus on the male as source of security, she cannot build mutuality with her fellow women.

Ironically, woman's greatest and most universal exile occurs

* Morgan, *Sisterhood Is Powerful*, pp. 565, 233, 306, 219, 128 f., 165, 171, 373.

precisely where she is supposed to be most at home, namely, in marriage and family life. In his study of *The Origin of the Family, Private Property, and the State*, Friedrich Engels already identified the family as the basic unit of capitalist society and of female oppression. The family is founded upon the open or concealed domestic slavery of the wife, and society is founded on a multiple of families. In the family the husband is the bourgeois, the wife, the proletariat. There is no free marriage contract unless both are free in every respect, including the economic. The same situation prevails today. A great many American men are not accustomed to doing monotonous, repetitive work and are loath to realize that in their daily lives they have been accepting and implementing the very oppression and exploitation that they deplore in public life. "All men everywhere are slightly schizoid —divorced from the reality of maintaining life," says the author of "The Politics of Housework." By foisting the housework onto his wife, he gains seven hours a week to play with his mind and not his human needs, hence "the horrifying abstractions of modern life." The family is supposed to be the place where everyone can find relief from the commodity relations that dominate the rest of society, but it is not so; for family functions and woman's functions are almost synonymous. The nuclear family unit forces woman "into a totally dependent position, paying for her keep with an enormous amount of emotional and physical labor which is not even considered work." Women have to purchase from men what should be theirs by right—equal opportunity for making money, for doing work they like. "Sex and love have been so contaminated for women by economic dependence that the package deal of love and marriage looks like a con and a shill." "The whole business of the white family—its softened men, its frustrated women, its angry children—is in a state of great mess," testifies a black sister.*

Simone de Beauvoir's classic book *The Second Sex* casts light on many other aspects of the exile of modern woman. Constantly

* *Ibid.*, pp. 486, 451 f., 465, xxxii, 28, 54, 357.

tempted by her whole upbringing and by all that surrounds her
to see her true role as submission, woman is never impressed
with the necessity of taking charge of her own existence. If she
hopes for self-realization without *doing* anything, man tempts
her to see herself in this way. The result is that each blames the
other for the ambiguity of "give-and-take." "She complains of
giving her all, he protests that she takes his all." Men are sometimes justified in their complaint in the sense of woman's active
complicity in her own oppression and of the tyranny she exercises over him in dominating him, monopolizing him, using him,
possessing him, criticizing and mutilating him. Yet both complicity and tyranny are marks of woman's dependence on man,
her alienation from herself, her weakness in the parasitic relationship, and the torment she suffers from the institution of marriage shaped as it is according to the masculine code, developed
by males and in their interest. What we have is a double alienation based not only upon preexisting institutions but upon the
inauthenticity of both man and woman: "Woman is pursuing a
dream of submission, man a dream of identification," and "each
blames the other for the unhappiness he or she has incurred in
yielding to the temptations of the easy way." Man in particular
squanders an enormous amount of time and energy in trying to
appear male, important, and superior, in talking about women,
in seducing them, in fearing them. "He would be liberated himself in their liberation. But this is precisely what he dreads."*

In her remarkable book *The Dialectic of Sex*, Shulamith Firestone, one of the young leaders in the Women's Liberation
Movement, gives us further insight into the exile of modern
woman. In order to be acceptable in the eyes of men, woman
must force and mutilate their bodies. Love and status are so
intertwined for woman that she is never free to choose love for
its own sake. But male culture, too, is parasitical. It takes from
woman without giving and flourishes on the confirmation and
support that women give to men. What is worse, woman cannot

---

* Simone de Beauvoir, *The Second Sex*, trans. and ed. by H. M. Parshley
(New York: Bantam Books, 1961), pp. 679, 454, 677.

see herself directly but only through the eyes of male culture, and values herself accordingly. Yet through the blindness of "sex privatization," women imagine themselves to be related to as individual persons and do not perceive that men treat them in terms of their class generality.[*]

Outside of marriage as well as in, woman, while not being allowed to have control over her body, is held responsible for its products, for her pregnancy. There are numerous women who have been granted hospital abortions only on the condition that they agree to be sterilized, i.e., to be permanently punished for sexuality or for daring to do something active about not wanting a child. Among Puerto Rican women in New York City *La Operación* has been so encouraged that between a fifth and a third of them have been sterilized. Not unconnected with this surely is the fact that in a recent three-year period 79 percent of New York City's abortion deaths occurred among black and Puerto Rican women. The abortion death rate was 4.7 times as high for Puerto Rican women and 8 times as high for black women, as for their white sisters. "It is obvious," concludes Lucinda Cisler, "that poor women have almost no access to information about legal or safe illegal abortion sources, to friendly doctors who do abortions, or to the money to pay the exorbitant charges involved."[†] Sadly the repeal of the New York State antiabortion law has not made that much difference in this situation.

The situation of black women and Puerto Ricans and Chicanos, while testifying to the common oppression of women, is sufficiently unique to discourage too many claims that the Women's Liberation Movement is or can be one unified movement of all women. Black women, for example, have very specific problems arising from their situation that other women do not. Doubly oppressed and doubly burdened, they have for the most part chosen to fight beside their black brothers, fighting racism

[*] Shulamith Firestone, *The Dialectic of Sex: The Case for Feminist Revolution* (New York: Bantam Books [paperback], 1971), pp. 127, 139, 149, 152, 157.
[†] *Ibid.*, pp. 107, 257.

as a priority oppression. "Most black women have to work to help house, feed, and clothe their families." "Black women make up a substantial part of the black working force." Black woman in America is justly called "a slave of a slave," says Frances Beal, since she has so often been used "as the scapegoat for the evils that this horrendous System has perpetrated on black men." For these reasons black women cannot identify in their struggle with any white women's group that does not have an anti-imperialist and antiracist ideology but lays oppression simply to male chauvinism.* Mattie Humphrey sees the black woman's situation as even more exposed: Caught between the black-consciousness struggle and the struggle for women's equality, the black woman must recognize that she can benefit only indirectly from either movement and that she may be accused of betraying the other movement in the process.†

The exile of women in the professions and in other labor is perhaps too well known to need many indications here. Although thirty-five million women work and do so out of sheer economic necessity, women everywhere represent only a small percentage of the professions—law, medicine, chemistry, editing, journalism, university teaching—and their jobs are less responsible and interesting and their pay notoriously lower than that of men. Though more women proportionately are in secretarial, clerical, service, and factory occupations, their treatment and their pay are no better, indeed far worse. Quite regularly, women do not relate directly to their work as their accomplishment but only through the men, and many of the petty jobs women do seem to have no purpose other than emphasizing, as one secretary puts it, that "women are shit and men are king." In any case, the much heralded entry of woman into man's world has not meant either the end of "shitwork" for the woman or in most cases that she is really accepted as a man's equal. Women with Ph.D.s make less money than men with B.A.s. There are also countless women who cannot get steady employment but

---

* *Ibid.*, pp. xxvi, 260 f., 559, 341–343, 350–352.
† Humphrey, "The Black Woman's Survival Kit," p. 21.

who occupy the position of a reserve labor force that can be used, in almost classical Marxian fashion, to hold down the wages of others.

> Considered as a whole, female employment in Britain and the United States displays the same basic character, that of an inert, unvalued though essential force, considered as temporary labor, docile, ignorant and unreliable. Because more than half the working women are married, the assumption arises that the family is their principal concern, that work outside the home brings in a little extra spending money, that they have no ambition. Not only are women paid less than men in most of the instances where they do work identical with men, but most women work at a lower level than men in the same industry, so that the question of parity can never arise.*

Even in the radical movement, as Marge Piercy testifies, the relationship of men to women is still predominantly a sexual one. Women are used to prop up men, used up and cast aside, and they are "not able to keep tenderness and sensual joy from being converted into cooperation" in their own manipulation. The women the radical movements want to reach—the working-class women and those on welfare—will have to have a movement for liberation which will take a whole new form, attacking exploitation on the job and in the home together in a way that neither traditional male unionism nor middle-class feminism can do.†

Contemporary woman is a "problematic rebel," as many women themselves recognize. Sally Kempton, a well-known writer whom I knew when she was an undergraduate at Sarah Lawrence, reports in the July, 1970, *Esquire* that she is not sure whether being married and belonging to the Women's Movement are compatible but that in any case she does not know what to do with the rage and resentment with which acting out the role she felt her father and her boyfriends expected of her has left her burdened. Woman has doubted her own motives for

---

* Greer, *The Female Eunuch*, pp. 112 f.
† Morgan, *Sisterhood Is Powerful*, pp. xxvii, 37–40, 43, 94, 96, 99, 115, 118, 422, 424, 428, 431, 436, 462, 562.

so long and been ridden so long by her guilt that she is tempted
to try to throw off both self-doubt and guilt in an apocalyptic
"liberation" that can lead to little else than destruction and emptiness. Contemporary woman knows the inner division that
comes from not having been given an image of woman, an
image of the human. She knows the paradox of the person in the
modern world who needs to have a calling to be a person and
yet she herself has to make the assertion that she is called, and
she has to make that assertion stick—whether as wife, mother,
mistress, call girl, business executive, concert performer, or
actress.

Here too we must distinguish between the two types of Modern Rebel to which I have pointed—the Modern Promethean
and the Modern Job. The Modern Promethean and the Modern
Job are ideal types. They do not exist in pure form. But they are
useful nonetheless in helping us distinguish between two quite
different attitudes, both of which abound in every form of rebellion, often mixed together not only in the same movement and
platform but frequently in the same person. The Modern Promethean can be recognized, as we have seen, by his Either/Or
approach to what oppresses him. At its most extreme, he believes
he must destroy the reality that confronts him or be destroyed
himself. Less extremely, he sees the other as evil or ignorant, but
in any case as in the wrong and to be put down. The Modern
Job, in contrast, holds the tension of contending *and* trusting by
bringing them both within the dialogue with the other, even
when that dialogue is a Dialogue with the Absurd. He does not
wish to destroy but to confront in such a way that from pseudoharmony and pseudodialogue there may arise real recognition of
otherness, on the one hand, and genuine dialogue, on the other.

These two attitudes are not only often mixed, but usually it is
necessary to go *through* the Modern Promethean to reach the
Modern Job. Someone who rebels is usually in a weaker position
and has to rebel irrationally and even unfairly in order to throw
off the weight of guilt and resentment that has been keeping him
passive and oppressed and find a ground of his own from which

he can come back to a stronger and more open confrontation
with his former oppressor. You cannot have a measured rebellion. The hurt has to be brought out first. Those who will not
hear the hurt because it is expressed angrily or with hostility
help destroy the possibility of moving to the next stage where
women, feeling a firmer ground under them, will enter into a
stronger dialogue. At the present stage, women are a long way
from having expressed their resentment, and there is nothing
men are more deathly afraid of, even when they joke about it,
than the resentment of women. Woman "must recapture her
own will and her own goals, and the energy to use them," writes
Germaine Greer, and "in order to effect this some quite 'unreasonable' suggestions, or demands may be necessary." "The key to
the strategy of liberation," she adds, "lies in exposing the situation, and the simplest way to do it is to outrage the pundits and
the experts by sheer impudence of speech and gesture, the exploitation of cliché 'feminine logic' to expose masculine pomposity,
absurdity and injustice."*

If we bear in mind the fact that at present and for some time
to come the Women's Liberation Movement may have to go
through the Modern Promethean before it can reach the Modern
Job, we may be able to distinguish, however roughly, between
these two basic attitudes as they are expressed in statements on
women's liberation. We may just thereby come to recognize the
crucial importance of the Women's Liberation Movement eventually maturing from and through the Modern Promethean to
the Modern Job.

There is no lack of Modern Prometheanism in the Women's
Liberation Movement. Indeed, some of the radical sects in the
movement are ideal prototypes of the Modern Promethean.
"Don't accept rides from strange men," says Robin Morgan in
the poem-letter at the end of her Introduction to *Sisterhood Is
Powerful*, "and remember that all men are strange as hell." On
the pages before, she advances rather hesitantly the notion that

* Greer, *The Female Eunuch*, pp. 112 f.

men ought not to exist. Some of her sisters in the movement are
not hesitant at all. Not content to point out the obvious exploitation of women by men, they rush to characterize *all* relationships
between a man and a woman as class relationships and as such
"no more or less personal . . . than is the relationship between a
woman and her maid, a master and his slave, a teacher and his
student." Roxanne Dunbar states that "*all* men enjoy male supremacy and take advantage of it to a greater or lesser degree
depending on their position in the masculine hierarchy of
power." SCUM—the Society for Cutting Up Men—comes out in
its manifesto with an explicit proposal for the destruction of
the male sex, the man being anyway only "an incomplete female,
a walking abortion, aborted at the gene state." Every evil trait is
laid at the doors of the male, including distrust, ugliness, hate
and violence, disease and death. Yet the women of SCUM, after
dismissing contemptuously the "approval-seeking Daddy's Girls"
as "millions of assholes" whose debrainwashing is not worth
waiting for, set forth a program for systematic sabotage of the
economic system, cars, great works of art, the monetary system,
capped by the reduction of men to walking automata, to a male
auxiliary that will work for their own elimination, or to those
who "can go off to the nearest friendly neighborhood suicide
center where they will be quietly, quickly, and painlessly gassed
to death."* Need we pause to remark that this program aims at
that very extermination of man and the image of the human that
the Nazis undertook?

Less extreme perhaps but also clearly of a Modern Promethean vintage are the New York Radical Women who "are critical of all past ideology, literature and philosophy" as products of
"male supremacist culture," or the Redstockings who also proclaim every relationship a class relationship, women's oppression
as total, male supremacy as the oldest and most basic form of
domination, all men as benefiting from male supremacy and as
having oppressed women, and women as not suffering from

* Morgan, *Sisterhood Is Powerful*, pp. xl, xxxv, 59, 479, 514–519.

brainwashing but from the daily, continual pressure of men. With true Modern Promethean rhetoric they, and many others in the movement, repudiate all divisions among women and claim solidarity with all women, a claim which black women, as we have seen, must deny. The Witches—Women's International Terrorist Conspiracy from Hell—pronounce themselves "Free Human Beings," denounce marriage as legal whoredom for women, and pronounce both hex and curse on their masculine oppressors: "DEATH TO MALE CHAUVINISM."*

There are traces of the Modern Promethean even in far more moderate members of the movement. At a conference on women in the churches in New York in April, 1971, Mary Daly declared that the peace and ecology movements are coopting women if they do not "explicitly have the liberation of women as their aims." The sentiment behind this statement is understandable, just as is the refusal of a person primarily concerned with the black revolution to take part in any movement that does not make that one of its goals. At the same time it does not allow to others, including other women, the freedom to focus on peace or on ecology if this is *their* primary concern. It is of the old vintage, "If you are not for us, you are against us." "If you are not part of the solution, you are part of the problem." Carried to its worst, this becomes a party line in which every word, action, or gesture is *politicized*, and men and women alike are under a constant inquisition as to whether or not they are devoting all of their energies to what has been defined *for* them as *the* cause. I have the same reaction to Mary Daly's statement that "Sisterhood means revolution in the deep psychological sense because it means the bonding of the oppressed which is not implied in brotherhood." If she wishes to say that women in general are more oppressed than men, we can agree. But wherever throughout history men have bonded together in the name of brotherhood, it has almost invariably been a bonding of the oppressed against some common oppressor. Also Modern Promethean in

* *Ibid.*, pp. 492, 520, 533 f., 538, 540, 543, 547, 553.

tone is Rosemary Ruether's statement in a symposium on *Women's Liberation and the Church** that the liberation of women is the most profound of all movements of liberation because it gets to the root of the impulse of domination as well as to the causes of our alienation from one another. *Every* movement of liberation touches on the roots of the impulse of domination and the causes of alienation. The Women's Liberation Movement *may* be the most important and profound at *this* moment in history, but are we going to say that it is necessarily more basic than the movement against slavery was in the past?

Is the sexual the most basic oppression and is it the cause or root of all other types of oppression, as so many women in the movement claim? In one part of her introduction to *Sisterhood Is Powerful*, Robin Morgan says that *sexism* and *racism* predate corporate capitalism and have postdated socialist revolutions. But three pages later she quotes with approval "the profoundly radical analysis beginning to emerge from revolutionary feminism: that capitalism, imperialism, and racism are *symptoms* of male supremacy—sexism."

> Racism as a major contradiction, for example, is surely based on the first "alienizing act," the basic primary contradiction that occurred with the enslavement of half the human species by the other half. I think it no coincidence that all the myths of creation, in all religions, have to do with a "fall from grace" simultaneously with the emergence of set sexual roles.†

This is not much different from Freud's seeking to bolster his claim that the Oedipus complex is the basic human reality by reading a "myth" back into prehistory—the primal event of the slaying of the father by the fifty sons that he recounts in *Totem and Taboo*. Both are Modern Prometheans in that both seek to lodge a monolithic claim on the spurious grounds of speculating

---

* Quoted in Miriam Carroll, "Female Rebels Chart Their Course," *Catholic Star Herald*, March 26, 1971. I am also indebted to Miriam Carroll for her write-up of Mary Daly's speech at the conference on women in the churches, New York City, April, 1971.

† Morgan, *Sisterhood Is Powerful*, pp. xxxi, xxxiv, 355.

as to what was "in the beginning" and therefore presumably is most basic. The plain fact is that we do not know man in a state of nature or even in prehistory but only, basically, as he is given to us now. That means we know nowhere of a family structure minus a culture any more than we know a culture minus one or another type of family structure. Writing on women in black liberation, Frances Beal says: "Racial oppression of black people in America has done what neither class oppression nor sexual oppression, with all their perniciousness, has ever done: destroyed an entire people and their culture."*

Using the literature of the French playwright and novelist Jean Genet as her springboard, Kate Millett maintains that "sexual caste supersedes all other forms of inegalitarian stratification: racial, political or economic."

> *The Balcony* demonstrates the futility of all forms of revolution which preserve intact the basic unit of exploitation and oppression, that between the sexes, male and female, or any substitute for them. Taking the fundamental human connection, that of sexuality, to be the nuclear model of all the more elaborate social constructs growing out of it, he perceived that it is in itself not only hopelessly tainted but the very prototype of institutionalized inequality. Genet is convinced that in dividing humanity into two groups and appointing one to rule over the other by virtue of birthright, the social order has already established and ratified a system of oppression which will underlie and corrupt all other human relationships as well as every area of thought and experience.†

Far more sophisticated and plausible than the similar arguments of Robin Morgan, Kate Millett's thesis is only valid as far as her example reaches—Jean Genet's experiences in the homosexual world and the satiric light they cast on "normal" male-female relationships. It does not, in fact, show that everywhere and always sexual exploitation is the most basic. Nor need we follow Kate Millett in calling sexuality the fundamental human connec-

* Morgan, *Sisterhood Is Powerful,* pp. xxxi, xxxiv, 355.
† Millett, *Sexual Politics,* p. 20.

tion; for then everything depends on what you mean by "sexuality," and if you include in it a strong measure of violence, cruelty, sadism, masochism, oppression, and struggle for power, it is more reasonable to say that these are aspects of the evil of dominating and being dominated that have become associated with sexuality and often manifest themselves that way, rather than that sexuality includes them as its invariable concomitant.

It is no accident that Genet is Saint Genet to Sartre, hero, saint, and image of man; for this world is indeed close to Sartre's understanding of sexuality as we have seen it. No more than Freud can Kate Millett validly isolate sexuality from the rest of human experience and make it the root and not the concomitant or fruit of the "sick delirium of power and violence." In a competitive game of volleyball played by both men and women, it is not uncommon to see the more skilled player shouldering aside the less skilled, some of whom are usually women. But the less-skilled men are shoved aside quite as readily. The problem turns not on the man-woman relationship but on dominance—on shoving people aside because one wants to win the game more than one cares about the person whose feeling of not being able to play may be reinforced by such behavior. In the relationship between black men and black women the matter is still more complex. The attitude of the black man toward the black woman grows in no small part out of the unequal relation between white and black—the continual put-down which the black man often has to face in the world outside the home. It is true that these relations in turn are reinforced by traditional sexual roles for white men and women and black men and women that grew up on the plantation, but these roles in their turn were the product of slavery and not of a direct, unmediated relationship between the sexes. In any case, what we have here are corollaries. There is no simple cause and effect. The Modern Promethean in Women's Liberation must take her place alongside the great simplifiers such as Marx and Freud, each of whom wants to reduce what is determining in the human condition to one basic factor —economic, Oedipal, or sexist. None of this is to gainsay the oft-repeated assertion that only a revolution of which the liberation of women is an integral part can lead to the freedom, dignity, and equality of all human beings.

Wherever it is held that the dignity of anyone—women or blacks or youth—can be attained simply through attacking, putting down, rejecting, hating, and eliminating one's opponent, we have the Modern Promethean—the unconscious Manichaean who believes, like Sartre's anti-Semite or like Captain Ahab in his search for vengeance on Moby Dick, that the "good" can be automatically established through the purely negative act of destroying the "evil."

One might describe Shulamith Firestone's *Dialectic of Sex* as an attempt to reach the goals of the Modern Job by using the means of the Modern Promethean. Although she attempts to show that racism is a sexual phenomenon, that it is sexism extended, what is really basic for her is power and politics: "This power hierarchy creates the psychology of racism, just as, in the nuclear family, it creates the psychology of sexism." This focus on power includes man's power over nature which she, with the naiveté of the most enthusiastic of Modern Prometheans, imagines to be on the brink of becoming total. Within a century she anticipates the achievement of "the goal of Empiricism: total understanding of the laws of nature."

> The nature of aging and growth, sleep and hibernation, the chemical functioning of the brain and the development of consciousness and memory are all beginning to be understood in their entirety.

As a part of the feminist revolution, she envisages an androgynous culture which will abolish itself. Culture will not be missed when it disappears; for "by then humanity will have mastered nature totally, will have realized in *actuality* its dreams." By then, too, humanity will have overcome through technology the double curse proclaimed in the myth of Adam and Eve: the curse of work and the curse of childbearing. The essential mission of the feminist movement, indeed, will be to create cultural acceptance of this new ecological balance necessary for the survival of the race in our century. Through cybernetics and control of birth and genetics, "we now have the knowledge to create a paradise on earth anew." The division of work implicit in the family structure will no longer have any meaning. Then and then only will a socialist revolution be possible; for "the family structure is the *source* of psychological, economic, and political oppression."*

In *The Dialectic of Sex* we also find utterances that could be taken in the spirit of the Modern Promethean *or* that of the Modern Job. Certainly this is true of the four principles which Firestone expounds as prerequisites for any alternative system:

> 1) The freeing of women from the tyranny of their reproductive biology by every means available, and the diffusion of the childbearing and childrearing role to the society as a whole, men as well as women.
> 2) The full self-determination, including economic independence, of both women and children.
> 3) The total integration of women and children into all aspects of the larger society.
> 4) The freedom of all women and children to do whatever they wish to do sexually.†

Her vision of the larger "household" unit that will replace the nuclear family is also one that could be either Modern Promethean or Modern Job, dependent upon the spirit and manner in which it would be carried out:

> The birth of children to a unit which disbanded or recomposed as soon as children were physically able to be independent, one that was meant to serve immediate needs rather than to pass on power and privilege (the basis of patriarchy is the inheritance of property gained through labor) would eliminate the power psychology, sexual repression, and cultural sublimation. Family chauvinism, class privilege based birth would be eliminated.‡

* Firestone, *The Dialectic of Sex*, pp. 108, 180, 190, 202, 212, 242.
† *Ibid.*, pp. 206–209.
‡ *Ibid.*, p. 241.

Since the Modern Promethean and the Modern Job are ideal types, it is not surprising that in many cases they are both present, and since they are basically attitudes rather than systems it is not surprising that many aspects of the Women's Liberation Movement can express as well as lead to one attitude or the other. A case in point is the "consciousness-raising" group which has been a standard form of organization for the radical branches of the movement since 1966 at least. On one level, these groups simply fulfill the need of people who share a common oppression, but have not been in dialogue, to enter into real communication about their feelings and their situation, and in that sense they are essential for any rebellion, including that of the Modern Job. Women talk but do not really communicate at a deep level, says Beverly Jones, author of an article on "Marriage and Motherhood." Not trusting or respecting each other, they keep their dialogue on a superficial level, and this stands in the way of their realizing a common identity.* The Women's Collective of the New York High School Student Union also sees these groups in terms of the Modern Job since it emphasizes their value in helping women realize that they do have a ground to stand on from which to confront and enter into dialogue with men:

> Getting together and rapping about hang-ups that have arisen as a result of being females helps us to realize that we aren't shits, that we aren't docile and reticent because of something fucked up inside us, but it's like that because we have been *programmed* into that.†

These "consciousness-raising," or "bitch," sessions only go over to the Modern Promethean when they become, as they often have, a technique with a definite process and goal, such as moving from A. "Ongoing consciousness expansion" to B. "Classic forms of resisting consciousness, *or* How to avoid the awful truth," to C. " 'Starting to stop'—overcoming repressions and de-

* Morgan, *Sisterhood Is Powerful*, p. 60.
† *Ibid.*, p. 374.

lusions," to D. "Understanding and developing radical feminist theory," to E. "Consciousness-raiser (organizer) training." The same might be said about the whole topic of the expression of hostility, which is one thing when it is spontaneous and the result of overcoming of oppression and another when it is planned and programmed, as with SCUM, WITCH, Redstockings, and the radical Lesbians in their hatred of the male oppressor. Perhaps somewhere between the two is the suggestion of Florynce Kennedy that women can be readily brought into the liberation struggle if they direct their hostility from the vertical *down* (the kids, the merchants, the family, co-workers, and other women), and the horizontal—to the vertical *up*, which, according to her, means systems and institutions less than it means people. "Kicking ass should be only where an ass is protecting the system."* Parenthetically, in the midst of so much colorful language, I wish someone would invent a single word for human being which does not confuse the generic with the gender, as does the term *man*.

Perhaps nowhere more clearly than in this thoroughly confused and mixed-up area does the contrast between the Either / Or of the Modern Promethean and the Both/And of the Modern Job emerge. If "black is beautiful" does not necessarily mean "white is ugly," neither does the appreciation of "the hitherto unrecognized culture of women" with its "intense appreciation for life," "its sensitivity to unspoken thoughts and the complexity of simple things," and its "powerful knowledge of human needs and feelings" necessarily mean, as the New York Radical Women suggest, that all past ideology, literature, and philosophy must be put down as "products . . . of male supremacist culture."

A similar problem arises when we turn to the question of how one may remedy the present lamentable situation vis-à-vis women. Insofar as one is content to start with the concrete situation and the given, one is in the realm of the Modern Job, no matter how much one rebels against that situation. Insofar as

* *Ibid.*, pp. xxiii f., 514–520, 533–553, 445.

one falls into utopian thinking which simply replaces the unde-
sirable given with a desirable ideal, one falls back into the realm
of the Modern Promethean. That society is not properly organized to permit woman to combine a career with her role as wife
and mother is, for most women, an unassailable statement of
fact. What one does with this fact determines whether one is
simply a conformist, a Modern Exile, a Modern Promethean, or
a Modern Job. Simply to use this fact as a means of attacking
and accusing the men of our society, as is sometimes done by
women who consider this their trump card in determining where
a man is "at" vis-à-vis the movement, suggests the all-or-nothing
attitude of the Modern Promethean. To start with the situation
as it is and explore other possibilities of social organization, as
the kibbutzim did in Israel and as is being done in communes
and cooperative communities throughout America, suggests the
Modern Job. The same ambiguity clings to the unexceptionable
statement that woman's place, like man's, must not be dictated
arbitrarily by sex, race, or family background but by the unique
talents of each person. This is a desirable goal for all, but one
that must be achieved in tension with the fact that each man and
woman does exist in social categories, does fulfill social roles,
however dynamic, and does have to fight within whatever structure he or she finds himself for the recognition of the *unique*
contribution that he or she can make to this structure. If men are
better off than women, it is nonetheless also not true of men in
general that their place is dictated by their unique talents minus
consideration of their race, family background, social position,
and a host of other categories.

In Simone de Beauvoir's *The Second Sex*, the *positive* role of
the rebellion of the Modern Promethean as a step toward that of
the Modern Job emerges clearly. Up till now woman, shut up in
the immanence of family and social role, has endeavored to hold
man in that prison too, doing away with her own inferiority by
destroying his superiority—mutilating, dominating, and contra-
dicting him, denying his truth and his values. Today woman tries
to escape her prison instead, and a new conflict arises as he

refuses to accept her as an equal in any concrete way and she
becomes aggressive in her turn and tries to dominate him. But
this new conflict will be no more fruitful than the old if it does
not lead her not only to strength and self-assertion but also to
that love between equals that such strength makes possible.
Woman must rebel for herself and in the name of her own worth
and dignity but not for the purpose of remaining with herself:

> On the day when it will be possible for woman to love not in her
> weakness but in her strength, not to escape herself but to find
> herself, not to abase herself but to assert herself—on that day
> love will become for her, as for man, a source of life and not of
> mortal danger.*

Thus the rebellion of modern woman against her exile will in
the first instance take the form of the Modern Promethean, but if
it does not want simply to deepen the exile, it will move from
there to the form of the Modern Job. This Simone de Beauvoir
makes repeatedly clear. In marked contrast to Sartre, to whom
she is otherwise so close, de Beauvoir holds that "it is possible to
avoid the temptations of sadism and masochism when the two
partners recognize each other as equal." With a little modesty
and generosity love is changed from a matter of victory and
defeat to a free exchange. For such free and equal mutuality to
come into being, it is necessary that each partner stop projecting
on the other the repudiated part of his own self and instead live
out the ambiguities of the situation with authentic pride. Authentic love is not a mode of salvation, but "a human interrelation." It bears not only its own ambiguities but also the lacks,
limitations, and gratuitousness of the other. Such love respects
the otherness of the other, but it does not proclaim woman as set
in opposition or hostility to man: "Let her have her independent
existence and she will continue none the less to exist for him
also: mutually recognizing each other as subject, each will yet
remain for the other an *other*." Here is a teaching of confirming
the other in his otherness far closer to Buber than to Sartre: To

* Beauvoir, *The Second Sex*, pp. 675, 629.

establish liberty in the world of the given, it is necessary "that by and through their mutual differentiation men and women unequivocally affirm their brotherhood."*

The battle cannot be won through relegating the blame to men *or* women but through seeing the task as a common one—a task of the "between" to be shared by men and women in their relationship to each other in the concrete situations of their lives. Here first do we stand on the ground of the Modern Job. The plea that women be given the freedom and life-space necessary to express their life-experience *as women* without being downgraded by men or forced to conform to existing male structures, is not the Modern Promethean cry of "willful and independent women." Women stand in need of dialogue with and confirmation by men if they are to become what they are called to become as persons: "Women be-ing or bring-ing the New Woman into being," says Miriam Carroll of the Philadelphia Task Force for Women in Religion, "depend on a response—a dialectic with men for the process to continue or go to completion without damaging or wasteful detours." Rebellion, says Rosemary Ruether following Camus, is an affirmation of a common humanity —a breaking of the silence between oppressed and oppressor that is the beginning of humanization. It is no accident that in *Problematic Rebel* I pointed to the identical teaching of Camus as an example of the Modern Job; for wherever the struggle for liberation is a fight for the human and not just for one group against another, the Modern Job is present. The chief act of rebellion for a woman, according to Ruether, is an internal grasping of faith in full personhood and a rejecting of the limiting self-images that women have taken over and internalized.†

"If women are to be better valued by men they must value themselves more highly," writes Germaine Greer, and take the responsibility for their sexual life that will free them from thinking of themselves with shame *and* from emotional blackmail against men. If women do not want to be belittled, they must

* *Ibid.*, pp. 651, 685, 615, 688 f.
† Paraphrased in Miriam Carroll, "Female Rebels Charts Their Course."

themselves stop panhandling: "In their clothes and mannerisms women caricature themselves, putting themselves across with silly names and deliberate flightiness, exaggerating their indecisiveness and helplessness. . . . They ought to take advantage of the genuine praise of women which is appearing, though fitfully, in contemporary culture."*

The stance of the Modern Job in the Women's Liberation Movement also means, at some point along the line, a conscious rejection of the Either/Or of the Modern Promethean. "The women's liberation movement must seek the liberation of all people, men as well as women," writes Florence Bryant. "This putting down of men must stop. . . . One can only be as free as one allows others to be." This freedom for both men and women is not just laissez-faire: It is interdependence, cooperation, dialogue. Starting with the, to me, indubitable fact that, "Men and women as they are, are the products of complex social relations in an ongoing historical process," Mary Daly stresses that personal liberty and growth are not opposed to, but essential to, love and commitment. The way forward, for her, is the way of the "between," rejecting "the old obsession with sex roles, in order to focus upon the problems of persons in relation to others."

> We should strive, therefore, toward a level of confrontation, dialogue, and cooperation between the sexes undreamed of in the past. . . . The directing principle . . . should be commitment to providing the possibility of ever more profound, complete, dynamic and humanizing relationships.†

Although I have spoken of Shulamith Firestone as one who wishes to reach the goal of the Modern Job through the means of the Modern Promethean, there are emphases in her *Dialectic of Sex* in which the stance of the Modern Job emerges unmistakably both as means and end. She sees the feminist movement

* Greer, *The Female Eunuch*, pp. 264, 268.
† Bryant, "A Liberated Woman Looks at Woman's Liberation," p. 14; Mary Daly, "Women and the Catholic Church," in Morgan, *Sisterhood Is Powerful*, pp. 131 f.

as the first to combine effectively the "personal" with the "political." It is developing a new way of relating, a new political style "that will eventually reconcile the personal—always the feminine prerogative—with the public, with the 'world outside,' to restore that world to its emotions, and literally to its senses." To reintegrate the emotional with the rational is to reintegrate the female principle with the male. What is more, she insists on including the oppression of children in any program for feminist revolution. Otherwise, women will be open to the accusation of missing an important substratum of oppression merely because it did not directly concern *them*. Only the elimination of the very conditions of femininity and childhood themselves will clear the way for a fully "human" condition, she says. The most important characteristic of revolution, according to her, is flexibility*—an emphasis rare among revolutionaries and one that, if taken seriously, points the way toward the Modern Job.

Germaine Greer is to me a particularly impressive example of the Modern Job because she combines radical rebellion with a total absence of resentment and because she expresses the attitudes of the Modern Job so fully and consistently with no trace of the Modern Promethean except the recognition that women must place "unreasonable" demands if they are to be heard. "The first exercise of the free woman is to devise her own mode of revolt," she writes, "a mode which will reflect her own independence and originality." Precisely, therefore, she opposes training women as a task force in battle: "The consequences of militancy do not disappear when the need for militancy is over. Freedom is fragile and must be protected. To sacrifice it, even as a temporary measure, is to betray it." None of the feminist groups has so far emerged with a strategy for rendering physical violence irrelevant, Greer points out, "which is the only hope of any human being." For women to train themselves as a fighting force would mean adopting the manners of the oppressors and practicing oppression on their own behalf. Such an approach can

---

* Firestone, *The Dialectic of Sex*, pp. 38, 210, 104, 227.

only grow out of confusing revolution with reaction and rebellion. It would be genuine revolution if women would stop loving
the victors in violent encounters and admiring the image of the
brutal man. Women's revolution is not ideology and universally
valid strategy. It is necessarily contextual. By the same token
women "must fight against the tendency to form a feminist élite,
or a masculine-type hierarchy of authority in our own political
structures, and struggle to maintain cooperation and the matri-
archal principle of fraternity." To abandon her slavery, woman
must renounce the chimera of security and accept a measure of
social ostracism in the process of achieving liberation. But Greer
also foresees for the revolutionary woman joy in the struggle,
purpose and integrity, pride and confidence, communication and
cooperation, magnanimity, generosity, and courage.

Germaine Greer has been criticized for lacking an overall revolutionary theory. But, she herself points out, it is not true that
to have a revolution you must have a revolutionary theory. What
is more, it is likely that "a theory devised by minds diseased by
the system will not be able to avail itself of the facts of a changing situation." Above all, women ought not eschew sex because it
is now enslaving; for sex is the principal confrontation in which
new values can be worked out. The Modern Prometheans among
the Women's Liberationists to the contrary, men are not the
enemy: "Men are the enemy in much the same way that some
crazed boy in uniform was the enemy of another like him in
most respects except the uniform. One possible tactic is to try to
get the uniforms off." Against men's probable desire that if they
are not free, women should not be free either, Germaine Greer
replies that by securing their own manumission, women "may
show men the way that they could follow when they jumped off
their own treadmill." In the end the task is not that of women
alone, of course, it is a task of the "between." To achieve a stable
relationship between the forces of creation and destruction, we
have to abandon the polarity of male sadism and female masochism and translate a universe of aggressors and victims into a
cooperative endeavor. "The great renewal of the world will per-

haps consist in this," Greer quotes Rilke, "that man and maid, freed from all false feeling and aversion, will seek each other not as opposites, but as brother and sister, as neighbours, and will come together as human beings."*

Perhaps most remarkable and gratifying of all is to find the attitude of the Modern Job so clearly expressed by Mattie Humphrey, a militant worker for community health, educational reform, black revolution, *and* women's liberation. The plight of the black woman caught between a male-dominated black revolution and a middle-class white feminist movement does not lead her to reject one or the other but to affirm both and the struggle of youth as well, and her affirmation of them all is for the sake of a rehumanizing of America—the revealing of the image of the human that has been so obscured by "this brute-force, authoritarian, chauvinistic, egotistical caricature who now sits in all the power seats of the American empire . . . oblivious to his own humanity or to any kinship within the human family." Affirming the black-consciousness movement and the Western women's liberation struggle as well as the openness and creativity to be found in the liberation struggle of youth are, for Mattie Humphrey, all part of "our struggle . . . to inspire a fuller vision of humanity." It means the affirmation of black and white, men and women as one species. Without such affirmation the black woman cannot be wholly human. Knowledge, understanding, wisdom, and vision mean, for her, that the greed for things must be "displaced by an urgency for shared human feelings and for understanding of motivations and aspirations."†

For Kate Millett too, in *Sexual Politics*, the sexual revolution means a liberation of men as well as women, of the slavery of the master to his domination over the slave. When male su-

---

* Greer, *The Female Eunuch*, pp. 10 f., 303, 313, 315, 325–329, 85, 109. The Rilke quotation can be found in context in Rainer Maria Rilke, *Letters to a Young Poet*, trans. by M. D. Herter Norton, rev. ed. (New York: W. W. Norton & Co., 1954), Letter No. 4, pp. 38 f. Greer left out the significant end: "in order simply, seriously and patiently to bear in common the difficult sex that has been laid upon them."

† Humphrey, "The Black Woman's Survival Kit," pp. 21–24.

premacy is overthrown, it will be possible to replace the present
constriction of roles by a reevaluation of "masculine" and "feminine" traits which might reject violence and excessive passivity in
either sex and encourage intelligence, tenderness, and consideration as appropriate to both sexes. This is surely the attitude of
the Modern Job as is Mary Daly's statement, "Individual men
and women find themselves not in static conformance to roles
but only in dynamic relationship to each other." But Mary Daly
also calls for a striving for authenticity which recognizes "the
ambiguity of concrete reality, which cannot be contained in abstraction."* Precisely because of this ambiguity, we cannot altogether dispense with the idea of the "social role," though we can
guard ourselves against taking it as the reality itself and see it
instead within the dialectic between more or less static conceptions of roles and the actual dynamic of our relationship to them.
We cannot deny the specialization of labor and the continual
rationalization of that specialization in terms of job descriptions,
problems of the exercise or sharing of decision-making and authority, and the obvious need to call for people not as the unique
persons they are but as abstractions, such as professor, secretary,
machinist, crane operator, doctor, or bank clerk. What we need
not accept is that the convenient label and the social role either
adequately describe what in fact goes on or exhaust the reality
of the person for the hours during which he works. On the
contrary, his own unique relationship to his work is of crucial
importance not only for the success and meaning of the work but
for the human reality that is here becoming event. What is more,
we can recognize the necessity for a continual critique of abstractions to make them more and more flexible and more and
more in line with the actual situation at any one time. In terms
of this critique, it is a part of the task of the Modern Job—man
and woman alike—to reject the unfair "burden of always responding to a situation in a catalogued way." But this means to
reject a life in which the human has been all but smothered

---

* Morgan, *Sisterhood Is Powerful*, p. 131.

under the weight of technical, social, and bureaucratic abstractions, and this is a cultural and spiritual revolution which must concern us all. Indeed, this, if I may be so bold, is the deepest level underlying all the rebellions of our day—those of the blacks, of women, of youth, and of the Third World.

In each of these spheres we come upon the plain signs of the fragility of our life together, of the life between man and woman and between man and man. Our hope for the "greening" of America or the world can only be meaningful if we begin with the realism which shows us caught in an immense corporate state or complex of military and industrial complexes in which the pervasive alienation removes our being with one another in community, not to mention our realization of our personal uniqueness in that being together, and leaves us only pseudo-freedoms that we imagine we enjoy. But if there is a fragility in our life as human beings there is also strength. The deeper the human image is hidden, the greater the possibility that resources may arise from the depths through which we can rediscover in each situation the human being, man and woman. It is a battle, a contending, a never-ending struggle, and it is a fight that cannot be won through setting oneself proudly against others and saying, like the Modern Promethean, "I represent the human." But it is a fight which offers the Modern Job hope that that through which we dehumanize ourselves may also be the road through which we can rediscover our humanity—while there still is a humanity to rediscover.

THE
CONTEMPORARY
CRISIS OF
VALUES

THE CRISIS
OF VALUES AND
THE HUMAN IMAGE

The inescapable corollary of the "eclipse of God" is the eclipse of the human. This is not a theological matter but a human one. It has nothing to do with belief or disbelief in God but with the loss of that courage to address and to respond which is the heart of existential trust. If our touchstones of reality are shattered, if we can no longer summon the resources to go out to meet the new situation in whatever form it takes, then our image of the human—our stance as human beings—is also imperiled.

The waning of genuine dialogue between man and man is the symptom, writes Buber, but a pervasive "existential mistrust," such as has never before existed, is the disease itself. The Absurd is not just the infinite universe, but also the all-too-finite social integument in which modern man finds himself. If the "death of God" means that there is now no longer any absolute to which man can appeal for reality, meaning, and value, the Modern Promethean concludes that man must himself create meaning through his own will to power or invent it through his responsible and conscious choice. Through refusing any longer to accede to the alienation of reality from the human world, the Modern Promethean seemingly overcomes his and our own exile. In fact, however, he often deepens it; for his sense of alienation may ultimately lead him to an Either/Or which demands the destruc-

tion of the "Other" as the indispensable prerequisite of his own
continued existence. The Nietzschean contrast between the master morality and the slave morality does not lead merely to social
tyranny but also to absolute, metaphysical self-affirmation. This
does not mean in practice that man as such is deified. "Before
God we are equal," says Zarathustra, "but now God is dead, we
will not be equal before the populace." The fundamental *inequality* of man is the teaching not only of the nineteenth-
century Grand Inquisitor but of his twentieth-century counter-
part—the dictator of the totalitarian state.

Nazism made this teaching so consequent that the literal *and*
the long-range result was the eclipse of *man*, the denigration and
destruction of the human image. The precedent which the Nazis
set in their scientific extermination of millions of human beings
has not been lost on subsequent history. In the war in Indochina
the country with the highest standard of living in the world has
"liberated" an unimaginably impoverished people by destroying
it—burning its children to the bone with napalm. Even those
white Americans who have accepted the Negro as a man have
for the most part not really accepted him as a black but as
someone making his way into the white majority. If the Egyp-
tians did in fact have systematic plans for the extermination of
the Jewish population of Israel in the Six Day War, this was
only the logical further consequence of that destruction of man
that the Nazis, without serious opposition from the great democracies, successfully put into effect on a scale that still outruns the
imagination. The next step, still more grotesquely beyond our
imagination and just therefore all too possible, is the nuclear war
in which man can simultaneously destroy himself and his image.

A special aspect of the eclipse of man is the relativization of
responsibility and guilt. All too often they are relegated to
merely external social taboos, to internal psychological compul-
sions or "hang-ups" or to both, with no room left for free and
responsible dialogue of the person with the situation that confronts him and demands of him response. Lacking a direction-
giving image of meaningful and authentic human existence,

modern man experiences an inner bifurcation and fragmentation which makes it impossible for him to take his own or others' motives at face value. Humility, love, friendship are regularly seen as masking resentment, hatred, or hostility. The very mistrust which drives us to unmask our bad faith is itself often a part of it. We try to avoid the anxiety of personal responsibility by asserting that we are all just men and therefore no one can be guilty, as does Joseph K. in Kafka's novel *The Trial*; or we affirm our guilt and that of everyone else and surrender the tension between what we are and what we might become, as does Jean-Baptiste Clamence in Camus' novel *The Fall*.

Those who have offered us contemporary images of man as "live options" do, of course, believe that they are just that. Yet some of these options, so far from overcoming the contemporary crisis of values, only serve to deepen it: Some both move us forward and set us back, while some serve as indispensable elements in the rediscovering of values without offering us the direction of authentic existence essential to such rediscovery.

The Modern Vitalist contributes to the rediscovery of values the image of abundant life, of creativity and dynamism, of energy as evil only when suppressed. He begins with the dynamic, but he leaves the ground of the concrete—reality seen from within the standpoint of actual human existence, which is always personal, separate, and in relation, and never merely a flowing totality. As a result, he offers no real direction for one's potentialities, no guidance in response to particular situations and in the movement toward authentic, personal existence. He leaves us with no protection against the Nazi conversion of vitalism into unlimited demonry, for he has failed to grasp Tillich's insight that vitality is never separable from intentionality.

The Modern Mystic puts forward the great mystics of the ages as contemporary images of man. Yet he is often concerned with the mystic only in terms of his individual "experience," extracting him from the context of his religion, his culture, and his own set of personal meanings and relationships. As such, mysticism is transformed and distorted by that modern valuation of experience for experience's sake which would have been so utterly unthinkable to any of the great mystics of the past. It is, in fact, a part of that modern *psychologizing* of reality that leads contemporary man to convert the meaning of the events which he lives through in common with others into inner psychic experience—enriching, interesting, or even terrifying. The current fascination with mind-transforming drugs as an automatic source of "religious experience" is an excellent example of this trend. One's personal existence in relation to what is *not* oneself—nature, other men, the world, God—is now reduced to what is *within* one.

What stands out above all else in the Modern Gnostic is the absence of any genuine otherness. Other people always prove to be hierophants who guide the self to its path or shadow figures on which he works out his inner destiny. Impulses for "evil" may be acted out, since other people are seen as functions of one's own individuation, as one is of theirs. Ultimately, the integration and individuation which the Modern Gnostic offers us is nothing other than a free experimentation with the self. If it removes the illusion of the persona, or mask of outer personality, it also destroys the unity of the self by dividing it into the observer and the observed, the experimenter and what is experimented upon!

The Modern Pragmatist rests his morality on pragmatic consequences without adequate concern for the task of making a moral decision *in the present*. His ethics of potentiality makes all things serve the purpose of releasing and fulfilling potentiality, but leaves "potentiality" itself a vague, neutral term without any value direction of its own. He thus falls into the dilemma of defining values in terms of a functioning which itself implies other, assumed values. These latter remain hidden and unclear, vacillating between human relationships seen as of value in themselves and as mere means to the end of self-realization. It is not enough to tell me that my relations to people and work will help me to become mature, integrated, creative, and productive. If I have a genuine moral concern, I may not reduce the situation to a function of my becoming; for I am concerned about whether a certain action *toward others* or *between* them and myself is right or wrong.

The Atheist Existentialist recognizes, as the Modern Pragmatist does not, that there are real, inescapable consequences of the "death of God," that we cannot cling to the same old values when that relationship to reality that undergirded and informed them has atrophied or disappeared. He thus sees the problem of finding authentic personal direction with utmost clarity. Yet he gets no further than the creation or invention of new values through one's own will to power or conscious choice. He denies the charge of arbitrariness since he defines man in relationship to his involvement, yet he tends to truncate this involvement. Either he sees valuing as the upward movement of the will to power, which must itself imply value and direction if it is to have any meaning other than a purely vitalist one, or he sees it as the minimizing of self-deception (*mauvaise foi*), which makes value primarily a relationship to oneself alone and only secondarily to the world in which one is called upon to act and decide. In either case this means to divest of full moral seriousness one's relationship to what is not oneself.

Many in our age have pointed "beyond morality" as the source of the ethical without noticing how they have undercut the very basis of ethics in so doing. Nietzsche's transvaluation of values is an excellent example of this. His rejection of the old morality takes place on the basis of implicit moral values (the higher selfishness, the right kind of chastity, joy in life, world-affirmation), yet that transmoral sphere in the name of which he transvalues values is not itself moral. It is instead a circular process in which values are the product of a "will to power" which justifies itself by the creation of new values and the progress toward the "superman"—an undefined direction which we can only assume to be upward if we take for granted the very values that are to be created. That Nietzsche himself doubted that his nihilism has actually laid the ground for a higher value is suggested by his teaching of the "eternal return" of all things in which the only exercise for the will to power is the redemptive affirmation of

what was—an *amor fati* which finds mystic joy in the ring of
eternity but is no longer able to make those real decisions and
perform those real actions in the world which would bear out
Nietzsche's definition of man as "the valuing animal" and his
claim that "without valuing the nut of existence is hollow."

Carl G. Jung represents a psychologically oriented attempt to
establish a "transmoral morality." In Jung's psychology of religion the place of God is taken by the deified Self produced in
the depths of the unconscious by the integration of the personality. To be a person means to have a vocation, writes Jung, but
for Jung the voice that calls to vocation comes from within the
unconscious. The unconscious is the potential arena of the true
self and the source of its moral values. It is the unconscious
which calls and guides, the conscious which listens and obeys, or
if it fails to obey, pays the price of neuroticism. Good and evil
are both relativized here to mere functions of wholeness. Jung's
"individuation" has no direction, guide, or criterion by which to
distinguish one voice of the archetypal unconscious from another. By making man's relations to other men largely extrinsic
and instrumental, it destroys man's personal wholeness, dividing
him into an essential inner self and an inessential social self—a
mere persona, a mask or social role. Jung's archetypal psychologism thus becomes a transmoral sanction for reducing the moral
conscience and the situation between man and man to psychological corollaries.

A more profound but still more disturbing attempt to reach a
transmoral morality is Martin Heidegger's concept of "conscience" as the recall to one's ownmost, not-to-be-outstripped,
nonrelational authenticity. The fact that our existence is *zum
Tode*—toward death—leads Heidegger, as we have seen, to en-
throne one's resolute anticipatory relationship to one's own death
above all dimensions of *Mitsein*, or being with others. "When the
call is understood with an existentiell kind of hearing," writes
Heidegger in *Being and Time*, "such understanding is more authentic the more non-relationally Dasein hears and understands
its own Being-appealed-to." Conscience, as a result, becomes

identical with an essentially self-related authenticity. "Only by authentically Being-their-Selves in resoluteness can people authentically be with one another," writes Heidegger, thus making the authentic Being-one's-Self the explicit transmoral source of morality. Yet he undercuts this morality by the same token since he does not recognize solicitous "Being-with" as an ultimate ontological category but only as a part of *Dasein*'s "being-in-the-world." "With death, Dasein stands before itself in its ownmost potentiality-for-Being," writes Heidegger. "When it stands before itself in this way, all its relations to any other Dasein have been undone. This ownmost non-relational possibility is at the same time the uttermost one."*

In his book *Morality and Beyond*† Paul Tillich avoids all these pitfalls except one: the attempt to define the moral imperative as self-realization. Even his definition of this imperative as "the command to become what one potentially is, a *person* within a community of persons," does not change the fact that he has subordinated the moral to a transmoral reality which replaces the intrinsic value of moral action by its function in leading to one's integration and self-realization. The dualism that Tillich establishes here between "external law, human or divine," and "the inner law of our true being, of our essential or created nature," only serves to relativize both. Such relativization leads Tillich to the assertion that the unconditional character of a moral decision refers not to its content but its form and that "the doubt concerning the justice of a moral act does not contradict the certainty of its ultimate seriousness." "We can lose our salvation even when we do something objectively right, if we do it with an uneasy conscience," writes Tillich. "The unity and consistency of the moral personality are more important than its subjection to a truth that endangers this unity."‡ This opposition between the subjective unity and the objective right is a false

* Martin Heidegger, *Being and Time*, trans. by John Macquarrie and Edward Robinson (New York: Harper & Row, 1962), pp. 325, 344, 204.
† Paul Tillich, *Morality and Beyond* (New York: Harper & Row, 1962).
‡ *Ibid.*, p. 69.

dichotomy which takes the heart out of an ethical action, in which my conviction of the rightness of my act must include the fact that I am called to respond in my own way and with my whole self to a transubjective demand which is not dependent upon the consistency of my moral personality.

For all this, Tillich is more successful than any of the other thinkers we have discussed in establishing a transmoral source of morality which is itself moral. This is clearest in his discussion of justice and love. Tillich sees love as supplementing abstract justice by mutual participation, involvement, and communion. "Justice is taken into love if the acknowledgment of the other person as person is not detached but involved. In this way, love becomes the ultimate moral principle, including justice and transcending it at the same time."* Such love enhances justice while the justice in it is an unconditional element that protects it against its own sentimentalization. Love "listens" to the particular situation as abstract justice cannot do, and acts in relation to the concrete demands of this situation. Love, therefore, becomes the alternative to moral universalism and moral relativism: It preserves the eternal yet changes in response to the unique. At the same time moral habit, "the tables of laws," is a gift of grace so long as it is not elevated to absolute validity and substituted for agape and its power to listen to the voice of the "now."

But can we really accept Tillich's assumption that "the presence of the divine Ground of Being toward and in the human spirit opens man's eyes and ears to the moral demand implicit in the concrete situation"? Are Tillich's "Ground of Being" and his "true and essential self" sufficiently grounded in the concrete situation of address and response that his agape-filled man will be able to experience the other's side of the relationship and know him not as a "person" in general but as a unique and concrete "Thou"? We must also ask whether Tillich has not gone too far toward removing the "fear and trembling" of the moral conflict when he defines the "good conscience" of agape as being

---

* *Ibid.*, p. 39.

as much *above* the moral realm as the "bad conscience" of the law is below it.

These questions lead to a still more basic question concerning the Pauline dualism between law and grace which lies at the heart of Tillich's "beyond morality." The commanding law drives man to evil, says Tillich, because it is "the expression of what man essentially is and therefore ought to be, but what he actually is not."* Grace permeates everyone's life as the healing powers that overcome the split between our essential and actual being and make it possible to fulfill the moral command. Or rather it is fulfilled for us. "What was demanded, now is given. . . . We ask for a grace as unconditional as the moral imperative and as infinite as our failure to fulfill it." This is asking too much of grace and too little of ourselves. The moral command is not fulfilled *despite* our failure but with our spontaneity and freedom, sustained as it is by the grace that comes to us from within and from without.

"Morality does not depend on any concrete religion," writes Tillich; "it is religious in its very essence." Yet the ultimate ground of morality, for Tillich, is beyond the moral, and the moral itself tends to be devalued into a lesser, external, objective sphere of human existence to be distinguished from the inner sphere of authenticity, love, and grace.

> The question of moral motivation can be answered only transmorally. For the law demands, but cannot forgive: it judges, but cannot accept. Therefore, forgiveness and acceptance, the conditions of the fulfillment of the law, must come from something above the law, or more precisely, from something in which the split between our essential being and our existence is overcome, and healing power has appeared.†

Tillich not only splits the self, he splits God—into one who judges and one who forgives. "Torah" in the Hebrew Bible, in contrast, means neither isolated law nor isolated grace nor a

* *Ibid.*, p. 53.
† *Ibid.*, p. 64.

combination of the two. It is not a sphere of "unbearable tensions," as Tillich sees it, but the life-giving stream through which man attains to authentic existence. It is not objective and universal any more than it is subjective and merely particular. It is God's instruction and demand in the concrete historical situation.

Martin Buber understands conscience not as originally bad, as Tillich does, but as "the individual's awareness of what in his unique and non-repeatable created existence he is intended to be." It is this same conscience which summons us to "obedient listening," to "experiencing the other side of the relationship," and to responding to the address that comes to us through the unique other in the concrete situation. "It is always the religious which bestows, the ethical which receives," writes Buber. "Every ethos has its origin in a revelation." But the religious to Buber means a personal relationship with the Absolute, a bond between the Absolute and concrete in which the immediacy of religious reality is the ever-new source of the ethical. The good grows out of the actual present concreteness of the unique direction toward God which we apprehend and realize in our meeting with the everyday. "Every revelation is revelation of human service to the goal of creation, in which service man authenticates himself."* One cannot meet the eternal Thou by turning away from the temporal Thou: One cannot find one's direction to God apart from "the lived concrete."

There can be no split for Buber, therefore, between the religious and the ethical, no "transmoral conscience" which lends the moral a conditional validity. Ethical decision for Buber is both the current decision about the immediate situation that confronts one and through this the decision with one's whole being for God. I experience my uniqueness as a designed or preformed one, entrusted to me for execution, yet everything

* Martin Buber, *Eclipse of God: Studies in the Relation between Religion and Philosophy* (New York: Harper Torchbooks, 1957), "Religion and Ethics," p. 98; Martin Buber, *Good and Evil: Two Interpretations* (New York: Scribner's Paperback, 1961), p. 142.

that affects me participates in this execution. I discover the mystery waiting for me not in myself, therefore, but in the encounter with the other that I meet. The "suspension of the ethical," writes Buber in a commentary on Kierkegaard's *Fear and Trembling*, in our age leads to honest men who lie and compassionate men who torture—to men who sincerely believe that brother-murder will prepare the way for brotherhood. The cure for this situation is the rise of a new conscience which will summon men to guard with the innermost power of their souls against the confusion of the relative with the Absolute. But man's meeting with the Absolute means to Buber just the fundamental ethical, the lived concrete, the covenant with the present and the unique that lies at the heart of the life of dialogue.

That the doctrine of a transmoral conscience is a dangerous one that may mean the destruction of morality, Tillich recognizes in the cases of Luther and Heidegger. Yet he does not take the problem further than to state that we cannot dismiss the transmoral conscience without dismissing religion and depth psychology at the same time. "It is impossible *not* to transcend the moral conscience because it is impossible to unite a *sensitive* and a *good* conscience," Tillich writes. But what if the *best* conscience were precisely the one which refused to transcend and did not want to reach a "joyful conscience" that may accord well with one's inner state but not with moral conflict and tragedy?

The title of Paul Tillich's book is *Morality and Beyond.* "Transmoral morality," in subtle contrast, implies that there is a morality which transcends the "moral," in the limited sense of the objectified, the articulated, the codified, the legalized, but that at the same time there is no area of *human existence* that is "beyond the moral." The attempt to establish a transmoral area of human existence, even as the source of the moral, falsifies the human situation and endangers all morality. Even Søren Kierkegaard's "suspension of the ethical" in the name of an unmediated, I-Thou relationship to God (*Fear and Trembling*) ultimately means a disastrous relativization of the ethical—the choice *between* God and creation, the rejection of society and culture for the lonely relation of the "Single One" to God, losing thereby all check on the reality of the voice that addresses one.

For some the form of the crisis of values in our time is a religious one: When they no longer have a concept of the Absolute or a sense of divine revelation or belief, they feel shaken. But actually we are all inheritors of this crisis whether we believe or not and whether we care about the question of belief or not. There is no one in the modern world who can claim to live in any other culture than a purely secular one. Thomas Merton was a man who spent a good deal of his life in a Trappist monastery. But his greatness is that he never left the secular world. He never ceased to contend in it, in book after book, until his unfortunate death. We cannot leave the world for someplace holy. We are all sharers in the crisis of values. We are sharers of the eclipse of the human.

EDUCATION

Apart from everything that we might have to say about the special eclipse of modern man, what makes it necessary to speak of the human image and what is the heart of its hiddenness is that the human is not given either in myself or in the other or in all of us put together. I cannot capture the "human" either in sociology or anthropology or psychology or philosophy. I cannot get the human by any of these conceptual attempts, I cannot locate the human. I am thrown back on the image precisely in its hiddenness.

Is the "hidden image" a contradiction? On the contrary, the nature of an image is precisely that it comes into being and ceases to be. The image needs its hiddenness for its revelation. The central paradox of the Hebrew Bible is that man is created in the image of the imageless God. A similar paradox lies at the heart of the human image and education: The human cannot be revealed in the sense of bringing an already finished product out of the closet and laying it on the table. I have no right to say that man *is* before man *becomes* in each new situation, and what man becomes in each new situation I cannot say was *in* him potentially and is now actual. It exists *between* and *among* us. History is not carried in the history books. It is carried in and by us, and it also carries us. The same is true of the human image of which history is a part. It is carried by us, and it carries us.

The word *education*, taken back to its Latin roots, is closest to *educe*. Scientific method at its best is a combination of deduction —deducing from a general law to a particular—and induction— the empirical method which moves from many particulars to a generalization which, in the form of a hypothesis, one may again use in deductive form as a general law. But when Socrates was the gadfly of Athens who buttonholed the young men and asked them, "What are you doing and why are you doing it?," he was not deducing and he was not inducing. He was *educing*—drawing forth, drawing out of—and that is the meaning of education. He was, by the same token, educating himself; for education is a two-way street. His dialectic was so much a value in itself to him that he looked forward to nothing better or other than that in the Elysian Fields, if indeed there were such. He would seek out Achilles and the other great heroes and carry on his "educing" with them!

In what way is this drawing forth accomplished in education? Despite the bewildering variety of the goals of education, all of them may in the end be subsumed under the tendency of every society to educate its young into *its* image of man. For the Spartans this means the image of a certain sort of warrior and by the same token the repression of any artistic or imaginative traits that might make a man less martial. In Athens at its glory we have poets, sculptors, mathematicians, and philosophers of a depth and brilliance that have never again been equaled in world history. This image had greater flexibility than the Spartan, though we must not forget, as John Dewey tirelessly pointed out, that the whole of this great culture existed on the foundation of slaves. It took for granted, therefore, *two* images of man, one of whom, the barbarian, was born to serve, by hard and unremitting toil, to give the foundation to the life of leisure, freedom, and contemplation of the other. Hence contemplation was considered dignified and activity mean and slavish. The Romans had the image of the citizen—both active and thoughtful. The Chinese had the scholar, and the Israelites a man open to the deepest of emotions who could live and decide in the face of nature and history.

Our culture is no less bewildering, indeed more. We have pictures on television of a child in some Communist-dominated country being taught that capitalism is bad, Communism good. This is "propaganda." Such a child is "brainwashed"—as if children in America are not taught that Communism is bad and capitalism good! To some the goal of education is adaptation and adjustment to the culture, to society—a fallacy in itself, since society is continually changing. There are people who have a comfortable image either of a society that does not change, would not change, should not change, or once, in "the good old days," did not change.

A second group are those who regard education as a training in specialization. It is a well-known fact that man has become man in part through specialization, that we could not have the civilization that we have, including flights to the moon, without a complexity of specialization of labor far beyond the dreams of Adam Smith. Then education becomes training people to realize their potentialities and hopefully, by the theory of laissez-faire, to contribute to the harmony of the whole; or training people to fulfill the needs of society through supply and demand, subsidization, or pressure.

Then, of course, there are those who feel the threat of the change of values, particularly social and political values. They believe that education ought to be education for one or another sort of conformity, like Governor Ronald Reagan who does not believe that professors should be given tenure since tenure makes it difficult to get rid of those people who raise questions in the minds of students. At the time the local branch of the American Legion in Bronxville, New York, attacked some of my colleagues at Sarah Lawrence for participating in a banquet at the Waldorf Astoria, I got the overwhelming impression, through reading what the Legion wrote, that they thought it was un-American to teach people to think because you could not be sure that the conclusions would turn out to be the "right," the "patriotic," the American Legion type of conclusions. By this standard, "propaganda" is teaching students to think since they may draw the "wrong" conclusions, and "education" is teaching them the "right" conclusions, those that agree with the American Legion!

Being myself a product of progressive education, I can at least make the contrast. We were taught that "Thinking is seeing relations," and we saw relations in everything. We were encouraged to be socially aware and socially conscious without adequate preparation for the conflicts such awareness might lead to. Progressive education was based in important part on the educational theory of John Dewey. Dewey had an enormous impact on American and even some European education, in particular his notions of "learning by doing" and not detaching a man's education from his environment. Rather a man should evolve in such a way that he can by conscious adaptation do what animals must do much more painfully over aeons of evolution. Therefore, education becomes a type of flexible, conscious adjustment to the problems that confront man in the situation. This is an organic, evolutionary, process view of education, which holds that mind and body, action, and thought are by no means separate.

One thing that the Deweyite approach and the Great Books approach have in common is that they tend to locate *where* education takes place. The Hutchins approach locates education in the books, in the universal ideas, and man's mind becomes a sort of wax that may be imprinted or formed. To use an analogy of Martin Buber's, the old education is like a funnel through which you pour ideas into the student's mind. For John Dewey and the progressivists, in contrast, the education is in the child, waiting to be unfolded. The teacher is only the person who pumps up what is already there.

Applying the image of man to education, I would say that education cannot be located anywhere. Education in a deliberate, selective, and intentional form goes on in a classroom, between a teacher and a student, between students, in a laboratory, on a fieldtrip or wherever. More important, who is to say that when someone reads a book or plays a musical instrument or performs a scientific experiment that the education is in the experiment or in the experimenter or in the teacher? Obviously what is taking place is happening in all these together and obviously too not as a mere sum of them. What happens is an event of the "between." It is in this sense, and not as either funnel or pump, that the teacher must be understood. We have said that moral values rest on the image of man in such a way that there is no higher abstract formulation or even authority for morality. But what about those who live in situations where they have only destructive images of man? Such a person may not be hermetically sealed in these images; yet it is still something of a miracle or grace if he is able to respond beyond them. What sometimes happens, however, is that such a person stays shut up within himself until the time that a teacher senses a possibility within him that no one has ever sensed. Perhaps it is a bit of inwardness that only waits for an invitation to become embodied in a response. Perhaps it is an interest in music or in art or a poem or doing a puzzle. These are some of the great, not only educating but *humanizing*, events in the lives of children— because here and there there is such a teacher.

One of the most meaningful things that a teacher can do is to open to the student images of man that would not be accessible to him without their having come alive to the teacher first. This can happen in the way a teacher reads a poem or dramatizes an event or helps the student to see Lincoln in his historical situation so that suddenly Lincoln is present to the student and speaks to him.

But what about the paradox that in our day the very attempt to bring forth the image of man from its hiddenness often leaves it more hidden? We live in the age of mass education, and we cannot settle anymore for the idea that only certain people deserve to be educated. Yet the consequences of mass education are sometimes quite incredible. I find it hard to comprehend a class of two thousand as being a class at all. Other places there is not even a class. Instead there is a TV hookup. There is nothing wrong with TV. Like other audiovisual techniques, it can bring a far more widespread image than the traditional classroom makes possible. But it is disastrous if you substitute TV for the presence of the teacher who knows the student. Or if you have a brilliant lecture and you do not have some way in which the student can give back his impressions and wrestle with the teacher. Only the latter can teach him that it is not a matter of getting the subject right or wrong but of making it his own, bringing himself in relationship to it, and discovering that most difficult problem of all—what to select and what to let lie.

Most of our education is a problem of selection. We are bombarded not just by TV and radio but even by our education itself. It is absolutely overwhelming, compulsive, obsessive. The average education is calculated to stultify the minds of most students by its sheer mass *and* because the student is taught to abstract the person from what he says. He is taught to lift out ideas and information as intellectual questions and therefore not to hear them from where the person says them. The student is taught the methods of monologue. He learns to conduct a brilliant dialectic with no sense of the other person, whether it be the writer, his teacher, or his fellow student.

Then perhaps it may happen that the old-fashioned teacher, who really cares and who is laughed at by his colleagues who are busy getting ahead, will give back to the student the human image. This image of the human is at the same time an image of otherness. It is not you that is given to you. It is something, someone to whom you can respond. Even in those human sciences that try to be most scientific today, such as psychology, sociology, political science, and economics, leaving out the image of man as a center introduces a fundamental distortion which can hardly be corrected. For in the end you are going to see whatever you see—whether it is the tribe that is being investigated or sociological man that is being sliced up—in abstraction from the human image in its wholeness and uniqueness *and* from the personal standpoint from which you go to meet what you investigate. You cannot know the human except as *you* take part. That is what the good teacher invites you to do. Like the Mock Turtle, he says, "Will you, won't you, will you, won't you, will you, won't you join the dance?" If you do not join the dance, then you may know an enormous amount, but you have never acquired any education. For true education does not mean stamping on you this culture and this society. It is drawing forth what you can become in response to tradition.

There is no choice necessary here between tradition, on the one hand, and freedom and creativity, on the other. On the contrary, tradition is the very stepping-stone to freedom and creativity if it is presented and met in such a way that your response to it is your fresh creation. There ought to be a new presentation of the Civil War every year, for every new class of students, for every single student. Each poem should take on new meaning every time a new student reads that poem and another teacher teaches it.

When I first came to teach at Sarah Lawrence College, I thought that the only real teaching possible was in classes of twelve or thirteen and in individual conferences. I no longer think that that is true. Real dialogue, real teaching, the real coming forth of the hidden image are possible in many places. But I do believe with all my heart that one has to fight within the structure, to know one's actual situation, *and* to admit to oneself when it becomes impossible to make teaching meaningful within the structure. You are a part of the structure, and it is no good saying to yourself, "If only I were someone else!" You are yourself, and you must discover what *you* can do in this structure. This does not mean the abolition of all educational structures. No one can take Mark Hopkins literally when he says, "A college is a log with a student on one end of it and a teacher on the other." We are all part of a structure or institution. We have to work with this structure or change it to a new, more meaningful one. Yet no structure is meaningful in itself, but only as we bring our trusting and our contending to it. Within whatever structure we find ourselves or whatever structure we build, what we fight for is the revelation of the hidden human image.

How about those who feel today in ever-growing number that there is *no* good structure, that "compulsory miseducation" obscures the hidden image and that "deschooling society" is the only way to the liberation of man? School, the very institution which above all ought to reveal the hidden image of man, is one of the chief instruments of its eclipse. The fault lies not with the teachers, says George Leonard, but with the society which requires its educators to *prevent* the new generation from changing in any deep or significant way. The IQs of high-school dropouts are higher than the IQs of high-school graduates, but both experience alike that fragmenting of their lives which school teaches—"segregating senses from emotions from intellect, building boxes for art and abstractions, divorcing the self from the reality and the joy of the present moment." The absence of joy decreases the effectiveness of the learning process "until the human being is operating hesitantly, grudgingly, fearfully at only a tiny fraction of his potential." At the same time the perception of the student is progressively narrowed: "The entire education process . . . may best be viewed as a funnel through which every child is squeezed into an ever-narrowing circle; at the end there is room only for a single set of 'right answers.' " Of all the wrongs with which the world is filled—war, disease, famine, slavery—"none is deeper or more poignant than the systematic, innocent destruction of the human spirit that, all too often, is the hidden function of every school."*

Charles Reich in *The Greening of America* puts the paradox of the schools into a total theory—that of the Corporate State which molds not only producers but consumers and destroys any real personal life in the process. The student is trained for his place in the machinery of the State not merely by learning to perform a function but by being made to become that function: "to see and judge himself and others in terms of functions, and to abandon any aspect of self, thinking, questioning, feeling, loving, that has no utility for either production or consumption

* George B. Leonard, *Education and Ecstasy* (New York: Delacorte Press, 1968; Delta Books [paperback], 1968), pp. 7, 11, 20, 110, 112.

in the Corporate State." Consumer training, no less significant than job training for the loss of the self, consists in school "of preventing the formation of individual consciousness, taste, aesthetic standards, self-knowledge, and the ability to create one's own satisfactions." Solitude, separateness, undirected time, silence, activity, and initiative are not permitted, since these might get in the way of the self's dependence upon the State and of the development of a substitute self which, appropriately approved and rewarded by the State, will get along better than the real self that might-have-been. Textbooks and examinations teach students to stop thinking and to start obeying. "Public school is 'obedience school' "—unquestioning acceptance of and respect for authority in all areas, including facts and ideas, simply because of its position. Everything is hierarchy—competition for one's "place in life"—similar to what the student will encounter in the outside world. The school keeps the child off the streets and remolds his thinking through force-feeding a whole set of values about business, competition, success, and the American way of life—all "amid a pervasive atmosphere of dishonesty and hypocrisy." The school is the beginning of the "meritocracy" of functional usefulness. "The youngster who gets A's is well on his way to being suitable material for the Corporate State." Although there are no prison bars or locked doors, the student is no freer than the inmate of a penitentiary or insane asylum, and like him is denied the privacy, liberty, solitude, freedom to try different forms of relationship, and the degree of sovereignty which the self needs to develop. "The school is a brutal machine for destruction of the self, controlling it, heckling it, hassling it into a thousand busy tasks, a thousand noisy groups, never giving it a moment to establish a knowledge within."*

> Probably the saddest thing in America is the fate of most of its teenagers. At mid-teens, no matter how oppressive the Corporate State, there is still a moment when life is within their grasp. There are a few years when they pulse to music, know the

* Charles A. Reich, *The Greening of America* (New York: Random House, 1970), pp. 130–137.

beaches and the sea, value what is raunchy, wear clothes that express their bodies, flare against authority, seek new experience, know how to play, laugh, feel, and cherish one another. But soon their senses are dulled, their strength put under restraint, their minds lobotomized; bodies still young, cut off from selves, they walk the windowless, endless corridors of the Corporate State.°

In *Deschooling Society* Ivan Illich recognizes that what is at stake in the cultural revolution for which he calls is nothing less than the liberation of man, the image of man, man himself. Not only do the poor get no equality from obligatory schools with their myth that education is tied to school and learning to teaching, but the mere existence of school has an antieducational effect all over the world by discouraging and disabling the poor from taking control of their own learning. What is more, the very existence of obligatory school divides any society into the two realms of the "academic" and the "nonacademic," with the result that education becomes unworldly and the world becomes noneducational and uncreative. Illich objects to this split in as strong terms as Buber and Bonhoeffer have objected to the split between the "holy" and the "everyday." School by its very nature makes a total claim on the time and energies of students, which makes the teacher into custodian, preacher, and therapist, cancels out the student's freedom in every sphere, and warps his nature. The distinctions between morality, legality, and personal worth thereby blurred, every transgression becomes a multiple offense—breaking rules, acting immorally, and proving oneself personally worthless all at the same time. Only the segregation of children within the magic womb of school with its primitive and deadly serious otherworldly atmosphere could make possible the child's submission to such authority and his internalizing of it until he shares the prejudice of society against those discriminated against and the extra recognition which is accorded to the privileged!†

° *Ibid.*, p. 156.
† Ivan D. Illich, *Deschooling Society* (New York: Harper & Row, 1971), pp. 8, 24, 30–33.

One of the value myths that schools instill in young people is that everything can be measured, including their imaginations and man himself. "In a schooled world the road to happiness is paved with a consumer's index." Schools break learning up into subject "matters," build their curricula on these prefabricated blocks, and teach the students to "think" in the same way. "People who have been schooled down to size let unmeasured experience slip out of their hands." The pedagogical hubris of school—manipulating others for their own salvation—carries over logically to warmaking and civil repression. "Pedagogical warfare in the style of Vietnam will be increasingly justified as the only way of teaching people the superior value of unending progress." The hidden curricula of schooling implant in the citizen the myth that bureaucracies are benevolent and that increased production will provide a better life, while developing in them the habit of self-defeating consumption of services and alienating production. Needs are created faster than satisfactions can be, and the earth is consumed in the process of trying to meet these artificial needs. "Everywhere nature becomes poisonous, society inhumane, and the inner life is invaded and personal vocation smothered." By discouraging the pupil from taking personal responsibility, the school leads many to a kind of spiritual suicide which is the logical corollary of the ethos of ever-increasing consumption that is at the root of physical depredation, social polarization, and psychological passivity. Finally, Illich sums up the obscuring of the hidden image in the very mythical figure that I have used as a symbol of the sterile rebellion of modern man—the Modern Prometheus. When man's value is measured by his ability to consume, man becomes the idol of his handiworks, or more exactly the furnace which burns up the values produced by his tools. At the heart of the Promethean fallacy, says Illich, is the consumer ethos, and this ethos is itself "a corruption in man's self-image." *

Ivan Illich's call for the "deschooling of society" and the "de-

* *Ibid.*, pp. 40, 50, 60, 74, 110, 113 f.

institutionalization of values" appears at first glance to be an effort to abandon all formal education in favor of that spontaneous and unplanned education outside of school, which is, as he repeatedly asserts, where most real learning takes place. We have, indeed, honed our paradox to such a fine point that it might seem as if all that is left of it is that attempts at deliberate education, while undertaken in the name of revealing the hidden human image, in fact work only to obscure it. Yet none of these authors would disagree with what we earlier said about the necessity of structures within which we fight for meaningful education. None would say that we must entirely abolish deliberate, planned education, though most would want to abolish *compulsory* education. All would affirm our original approach to genuine education as the revealer par excellence of the hidden human image.

Ivan Illich not only calls for radical innovation in formal education accompanied by radical political changes and changes in the organization of production. He also calls for "radical changes in man's image of himself as an animal which needs school." This implies the rejection of the almost universally held notion that qualification must precede employment, that schooling must precede productive work, that men are prepared for the "secular world" by incarceration in any sacred precinct, be it monastery, synagogue, or school. He believes instead that the education that schools are failing to provide could be acquired more successfully in the setting of the family, of work and communal activity. This not only means education *in* the world. It also means education with and by the world through allowing ourselves to be surprised by otherness and by the Other, for "it is precisely for surprise that true education prepares us." This dialogue with the Other also includes a genuine dialogue with tradition, with communal memories, whether they be stored in a library or the workings of a factory:

> Education implies a growth of an independent sense of life and
> a relatedness which go hand in hand with increased access to, and

use of, memories stored in the human community. The educational institution provides the focus for this process. This presupposes a place within the society in which each of us is awakened by surprise; a place of encounter in which others surprise me with their liberty and make me aware of my own. *

Every society has an image of man it wishes to educate in its young, and the teacher properly represents the society in this task. Yet he does not fulfill his task through imposing an image but through confronting his student with it and through allowing him to develop in free dialogue with it. Nor will the image the student develops ever be identical with that of the teacher or the society he represents. It can at best be a creative response to that image. Education must certainly be social and political education for life in a democracy. But it cannot be an "instrument of national policy," as James Bryant Conant, Dwight Eisenhower, and some prominent educators once suggested.†

The true teacher has always been aware that above all he is confronting his students with images of man and that it is precisely through this confrontation that he *educates* the student. The unique response of every student to the image of man is what draws out of him the potentialities of becoming and makes him at last into an "educated" man—one who has made tradition his own and thereby has become more uniquely himself. This is clear enough in the study of literature, but it is also central in philosophy, the social sciences, and even in psychology when it is approached in a humanistic fashion. This recognition of the central significance of the image of man is opposed, of course, to the view of education as mere training in techniques or adaptation to the environment. It is equally opposed to the focus on the classics or the Great Books as abstract, objective truth to be apprehended by the analytical intelligence and stamped on the unformed mind.

* Ivan D. Illich, *Celebration of Awareness: A Call for Institutional Revolution*, with an Introduction by Erich Fromm (Garden City, N.Y.: Doubleday & Co., 1970).
† Report on "American Education and International Tensions," approved by N.E.A. at its annual meeting in 1949, signed by Conant, Eisenhower, et al.

Education must, of course, help the student to become a mature adult, an active member of family and community groups, a citizen of democracy. But it must also educate him to live in a world of stresses and strains, of crises and wars—a world of "the death of God" in which we no longer have a direction of authentic existence, in which not only our values but the source and ground of these values is relativized, called in question, shattered, or rationalized away. Our greatest educational need today is precisely the education of character, the education of men who will be ready to respond to unforeseen historical and personal situations with integrity, with flexibility, with openness, with strength.

The image of man offers a fruitful alternative to three classical educational dilemmas. It does not have to ask whether human nature is *evil* and to be controlled or *good* and to be developed. Rather it confronts and evokes, trusts and encourages, guides and sustains. Secondly, it need not be hung up on the question of whether education is for the sake of preserving the traditions of the past or creating the future. It sets the student in creative relation to the past and just thereby enables him to respond to the new situation from the ground of basic attitudes which his dialogue with the past has engendered in him. It frees him from the sterile conflict between conformity and rebellion and allows him to find a ground of his own from which to relate and contribute to the social whole. Thirdly, it need not anguish over the question of whether the teacher is educator or propagandist so long as it makes the heart of education that genuine dialogue in which the teacher presents and points to images of man, yet encourages the student to respond to them—accepting or rejecting—in his own unique way. The image of man avoids the fallacies of social psychology and educational theory that have plagued American education—the fallacies of education for adjustment, of the introjection of the Generalized Other, of instrumentalism and environmentalism, of "culture" and the Great Books, of education as the development of potentialities, the realizing of the self, or the forwarding of national policy. Education which simply adapts one to society does not fit one to live in and contend with society. It robs society itself of the creative and unique contribution that a modern Socrates or a modern Amos might make who stood his ground and witnessed for a true word in a historical situation. Even education for the space age must be subject to the challenge and test of what it is in our national way of life that, through the competition of science and arms, we are trying to defend.

One of the sad things about even the best of educators at even the most enlightened and progressive of institutions is the tendency to keep educational values in one compartment and practical economic necessities in another. One of the reasons for this is the tendency in our culture to regard values as static ideals—a sort of inspirational icing on the cupcake of the quotidian— rather than as a direction of movement which informs one's decisions concerning change, starting from the situation in which one finds oneself. The very notion of the inherent conflict between the ideal and the practical assumes a static nature of both. No ideal that disregards the actual situation from which one starts is worth anything. But a "practicality" which regards the situation as unalterable and abandons the task of finding real direction in favor of meeting each crisis with ad hoc decisions is only specious.

Another reason for the gap between educational values and practical economics is the problem of communication. The structures of most academic institutions, even the small ones, tend to obstruct quite as much as to promote communication. "Values" often become monolithic abstractions imposed from above by presidents, deans, and committees, and the real meaning of education to the student and even to the teacher is lost sight of. Instead of continuing dialogue between administration, faculty, departments, and students, out of which the practical implementation of educational values should arise, formalism and mistrust all too often become the order of the day.

When I spoke to a small group of professors and administrators at the University of California at Berkeley on Martin

Buber's approach to education, Chancellor Edward W. Strong said that he was fascinated with the notion of education as dialogue. It must be fine for a small college like Sarah Lawrence, he added, but he could not see how it could be applied to a large university like Berkeley. There can be dialogue in lectures, too, I replied, but the student must have some chance of checking what he has learned with the teacher. And if in the present structure he has no such chance, then some of the vast sums that go into buildings and scientific research should be diverted to this purpose.

I did not know at the time that Berkeley had classes of two thousand. But this conversation and the parting words of the chancellor—that he had to go to a meeting where he expected hidden microphones to be planted in the room by his opponents —came back to me with new meaning at the time of the Berkeley student riots. The large and impersonal nature of the University of California plus the atmosphere of mutual mistrust were quite as important factors in the rebellion as the issue of freedom of speech. It is ironic—indeed tragic—that an era of unprecedented expanding education should be an era of contracting contact between teacher and student. How can one reconcile education as dialogue with the programmed teaching box? With the competitive pressure of grades and examinations which results in the instrumentalization of knowledge, the dehumanization of the humanities, the false departmentalization and provincialization of knowledge? With the gap between the "two cultures"? Values cannot be just the possession of the elders who know better. However much the student rioters all over the country may be "problematic rebels," they are not rebels without a cause. Teaching, curriculum, requirements, grades, examinations, large classes—all suggest that even the cost of student protests and demonstrations may be a legitimate educational expense. This is true, of course, only if it promotes communication. But in a situation where there is no dialogue, sometimes even these negative forms, however distorted by subjective emotion and political motives, may be a beginning point of communication.

A prime cause for anxiety of the younger generation vis-à-vis the older is the confusion of equality with the rejection of authority, or the confusion of authoritarianism with legitimate authority. The sense of being dominated by a group that one finds alien and that one fears leads to the natural, but nonetheless false, notion that all that is needed is to establish complete power equality and there will be no further problem. On the contrary, there will still be the same problems of communication, the same questions of what do you do about these problems and where you go from the situation in which you find yourself. Nor does it follow that all authority is irrational, bad, and illegitimate. Sometimes one person washes the dishes and another wipes. Sometimes one person makes one suggestion and another person another. The belligerent rejection of elders as "irrelevant," as not having experience that counts, as deserving neither attention nor respect, leads not to freedom but to the tyranny of the peer group.

This can be a much more terrible tyranny than that of an authority above one. For one is delivered without appeal to the authority of those who dominate the group. In order to be "in" with this group one must go along with whatever they say. A Sarah Lawrence student came back from a ski weekend and confessed to her teacher in the "Marriage and the Family" class that she felt guilty because she was not willing to exchange partners as all the others did. She felt on the defensive because there was nothing in the atmosphere that confirmed her in her own life-style when it did not correspond to the group's idea of fun. The result is conformity masking as "doing your own thing." For what, in fact, does this famous slogan of youth mean if you do not know who *you* are? You cannot know who you are if you have not let yourself come forth in response to a call greater than yourself, or if you have simply concentrated on *not* doing what someone older than you has told you to do, defining your freedom as just that. It is very difficult to win a ground from which to take a spontaneous and free action. It is necessary to go through being a Modern Promethean before becoming a Modern Job. But it is wrong to call reactive rebellion real freedom. It is not a response from a ground of one's own but simply takes its cue and coloration from what one is reacting against. Its rejection of authority in the present is as automatic and unfree as its submission to it was in the past. Such rebellion takes place for rebellion's sake rather than because one really stands for something. Here if anywhere we find the "rebel without a cause."

All too often the modern university offers halfway measures as panaceas—survey courses, civilization courses, synthesis courses. When I left a gigantic state university, I was scheduled to teach an eleven-week course in the whole history of the humanities to make up to science seniors for the liberal arts that they had not had! In a small and topflight college that I visited recently, on the other hand, the standards were so high and the requirements so rigid that anything that might decently be called liberal arts appeared to be choked out by the goal of preparing a few students for graduate school. One of the most serious issues of the economics of the quality of education is the encroachment on liberal arts education by technical training, early specialization, graduate-school preparation, and a whole atmosphere of competitive pressure that makes study for its own sake almost an impossibility. Equally serious is the fragmentation of the liberal arts so that they themselves become mere special fields of study, and the wholeness of man—the human image—is lost sight of. Worst of all is the fact that the serious but economically deprived student often feels himself compelled to be purely technical and practical, whereas the economically privileged student often regards education as the "cultural" ornament of the leisure class.

The title of a recent essay, "The Student as Nigger,"* dramatizes the revolt on the campus, a phalanx of the army of young rebels that is even more significant than the subculture of the hippies. When I asked the president of a small but highly respected men's college in the East what changes he had observed in his college since the last time I had lectured there, he did not

* Jerry Farber, The Student as Nigger: Essays and Stories (New York: Simon & Schuster Paperbacks, 1970).

speak, as I expected, of the heightened sense of aliveness, the greater social concern, the increase in the intellectual seriousness of faculty and students. Instead he put forward just one word: *hostility*. To him the dissident students, the new political awareness and activity, the insistence on student participation and representation in important decision-making, the protests and demonstrations, the New Left politicos, and the anything–but– Ivy League costumes of the demihippies all spell the disruption and dissolution of the happy communal harmony that this relatively isolated and homogeneous college once enjoyed. But it is in the great multiversities—the Berkeleys and Columbias—that the revolt on the campus has erupted into the direct action of sit-ins and "confrontations." At times the politicization and polarization are so great as to destroy rather than create any possibility of mutual trust. Yet the "free universities" that are springing up around the country can also be creative forms of protest against academic rigidity and irrelevance and so can dropping out if it does not simply lead to tuning out. It is a good thing that we have so many dropouts today. Perhaps it will account for a lessening of the terror of not "making it." "Making it" is one of the obscenities of our society. What could be more empty than making it in this external sense?

One aspect of the revolt on campus and the free university that is of particular interest is the growing positive trend of a new type of education which might be called "education for openness." At its best this new trend means a growing concern on the part of both teachers and students for genuine dialogue and open learning in the classrooms, for education of sensory awareness, for the recognition that even though the goal of education cannot be the same as that of group therapy, there are dynamic group processes that take place and that may be recognized and understood without manipulation of or threat to the students. At its worst, the goals of this education for openness become too confused, and any experience, however joyful or terrifying, any breakthrough of suppressed consciousness or emotion, any gut-level hostility is accounted of value in itself and a magic substitute not only for the established academic disciplines but even for the most elementary faithfulness. The student no longer finds it necessary or even desirable to be open and respond to what a writer, a painter, a teacher, or a fellow classmate may be saying. The revolution in education at whose doorstep we seem to be standing may lead to the release of untold potential for learning and understanding. But it also may lead to a new mindlessness in which all careful thought and patient learning are put down in favor of the easy insight or "spontaneous" feeling!

There is one dominant motif of the contemporary cacophony that young people have not only reacted to but appropriated as a drumbeat of their own life-music. This is the dualism between thought and feeling, that sickness which manifests with unmistakable clarity the absence of personal wholeness *and* the absence of genuine dialogue in our time. This dualism is expressed in the first instance in an overwhelming mass of technical data, miscellaneous information, specialized knowledge, academic thought, the largest part of which young people experience as either peripheral or entirely irrelevant to their lives. In reacting against this, however, they have attempted to break through to "pure feeling," real contact, "joy," nonverbal awareness, "gut-level hostility," and have thereby perpetuated and intensified the very dualism that they thought to overcome. The sickness of thought divided from feeling is not cured by turning the psyche upside down. The illusion of pure feeling or of total contact without words is as much a symptom of this illness as detached intellectuality. Both represent an elemental shut-inness which prevents full awareness of the concrete situation, of the other persons and groups, and through them of oneself.

The dangers of this false dichotomy have been pointed out with great clarity and personal honesty by William Bridges, coordinator of the Education Network of the Association for Humanistic Psychology. "Ten years ago I was dismayed to hear Carl Rogers tell a Harvard audience, 'Teaching is, for me, a relatively unimportant and vastly over-rated activity,'" Bridges writes. "Yet, in the next several years, I slowly stopped 'teaching' . . . and gradually shifted to the role of facilitator—the one who helps students learn what they want or need to learn without 'teaching' it to them. . . . I began to acquire . . . a sizeable repertoire of techniques drawn from Gestalt therapy, encounter, psychosynthesis, sensitivity training. . . . Each semester a higher percentage of my class meetings included some unexpected 'experience' for the students. . . . More and more time was spent on ourselves and less and less on literature."

Looking back at this shift from "teacher" to "facilitator," Bridges now recognizes that "there is an implicit conflict between the exhortation to be nonprescriptive and the desire to introduce to the class those wonderful 'experiences' that one enjoys so much." Actually, there is not much difference between taking the class on a fantasy trip and assigning pages and exercises. Bridges also recognizes that there is "an implicit conflict between the humanistic ideal of working with students *where they are* (as the real individuals that they are right now) and the fact of laying a very heavy trip on them (a set of expectations that masquerade as total freedom)." Students who genuinely desire to learn literature rightly feel upstaged when the focus of the class shifts permanently to the group itself and literature is merely used as the jumping-off point for an encounter group.

So-called humanistic education has labored under the erroneous impression that there are "basically only two kinds of learning: experiential and personal learning of the sort that goes on in therapy or in an encounter group, and the acquisition of information about the extra-personal world." "If you accept this view," writes Bridges, "it is natural to conclude that teaching gets in the way of learning because it predetermines the information and precludes intrapersonal encounter." This falsely polarized picture makes it impossible for the teacher to help the student learn to do and perceive in ways that unlock his innate human potential.

I was once present at a demonstration of "open learning"

when the facilitator (a gifted poet who has since given up teaching for therapy) was asked what was in it for him. "I have always found it difficult to express my feelings directly," he responded. "I want to help my students get in contact with theirs." The open-learning teacher tends to live vicariously through his students, as Bridges points out: "We project onto them the hope of and responsibility for finding the relation to reality that we ourselves cannot find." The humanistic ideal all too often "provides an unfortunately convenient rationale for abandoning the learner to his own devices," misrepresenting that loss of meaning which is common to teacher and student "as a guided experiment in freedom and self-discovery."*

In the end the economics of the quality of education means the economics of becoming human in our society. Is our goal "know-how" and success or is it openness and response? Are we educating smart-dealers who know how to turn everything to account or are we educating men and women who will bring themselves in good faith to the meeting with the world that calls them—and us—out? The ultimate economic value of education is the human image—bringing it from hiddenness to manifestation.

* William Bridges, "Thoughts on Humanistic Education, or, Is *Teaching* A Dirty Word?" *Journal of Humanistic Psychology*, Vol. XIII, No. 1 (Winter, 1973), pp. 5, 7 f., 10, 12.

THE
"IVORY TOWER"
AND THE
"WORLD"

From our knowledge of "primitive" religions we are acquainted with *rites de passage,* communal rituals that are designed to help the individual in his perilous transition from one stage of existence to another, as at birth, puberty, marriage, and death. While he is in each stage, the individual possesses the security afforded by the community. His way from stage to stage, in contrast, he has to make as an individual, and the only help the community can offer is its magical rites.

The analogy with our modern commencement exercises is evident. Our more civilized and elaborate rituals are designed to help the graduating student in his solitary and perilous transition from one communal state to another. Both the stage that he is leaving and the one that he is entering are parts of our overall society; yet one of them, curiously enough, is often referred to as an "ivory tower" whereas the other is often referred to simply as "the world." The meaning of this dualism between "ivory tower" and "world" becomes clearer if we look at the similar dualism between the Castle and the Village in Franz Kafka's novel *The Castle.*

In this strange and haunting work the great Czech-Jewish writer depicts the attempt of a man, simply named K., to attain some position in a world in which he has newly arrived, a world in which he is a stranger, an exile, a disreputable man without a recognized place or social role. Denied the right even to spend a night in the Village, K. claims he has been sent for by the Castle in order to be the land surveyor of this Village. This claim, we soon realize, is one that will never be either verified or denied by the Castle itself. It is up to K. to prove his claim by his own actions and attitudes. Like the young man or woman who enters on a vocation, K. begins his stay in the Village with the assertion that he has a calling to which he is called—an assertion which must often seem a ridiculous piece of playacting to the doctor, lawyer, psychotherapist, teacher, or minister who plays his role for the first time. For K., as for them, the problem is to "make good"—to make his assertion stick.

If one does succeed in making one's assertion that one is a doctor, a lawyer, or a businessman "stick," this does not mean that he will have escaped for good from that painful loneliness and responsibility that comes of being a "single one," a separate individual who, if he is a real person, must acquire the courage and the strength both to meet others and to hold his ground when he meets them. To be confirmed in one's social role is not necessarily the same as being confirmed as a person—as the unique person who you are, apart from all social classifications and categories. It may even happen, on the contrary, that the more successful you will be in your social role, the less you will feel confirmed as a person. This is bound to be the case where your social role remains mere "role-playing" and is never integrated in any thoroughgoing fashion with your existence as a person. It is particularly true, unfortunately, of those whose social roles elevate them above the populace and make it necessary for them to profess attitudes, convictions, and ideals that they may not really hold. But it is also likely to be true of anyone who, in his desperate need for the confirmation of others, prefers to sacrifice his personal integrity rather than run the risk of not being established in a definite, socially approved position.

He who enters the transition stage stands, therefore, in the tension point between personal and social confirmation. He cannot resolve this tension by renouncing social confirmation, for no man can live without it: Everybody must play a social role, both as a means to economic livelihood and as the simplest prerequisite of any sort of relations with other people in the family and society. On the other hand, he cannot resolve the tension by sacrificing personal confirmation, for this suppression of his own uniqueness will result in an anxiety that may be more and more difficult to handle as the gap between what he is as a person and the role that he plays widens. Charles Reich, a professor at the Yale Law School, illustrates this very point with the example of a law student:

> The deepest form of role-constraint is the fact that the individual's own "true" self, if still alive, must watch helplessly while the role-self lives, enjoys, and relates to others. A young lawyer, out on a date, gets praised for his sophistication, competence, the important cases he is working on, the important people he knows, his quick and analytical professional mind. His role-self accepts the praise, but his true self withers from lack of recognition, from lack of notice, from lack of appreciation and companionship, and as the young lawyer accepts the praise he feels hollow and lonely.[*]

The more he is confirmed in his social role, the more he is aware in the depths of his being that he, as a person, is not confirmed. But this split between the "true self" and the "role-self" is not inevitable. It is possible for those who have the courage, strength, and personal resources to hold the tension between the two. To stand faithfully in this tension is to insist that one's confirmation in and by society be in some significant sense also a confirmation of oneself as a unique person who does not fit into any social category.

The problem that confronts the person in transition is not a simple passage from a university which provides a secluded shelter for ideas and ideals to a world of stern social and economic realities in which one can only make out by becoming an "or-

[*] Charles A. Reich, *The Greening of America* (New York: Random House, 1970), pp. 140 f.

ganization man" or assuming a "corporate image." The university is not so different from the corporation as all that; nor is the corporation a world hermetically sealed to those personal values and social ideals that the university fosters, along with the advancement of science and culture. Far from being complete opposites, these two worlds each possess a large admixture of the other. The problem of the university intellectual is that of specialized vocabularies no different from the technical universes of discourse that are to be found throughout industry and science. His problem, thus, is the problem of communication, and communication means not only a defined set of terms through which experts may reach practical agreement, but genuine contact between person and person, in which each shares with the other his own relationship to reality. The danger of the university intellectual, on the one side, is that he tends to concentrate on such a specialized and abstract sphere of reality that only a few even of his colleagues can understand the monographs in which he imparts the "more and more" that he has found out about the "less and less." On the other side, however, he tends to fall into that general condition in our culture in which the fact of communication is more important than what is communicated.

The attitude toward popular culture that has made it into a big business of "mass communication" creates even in the universities the incessant danger that education will imperceptibly go over into public relations, concern with the issues of culture into concern with *having* culture, concern with witnessing for and sharing convictions into concern with reaching the widest audience and influencing the largest numbers. A rigged television quiz show is only an obvious symbol of that prostitution of culture that seems to be implicit in the very media in which culture is transmitted. *What* is communicated by our mass media tends to be subordinated to *the way* in which it is communicated. The particulars are less important in themselves than our expectation that there *will* be clever captions in *Time*, sophisticated cartoons and chatter in *The New Yorker*, slick pornography in *Playboy*, and entertaining shows on TV.

A number of years ago I had lunch with a man from *Reader's Digest* to discuss the possibility of an article on Martin Buber, the great contemporary Jewish philosopher to whose thought I had already then devoted ten years of my life. I had many anecdotes I might have told him as to why Martin Buber was to me "the most unforgettable person I have met." Rather than asking me about these, he suggested that I make up a story to the effect that I had been having problems with my wife and had gone to Martin Buber for help with them. Instead of listening to the real events that made this man so remarkable and so unique, the editor wished to fit him into an already formed category of known reader interest. A little later the free-lance journalist who had brought us together said, "What has impressed me about Martin Buber is that he really *listens* to what the other person is saying." At this the editor showed some interest and turning to me said, "Can you give me four rules for listening?" Thinking of the *Reader's Digest* advertisements I had seen on the New York City subways announcing four rules for better sex, four rules for better spelling, four rules for a better vocabulary, I replied, "If I could give you rules, it wouldn't be real listening!"

The clearest mark of the man of our time, says Martin Buber, "is that he cannot really listen to the voice of another. . . . The other is not the man facing him whose claim stands opposite his own in equal right; the other is only his object." In almost the same words, Clara Mayer, for thirty years dean of the New School for Social Research, said to me, "The frightening thing about our culture is that no one listens, no one really *hears* others." In the discussion period after a lecture on youth at a Boston university, I was confronted by nothing but programmed listening. The student who edited the student newspaper said that I had mentioned Job, and Job is a "cop-out." A young woman said that you cannot possibly have dialogue with teachers because they have the power. Another young woman in her midtwenties who had come as my guest asked me, "What *do* you mean by God?" When I said I could not respond to the question put in that way, she rejoined, "That's the trouble with the Establishment. They always want the dialogue on their terms!" Finally, the chancellor, who was present, said, "As I see it, you want the Establishment to be rigid so that youth can have a healthy rebellion." When I say there is no real listening to the other in his otherness, this goes all the way from those who do not even bother to check what the other person means by the terms he uses to those who actually mishear what he says. We are just on the line between not listening and willful misunderstanding, and all too often it is willful misunderstanding that prevails.

At the very time when our communication has become not merely massive but worldwide, actual dialogue between man and man is at a minimum. One reason for this is that in the very act of communicating, our culture objectifies what is communicated so that the person addressed is always everyone and no one but never really you as the person that you are. "You ought to use Stoppette," says the beautiful blonde in the TV program between tabulation of the votes in a national election, and for a moment her brilliant smile and "market personality" make you think she really means you. But the next moment we recall our anonymity or complain, like the brother in the play *A Hatful of Rain*, "I have voted twelve times for Miss Rheingold, but does *she* care about me?"

When one feels oneself addressed only as the anonymous member of a crowd, one loses one's sense of personal responsibility. The man who does not listen is also, as Buber has pointed out, the man who does not feel himself accountable. Unwilling "to answer for the genuineness of his existence," the typical man of today "flees either into the general collective which takes from him his responsibility or into the attitude of a self who has to account to no one but himself." The name with which our age ennobles this unwillingness to answer for the genuineness of our existence is "self-realization." The positive emotional aura that clings to this term takes the place of the difficult task of discovering a direction of meaningful personal existence. In the place of an image of man we substitute an image of our self.

This self, curiously enough, is never really a unique personal self but only a collection of potentialities viewed from the outside. "You can tap creative resources you did not know you possess," we are told in one month's advertisement for *Reader's Digest*. Another month we are told that for a better-paying job, more self-confidence, and higher grades we should "discover the *easier way* to build a better vocabulary." A world of sheer manipulation of impersonal objects unfolds in which one's vocabulary is an acquired technique rather than a means of again and again entering into dialogue with other persons who have a point of view and a right of their own. Even when the other is recognized not merely as a subject of manipulation but as someone necessary for one's own development as a person, he still remains merely a function of one's own self-realization rather than an independent person of value in himself. If you do not want to be cold and withdrawn, said another *Reader's Digest* advertisement, "get involved with people up to the hilt"!

The assertion that one is answerable only to oneself for the genuineness of existence is tantamount to the claim that one owes no real response to the address of others. This denial of response to others ultimately means the denial of responsibility to God. God, in our age, tends to become identical with our highest ideals and inspirations. He is no longer the reality that we meet in the new and unique situations that confront us. We affirm God only after we have identified him with our selves; we remove the reality that *faces* us into a process *within* us and just thereby undermine the ground for all true existence. God, in our age, places no demands upon us. He is the symbol of good Americanism, of successful living, of self-realization, of the progress of civilization. Created in man's image, he can no longer stand as the Meeter through whose meeting we find an image of man, a direction of authentic existence. While we may still define the aim of our religion, like Erich Fromm, as that "of becoming what one potentially is, a being made in the likeness of God," we also tend, like Fromm, to regard God as merely "the symbol of man's own powers"!

Modern thinkers, from Feuerbach, Marx, and Nietzsche to

Freud, Fromm, and Sartre, hold that man need only deny any reality transcending him in order to recover his alienated creativity and freedom and become himself. The "death of God" which these Modern Prometheans proclaim has been actualized in our day, by the most tragic of ironies, in the eclipse of the human. What is at issue here, as we have seen, is *not* belief in God but the loss of existential trust—the denial of all partnership of existence. When this trust disappears, real personal confirmation, genuine dialogue, and true community become ever more difficult. "In our age," says Buber, "the true meaning of every word is encompassed by delusion and falsehood and the original intention of the human glance is stifled by tenacious mistrust." The denial of the reality of our meeting with transcendence, corrosion by existential mistrust, and the widespread emphasis upon aiming at the self have all worked together to help produce this "eclipse of man."

The task of our age is to recover man's eclipsed humanity. To do this we must rediscover the hidden human image—an image of authentic human existence that may help us realize ourselves as unique persons, as partners in dialogue, and as genuinely human beings. Some past ages knew what sort of man they were trying to educate. Our age does not. Without such an image of man, education becomes either unrelated to practical life or merely technical. Only an image of man provides that central direction that stands at the core of all true education. The image of man is the most important link, in fact, between the various disciplines of the university. It is also the essential link between the university and the world which the student enters upon graduation. When an image of man is lacking, these disciplines fall apart into areas of specialization that can no longer communicate with one another, and the universe itself becomes an "ivory tower" which has only a technical relation with society.

The most frightening example of this technicizing of intellectual life is the modern game theorist, such as Herman Kahn, who, in the name of scientific objectivity, foresees the sacrifice of the lives of sixty million Americans and the physical soundness of countless millions of the generations to come as not too great a price to pay for our success in the thermonuclear war for which he calmly urges us to prepare! In such times society itself replaces the image of man with the image of the corporation man who "follows suit" even when it is a question of rigging prices in direct defiance of the law or of the Lieutenant Calleys who become heroes to many Americans because their training and conditioning to murder has led to just that. To say, as *The New York Times* commented, that the seven vice-presidents of General Electric and Westinghouse who were sent to jail did not "look like lawbreakers," or to stress, as their attorneys did, that each and every one of them was a "pillar of society"—president of the Bank, head of the Little League, the Community Chest, or the Chamber of Commerce—is only to emphasize the confusion in our society caused by the lack of any real direction toward the genuinely human. If these men, unlike Kafka's K., all appeared "respectable," it is because *we* confirmed them in their seeming, in their dualistic roles, in their claim to represent the sort of man that our society has tried to produce. In the case of Lieutenant Calley we have even celebrated his murdering of women and little children in a hit tune, and our President—Nixon—has leaped on the bandwagon to nullify the attempt of the court-martial to distinguish between the killing of enemy soldiers and totally unjustifiable murder of civilians!

What is the responsibility of the person in the modern corporation or in the modern state? When Eichmann justified his part in the extermination of six million human beings on the plea that he was only obeying orders, he denied the dignity and meaning of human existence in a more fundamental way than anyone has ever dared to do. He denied both personal responsibility and the existence of persons to respond to. The Nuremberg trials established the principle of a common humanity higher than the orders of generals, but the presidential and, to some degree, public "acquittal" of Lieutenant Calley reversed this in favor of the consummate naturalness of killing the very Vietnamese whom our soldiers had come to save because these sol-

diers were trained to see the Oriental as the "enemy"! In our day
men have not only manipulated and exploited the other person,
they have, with impunity, treated him as *by his very nature* an
object, reducing him to cakes of soap, or burning and disfiguring
him with napalm bombs. The very basis of human moral worth
disappears along with the human image.

By the same token the moral worth of man reappears when
men like Martin Luther King stand up and let themselves be
counted in a situation in which, in the first instance, it is not the
impersonal law but the personal witness which is effective.
" 'The scourge of our time,' " says Pietro Spina, the hero of Ignazio Silone's novel *Bread and Wine,* " 'is insincerity between
man and man, lack of faith between man and man, the pestilen-
tial . . . spirit that poisons public and private life.' " The cure for
this scourge, accordingly, is not a new set of words but a new
kind of relationship, a new image of man. " 'No word and no
gesture can be more persuasive,' " says Pietro Spina, " 'than the
life, and, if necessary, the death of a man who strives to be free,
loyal, just, sincere, disinterested; a man who shows what a man
can be.' " Erich Fromm also points to the image of man as the
only means of giving meaning and continuity to our culture:

> While we teach knowledge, we are losing that teaching which is
> the most important one for human development: the teaching
> which can only be given by the simple presence of a mature,
> loving person. In previous epochs . . . , the man most highly
> valued was the person with outstanding spiritual qualities. Even
> the teacher was not only, or even primarily, a source of informa-
> tion, but his function was to convey certain human attitudes. In
> contemporary . . . society . . . those are essentially in the public
> eye who give the average man a sense of vicarious satisfaction.
> Movie stars, radio entertainers, columnists, important business or
> government figures—these are the models for emulation. Their
> main qualification for this function is often that they have suc-
> ceeded in making the news. Yet . . . if one considers the fact that
> a man like Albert Schweitzer could become famous in the United
> States, if one visualizes the many possibilities to make our youth
> familiar with living and historical personalities who show what

human beings can achieve as human beings, . . . there seems to be a chance of . . . keeping alive a vision of mature life.*

The image of man to which I should like to point is that of living in the creative tension between the Castle and the Village. It is the image, to vary the literary figure, of Doctor Rieux, the hero of Camus' novel *The Plague*, the man who sees no reason for giving up the struggle despite the fact that his victories over the plague are never lasting. Rieux is not a saint. He is a healer, a man who shows what it means to be human in a situation in which most men tend to lose their birthright as human beings. Even while he accepts the never-ending struggle with the plague as the inescapable human condition, Rieux also affirms the meaning that emerges from that struggle.

Our own plague, the corruption of our culture, is not so much the obvious exploitation of one man by the other as the subtle turning of everything to account. It is the loss of innocence, spontaneity, and immediacy that colors even our enjoyment of the simplest pleasures, that makes gamesmanship, name-dropping, and role-playing more important than direct living, and that makes the sort of person that one *seems* more important than the sort of person that one *is*. The very subtlety of this mixture of the authentic and inauthentic offers hope. Even though the fact of communication *tends* to become more important than what is communicated, one *can* stand one's ground, even on a television program, and say a genuine word—the truth that one has to say in response to a concrete situation. No man is so purely a "corporation man" or "organization man" that he is incapable of some personal response and personal responsibility. Technical achievement and mass communication do not threaten us in themselves but only in their tendency to become independent of the direct human dialogue that they were meant to serve. In every situation in which we find ourselves there is some breath of air, some moment of freedom that makes it possible to

* Erich Fromm, *The Art of Loving* (New York: Harper & Bros., 1956), pp. 117 f.

move in the direction of authenticity. We can move *toward* using for purposes of true interhuman communion those techniques of communication that tend to become ends in themselves.

If the university is not an "ivory tower," hopelessly withdrawn into a realm of abstract ideas and unrealizable ideals, neither is the world to which the student goes outside the university one that is inauthentic by its very nature. The link between these two worlds is the human image—the image of a meaningful personal direction that helps each one of us realize in his own situation his uniqueness and his humanity. Our task is not to reject the Village for the sake of the Castle or the Castle for the sake of the Village, but to bring the Castle and the Village into fruitful interrelationship with each other. We do not find true existence by leaving the ground of the actual for the ideal or for a solitary relationship with God. We find it by "hallowing the everyday." The treasure, says Martin Buber, is "here where we stand where we live a true life."

> The environment which I feel to be the natural one, the situation which has been assigned to me as my fate, the things that happen to me day after day—these contain my essential task and such fulfillment of existence as is open to me. . . . If we think only in terms of momentary purposes, without developing a genuine relationship to the beings and things in whose life we ought to take part, as they in ours, then we shall ourselves be debarred from true, fulfilled existence. . . . The highest culture of the soul remains basically arid and barren unless, day by day, waters of life pour forth into the soul from those little encounters to which we give their due. *

Here where we stand, however, is precisely that social reality that at first glance may seem so alien and stubbornly resistant to any ideas or ideals that we may bring to it. "We cannot 'escape History,' since we are in it up to our necks," writes Albert Camus.

* Martin Buber, *Hasidism and Modern Man*, ed. and trans. with an Introduction by Maurice Friedman (New York: Harper Torchbooks, 1966), "The Way of Man," pp. 172 f.

"But one may propose to fight within History to preserve from history that part of man which is not its proper province."

> We live in a world of abstractions, of bureaus and machines, of absolute ideas and of crude messianism. We suffocate among people who think they are absolutely right, whether in their machines or in their ideas. And for all who can live only in an atmosphere of human dialogue, this . . . is the end of the world.

"Some of us," Camus nonetheless urges, "should . . . take on the job of keeping alive, through the apocalyptic historical vista that stretches before us, a modest thoughtfulness which, without pretending to solve everything, will constantly be prepared to give some human meaning to everyday life."*

The human image that in our day promises to make the tension between the "ivory tower" and the "world" most realistic and fruitful is that of the person who takes on himself the modest but essential task of wresting meaning from the dialogue with the concrete, and sometimes absurd, situations in which we find ourselves.

---

* Albert Camus, "Neither Victims Nor Executioners," trans. by Dwight Mac-Donald, in Paul Goodman, ed., *The Seeds of Liberation* (New York: George Braziller, 1964), pp. 41 f.

15

AIMING AT THE SELF:
The Paradox of
Psychologism and
Self-Realization

"I believe," wrote James Agee, "that every human being is potentially capable, within his 'limits,' of fully 'realizing' his potentialities; that this, his being cheated and choked of it, is infinitely the ghastliest, commonest, and most inclusive of all the crimes of which the human world can accuse itself. . . . I know only that murder is being done against nearly every individual on the planet."*

The concept of self-realization has its earliest philosophical roots in Aristotle's doctrine of entelechy, according to which every individual being needs to realize its own telos, or goal. Since then it has developed through innumerable variations of humanism, mysticism, vitalism, pragmatism, psychologism, and existentialism. It lies at the heart of Sartre's "project," of Heidegger's realization of one's ownmost, not-to-be-outstripped, nonrelational possibility, of John Dewey's ethics of potentiality, and of the thought of such varied psychologists and psychoanalysts as Rollo May, Carl Rogers, Medard Boss, Erich Fromm, Karen Horney, and Abraham Maslow. As a holistic approach to the person which sees his future actuality as unfolding from his

* Quoted with no reference in George B. Leonard, *Education and Ecstasy* (New York: Delacorte Press, 1968; Delta Books [paperback], 1968), p. 24.

present possibility, it represents a decisive step forward toward the human image. Nevertheless, it leaves much to be desired by way of a fully concrete and serious grappling with the problem of finding authentic personal direction. Erich Fromm, for example, defines "a genuine ideal as any aim which furthers the growth, freedom, and happiness of the self," and values in terms of "the mature and integrated personality" and "the truly human self." Yet the very meaning of each of these terms depends upon one's image of the human and one's sense of one's own personal direction.* Nor can values be based on self-realization, as Karen Horney does in her ethic of "self-realization," with its assumption of an already given "real self" contrasted with the pseudoself erected by neurotic pride and striving for perfection.† On the contrary, we cannot define ourselves or our potentialities apart from the direction we give them, apart from what we become in relation to others.

The Viennese logotherapist Viktor Frankl serves as a useful counterbalance to the psychologists mentioned above on the subject of self-realization. The main cause of neuroses in our age, he suggests, is the existential frustration that arises from not being able to find a meaning in life. The therapist cannot give a meaning to his patient. "It is up to the patient himself to 'find' the concrete meaning of his existence." In conscious opposition to Sartre, Frankl sees this meaning as one that is discovered and not invented. Potentialities, too, Frankl sees as inseparable from the demand that life places on us to make meaningful and valuable and thus existential commitments. The individual has many possible choices, but at any given time only one of them fulfills *the necessity* of his life task. Responsibility and maturity mean choosing one potentiality which shall be actualized, one which is

* For a full-scale discussion of Fromm in this context, see Maurice Friedman, *To Deny Our Nothingness: Contemporary Images of Man* (New York: Delacorte Press, 1967; Delta Books [paperback], 1968), Chap. 13, "Erich Fromm and 'Self-Realization.'"

† Karen Horney, *Neurosis and Human Growth: The Struggle toward Self-Realization* (New York: W. W. Norton & Co., 1950), pp. 13–18, 384 f., 388–390, 375–378.

worth actualizing, and relegating the rest to nonbeing. *"Thus the problem really just begins when potentialism ends."* *

The road beyond potentialism is the direction-giving human image. Real values, the values that are operative in our lives, are brought into being through our ever-renewed decision in response to the situations that we meet. These values become touchstones of reality for us. We carry them forward not as abstract principles but as basic attitudes, as life-stances that we embody and reveal in ever new and unexpected ways. They remain with us, latent in the deepest levels of our being, ready to be evoked and given form by the situations that call us out. These basic attitudes are the images of the human that unite one moment of lived dialogue with another, for it is not abstract consistency of principles or ideals but faithfulness in responding to the present with the touchstones that live in us from the past that gives unity and integrity to our lives as persons. In contrast, therefore, to those psychotherapists who seek to derive a direction-giving image of the human from the concept of "self-realization," we must recognize that self-realization cannot be made *the goal* either of therapy or of life, however indispensable it is as a by-product and corollary of a true life. Self-realization is corrupted into psychologism, in fact, precisely at the point where one aims at oneself. For this is the age-old paradox! We are called upon to realize ourselves, yet to aim directly at so doing is always self-defeating. You *begin* with yourself, but you do not *aim* at yourself, as Martin Buber says in his little classic *The Way of Man*. You must recognize the contribution of your inner contradiction to the conflict between you and other men, yet you must not bog down in being preoccupied with yourself. Of course, it is not enough to say, "Forget about yourself and be nice to others," for we often relate to others mainly as a way of evading ourselves. For all that, once we make ourselves the goal

---

* Viktor Frankl, "On Logotherapy and Existential Analysis," *The American Journal of Psychoanalysis*, Vol.XVIII, No. 1 (1958); "Beyond Self-Actualization and Self-Expression," *Journal of Existential Psychiatry*, Vol. I, No. 1 (Spring, 1960); italics mine.

—even if we do so in the hope of becoming more of a person and thereby being able to help other people more effectively— we embark on a path that is not likely to lead us beyond ourselves to genuine dialogue with others. Instead, we are more and more apt to tot up our relations with others in terms of the progress of ourselves toward becoming whatever we feel we should become.

Many years ago, when I was immersed in mysticism, a Quaker Jungian psychologist said to me, "The only difference between the Jungians and the mystics is that the mystics look at the sun while we look at our skin as the sun tans it." Only later did it strike me how misleading this analogy is when applied to the life of the spirit. From the standpoint of the true mystic, as opposed to the occultist, it is only in focusing on the sun and forgetting yourself—it is only in cleaving to God and forgetting about your spiritual progress—that you experience any transformation. But this is not so easy for modern man. When I read Gerald Heard's adaptation of the ten steps of Saint John of the Cross, I perceived only the spiritual techniques and maps and not the total immersion that produced San Juan de la Cruz' marvelous lyric poetry about "the dark night of the soul." For me it turned into a way of self-perfection, and even the desire for spontaneous ecstasy became a "planned spontaneity," or at least a longed-for one. The first time that I felt a mystic ecstasy rising in me it came as a complete surprise. I never set out deliberately to recapture it, but nonetheless in the future there was always one part of me which was wondering whether it would come and watching for any signs of it.

It is not possible to be human and live with continuous spontaneity. To live with no spontaneity at all is not to be human. But to know that true existence has passed you by and to set out to be "spontaneous" is to fall lower still. When you make self-realization your goal, whether mystically or any other way, you fall into the ironic paradox that you then inevitably become divided into two parts, one part of which is the observer which, like it or not, sits back to see if anything is happening.

This is the problem shared by the Modern Vitalist, the Modern Mystic, the Modern Gnostic, and to some extent by Psychological Man and the Modern Pragmatist, as I discuss the types of contemporary images of the human in *To Deny Our Nothingness*. If you set out to be a vitalist, you may think that you are getting back to a happy paganry, but it is more likely to end up like the Nazis or like D. H. Lawrence's late novel *The Plumed Serpent*—a hothouse spontaneity in which one strains and strives to find the missing life and misses it all the more thereby. Or one may end up like the boss in Kazantzakis' novel *Zorba the Greek*, who does not even try to become Zorba but is content to turn Zorba into a myth that he celebrates in literature and with his friends.

The same applies to the Modern Gnostic. If you say to yourself, like Harry Haller in Hermann Hesse's novel *Steppenwolf*, that all the thousand pieces of life's game are in your pocket, that you can open any door of the "magic theater" and all girls will be yours, all missed experiences will be realized, all unactualized possibilities actualized, you will have spatialized time and taken the seriousness out of both decision and the existence that demands it. Even those today who cultivate getting beyond the mind, beyond intellect, beyond words, are often not feeling but taking intellectual, and usually highly verbal, positions about the *importance* of feeling.

If psychologism be defined as the tendency to convert events that happen between oneself and others into psychological happenings or categories, then we must say that all modern psychology, psychotherapy, and psychoanalysis run the risk of falling into precisely this. The very attempt to look at the person in abstraction from his relations to others, as a more or less isolated psyche, means this. In the analytical psychology of Carl Jung, however, the danger is doubled, because for him self-realization is the goal and the means toward that goal is a turning inward to a larger-than-life-size Self to be integrated in the depths of the Objective Psyche, or Collective Unconscious. When the person is thus focused on these inward processes, there is the danger that everything else and everyone else consciously or unconsciously become the means to the end of *your* individuation, or integration, the function of *your* becoming. Jung, like other Modern Gnostics, emphasizes the inner in such a way that the outer becomes either an obstacle to or a function of the inner. In the face of this approach, it is not possible to say with the poet Richard Wilbur, "Love is for the things of this world," much less "for the people of this world."

The Jungian will point out, of course, that you cannot relate genuinely to others without first removing the "projections" which distort one's image of them and that when you have removed these projections and become individuated, you will then go out and have a true relationship with the world. But I think that the means must be like the end if the end is to be reached. If I relate to you now in order to become whole, I doubt that I shall be able to come back later and relate to you as if the relationship were of value in itself. When it was pointed out to me in connection with a criticism that I published of Jung, that Jung was enormously concerned with others because in others we find our own shadows, animas, and animuses, I replied that it was precisely this that I objected to: that he was not concerned with the other in his otherness, his uniqueness, but primarily in terms of the becoming of one's self. I do not think that there is such a thing as personal wholeness, or integration, minus a direction—and that direction is your unique direction discovered ever anew in your response to the world that calls you out. I would go even further and say that we are not given to ourselves in abstraction from the world. We may put brackets around ourselves for certain purposes, such as the recognition of our own "hang-ups." There *is* a proper time for concerning oneself with one's projections, introjections, shadow, anima, and animus. But even our hang-ups, projections, introjections, and complexes begin in relationship with others and only later become our "shadow."

The same objection applies to psychedelic drugs. If a friend of mine witnesses that he would have left the Society of Friends but for the deepening experience of LSD, I take that very seriously as I do the reports of mature friends of mine, some of whom had genuinely religious responses to their "trips." The only thing I object to is the notion, popular a few years ago, that taking LSD automatically produces a religious experience. To seek to "have" an experience is already to risk not having it; for the more we focus on it as a goal, the more we are in danger of removing it into ourselves, of psychologizing it. The word *psychologism* is in no sense an attack either on psychology or psychotherapy when these observe their proper limits. It is an attack on the tendency to make the reality of our relationship to what is not ourselves—persons and cats, sunsets and trees—into what is essentially *within* ourselves.

The very notion of *having* experience, whether it be psychedelic, mystical, sexual, travel, or adventure, robs us of what experience once meant—something which can catch us up, take us outside ourselves, and bring us into relationship with the surprising, the unique, the other. Secondly, it robs us of spontaneity; for one part of us will always be planning the experience, observing it as it is taking place, checking it out to see whether it is working. One may have a religious response—the response of the whole person in the situation—to anything: pain, sickness, death, suicide, LSD. But one does not have it automatically, and one does not have it as an "experience."

Psychologism is a habit of mind. It is the tendency to divide the reality that is given to us into two parts—one of which is an outer world into which we fit ourselves and the other of which is an inner psyche into which we fit the world. This is an understandable division. Much of our lives is lived in terms of it. But the wholeness that is possible for us as human beings can never be found by regarding the outer as a mere reflection of the inner, as the Modern Vitalist, the Modern Mystic, and the Modern Gnostic tend to do, but only by overcoming the division itself. The real person—and by "person" I do not mean Jung's "persona," the mask, or social role—has to live with that inner brought into relation to the outer. If we have "vocation," a term which Jung also uses, it is because we are called, and that call cannot come to us only from within. Even if the call comes in mystic ecstasy or in a dream, we do not have the right to say that it is simply *in* us. We do not actually exist divided into "inner" and "outer" except for certain useful purposes. In reality we are a whole in every moment in streaming interaction with everybody and everything.

"By never being an end in himself," Lao-tzu said of the "sound man," "he endlessly becomes himself." We cannot ask in all seriousness and concreteness what we mean by the term *self-realization* until we cease to use the term for its emotional value and really care about it, care deeply, like Celia in T. S. Eliot's *The Cocktail Party*, because there is some omission in our life, some call we have not answered, because our guilt is not just committing adultery with Edward but our failure to become the persons we were called to become. To exist is not to realize potentiality, it is to make decisions and find direction. What we call our potentiality, we only discover when we are faced with actuality, i.e., in the course of making decisions and finding direction in the situations which call us out. We do not really know our resources— our "potential"—in advance of that call. Every one of us knows that in time of crisis we shall find ourselves capable of a great deal more than we now think possible. And most of us also know how often we make the mistake of plotting our future on the assumption that we will be up to something that we may not be up to at all when it arrives.

When I was a freshman at Harvard, I lived with a number of very bright students, all of us on scholarships, at the top of Weld Hall in Harvard Yard. My friends all had what I came to call "the conceit of innate superiority"; whereas I only had "the conceit of accomplishment." Their IQs were so real to them that they did not feel that they needed to work or study. For them their potentiality, as measured by their IQ, was their reality. One of my friends dropped out of Harvard when he was a sophomore because he felt that there was a *qualitative* difference between him and his professors of philosophy. Yet that year, in addition to Raphael Demos and the regular faculty, there were present at Harvard Bertrand Russell, Alfred North Whitehead, G. E. Moore, William Ernest Hocking, and Rudolf Carnap—the greatest collection of Western philosophers that could be found in the world at that time! My friend dropped out of Harvard because his image of his self had always been bolstered by being told that he was a prodigy with a fine brain. It never occurred to him that one of those philosophers might have been no better than he when he was an undergraduate and that in any case genuine education has nothing to do with comparing oneself with others but only with becoming what one is called to become.

He was only the most extreme. All my friends mourned as freshmen because T. S. Eliot had written "The Lovesong of J. Alfred Prufrock" when he was seventeen and Mozart had written any number of great symphonies, and they had nothing to show at the same age! One of them, who was an excellent writer, once confessed to me that he could not become a novelist because he wanted to begin by writing *The Brothers Karamazov* and could not, like Dostoevsky himself, make his way there by writing lesser novels. So instead he worked fifteen years writing advertising copy for *Time, Life,* and *Sports Illustrated.*

We live in a culture in which potentiality is regarded as some sort of solid object that we may take to ourselves as our possession. Actually our potentialities are not something we even have control over most of the time. They are not *in* us; they are between us and what calls us out. After I had delivered a convocation speech at a California state college, I was horrified to discover that, without any advance notice or chance for preparation, I had been scheduled to address three classes in a row—one on ethics, one on political science, and one other, plus an honors seminar on existentialism in the evening. When I had got through all that, I was told I was to lecture to a class in the morning on "medieval philosophy." "I don't know a thing about it!" I objected, but finally agreed when the coordinator promised that I could then return to San Francisco. Out of nowhere there came to me a lecture ranging from Job and Oedipus, Meister

Eckhart and Saint Thomas Aquinas, to Descartes and Pascal. When I made my way painfully to the drinking fountain in the corridor, exhausted to the very depths, I heard again Martin Buber saying to me, "I wish people would ask me more questions." I understood now what he meant as I never had before. He was not saying, "I am a wise man. I know a lot. It is a pity people are not taking advantage of it." He was saying, "If people would come to me with real questions, something would come into being between them and me that does not exist now." The questioner is just as important as the answerer. A wise man is not a fount of knowledge. On the contrary, he is helpless until someone brings to him a question great enough to evoke a profound response. He does not *have* the wisdom. It literally happens, comes to be, in the *between*.

The word *self* has no meaning, I submit, apart from the way in which we bring our deep responses to life situations. Jesus said, "He who would find his life must lose it." But if you set out to lose your life *in order* to find it, you will not really have lost it and therefore *cannot* really find it. This is the paradox of aiming directly at self-realization as a goal instead of allowing it to come as a by-product of living itself. If I follow Fromm and other psychologists who tell me that it is important to have good relationships with other people that I may be a mature and productive person, then the relationships are merely functional, and I shall not even become the person I aim at being. Only when I forget myself and respond with *all* myself to something not myself—only then do I even have a self, for only then does my true uniqueness emerge. It is, of course, possible for a relationship that starts out as merely functional to end by being organic, as my friend Richard Huett has pointed out to me. In that sense, Fromm's advocacy of good relationships with other people "may well prepare the proper climate for the burgeoning of the deeper relationships," as Huett says. But this depends upon our forgetting our original motivation at some point and getting caught up in the relationship as something of reality and value in itself.

By robbing us of these simple contacts with what is not ourselves and the touchstones that emerge from them, psychologism robs life of its finest reality. This is a reality which we cannot sustain and maintain, to be sure, a reality which does not relieve us of the task of working with and on ourselves when we are brought back to ourselves. Nonetheless, the possibility is there of finding real life—of revealing the hidden human image—not by leaving our inwardness behind but by bringing it with us as a whole in our response to whatever comes. This is not a question of "inner" versus "outer." We need all our inwardness, for it is an integral part of our wholeness as persons. Our wholeness is not a state of being but a presence, an event, a happening that comes into being again and again in our contact and response.

At the end of a one-day seminar that I led, I suggested that the people present break up into small groups, one of which I joined as a participant-observer. In that small group there were two people, a woman and a man, who had the same complaint— that they continually observed themselves in all that they were doing and therefore never did anything freely, spontaneously, with their whole being. "My problem is that I am really a very good psychological analyst, and I know it," said the woman. "I bring it to all of my relations in life," she added, "and therefore I never feel anything that catches me up." She brought to my mind Virginia Woolf confessing with shame in her diary that she could never meet a friend without thinking, "How can I use her in my novels?" The man leading the small group asked her, "Is there any place where you do, in fact, come out of this?" "Yes," she answered, "if I go to a ballet, or if I get angry." Here at least—caught up by beauty or taken over by anger—she forgot herself and broke out of the vicious circle!

Even this hope seemed denied to the man in question. After my talk to the group as a whole, he had asked me, "Isn't the most important thing to discover your conflicts, your defensiveness, and work on that?" "Yes," I replied, "that is true. Yet you may never get beyond that." He had been with enough groups, he continued, to become aware that he was a defensive person. His problem, he realized, was that he did not hear things as they were said and respond to them spontaneously but heard them only in reference to his own feeling of being vulnerable. He wanted to get out of this by focusing on the fact that he was defensive. But this was equally self-preoccupation. The story he told our small group—of his one and only encounter, in which he got everyone so angry that they stripped him naked and threw him into the hall!—was told so matter-of-factly and impersonally that even this sharing could not break him out of the circle. He was wrapped up in his image of himself. "Rake the muck this way, rake the muck that way, it is still muck!," said the Rabbi of Ger. "What does Heaven get out of it? While we are brooding over our sins, we could be stringing pearls for the delight of Heaven!"

I am not attacking self-realization as such, therefore, or the desire that people in our day have for a true life. I celebrate life too. I wish we could have joy, feeling, touch, expanded consciousness, true community. Yet setting out directly to attain these things leads to a planned spontaneity which again and again defeats itself and abstracts us from the real situation in which we are set. There are techniques for dieting, for playing the piano, for dance, but there are no true techniques for self-realization. Self-realization should not be our concern. We should be, rather, like the man in Hawthorne's story "The Great Stone Face." He sees the face carved on the mountain day after day and responds to it, but with no thought that he wants to be like it. Yet when he lies dead, people look at him and realize that his face has become that of the Great Stone Face!

ENCOUNTER GROUPS AND THE HUMAN POTENTIAL MOVEMENT

Many of the ever-growing number of people who are associated with what is called the Human Potential Movement would probably object to our call to go beyond potentialism and aiming at oneself. Between 1965 and 1974 well over a hundred "growth centers" sprang up in all parts of America as well as in England, Japan, and elsewhere. The forms of these centers, to which by now more than a million and a half people have come, are variegated in the extreme. The techniques used may include sensory awareness, relaxation, breathing exercises, direct confrontation, theater games, Gestalt exercises, guided fantasy, and nonverbal communication.

In most encounter groups the "here and now" is emphasized and past experiences, including early trauma, are minimized. A corollary of this emphasis is the focus on personal responsibility for one's fate as opposed to accepting historical explanations or excuses. Rather than harping on past experiences and magnifying mistakes and inadequacies, encounter groups focus upon capacity for love and joy and other positive aspects of living. Yet this is equated by many facilitators with concentration on the future and on one's potential rather than on the present and the unrepeatable reality of *this* group.

Jack Gibb, one of the pioneers in "T groups," distinguishes therapy from training groups by the fact that the latter focus upon personal growth and increased human potential rather than upon remedial or corrective treatment, upon interpersonal data rather than analysis of the unconscious, upon group processes and intermember interactions rather than leader-patient relationships, upon trying out new behavior rather than achieving new insight or motivation.* William R. Coulson, one of the leaders of the La Jolla Program, sees encounter groups as a natural corrective to the goals of education in our society. By teaching students to hide their feelings, to be knowledgeable not ignorant, to say only what can be said well and to show only those sides of themselves that are guaranteed approval, schools leave a learning niche that encounter groups had to be invented to fill. Schools do not teach us to express negative feelings or positive ones or to communicate creative thoughts and half-formed ideas that cannot be clearly articulated.†

One of the most important claims that encounter and marathon groups make is that they promote the achievement of true, intimate human contact through mutual self-disclosure, emotional expression, and acceptance of self and others—all of which leads to further development of the capacity to love and be loved. Carl Rogers attributes the phenomenal growth of the intensive group experience to the discovery by ordinary people "that it alleviates their aloneness, and . . . brings persons into real relationships with persons." Freed to become aware of his isolation amid affluence and the role-interacting-with-role, mask-meeting-mask character of most of his life, he learns also that this tragedy of life is not *necessary*, that he can modify his existential loneliness through the "intensive group experience,

* Jack R. Gibb, "Sensitivity Training as a Medium for Personal Growth and Improved Interpersonal Relationships," *Journal of Interpersonal Development*, Vol. I (1970), p. 7.
† William R. Coulson, *Groups, Gimmicks, and Instant Gurus: An Examination of Encounter Groups and Their Distortions* (New York: Harper & Row, 1972), pp. 25 f.

perhaps the most significant social invention of this century."*
One wonders if many people in the encounter movement do not
confuse the reciprocal release of pent-up emotions and deeply
repressed feelings with genuine relationship. Openness in communication is an important part of genuine dialogue, to be sure,
but many encounter leaders seem to be mostly concerned about
each person's expressing his feelings honestly and expect real
mutuality to emerge of itself from this self-expression.

In the encounter movement too, the search to bring the
human image out of its hiding not seldom leads only to greater
eclipse. I have myself witnessed poor, insensitive, or authoritarian leadership dovetailing with cliché demands and expectations on the part of participants plus the tendency of leaders
and participants alike to rely on *techniques* as opposed to mo-
ment-by-moment awareness of the concrete situation. Carl Rogers
criticizes "the manipulative, interpretative, highly specialized ex-
pertise which appears to be more and more prominent in the
training of group leaders" and "the 'exercises' which have become
such a large bag of tricks for many group leaders."† The authoritarianism on the part of such leaders may mesh with a corre-
sponding authoritarianism on the part of participants who not
only suspend their own responsibility in the leader's favor but
use what they take to be his rules as clubs with which to attack
one another. "Group work offers infinite opportunities to slip into
a well-disguised, smoothly rationalized authoritarianism," writes
Thomas C. Greening, especially on the part of trainers and participants eager to pursue a predetermined goal of emotional intensity and sensual awakening.‡

Basic encounter groups seem to offer many people who are

* Carl R. Rogers, "Ethical Questions of the 21st Century," a paper for the
Humanist Institute of San Francisco (unpublished).
† Carl R. Rogers, *Carl Rogers on Encounter Groups* (New York: Harper &
Row [paperback], 1970), p. 157.
‡ Thomas C. Greening, "Encounter Groups from the Perspective of Existen-
tial Humanism," in Thomas C. Greening, ed., *Existential Humanistic Psy-
chology* (Belmont, Calif.: Brooks/Cole Publishing Co. [paperback], 1971),
pp. 84 f.

intellectually detached or in some other way cut off from their emotions the hope of getting back to what they "really feel." Actually, many such people are as cut off from the feelings of others as their own, in addition to which they are programmed to listen for cues and to put other people on pegs rather than really hear them. They not only miss the feeling with which and out of which the other speaks; they miss the plain meaning of what he says, the standpoint from which he says it, and not infrequently the very words that he utters. No wonder that in trying to cure this condition, people not only turn *to* feelings but *away* from words. The danger of this emphasis on feeling *at the expense of thought* is that we may cease to struggle for the word and take it seriously. There are few places left for the person who cares about the *whole human being*, the person who brings himself and wrestles with the word. What such a person says is all too often reduced by those who have jumped on the bandwagon of "Feeling = reality" to "Those are just words" or "You intellectuals always think in terms of labels." Those who do this, I have often observed, act as if *their* words are really feelings, whereas the words of those they are attacking are "merely words."

Our feelings are important, of course. We must go back to them and start there. But there are many people today who seem to want to end there. When we have a deep and perhaps violent emotional breakthrough, it is a revelation of something hidden in the depths of our souls, something heretofore perhaps entirely unsuspected. This can mislead us into seeing the emotions that are thus brought to light as the *only* reality and into depreciating what was accessible to the conscious mind before. An equal and corollary danger is to see the breakthrough as complete in itself, instead of seeing it as a little light lighting up a long, dark road up a mountain and down into a canyon—a road which you have to walk in your everyday life before this "breakthrough" can be made lasting and meaningful.

The concentration on feeling most often means the concentration on *individual* feeling, the feelings experienced *within* you and expressed to others. This dualism between "inner feeling" and outer "facade" raises serious questions about the claims that are made for the carry-over of encounter group experiences into everyday life. In many encounter groups an individual is taken out of his world and is identified with feelings that he can only express outside of any situation which places a demand on him as an active person working together with other persons. Our chances of infusing our stance in the world with genuine personal wholeness are far greater, it seems to me, if we hold the tension of the unique person and the social role in such a way that even in the dialogue with bewildering social hierarchies we become more and more ourselves. "Most sensitivity training, as now practised, is too short in duration to be of optimal enduring effects," writes Jack Gibb, and adds, "The effects of training seem to be more enduring when integrated in long range programs of institutional change and growth," thereby becoming an organic part of management, organization, family life, or whatever subculture may be involved.*

The result of the location of feeling *within* is that experienced encounter-goers and even experienced encounter leaders often tend to see the expressions of others as being important to the individual mainly as "feedback" that will enable him to come still more into touch with his inner feeling. This tendency to view the interaction with others as "feedback" sometimes gives rise to a gambit which I witnessed in an interchange with the experiential leader of a weeklong Esalen seminar on "Theological Reflections on Human Potentiality," the "nonexperiential" part of which was co-led by the poet-monk Brother Antoninus and myself. During the first evening of five hours of experiential exercises we split, at the leader's request, into groups of five or six. I found myself with the leader and four others. The initial conversation was between this handsome and striking man and a young man who, in expressing admiration for him, felt compelled to ask him how he could avoid "blowing it." After the

* Gibb, "Sensitivity Training," pp. 22 f.

term was used several times, I found myself imagining "blow it" as meaning everything from going mad to failing in responsibility. When I asked the young man what he meant by the term, the handsome leader turned to me and said, "You are interrupting our dialogue with your academic questions." "I was not being academic," I replied. "I just wanted to know what the phrase meant so I could follow the conversation." At this, he drew himself up and replied with hauteur, "Among me and my friends, one does not question the feelings of another person." Now I at last understood the full implications of his opening statement, "You are the world's foremost expert on your own feelings." He was free to put me down, but I was not free to reply to that put-down since it was really an expression of *his* feelings and did not concern me!

From this gambit, which is a far more common ploy than one would imagine, it is only one short step to a solipsistic hell in which we imagine that feelings are only *in* ourselves and that the feelings of others concern us at most only as reflections or projections of our feeling. You may be my "anima," to use Jungian terminology, and I may be your "animus," but there can be no direct contact between us as real persons. It is true that we *can* feel things within that no one else can feel equally well, but we do so not as "experts" but as persons, persons whose thoughts and feelings are tied up in the most immediate fashion with other persons.

One of the virtues of the encounter group is that it has room for hostility and anger as well as for "positive" emotions and does not trap people into repressing the negative because they think they *ought* not feel it. Yet even in the encounter group a hidden morality often exists which leads one to say to oneself, "I *ought* to feel gut-level hostility," or to say to someone else, "You can't be for real. You haven't expressed any anger or hostility." Even in the rare case where the leader, like Carl Rogers, is willing to allow the participant to remain psychologically on the sidelines and not commit himself to the group, the group is not likely to allow him to remain in this stance:

As time goes on the group finds it unbearable that any member should live behind a mask or front. . . . The expression of self by some members of the group has made it very clear that a deeper and more basic encounter is *possible*, and the group appears to strive intuitively and unconsciously toward this goal. Gently at times, almost savagely at others, the group *demands* that the individual be himself, that his current feelings not be hidden, that he remove the mask of ordinary social intercourse. *

How can one know that at this particular moment this is the right time for that person to get so involved? Maybe he is very sensibly protecting himself against being psychologically murdered. He may have taken the true measure of this group and know intuitively, if not consciously, that it does not have the resources to confirm his otherness, whatever its rules, aspirations, and stated intentions. Although I would not assume with Bernard and Constance Apfelbaum that holdouts *always* "express the inevitable presence of *real* risk in a group," my own experience as a member of a family therapy team leads me to agree that the "holdout" may sometimes be the "identified patient" in the family therapy sense, i.e., the one who is carrying the burden for the whole group and who, if helped sympathetically, may also help rescue the whole group. What the group member needs, first of all, is to trust, not the group, but *himself*. Only if the leader helps him see that his reactions to the group contain a grain of truth will he have a ground on which to stand, a ground from which "self-disclosure would no longer be so risky." How can encounter leaders assume, they ask, "that if a group member is uninvolved and guarded, it is his problem and not the group's?" Does not this imply an unstated assumption that "*if you can learn to trust the group first, then it becomes trustworthy*"? If this assumption is held, then there is a strong pressure on the facilitator to urge members "to take the risk, whether it be in the name of mental health, moral commitment, the courage to be—or, just not to let the rest of the group down."†

* Rogers, *Carl Rogers on Encounter Groups*, pp. 27 f.
† Bernard and Constance Apfelbaum, "Encountering Encounter Groups: A

The temper of the particular group and the emphases of the facilitator inevitably affect our *attitude toward* our own emotions so that what we express is not the raw emotion but the emotion shaped by our attitude as a member of *this* group. This means that there is a particular social matrix for the feeling that makes it different from what it would be if we were alone or with a friend or a member of the family. What you feel about your wife or husband, for example, is going to come out modified by the context of this group or by the leadership style of this facilitator. Your sense of the group's attitude in general and of the attitude of some or all of its members toward you in particular will affect the form, intensity, and even content of the feelings you express. This is seldom recognized. Instead, feelings, like potentialities, are treated as a substantive reality that is *in* us and only needs to be brought *out*.

Foremost among the factors which can prevent an encounter group from being real are the expectations which some participants bring with them of instant enlightenment, revelation, and joy. During one encounter group that I led at Big Sur, Esalen, we went around the room at the beginning asking each person what he or she hoped for in coming to the weekend. After hearing some of the others refer to my books, one woman said, "I don't want any lectures. [No one had any in mind.] I was here six months ago for a seminar with Will Schutz, and I got *joy*. I am a social worker, and I've come back to be recharged. I've got to get joy again this weekend." Such insistence on outcome and result means, quite simply, the unwillingness to start from where the group is and by the same token the impossibility of finding a genuine direction of movement in the present.

We cannot avoid the route of feeling, yet expecting and demanding feeling can get in the way of true spontaneity, of our really being open and really meeting one another. It may lead, indeed, to that supreme contradiction in terms—"planned spon-

Reply to Koch and Haigh," *Journal of Humanistic Psychology*, Vol. XIII, No. 1 (Winter, 1974), pp. 61–65.

taneity." It takes the most sensitive listening to distinguish between those feelings that really grow out of the group's being
together and those that arise as part of the effort to be "groupy."
It takes a great deal of listening to allow what happens to come
forth spontaneously—not inhibited by the self-images of the participants, which tell them in advance what their strengths and
weaknesses are supposed to be, but *also* not inhibited by the
group pressure to get down to the "true self" and express the sort
of emotions that the group holds to be "real." Putting the paradox another way, to deal directly with feelings is often to deal
indirectly with them. Talking *about* feelings does not necessarily
mean expressing them. At times group members have said to me,
"You are not showing your hostility, or your anger," and I have
replied, "Certainly I am! I don't have to say 'I'm angry' to express anger." In fact, if I say I feel angry, already I am likely
to be a little less angry; for by putting a label on my emotion, I
have to some degree taken myself out of the situation.

Rogers recognizes this danger of hothouse spontaneity quite
explicitly and links it with the "old-pro" phenomenon, those veterans of previous encounter groups who "feel they have learned
the 'rules of the game,' and subtly or openly try to impose these
rules on newcomers."

> Thus, instead of promoting true expressiveness or spontaneity,
> they endeavor to substitute new rules for old—to make members
> feel guilty if they are not expressing feelings, or are reluctant to
> voice criticism or hostility, or are talking about situations outside
> the group relationship, or are fearful to reveal themselves. These
> "old pros" seem to attempt to substitute a new tyranny in inter-
> personal relationships in the place of older conventional restric-
> tions. To me this is a perversion of the true group process. We
> need to ask ourselves how this travesty on spontaneity comes
> about.*

Another "travesty on spontaneity" to which Rogers points is
the way in which some facilitators *make* the group reach the
"emotional openness" that they desire:

* Rogers, *Carl Rogers on Encounter Groups*, p. 55.

I am well aware that certain exercises, tasks set up by the facilitator, can practically force the group to more of a here-and-now communication or more of a feelings level. There are leaders who do these things very skillfully, and with good effect at the time. . . . At its best it may lead to discipleship (which I happen not to like): "What a marvelous leader he is to have *made* me open up when I had no intention of doing it!" It can also lead to a rejection of the whole experience. "Why did I do those silly things he asked me to?" At worst, it can make the person feel that his private self has been in some way violated, and he will be carfeul never to expose himself to a group again.*

What began as a chance to recover the freshness of being together with others without performance expectations and with the possibility of making mistakes is in danger of becoming an institution, Coulson points out, "with new rules of procedure, recognized centers for doing it, gurus, formulas, known truths, hierarchies in charge, and credentials for being a practitioner." "To be frank, encounter groups are now drowning in gimmickry."†

We would like to live more intensely, more vitally, more fully. We would like to touch and contact others. We would like to share love and joy. Sometimes within encounter groups this is exactly what happens. But the more we *aim* at this goal, the more one part of us will be looking on from the sidelines, anticipating and measuring results, and for that very reason not living fully in the present. Our problem is that we are divided within ourselves, that we are not in genuine dialogue with one another, and that we live immersed in a deep existential mistrust. These sicknesses of our human condition cannot be overcome simply by the *will* to wholeness, openness, and trust, or by the magic of technique.

It makes no sense to talk of pure spontaneity, for structures are necessary and without them we would not have that margin within which spontaneity can arise. But there is an all-important difference between the structure which *makes possible* spon-

---

* *Ibid.*, p. 48.
† Coulson, *Groups, Gimmicks, and Instant Gurus*, pp. 5, 56, 165.

taneity and that which *takes its place*. There is nothing wrong
with planning as long as we do not try to plan the spontaneity
itself, or what amounts to the same thing, bring such strong
expectations of specific results that one type of event is reinforced
whereas another is played down or ignored. It seems to be our
human fate that again and again the structure goes over from
something that is life-promoting to something that gets in the
way of life. Here we touch again on the paradox that some of
the very things that we try in order to reveal the hidden human
image hide it still further. Rogers sees the encounter movement
as "a growing counterforce to the dehumanization of our culture." Yet, as he himself recognizes, it may, in fact, promote that
dehumanization because of the tendency to turn structures that
arise organically out of a unique group in a unique situation into
omnicompetent techniques that may be carried over to any occasion. Sensitivity training is no substitute for sensitivity, openness, and responsiveness, and that always means to the unique,
concrete situation in all its fullness and not just to what one is
looking for. True sensitivity is wedded to the moment. Coulson,
in this spirit, chides a fellow facilitator for suggesting a risk to
two people rather than allowing it to be produced *between* them
and quotes Buber's statement in *Between Man and Man* that
"every living situation has, like a newborn child, a new face, that
has never been before and will never come again. It demands of
you a reaction which cannot be prepared beforehand. It demands nothing of what is past. It demands presence, responsibility; it demands you."*

By far the most forceful and eloquent statement of the paradox of the hidden human image as it has been manifested in
many encounter groups is that of the psychologist and educator
Sigmund Koch:

> The group movement is the most extreme excursion thus far of
> man's talent for reducing, distorting, evading, and vulgarizing his
> own reality. It is also the most poignant exercise of that talent,

* *Ibid.*, pp. 18, 20.

for it seeks and promises to do the very reverse. It is adept at the image-making maneuver of evading human reality in the very process of seeking to discover and enhance it. It seeks to court spontaneity and authenticity by artifice; to combat instrumentalism instrumentally; to provide access to experience by reducing it to a packaged commodity; to engineer autonomy by group pressure; to liberate individuality by group shaping. Within the lexicon of its concepts and methods, openness becomes transparency; love, caring, and sharing become a barter of "reinforcements" or perhaps mutual ego-titillation; aesthetic receptivity or immediacy becomes "sensory awareness." It can provide only a grotesque simulacrum of every noble quality it courts. It provides, in effect, a convenient psychic whorehouse for the purchase of a gamut of well-advertised existential "goodies": authenticity, freedom, wholeness, flexibility, community, love, joy. One enters for such liberating consummations but inevitably settles for psychic striptease.*

Koch attacks the debasing, schematizing, and vulgarization of language that the encounter movement has produced and still more "the reducing and simplifying impact upon the personalities and sensibilities of those who emerge from the group experience with an enthusiastic commitment to its values." Even more than behaviorism he sees the "entire, far-flung 'human potential' movement" as "a threat to human dignity" which obliterates the content and boundary of the self by transporting it into "public space." Self-exposure *functions* as a therapeutic absolute in the work of the movement, he claims, whatever the leaders consciously intend. The threads which Carl Rogers identifies in the encounter process are really "a kind of Pilgrim's Progress toward the stripping of self," e.g., cracking masks, positive closeness, here-and-now trust, and feedback. The uncritical approval of any kind of feedback, says Koch, makes "the chances for simpleminded, callow, insufficiently considered or reductive shaping" of the individual by the group high. Given the common factors of an adventitiously assembled face-to-face group, the

* Sigmund Koch, "The Image of Man Implicit in Encounter Group Theory." *Journal of Humanistic Psychology*, Vol. XI, No. 2 (Fall, 1971), p. 112.

encouragement by the leader of frank, direct, and uninhibited feedback, and the assumption that self-disclosure as facilitated by trust leads to the enhancement or realization of "human potential," these criticisms must apply, says Koch, not just to some but to *all* encounter approaches. While not denying that some approaches or leaders are "less 'bad' than others," he sees the danger in all encounter groups of "simplistic lexicons" through which joking or wit is interpreted as evasiveness, sleepiness, boredom, or torpor as withdrawal, a raised voice as hostility, blocking as defense, and abstract statement as intellectualist concealment, or "mind-fucking."*

In a reply to Koch, Gerard Haigh, past president of the Association for Humanistic Psychology, suggests that encounter groups do not necessarily violate the uniqueness of persons because they are not programmed to fit a predetermined model. Although Rogers and others predict what *may* happen in encounter groups, "the humanistic approach to leadership is not to *make the group process happen as predicted* but rather to *let it happen as it will*." While group facilitators in training often try to make things happen as a way of assuaging their anxious uncertainty about their own effectiveness, and some "old hands" even employ techniques which have proved effective in the past, most leaders, Haigh holds, are nearer the "facilitating-awareness" pole of the continuum. They approach their task "in the spirit of discovery, trying to allow the participants to unfold in their own way, or not to unfold, if they wish." "The beauty of encounter groups, approached in a spirit of discovery, is that they provide an endless opportunity to revise, expand, and deepen our image of man and our ways of growing toward it."†
Unfortunately, the paradox of our attempts to bring the hidden human image out of hiding cannot be resolved so simply as Haigh does, since he focuses on the leader's intentions and aspirations rather than on the climate of expectation. But neither

* *Ibid.*, pp. 112–116, 121, 123, 126 f.
† Gerard V. Haigh, "Response to Koch's Assumptions about Group Process," *Journal of Humanistic Psychology*, Vol. XI, No. 2 (Fall, 1971), pp. 129–132.

can it be resolved by Koch's insistence that *all* encounter groups are necessarily self-defeating!

Having imposed on me her own notion that being a scholar I must have an imperative need to lecture, the social worker seeking joy found herself feeling guilty by Sunday morning and came to me at breakfast to ask whether there were not something the group could do for me. Since I did not help her out with her guilt by asking for anything, she got the group to go through a familiar encounter technique. When we were all lying on the floor at the end of a nonverbal exercise that one of my facilitators led, she got several people to pick me up in their arms and rock me to and fro while singing, "Rock-a-bye, baby, in the treetop." I braced myself for the sudden fall when the branch broke, but quite unnecessarily since they put me down with extreme gentleness. Then the social worker came up to me and said, with a beatific smile, "Is there anything else we can do for you?" I saw no point in telling her that, however well-intentioned, her technique could not touch me at all, especially in the deep depression I was in through the news of an automobile accident that my wife had had. So I said, "You might let me talk for a few minutes." This the group accorded me, but no sooner had I started than a young woman burst into tears, exclaiming, "You have problems too!" We spent the rest of the morning on the relationship between her and her husband, who was also present and who left her two months later for another woman in the group.

One of the most important distinctions that can be made among encounter groups is between those that lead to the real openness of the "community of otherness," as I have termed a group in which each cares about the others for what they are, and those that lead to a cult, a community of the like-minded. Cults give their members the false security that *they* are in the know and everyone else is really outside. Cults destroy the person by destroying his or her responsibility before the other who does not fit the model of the group. They also destroy the reality

of the group because people do not meet each other in the
freedom of fellowship.

I encountered one such cult in the midst of the very first
encounter group I ever led—in the summer of 1961. An LSD
psychotherapist had come up from Los Angeles bringing with
her her own clique of five patients, including her husband. I had
been brought to California to give three weeks of seminars on
Buber. But when we went around the room asking each person
why he or she had come, the psychotherapist said, "I'm not
interested in Buber. I'm interested in gut-level hostility." This
was a self-fulfilling prophecy if ever there was one. She stopped
coming to my lectures in the evening, and I agreed not to speak
at all during our afternoon session. During this latter period I
witnessed strange scenes in which she would talk about her patients in their presence, telling the group things about their
mother complexes that she had never told them, or she or one of
her followers would attack the minister of San Francisco's Fellowship Church because he would not enter into an exchange of
hostilities. It was all I could do to restrain myself from asking
them if they had a license to practice voodoo! Several people left
in the middle of the week because they could not bear the
hostility.

Almost a quarter of a century before the Human Potential
Movement flowered into its present many-splendored form, I
took part, as I have recounted elsewhere,* in a "group psychodrama" in which Freud, the "group dance," intuition, insight,
"Jungian synchronicity," murderous hostility, and complete lack
of training were combined in equal portions. Looking back on
this "intensive group experience" from the perspective of its total
collapse and the consequences that followed, I came to think of
it as an example of what Martin Buber has called "the lust for
overrunning reality," in which the person "becomes at once
completely agitated and crippled in his motive power." It is a

* Maurice Friedman, *Touchstones of Reality: Existential Trust and the Community of Peace* (New York: Dutton Paperbacks, 1974), Chap. 4, "The
Shattering of Security."

crisis of temptation and dishonesty in which "the realms are overturned, everything encroaches on everything else, and possibility is more powerful than reality." Although today's Human Potential Movement is far, far more sophisticated and responsible than our disastrous "psychodrama," it may be helpful to ask, in each case, To what extent does it too represent a "lust for overrunning reality"—a lust for instant life, instant joy, instant intimacy, instant relationship? It is salutary, in the midst of our heightened mobility, to realize that there is an organic tempo to life, that not all human realities can be poured into an atomic crucible and transmuted with the speed of light, that some suffering and sorrow and pain must be lived through for *its* duration and not at the "souped-up" speed which we willfully will. The "Evil Urge," says a Hasidic master, goes around the world with his fist closed. Everybody thinks that just what he wants most in the world is in that fist, and so he follows him. But then the Evil Urge opens his hand, and it is empty!

It is not difficult to recognize in much of the encounter group movement the lineaments of the Modern Promethean, as I have described this figure in *Problematic Rebel*—the romantic all-or-nothing posing as heroic yet masking despair, seeking to destroy everything that confronts or limits it in the name of recovering man's alienated freedom, distorting the paradox of the person in the modern world into a set of simplistic either/ors: individual versus society, "true self" versus "social role," authenticity versus inauthenticity, "spontaneity" versus "structure." But it is also not difficult to recognize some of the same lineaments in Sigmund Koch's attack on *all* encounter groups. The only change is the reversal in who is Captain Ahab defending "humanity" and who is the White Whale—the "other" that must be destroyed if *we* are to be able to live and grow!

Encounter groups can serve the purposes of the Modern Job equally as well as the Modern Promethean, i.e., of that mature rebellion which takes place *within* the dialogue of trust and contending, which affirms where it can affirm and withstands where it must withstand. Such an attitude remains close to the concrete situation, respecting and responding to its uniqueness, rather than relying on programmatic ideologies and techniques for the liberation of the human. Encounter groups do not *necessarily* have to fall into planned spontaneity if the facilitator starts with the group where it is and does not try to push it to a deeper level than it is ready for.

In order to counteract the danger of "inappropriate self-disclosure, scapegoating, tyrannizing by the group, inappropriate reassurance, provocative behavior, tyrannizing by the leader, favoritism by the leader, and forced confession ('psychological rape')," Louis Paul sets forth a set of ethical principles for facilitators, the first of which is an encouragement of informed self-determination which will lead him at times to "endorse, protect, and value a member's choice to remain silent; to decline another's urging toward action; to deviate from the position of the majority; to remain an observer." The facilitator may wish to help the other enlarge his perceptions, options, and independence, but even this he does not force upon him. "The facilitator does not browbeat, intimidate, mystify, dazzle with his brilliance, or intellectually seduce." Neither does he take advantage of the awe in which the member may hold him to seduce or touch the other sexually, though he may touch the other as "a companion along the way." This touching is not exploitative but a genuine contact with reality. "To touch is human, humane. An alerting, a solace, a seeker connecting with the Other, flinging a bridge across the separateness."*

Much of what Greening and Coulson recommend for the practice of encounter groups also falls within the spirit of the Modern Job. For a facilitator to steer groups into being like ones he has known in the past, says Greening, is a "cop-out" "from the frightening existential challenge and responsibility to create one unique new being from the many potential beings." The unpredictable venture of creating relationships means a movement from marketing orientation to Buber's I-Thou meetings, says

* Louis Paul, "Some Ethical Principles for Facilitators," *Journal of Humanistic Psychology*, Vol. XIII, No. 1 (Winter, 1973), pp. 44–46.

J. V. Clark, whom Greening quotes, and this means, says Greening, "to gamble on the emerging humanness of the participants without taking over and trying to shape them in one's own image." Recounting the way in which a group led by Haigh worked through the problem caused by the presence of a disturbed member, Greening points to precisely what in *Touchstones of Reality* I call the "dialogue of touchstones" and to the possibilities of healing through meeting that are present in such dialogue:

> This capacity to trust and risk enabled him to offer her and the group the choice of valuing and exploring her emotion, rather than narrowing down her choices to either alienating herself from her feelings so as to "adjust" to the group or erupting with emotion while alienated from the group.*

Only an experienced facilitator and a group of people coming in touch with what is deeply genuine and meaningful in themselves and each other can break through the facade of "group games," "I-Thou jargon," and "peak experiences" to the real person inside, says Greening. Although the pressure to experience awareness undoubtedly exists, an effective group "will encourage deep and sustained confirmation of the authenticity of the awareness rather than hastily praise its semblance." It is "from one man to another that the heavenly bread of self being is passed," Greening quotes Buber, and he illustrates this by the very figure that I have singled out in *Problematic Rebel* as most clearly embodying the stance of the Modern Job—Dr. Rieux in Camus' *The Plague*. For centuries men like Dr. Rieux have been groping toward "islands of authenticity," such as encounter groups may represent in our plague-infested era. The challenge of the future, says Greening, will be "to create a world in which encounter will no longer have to be an encapsulated, specially arranged event." He sees this challenge as being met in part by those colleges and universities now offering intensive group ex-

* Greening, "Encounter Groups," p. 86.

periences in order to tap the vast potential for authenticity, re-
latedness, and creativity in their students.*

It is no accident that it is out of the very institution which
Greening sees as particularly rich in "the shared search for meaning"—Johnston College, a new experimental division of the University of Redlands—that there has emerged a truly Modern
Jobian reply to Fritz Perls' famous credo. "I do my thing and
you do your thing," says Perls, one of the gods of the Human
Potential Movement, in a poster to be found in innumerable
growth centers and "turned-on" homes. "I am not in this world
to live up to your expectations, and you are not in this world to
live up to mine. You are you and I am I; if by chance we find each
other, it's beautiful. If not, it can't be helped." Building on
Buber's understanding of dialogue and the mutual need for confirmation, Walter Tubbs, a fellow in psychology and philosophy
at Johnston College, rejoins:

> If I just do my thing and you do yours, we stand in danger of
> losing each other and ourselves. I am not in this world to live up
> to your expectations; but I am in this world to confirm you as a
> unique human being, and to be confirmed by you. We are fully
> ourselves only in relation to each other; the I detached from a
> Thou disintegrates. I do not find you by chance; I find you by an
> active life of reaching out. Rather than passively letting things
> happen to me, I can act intentionally to make them happen. I
> must begin with myself, true; but I must not end with myself: the
> truth begins with two.†

Greening also points to that existential trust which I have
characterized in *Touchstones of Reality* as "the courage to address and the courage to respond." Such courage is frightening,
he points out, for it entails vulnerability to disconfirmation. Too

---

* *Ibid.*, pp. 79 f., 82, 86, 88–96, 98–100.
† Walter Tubbs, "Beyond Perls," *Journal of Humanistic Psychology*, Vol. XII,
No. 2 (Fall, 1972), p. 5. The original, set in verse form, was fittingly placed
by Thomas Greening, the editor of the journal, as a prelude to my own
article, "Dialogue and the Unique in Humanistic Psychology," pp. 7–22.

often in everyday life the gestures of self-disclosure and humanness go unnoticed or are rejected, as a result of which people
develop a self-fulfilling prophecy which says that existential risk-
taking is useless. Greening recognizes, as I do, that there is no
guarantee that mutual confirmation will happen in encounter
groups, to which I add, in *Touchstones*, that the courage to
address and respond also includes the courage *not* to address or
respond when you are not really addressed as a unique person
but only triggered off. The encounter group *can* be, as Greening
himself concludes, a way toward the realization of the community of otherness: "Few social inventions can equal encounter
groups as a method for enabling people to learn from their
differences and discover or create their unity."*

William Coulson also points to the community of otherness in
his recognition that what matters is not so much whether words
hit or miss the mark as whether the members of the group really
care for one another. He also recognizes the all-important difference between providing an *occasion* for encounter groups and
structuring the encounter itself. An encounter group goes better
when the leader yields to the process and shares in its suffering,
vulnerability, and surprise. What is primary and healing, according to Coulson, is not professional training but the relationship
itself. Coulson makes an important distinction between the ir-
responsible release of possibilities which characterizes some
groups and the proving of one's humanity through the responsible return to the people given in one's life situation. If the leader
himself becomes involved in the suffering of the group activity,
he is less likely to stimulate the group into being overwhelmed
by new possibility and more willing to wait attentively and discover what he wants in gentle interaction with others. The facilitator helps others meet, not by arranging a cautious experience
as opposed to an experimental one, but by providing an occasion
for meeting, and *arranging* nothing at all. The foremost learning
of an encounter group, states Coulson, is that one can call on

* Greening, "Encounter Groups," pp. 101 f.

people. Encounter is not *useful*. "It is at most a celebration of the mystery that lies between us."

The La Jolla Program does not encourage participants to establish themselves as "encounter gurus" but "to apply their learnings to the settings *in which they already find themselves*." The value of the special encounter group is "getting people relating again person-to-person rather than function-to-function." The humanizing need within institutional life is for occasions for genuine meeting, for it is out of such meeting that real community will arise. Community means mutual teaching and learning, influencing and being influenced, letting others have a say and asking them to let you in, taking the time necessary to build up close, human, trusting relationships, helping each other to speak personally.* It is significant that Coulson ends his book not on the note of *encounter*, the word with which Walter Kaufmann renders Buber's *Begegnung* in his translation of *I and Thou,* but with *meeting*, the word Buber himself preferred. Unfortunately, it is less the rule than the exception that the spirit of encounter groups has been that of genuine meeting.

I have myself again and again attempted to guide encounter groups in the direction of meeting through establishing a third type of structure—neither merely academic nor merely concerned with feelings, but such that the participants will respond with personal depth to matters of common concern. If the *death* of dialogue is the split which leads one group to be entirely "objective" and content-oriented and another to be centered on looking at feelings, the *life* of dialogue might be a "basic encounter-discussion group" in which the members are called forth in such a way that they respond from the depths without making that response their conscious goal. This is a structure which makes spontaneity possible without taking its place. It has worked with heartening results during the several years in which my wife Eugenia and I have co-led discussions of Hasidic tales. One person brings in a tale that has spoken to his condition,

* Coulson, *Groups, Gimmicks, and Instant Gurus,* pp. 39, 41, 64, 66 f., 76–79, 95, 152–154, 157–159, 171, 173 f. 181.

reads it, discusses his relationship to it, and then the rest of the group enters in, with the story always present to return to as a center and ground. In contrast to the discussion of abstract concepts, in which people pass each other by without knowing it, the Hasidic tale gives a concrete check that helps the participants know where they stand in relationship to the story and to one another.

An English Quaker who made a great point of the fact that he was a humble member of the working class once read a story to the group about a man who refused to establish a congregation of his own, even though the Baal Shem twice insisted on it and threatened him with the loss of his share in the world to come. In the original tale, the man's reply was, "I will not do anything that does not befit me." But the English worker read it aloud, "I will not do anything that does not benefit me." No one in the group picked this up except myself, and I did not comment on it. We continued the discussion for a while, and then I asked him to read the tale again. This time every single person in the group caught his substitution simultaneously, and he himself said, "Maybe that says something about me"!

Once at Pendle Hill I counseled a young man whose life was going in a circle and getting nowhere. He had been a theologian, an English major, a pianist; he had taught in Africa; he had almost entered a monastery; he had a wife and child and was on the verge of leaving them. In the group he read a Hasidic tale about "True Sorrow and True Joy," which says of joy:

> He who is devoid of inner substance and, in the midst of his empty pleasures, does not feel it, nor tries to fill his lack, is a fool. But he who is truly joyful is like a man whose house has burned down, who feels his need deep in his soul and begins to build anew. Over every stone that is laid, his heart rejoices. *

I was familiar with that tale, but it had never struck me. Now, knowing this man as I did, it moved me a great deal. Ever since,

---

* Martin Buber, *Tales of the Hasidim: The Early Masters*, trans. by Olga Marx (New York: Schocken Books, 1961), p. 231.

I cannot read or hear it without its evoking that same poignant feeling created in me by his situation at that time. His reading that tale to the group and discussing it with them was, I suspect, the turning point when his life began to become a meaningful way.

One of the purposes of the "basic encounter-discussion group" structure is to encourage a return to wholeness beyond the tragic split between thought and feeling that marks our culture. But even *this* holistic structure cannot be imposed. In an Interdisciplinary Seminar on Religion and Psychotherapy that lasted a whole year, I found the group so evenly split between those who wanted academic content and those who wanted pure exchange of feelings that no one was ready for my third structure in which the two might be joined in a single response to the problems and issues shared by the group. But it is a goal that one can move toward, refusing to accept the split as a permanent one or as a description of how things are. I was gratified to learn that Carl Rogers shares this identical goal and the identical experience:

> In any group to some degree, but especially in a so-called academic course I am conducting in encounter group fashion, I want very much to have the *whole* person present, in both his affective and cognitive modes. I have not found this easy to achieve since most of us seem to choose one mode rather than the other at any given instant. Yet this still remains a way of being which has much value for me. I try to make progress in myself, and in groups I facilitate, in permitting the whole person, with his ideas as well as his feelings—with feelings permeated with ideas and ideas permeated with feelings—to be fully present.*

Like Rogers, I do not like any class situation which would exclude the personal and the emotional. In a seminar on existentialism it once became important for me to ask a young woman, "Why are you so angry at existentialism tonight?" It turned out that existential guilt was a sore spot for her. She was one of twenty-one semifinalists in a competition to go to Europe that

* Rogers, *Carl Rogers on Encounter Groups*, p. 46.

summer. They had been instructed by the church agency to spend a weekend together and decide through a basic encounter which eleven of them would get to go. She was feeling guilt because, as one of the people that won out, she could not help imagining how the excluded ten were feeling, particularly given the way in which the decision was reached.

Another aspect of the "basic encounter-discussion group," and potentially of any encounter group, is that it is a structure that will help to avoid the danger of looking at the interactions of the members of the group only in terms of the feelings that they produce *within* one and not as real events in themselves. The artificial time and space of the weekend or week group adds greatly to the danger that even the most profound interactions among the members are likely to have an unreal, set-apart quality radically different from a genuine commitment to and real concern for other persons. On the other hand, the idea of being in an "encounter group" may tend to obscure the unique and unrepeatable character of *this* group. It may tempt one to carry over what one has learned in one group as a technique to be applied to other, "similar" groups rather than as a "touchstone of reality" that can be made present again in a unique way in each new meeting. The very notion of coming together in order that each might realize his *potential*—as if this were a fixed substance within him that only needs to be liberated by some catalytic agent—promotes this turning away from real response to events and persons toward a focus on the impact of the group happenings on the individual psyche. When this takes place, the true meaning of the "here and now"—the sphere of the between that transcends all individual feelings and psychic aftereffects—is screened out of awareness and often irreparably injured.

It is not only psychologizing individualism that is at work here but a relation to time that robs us of true presentness. If our goal is to get rid of our hang-ups, to be turned on, to become free, then, like it or not, we are using ourselves and the other members of the group as functions of a process. But the reality of the group is not made up of the sum of the feelings of the people in it. It is *this* particular togetherness and interaction with its specific possibilities and limitations. There will be as much true openness as the resources of this particular group make possible *and no more.* True openness is not attained through the manifest or concealed pressure to "let go" and express emotions. Just as in individual therapy the patient often has dreams that fit the school of the therapist, so in encounter groups people often "express" the emotions that they feel are expected of them without ever sharing a moment of true presentness with the group. There has to be the reality, fully itself, of this group experience; there has to be intrinsic meaning, of value in itself as well as in its future effects, or the very stuff of life is being destroyed. This is as true for education, sex, and social action as it is for encounter groups.

Even the term *group process* obscures the concrete reality of what has come to be in *this* group that will never again exist in any other. If we take our "potential" seriously, we shall discover that it is not *in* us as something that we possess nor is it waiting to be pried out of us by one or another technique. It is what comes to be in the two-sided event, the grace that comes from both sides of the happening, from within and from without. Often it is true that all that is present in an encounter interchange is mutual projection which entirely obscures the unique person one is confronting in favor of some person or persons in our past. But we must not rule out a priori the possibility that many other things can take place. Perhaps two persons will break through to each other and then really oppose each other because each stands on a fundamentally different ground. This too is meaningful encounter and confrontation. But I have also observed that when an interchange which began in hostility and anger began to change into one in which one of the parties was beginning to sense the sorrow of the other from within, the group leader cut it off in favor of expressions of anger and hostility on the part of others in the group. A surgeon of about fifty-eight and a young woman of about twenty-two were having a bad time with each other because he was "establishment" and she, with her long skirts and motorcycle, was a "hippie." Yet they were deeply involved with each other, and they came to the point where she seemed finally to begin to sense the painful meeting from his side of the relationship. At this point the experiential leader deliberately cut it off, for he was looking for individual revelations and had ruled out in principle the "between."

We can and do experience the other side of the relationship—looking in each other's eyes, touching each other's faces, involving ourselves deeply with another's suffering, pain, or anger. Even when two people cannot stand each other, they can glimpse for a moment what it is like to be the other person. This glimpse is fully as real a part of the feeling aspect of encounters as those self-referring feelings that we entertain within ourselves and tend to make our goal. I would claim, in fact, that the deepest feelings arise not when we are focusing on our own feelings but when we are really responding to someone else. Is it really worth our while discovering that we can feel and touch if we do not use our feeling and our touching for real contact at this moment? The very notion of touching means touching what is not yourself. If instead we focus on *having* experiences of touching, or on *having* feelings, we cut off our contact with real otherness and isolate ourselves still more. "I have lost my sight, smell, hearing, taste and touch," says the old man in T. S. Eliot's poem "Gerontion": "How should I use them for your closer contact?" Coulson has expressed this paradox of touching turned in on itself with incomparable clarity:

> Sad it is that touch, which in our culture could imply the existence of an affection between people that is real and risky, which might take account of the individual uniqueness of both toucher and touched, . . . sad it is that this possibility for confirmation between persons has been appropriated as a gamer's self-display rather than as the knowing implication of a betweenness.
>
> This indiscriminateness of touch is sad for the recipient, for it implies the denial of his hope that what it is to be himself will not turn out to be interchangeable with what it is to be anyone else.

... The game-based touching is saddest, I think, for the toucher, for he misses the thrill of presence, which is only to be *found* between persons, never to be placed there. ... Cued by a voice from an electronic box, a man and a girl, strangers, embraced. Science had synthesized I-Thou.

Without time spent in working out mutuality and "gradually gaining knowledge of each other, there can only be blind guesswork, a mechanical forcing of one person on the other, in which both will be diminished."*

In a community of otherness, we start with the presupposition that even in a marriage or friendship, as close as it may be, we do not have a simple unity, but each goes out from his or her ground to meet the other in his or her otherness. This is not a matter of comparison and contrast but of seeing someone from where he or she really is. In many groups that I have been in, whether they called themselves encounter or not, something has happened which has gone beyond anything we can understand in terms of individual psychology, something which cannot be parceled out to the individual members of the group as the mere sum of their "feelings."

We can grow in the strength to be there for another, really there, in such a fashion that we are not at all concerned at that moment about whether we are realizing our selves or our potentiality. All great self-realization is a by-product of being really present in the situation in which we are involved. If we come to an encounter group with the concern, "How may I grow through this?" or "What can I get out of it?," we will not grow at all. The concern will stand in the way of our really being spontaneously and unself-consciously present for the other members of the group. Carried far enough, we will miss the trip entirely; for the present will be seen only as a means to the end, the future, and the group event will never seem real enough to call us out in our wholeness.

What is really called for is a faithful response to the situation,

* Coulson, *Groups, Gimmicks, and Instant Gurus,* pp. 53–55.

including the otherness of the people in it. Then in really meeting these people, in really being present for one another, our "shadow" also comes into play, and we begin to understand the reality of the interhuman more deeply than before. Such understanding includes a caring about the others for themselves, a caring that is sometimes strong enough to bridge the gap between one lonely person and another. If, in contrast, we look at the others merely as sources of "feedback," then we regard each person's words, gestures, and actions as useful bits of information about ourselves without any genuine response to them seeming called for. Thus the emphasis upon realizing our possibilities may profane the situation by turning it into a function of a self-becoming which is no true self-becoming since it does not grow out of faithful listening and response to the call that comes at every moment. Our resources for responding come into being as we are called out by the depth of our caring about someone or something not ourselves. "By never being an end in himself, he endlessly becomes himself."

Only when the encounter group is seen as a concrete happening, unique and unrepeatable, not subject to manipulation or techniques which will produce given results, can there be a really deep and lasting effect on all those who share in the group's life-reality. Carl Rogers testifies to "individuals for whom the encounter experience has meant an almost miraculous change in the depth of their communication with spouse and children." For the first time feelings are really shared—in the family, in business, in seminaries, in teaching. "I have seen teachers who have transformed their classrooms, following an encounter experience, into a personal, caring, trusting, learning group, where students participate fully and openly in forming the curriculum and all the other aspects of their education."*

I cannot testify to such dramatic changes, but I can share one group event among many which seemed to me so real that I cannot but believe that it had a lasting, if unmeasurable, effect

* Rogers, *Carl Rogers on Encounter Groups*, p. 71.

on a number of us who took part in it. In the final session of a leadership-training retreat which broke up into small encounter groups, an interaction between men and women evolved into an intensive rapport between the men. It was close to the time of year when I wear my father's Shriner ring in memory of his death, and I shared with the group how my father and I had failed to express our love for each other. I added my determination that this should not happen with my son. At this, a doctor who was experiencing the loneliness of a divorced life cut off from his wife and, most of the time, from his children, burst into tears and said that he would not fail to show *his* son how much he loved him. Then suddenly all the men of the small group were in a tight ring in the center of the room, embracing one another and sharing deeply in a manly sorrow that is almost always present but rarely ever expressed in the relationship between fathers and sons.

PART VII

SOCIAL
WITNESS AND
SOCIAL CHANGE

THE POWER
OF VIOLENCE
AND THE POWER OF
NONVIOLENCE

Nothing reveals what is hidden in man so much as violence.
Nothing hides the human image so much as violence.

Each day sees still more killings, maimings, and burnings in
Indochina, exchanges of bombs and gunfire in the Middle East,
starvation in Biafra and Bangladesh, murders, rapes, and mug-
gings on our city streets, gang wars, routine police beatings in
black ghettos, the endless misery of the Brazilian peasant, and
brutal manhandling of those everywhere who protest, strike, or
resist nonviolently for the sake of peace.

Racism, poverty, and war are already violence by their nature
and by their origin. The history of racism is a history of overt
and covert violence: the killing of millions of blacks in Africa,
the killing, maiming, subduing, dehumanizing of blacks in America through centuries of slavery, and another century of violence
after liberation from slavery. Poverty always means violence:
holding down the poor through intimidation and coercion. War
is inherently violence, though we have tried to forget this by
defining war as "containment" or "liberation" or "defense of the
peace" or "defending the free world."

It was the violence of the Second World War that led me to
the agonizing moral decision to become a conscientious objector.
Richard Gregg's famous book *The Power of Non-violence* helped

317

me to make this decision. Then the idea of nonviolence was known only to a few. Since then the whole world has been impressed by the power of nonviolence through the success of Gandhi's *satyagraha*, his nonviolent campaign and the final liberation of India; through Martin Luther King and the Civil Rights Movement, which began as a nonviolence movement; through many peace protests which also have been nonviolent. A great many people have adopted nonviolence as a technique of political and economic resistance in a spirit kindred to Herbert Marcuse's statement, "Non-violence is not a virtue; it is a necessity."

Today, however, we are absorbed by the power of violence which flames around us in ever more grotesque and omnivorous forms. What is more, those who have awakened to the imperative necessity for social change are less and less looking to nonviolence as the agent and more and more to dynamic violence as the response to the congealed and static violence of the *status quo*. Our understanding of the power of nonviolence must be deepened and toughened, therefore, through a new look at the power of violence.

Two of the great social theorists of all time, Thomas Hobbes and Jean-Jacques Rousseau, had completely opposite conceptions of violence. To Hobbes violence was the natural state of man and only a strong central authoritarian government could do anything about it, since in this state of nature man's life was nasty, raw, brutish, and short, a war of all against all. Rousseau, in contrast, imagined man in the state of nature as a good, spontaneous, loving creature. Only the chains of civilization turned him into the predatory animal that he now is. The English poet Alexander Pope was able to accept all evil in terms of the "great chain of being," and to tell us that whatever is, is right: "We are but parts of one tremendous whole, whose body nature is, and God the soul" (*An Essay on Man*). William Blake, also an eighteenth-century Englishman, had exactly the opposite view of violence: "A Robin Redbreast in a cage/Puts all Heaven in a rage." Confinement, imprisonment, destruction, mutilation are already violence and will produce more violence. "The Harlot's cry from street to street/Shall weave Old England's winding sheet" ("Auguries of Innocence"). As Blake walks down the "chartered streets" of London and sees the "mind-forged manacles" of woe, he understands that the tigers of wrath are wiser than the horses of instruction, and he cries out against "the human abstract," the deceit, mystery and humility, and pseudocharity, where "mutual fear brings peace, till the selfish loves increase," cries out against the violence done to the chimney sweep, who says in Blake's poem, "And because I am happy, & dance & sing,/ They think they have done me no injury:/ And are gone to praise God & his Priest & King,/ Who make up a heaven of our misery."

From Karl Marx to Herbert Marcuse, violence has been explained in terms of the economic system. The humanistic ideals of liberty, equality, fraternity, say Marx, Lenin, Marcuse, cannot be transformed into reality under a capitalist system the very nature of which is the exploitation of those below by those who control the means of production. Since the state in the capitalist system is there for the express purpose of keeping the control of these means of production in the hands of the capitalists, the entrepreneurs, and the managers, there can be no hope of gradual social change. One of the terrible ironies of this theory is that Marx believed that a socialist state would make unnecessary a police force and an army, that socialism would be followed by an automatic withering away of the state. Regrettably, that has not happened: Capitalists and Communists can claim equal honors in violence!

There really is a double standard, as Herbert Marcuse says, when you count only the violence that it takes to produce or perhaps even to carry along or conduct social change, when you do not count the far greater daily violence that is used to preserve and maintain the *status quo*. Violence is the monopoly of the *status quo*. Lao-tzu put it very beautifully a long time ago: "However a man with a kind heart proceed,/ He forgets what it may profit him;/ However a man with a just mind proceed,/ He remembers what it may profit him;/ However a man of conventional conduct proceed, if he be not complied with,/ Out goes his fist to enforce compliance." Our genteel society has that fist hidden just beneath the surface to enforce compliance. In Émile Zola's novel *Germinal*, in the French town where the people lived in great poverty, the grocery storekeeper would take out the credit that people owed him by sleeping with the men's wives. When finally rebellion came, this static violence produced actual violence. Not only was the grocery man killed, but the organ with which he had collected his credit was displayed on high.

In his essay "Violence: A Mirror for Americans," Ivan Illich suggests that violence is less likely to arise from purely economic or military causes than from the symbols that middle-class America is trying to sell to Latin America and to the black man in the American ghetto. From "a healthy though angry and turbulent rejection of alienating symbols" such violence is hardened through exploitation into hatred and crime, riots and vandalism. Violence is not caused by the American way of life but by the insistence that the superiority of this way of life be accepted by the billions of underdogs. Against this demand spontaneous violence always breaks out, and it is met in turn by planned violence that is "justified by the need to reduce a man or people to the service of the idol they threaten to reject." Nor is there any hope to be found in putting weapons into the hands of the people, for these will always be used against them. But the worldwide growth of two societies, separate and unequal—the immensely rich economy of the United States and the capital-starved economies of Latin America, the Third World, and the black ghettos—should make clear the dynamics that provokes violence between them.*

Father Philip Berrigan points out the institutionalized violence of prison, which claims to be a place of "rehabilitation," and his brother Father Daniel Berrigan points out the institutionalized

* Ivan Illich, *Celebration of Awareness: A Call for Institutional Revolution* (Garden City, N.Y.: Doubleday & Co., 1970), pp. 25–28.

violence of our system as a whole, which treats symbolic actions —such as the destruction of draft files—as the most heinous criminal offenses but overlooks "the crimes of our political and business leaders." "We don't send to jail Presidents and their advisers and certain Congressmen and Senators who talk like bloodthirsty mass murderers. We concentrate obsessively and violently on people who are trying to say things very differently and operate in different ways."* Robert Jay Lifton goes even further and concludes an extensive study of Vietnam War veterans by linking violence explicitly with the obscuring and eclipse of the human image. Although all wars leave problems of adjustment for the returning veteran, the war in Vietnam leaves a particular burden of guilt: "Both the veteran himself and society see him stained with a filthy, unnecessary, immoral war." Not only is the war itself not justified but the conduct of the war is such that it is a series of atrocities: "There is no distinction between an enemy who can be fired at justifiably, and people who are murdered in less than military situations." This results in the soldier carrying with him an uneasy sense of power, atrocity, and descent into evil which leaves him both victim and executioner. When such a soldier returns to society, he feels ready to murder the first person who crosses him. He carries over not only the Vietnam solution to problems but the "residual rage at having been victimized by society in having to fight an immoral, unnecessary war." He feels betrayed and betrayed in particular by those who will not believe or do not care about what happened over there. "People who resist the truth about American atrocities, who resist knowing what the war is all about, are preventing the veteran himself from confirming the truth that he has learned and sharing it with the large society. They are impairing his . . . return to accepting himself again as a human being." Judging from the responses to Lieutenant William Calley's admitted murders of civilians—women, children, and babies—there must be many such people. In the end, in fact,

* *Time*, March 22, 1971, pp. 16 f.

Lifton suggests that the obscuring of the human image in the veteran and his quest for rehumanization is simply an intensification of the problem of the whole society "which is now struggling with the excruciating process of recognizing, gradually and grudgingly, . . . that we are responsible for one long criminal act of behavior in Vietnam."* Not everyone, of course, will accept Lifton's judgmental language, but it is hard to deny the implication of American society as a whole in the violence that it has been content to lay on the conscience and consciousness of the young men whom it has sent to Vietnam to kill and be killed.

While revulsion against the violence of Vietnam and Indochina has become a cause with American youth generally, no individual case so dramatically illustrates the reaction to the sheer weight of escalated violence as the refusal of B-52 flight pilot Captain Michael J. Heck to bomb North Vietnam when President Nixon ordered the massive attack on Hanoi after the Christmas, 1972, truce. After six years in the Air Force and 175 flight missions, Captain Heck became "the first American pilot to have refused to go into combat since air operations began in Southeast Asia eight and a half years ago." Moved by the suffering in South Vietnam, he was pushed over the brink by the massive bombing of the North. In resigning from the Air Force and seeking noncombat status as a conscientious objector, he made it clear that if the Air Force court-martialed him, he could live with a prison term more easily than with taking part in the war. The thirty-year-old flight commander, winner of the Distinguished Flying Cross, the Air Medal with ten oak-leaf clusters, and two presidential unit citations, declared, "The goals do not justify the mass destruction and killing. It's torn our own country apart." With no illusions that what he was doing would shorten the war, he nonetheless affirmed the human image in his own witness that "any war creates an evil far greater than anything it is trying to prevent, whatever the reasons, even for the self-determination of South Vietnam." "A man has to answer to him-

* Robert Jay Lifton, "Violence, Guilt and the Vietnam Veteran," *Fellowship*, Vol. XXXI, No. 5 (May, 1971), pp. 5 f.

self first," he concluded, in striking contrast to all those—from
Eichmann to American bomber pilots—who have for so many
years justified their part in mass violence as "obeying orders."*
Perhaps the most remarkable insight into the nature and effects of violence is that given us by Robert Jay Lifton in that
discussion of the survivors of Hiroshima which we have already
touched on in Chapter 9, "Death and the Dialogue with the
Absurd." Lifton suggests that survivor guilt "may well be that
most fundamental to human existence" because of an unconscious perception of organic social balance that makes them feel
that their survival was made possible by the deaths of others.
The most macabre aspect of this guilt spawned by violence is that
it falls on the victims of the violence and not on the executioners! It is precisely this guilt that Elie Wiesel has again and again
pointed to in connection with the concentration camp survivors,
as Lifton recognizes:

> Recalling Wiesel's phrase, "In every stiffened corpse I saw my-
> self," we may say that each survivor simultaneously feels himself
> to be that "stiffened corpse," condemns himself for not being it,
> and condemns himself even more for feeling relieved that it is the
> other person's and not his own. It is this process of identification
> which creates guilt over what one has done to, or not done for,
> the dying while oneself surviving, and which leaves every survivor
> with his own intrapsychic version of "a wound in the order of
> being."†

As Lifton himself notes, his understanding of survival guilt
confirms Martin Buber's definition of existential guilt as an injury
to that order of being the foundations of which one recognizes to
be the foundations of one's own existence *and* of mankind in
general. The survivor's feeling that the eyes that accuse him
belong not only to those close to him but to the anonymous dead
shows his identification with all his fellowmen. "The extreme
experience thus demonstrates," writes Lifton, "that guilt is im-

* *New York Times*, January 12, 1973, pp. 1–2.
† Robert Jay Lifton, *Death in Life: Survivors of Hiroshima* (New York: Random House, 1967), pp. 56, 200.

mediately stimulated by participation in the breakdown of the general human order and by separation from it." The only possible antidote, Buber expounds, is the illumination of the existential guilt, the perseverance in that illumination, and the attempt to repair the injured order of existence. This attempt makes the *hibakusha* into "collectors of justice," seeking, beyond medical and economic benefits, "a sense of world-order in which their suffering has been recognized, in which reparative actions by those responsible for it can be identified."*

A second far-reaching effect of atomic violence is that "A-bomb disease" and "A-bomb neurosis" are inseparable. The original curse becomes an enduring taint of death which attaches itself to one's entire psychobiological organism and to one's posterity as well. The A-bomb disease, especially the keloid scars on the face, mars not only the bodily surface, but the entire idea of the self. What is more, "survivors are also subject to acute episodes of *symbolic reactivation* of their entire constellation of death anxiety and loss." A seemingly opposite, but even more deadly, aftereffect of such violence is psychic numbing, a form of symbolic death originally a protection against psychic death but often itself irreversible as in the faceless, thoughtless *Musselmänner* of the concentration camps. Products of a total "breakdown of inner imagery of connection, integrity, and motion, an absolute loss of the sense of human continuity," they are, for at least one survivor, the one image that could enclose all the evil of our time. Even when psychic numbing does not take such extreme form, one encounters in both Hiroshima and concentration camp survivors "a pervasive tendency toward *sluggish despair*—a more or less permanent form of psychic numbing which includes diminished vitality, chronic depression, and constricted life space, and which covers over the rage and mistrust that are just beneath the surface."

---

* *Ibid.*, pp. 496 f., 525. Cf. Martin Buber, *The Knowledge of Man*, ed. by Maurice Friedman (New York: Harper Torchbooks, 1966), Introductory Essay by Maurice Friedman, and "Guilt and Guilt Feelings," trans by Maurice Friedman.

Lifton considers psychic numbing to be one of the great problems of our age because, like survivor guilt, it spreads out in ever-widening circles. At the same time as it infects the victims, it also infects the exeutioners. "A grotesque example was provided by the Nazi physicians who conducted brutal medical experiments upon living human subjects, and by those who conducted the 'selections' which directly dispensed existence and non-existence." More indirectly, patterns of psychic numbing manifest themselves in those who create, test, and use, or plan to use, nuclear weapons. Their ideology coupled with their technical-professional focus exclude emotional perceptions of what these weapons do. And if it is not psychic numbing, it is a closely related phenomenon that leads to discrimination against and rejection of the survivor whose death-taint seems psychically contagious: "The young are forthright enough to say what many of their elders feel: the death-tainted are a threat, an enemy, and finally, an inferior breed."* The spiritually crippled survivor makes the air unfit for breathing, as Elie Wiesel puts it in *The Accident*.

Violence is the product of frustration, rage, shame, envy, the product of all those things that Rainer Maria Rilke called "unlived life." A man noted for his asceticism came to see a Hasidic rabbi, and the rabbi said to him, "Yudel, you are wearing a hairshirt against your flesh. If you were not given to sudden anger, you would not need it. And since you are given to sudden anger, it will not help you!" Another Hasidic rabbi said, "Anger injures and makes impure all the members of one's household as well as oneself." But he also said, "Since I have tamed my anger, I keep it in my pocket, and when I need it, I take it out." We must not identify anger and violence. Violence is often the result of repressed anger, repressed rage, what breaks out of you unexpectedly, suddenly, like the conflagration that comes when everything is dry and it takes one spark to set it off. William Blake's famous poem "The Poison Tree" originally bore the ironic subtitle "Christian Forbearance."

* *Ibid.*, pp. 130, 181, 485, 500–502, 504, 508 f., 171.

I was angry with my friend:
I told my wrath, my wrath did end.
I was angry with my foe:
I told it not, my wrath did grow.

And I watered it in fears,
Night and morning with my tears;
And I sunned it with smiles
And with soft deceitful wiles.

And it grew both day and night,
Till it bore an apple bright;
And my foe beheld it shine,
And he knew that it was mine.

And into my garden stole,
When the night had veil'd the pole:
In the morning glad I see
My foe outstretch'd beneath the tree. *

"Christian Forbearance" is one of the things which, along with slavery, the white man gave to the black man in the United States. He gave him a religion which promised him "pie in the sky by and by," but demanded of him Christian forbearance here and now. When Martin Luther stood before the German princes he said, "Here I stand. I can do no other." But when there was a peasant revolt, Luther was horrified. To the peasants he said, "As Jesus has written, you must turn the other cheek and obey your masters." But he said to the princes, "As Paul has written, the government is ordained by God, so you must crush the peasants without mercy."† This sort of double standard is also what America has applied to the blacks, the American Indians, and the Mexican-Americans.

Unlived life itself is something more than the failure to express

* William Blake, *Songs of Innocence and of Experience*, with an Introduction and Commentary by Sir Geoffrey Keynes (New York: The Orion Press, 1967), p. 49.
† Martin Luther, "On the Thieving, Robbing, Plundering Horde of Peasants" (tract).

yourself or to dominate others, though that is what the romantic often thinks. It is the failure to give our passions direction by bringing them into the dialogue with the other human beings with whom we live—in our family, in the community, in the neighborhood, in the city, and in the country. The failure to give our passions direction has to do with the fact that we do not take our stand, that we do not make our objection when we must, that we allow a pseudoharmony to continue to exist. Often we cannot do otherwise; for we do not even consciously know that we have another point of view from that of the dominant group. Or if we do know it, we know the consequences of not staying "in our place." This goes right through our society—not just the poor and underprivileged, but the worlds of business, commerce, and government. It is this that leads many young rebels not only to "drop out" but to adopt every way possible of not conforming and of showing "disrespect for their elders."

Rollo May has cast a profound light on the sources of violence in general and in America in particular in his book *Power and Innocence*. He sees violence as the response, provoked by the sense of powerlessness and apathy, to a situation which is felt to block off all other ways of response. Thus deeds of violence, despite their negative form, are potentially constructive in that they are a way in which people who feel impotent try "to establish their self-esteem, to defend their self-image, and to demonstrate that they, too, are significant." Curiously enough, even when as in America there actually is power, the denial of power in the name of a pseudoinnocence may lead to a feeling of powerlessness which produces an "explosion of impotence" as violent as real powerlessness. Violence also arises from mutual mistrust, including the mistrust of language: "When the bond between human beings is destroyed—i.e., when the possibilities for communication break down—aggression and violence occur." Violence unites the self on a level below the human one, says May. But since most people in Africa, Central and South America, and India live without consciousness and without personal dignity, it may actually *raise* undeveloped persons to a human

THE HIDDEN HUMAN IMAGE

level and thus serve a positive function. It may also be the only
way to wrench social reforms from the dominant group. If this is
true of the blacks in Africa, says May following Frantz Fanon, it
is also true of the proletarian class who, unable to communicate
with the tongue, may find in violence a necessary and appropriate form of communication.*

At the same time May understands the violence in Vietnam as
an *unnecessary* product of the violence America has repressed as
a nation because of its unwillingness responsibly to admit and
give direction to its power and its wish to cling to the mask of
pseudoinnocence that it has worn for so long:

> It is fantastic how the modern form of the age-old dragon is
> reenacted in an event like Vietnam, with the scorched-earth pol-
> icy, flame-throwing tanks, the fire and smoke laying waste to
> huge sections of land, the defoliation of the country, and, indeed,
> the mass murder of the Vietnamese people. Our modern Moloch
> is greedy. Which means we have much inner aggression and
> violence to project. We do it with protests and internal conflicts,
> resignation and apathy, but we still continue to do it.†

Jean-Paul Sartre in his Preface to Frantz Fanon's classic book
The Wretched of the Earth states the case for the power and the
necessity of violence still more trenchantly than May without
May's suggestion that the colonial exploiters might take up a less
exploitative posture toward the colonized and thereby mitigate
the violence that they have sown. The violence of the settlers
seeks not only to enslave and control the natives but to dehumanize them by wiping out traditions, taking away their language, destroying their culture, starving and flogging them,
shooting them if they resist, and degrading them if they submit.
The counterviolence of the natives is not only irrepressible, it is,
says Sartre echoing Fanon, the revealing of the hidden human
image—"man recreating himself." "No gentleness can efface the
marks of violence; only violence itself can destroy them. . . . The

---

* Rollo May, *Power and Innocence: A Search for the Sources of Violence*
(New York: W. W. Norton & Co., 1972), pp. 23, 44, 52 f., 67, 192 f., 245 f.
† *Ibid.*, p. 214.

rebel's weapon is the proof of his humanity. The child of violence, at every moment he draws from it his humanity. We were men at his expense, he makes himself man at ours: a different man, of higher quality." Nor does Sartre tolerate Camus' stance of "Neither Victims nor Executioners": Since the whole regime is conditioned by a thousand-year-old oppression, the passivity of the nonviolent simply places them in the ranks of the oppressors, of those who profit and have profited by colonial exploitation.*

The most impressive case for the necessity of violence if the humanity of the oppressed peoples is to be brought forth from its eclipse is that made by Frantz Fanon himself. A black psychiatrist from Algeria, Fanon has become the voice of the blacks in Africa and of the Third World in general. The French title of his book, *Les Damnés de la Terre*, is taken, like the English title, from the "Internationale": *"Debout les damnés de la terre, / debout les forçats de la faim!"* ("Arise ye prisoners of starvation, / Arise ye wretched of the earth!") Yet Fanon's Marxism is not based upon the proletariat of the advanced industrial countries but upon the peasants of the underdeveloped colonial countries. His book postulates "a murderous and decisive struggle" between the colonialist who made violence his ruling principle and the native who, ready for violence at all times, knows that his "narrow world, strewn with prohibitions, can only be called in question by absolute violence." Yet even as he proclaims the necessity of the counterviolence, Fanon explicitly dubs it, in true Modern Promethean fashion, as the reply to the living lie of the colonial situation by an equal falsehood—the Manichaeanism which sees the settler as simply the hunter who must be hunted, the oppressor who must be oppressed—the "absolute evil" whose rotting corpse must pave the way for new life for the native. Where before the colonialist said that the native understands nothing but force, now the native says the same of the colonialist. Lie though it may be, this violence in-

* Jean-Paul Sartre, Preface to Frantz Fanon, *The Wretched of the Earth*, trans. by Constance Farrington (New York: Grove Press, 1963), pp. 13, 18, 20 f.

vests the characters of the colonized people with positive and creative qualities, binds them together into an indivisible, organic whole, mobilizing them for the second phase of building up the nation through the fight against poverty, illiteracy, and underdevelopment.*

Fanon's plea for the liberation of the human image in his fellow blacks through violence is a damning indictment of the false humanism of European culture and a poignant plea for the new humanity that Africa has yet to produce. "At the level of individuals, violence is a cleansing force," he writes. "It frees the native from his inferiority complex and from his despair and inaction; it makes him fearless and restores his self-respect." "Leave this Europe where they are never done talking of Man," he cries, "yet murder men everywhere they find them, at the corner of every one of their own streets, in all the corners of the globe." For centuries European "humanism" has "stifled almost the whole of humanity": "When I search for Man in the technique and the style of Europe, I see only a succession of negations of man, and an avalanche of murders." Who would have the presumption to deny Fanon's call to "try to set afoot a new man," a call which he makes in the name not only of his comrades but of humanity and of Europe itself?† And who could deny that so much violence of the *status quo* must inevitably lead to an answering violence of those who, for life and dignity itself, must overthrow the *status quo*?

But when Fanon becomes programmatic and turns violence into a technique of carrying on the revolution as well as starting it, we may well question his Modern Promethean ideology. Fanon himself distinguishes between the spontaneous violence of reaction and the planned violence of the social theorist:

> Racialism and hatred and resentment—"a legitimate desire for revenge"—cannot sustain a war of liberation. Those lightning flashes of consciousness which fling the body into stormy paths or which throw it into an almost pathological trance where the face

* Frantz Fanon, *The Wretched of the Earth*, pp. 30 f., 33, 40, 42, 48, 65, 72 f.
† *Ibid.*, pp. 73, 252 f., 255.

of the other beckons me on to giddiness, where my blood calls for
the blood of the other, where by sheer inertia my death calls for
the death of the other—that intense emotion of the first few
hours falls to pieces if it is left to feed on its own substance.*

The realism that compels us to recognize that violence does
indeed lead to counterviolence does not compel us to follow
Fanon into abstract formulas for carrying forward the revolution
—formulas that are no longer tested by the new and unexpected
situation of each hour. Fanon's rhetoric is moving:

> Violence alone, violence committed by the people, violence or-
> ganized and educated by its leaders, makes it possible for the
> masses to understand social truths and gives the key to them.
> Without that struggle, without that knowledge of the practice of
> action, there's nothing but a fancy dress parade and the blare of
> the trumpets. There's nothing save a minimum of readaptation, a
> few reforms at the top, a flag waving: and down there at the
> bottom an undivided mass, still living in the Middle Ages, end-
> lessly marking time.†

But it is still rhetoric. Anyone who has followed the history of
the new African nations in the years since Fanon wrote his classic treatise will hardly be convinced that the fight against the
common oppressor has been enough to unite the black Africans
into national solidarity or save them from an internecine violence and counterviolence which can hardly be laid at the door
of European colonialism alone! Precisely where he remains close
to the concrete human situation is where Fanon is most significant. Precisely where he leaves it for general revolutionary the-
orizing is where he is least so. "Violence" can no more be made
an absolute and universal principle of social change than "nonviolence." Both are abstractions impermissible to the serious
thinker who, I still claim, must move forward to the concreteness
of the Modern Job.

Simone Weil defined violence as reducing a person to a thing,

* *Ibid.*, p. 111.
† *Ibid.*, p. 117.

the ultimate of which is killing, i.e., reducing a person to a corpse.* If that is so, then violence can no more be avoided in our culture or any culture than we can avoid what Martin Buber calls the "I-It relation," that is, the relation in which we use, and know, classify, and categorize one another; for this is an enormous part of our culture and becomes more so every day. It is these very categories, indeed, which lead us in the first place to prejudice, racism, and violence. But if violence means converting the human Thou into an It, then violence is no more always inevitable than the domination of the It. We live in an age, God knows, in which the machine, the corporation, and the technocrat dominate to an incredible degree. Yet a real possibility remains, through fighting and standing one's ground, of bringing these back into human dialogue. It remains with us and cannot be removed by the fist of any number of economic, psychological, social, military, or political realists who say, "This is the way it is." But if we are going to take this possibility seriously, then in each concrete situation we have to discover the hard way what the resources are for dialogue and what the resources are for creating something human and bringing the passion which explodes into violence into a real interchange.

It has taken us a quarter of a century, says Robert Jay Lifton, really to begin to feel the impact of Auschwitz and Hiroshima. It has taken us a quarter of a century to begin to realize that there are no limits to man's readiness to destroy himself and all other men. We cannot believe any longer that there is any limit to turning a person into a thing. Turning men into soap was done with the utmost scientific efficiency, as was the transplantation and freezing of genitals, and it was done with the practicality of modern business as when the skins of victims were made into lampshades and the hair of countless women into rugs. An SDS manifesto of 1962 reads, "Our work is guided by the sense that we may be the last generation to experiment with history." All of us, whether we know it or not, have lived in the shadow of the

* Simone Weil, *The Iliad, The Poem of Force* (Wallingford, Pa.: Pendle Hill Pamphlets, n.d.).

THE POWER OF VIOLENCE AND OF NONVIOLENCE 333

cold war and the atomic bomb. The real possibility of the extinction of the human race may account in part for the eruption of violence and assassinations, of small wars here and there all over the globe, as well as for revolt and revolution as a symbol of transcending death in a way that our old institutions and establishments in society do not seem able to do.

The black revolution begins with the fact of racism, both conscious and unconscious. It begins with the Negro ghettos, with living on welfare, with an enormously greater rate of sickness, death, unemployment, poverty, overcrowding, illiteracy, delinquency, mental illness—a daily life of daily violence beyond our capacity to imagine. This has led to a Civil Rights Movement and a movement for integration which then has been superseded by the Black Muslims and Malcolm X, by demonstrations and riots, by Black Power and black militancy, and by separation— the claim for the right to identity and pride and a separate power base. America has seen the assassinations of black and white alike, but always of those who are concerned with social change. What is more, a man who believes in nonviolence, and stands his ground and acts, is blamed when some violence accrues out of the reaction of both sides. That means that "violence" equals change in the *status quo*, whereas "nonviolence" means keeping the *status quo* unchanged even by use of violence!

What has concerned me most deeply in our time is the polarization of our situation, and this is why the old formulas of nonviolence no longer mean anything. Polarization is necessary to destroy pseudoharmony, but it always goes beyond that to false dichotomies, pseudocategories. Finally we get the *politicization* of all social reality: The polarization already implicit in poverty and racism is converted into political slogans and catchwords. Sometimes this is deliberate and tactical, done because people believe this is the only way, whether from the Right or from the Left. Often it is semiexpressive and symbolic, as when the students tell their faculty to go die. This leads to *willful* misunderstanding in which people *refuse* to see the position of others from within. Finally, politicized persons become programmed: Whatever they hear is fitted into the Either/Or of those who are *for* them or those who are *against* them.

When I came to teach at Sarah Lawrence College in 1951, I was dismayed by the utter lack of social concern on the part of the students even when their own boyfriends were risking their lives in the Korean War. By 1958 this situation had decisively changed with the Civil Rights Movement, the Northern Student Movement, SNCC, and the beginnings of the "freedom rides" in the South. This change has proved a lasting one, even when the emphasis has shifted from integration to the Vietnam War and from nonviolent direct action to the New Politics. It has done my heart good to see the "silent generation" of the late forties and early fifties turn into the rebellious generation of the late fifties and sixties. It is a gladdening experience, in particular, to find so many young people walking with me in their support of the Peace Movement and their opposition to the war in Indochina. But the joy of finding unknown comrades walking beside one must also include the courage to walk alone again if it should prove necessary. Both the Civil Rights Movement and the Peace Movement began as firmly committed to nonviolence. Today many in the Black Power Movement think there are much more effective techniques than nonviolence, and many young people in the New Politics confine their nonviolence to an attack on the "imperialism" of the Western nations and of Israel but otherwise support "wars of liberation" everywhere.

We have seen the rise of a generation of young radicals, but they are by no means all the same. Most of the black young radicals need to be concerned with food and shelter, for both personal and social reasons, whereas many of the white young radicals come from middle-class homes and do not need to be directly concerned with food and shelter. This makes a difference. Many of the white young radicals, Kenneth Kenniston has shown, actually have adopted the very ideologies of their parents. The only difference is that they try to live them, whereas they see their parents as selling out, as being content with merely stating their opinions. On the other hand, young radicals sometimes not only help polarize situations but also go far beyond the bounds of what is concrete, what can be got hold of. They point up one of the major and most problematic issues of our time: the relation of confrontation and dialogue. We have lived with so much pseudodialogue, so much false harmony, that it seems we have need for constant confrontation to show us where we really are, what the situation actually is. Yet many of those who are dedicated to presenting the real conflicts and issues often go beyond those issues into a politicization, a polarizing of the situation. Then political slogans and catchwords obscure the concrete situation, and the hostilities grow on either side beyond the bounds of the actual conflict.

When I spoke of my fear of this growing polarization to some leaders among the younger Quaker social actionists, I was startled to see my concern distorted into a plea for sweet reasonableness, a comfortable middle-class gradualism. Where real conflicts and abysses exist, and God knows there are enough of them, we cannot do other than start with that situation as it is. No reconciliation was ever achieved through ignoring real differences, or attempting to impose a sense of unity where there is none. But this is a very different thing from those who set out as a deliberate political tactic to sharpen and radicalize the polarities beyond the concrete realities of the situation. These have always been the favorite tactics of the Right, old and new, as of the old Communist Left. It is a painful thing to see them taken up today by the very young people who have been close to concrete social realities, in a way the young political actionists of my generation never were. The New Left, to be sure, has no comprehensive, systematic ideology such as Marxism and the various party lines provided the old Left, and its methods are still much more direct and immediate than the old political strategies. Yet the openness that was the very hallmark of the rebellion of youth only a few years ago seems in many cases to be supplanted by a new authoritarianism.

If social witness is to lead to meaningful and effective social change, it must mature through the rebellion of the Modern

Promethean to that of the Modern Job. The Modern Job can
stand his ground and contend, he can trust and in that trusting
fight and honor his opponent by opposing him. This is the link to
which Martin Buber pointed between genuine dialogue and the
possibilities of peace. Gandhi with his *satyagraha*, as V. V.
Ramana Murti suggested, was establishing dialogue with the
British in Buber's sense of the term because he was confronting
them with respect as an equal and bringing India stage by stage
to the place where there could be a real dialogue.

> The way of violence works as a monologue, but the nature of non-
> violence is a dialogue. . . . The technique of Gandhi's *satyagraha*
> is capable of creating the conditions that are necessary for the
> fulfilment of Buber's concept of dialogue. The history of non-
> violent resistance as it was practised by the Indian National Con-
> gress under Gandhi's leadership eminently proved this. . . . If
> Gandhi was able to carry on *dialogue* with England, it was only
> because of *satyagraha*. . . . The old relationship between master
> and slave was changed thereby into a new partnership between
> equals in a "dialogue." . . . Gandhi was able to win by his non-
> violent technique a progressive response from the British govern-
> ment that led to the development of a "dialogue." Each of the
> major campaigns of non-violent resistance evoked the necessary
> recognition of India's emerging nationalism by Great Britain at
> successive stages of the struggle. . . . There has not been a greater
> example of a genuine *dialogue* between two nations in recent
> times than that between India and Great Britain through
> Gandhi's *satyagraha*.*

Buber would not have agreed that invariably "*Satyagraha* is
the answer to the basic question that is inherent in the *Dialogue*," as Murti states, or that "The methods of *satyagraha* such
as non-violent non-co-operation, genuine self-sacrifice, and voluntary suffering" invariably "fulfil the great end of the *dialogue*." On the contrary, in his famous "Letter to Gandhi" Buber
rejected Gandhi's suggestion that the Jews in Germany could use

---

* V. V. Ramana Murti, "Buber's Dialogue and Gandhi's Satyagraha," *The
Journal of the History of Ideas*, Vol. XXIX, No. 4 (October–December
1968), pp. 608–612.

satyagraha effectively against the Nazis, since death in the concentration camps was anonymous martyrdom, not political witness.* But he did see nonviolent civil disobedience as something that was more and more likely to be the demand of the particular situation upon those contemporary men who are concerned not only for justice but for man as man. He also knew the meaning of tragedy where "each is as he is" and oppositeness crystallizes into unbridgeable opposition. This is a tragedy that Gandhi and Martin Luther King knew too—long before either was assassinated. There are tragic limitations to nonviolence, situations such as South Africa where the polarization has gone too far. Perhaps it has gone too far already in America—and even more ominously so in the Middle East. Much of what is happening today cannot be called either violence or nonviolence, and certainly it cannot be called dialogue—whether it is a climbing aboard the Polaris submarine or the occupation of the Pentagon, or spilling blood on or burning draft files. It is very hard, moreover, for any man in our time to make a personal or social witness that cannot be immediately corrupted and distorted by television and by the press.

Genuine dialogue, whether between persons, groups, or nations, means holding your ground, but also, in opposing the other, confirming his right to stand where he is. This approach is more fruitful than the one of violence versus nonviolence. Nonviolence often is not dialogue at all, but just monologue—an attempt to use a technique to impose something on someone else, underneath which there is often real hatred and congealed violence. Violence, on the other hand, is not always monologue. It usually is; for, as Camus says, it silences the other man: It reduces him to the place where he has to submit, where he cannot stand his ground. But there are situations in which violence too expresses a caring not just about yourself but about the relationship, about our society, about America, about the world.

* Martin Buber, *Israel and the World: Essays in a Time of Crisis* (New York: Schocken Books, paperback, 1963), "The Land and Its Possessors," pp. 227–233.

The danger today, though, is that violence too is politicized so that people set out to use it merely as a technique.

It is important to contrast dialogue with a word that has become very popular in our times, *confrontation*. The notion of confrontation as being anything real when the other is a caricature and you are a caricature and there is mutual mistrust—this is the thing we have to fight. Confrontation will come when people will not listen in any other way. But to turn confrontation into a slogan and a political technique, to say, as many who never understood the meaning of "dialogue" in the first place say, that the time for "dialogue" is over, the time for "confrontation" is here, means to politicize real polarity into a false Either/ Or.

What we need for our time is an openness, a flexibility, a willingness to resist and withstand the concrete situation. If dialogue means the recognition of real limits and real tragedy, it also means hope because it does not assume that what was true this moment will necessarily be true the moment after—hope, not as an idealism, therefore, but as a readiness to assess the new moment in its concreteness. This also means, of course, the readiness to know the needs of the other, like the first peasant who said to the second one, "Do you love me?" and the second one said, "Yes, I love you, I love you like a brother," but the first one replied, "You don't love me, you don't know what I lack, you don't know what I need." That is what the black man properly says to the white man: How can you say you are for brotherhood, peace, integration, progress, when you don't even hear me, when you don't imagine concretely what it means to live in the ghetto, to be black? Dialogue, therefore, has to include not just hope of something happening but hope that will enable you to enter again, both actively and imaginatively, into the concrete situation of the other—to witness, to risk yourself, to involve yourself, to stand there and discover in that situation what the resources are.

I believe that dialogue in this sense is a hope in the black-white confrontation. Neither integration as we have tried it in the past, nor separatism in the Black Muslim sense of giving to the blacks a few states, is ultimately going to work. Certainly the black man has to find the ground from which he enters into the dialogue. It is not the affluent white middle class that will determine about the black man; it is the black man who will determine about himself. Then the white man will discover how he can and may and must respond. The conflict in the Middle East is likely anytime to become as bad as Vietnam or worse. For many years I was chairman of the American Friends of Ichud, a group for Israeli-Arab rapprochement. I believed then, and I believe now, that Israel cannot live indefinitely in a sea of hostile Arab neighbors. I believed then and I believe now that there can be no reconciliation which acts as if there is only one side that is "right," whether it is that of the Arabs or of the Israelis. Whatever the opinions of either side, it is a basic fact that people exist face-to-face. You cannot properly reduce any conflict to one point of view, whether it is from above or from one side or the other. Until the Yom Kippur War, each day led to greater polarization, greater mistrust, and greater whipping up of hate in the Middle East. Yet through a change in the cold war between the United States and the Soviet Union a movement has begun in the only direction in which this conflict can move, short of plunging the whole world into war. That is in the direction of genuine dialogue, of people talking with each other, of cultivating the resources together, of recognizing, as the United States has finally done with Red China, the actual existence of the other, of confirming the otherness of the other even in opposing him.

We have been deluded by the notion that political power is the only power. Of course, political power is great power, and usually behind it are economic power and military power. Yet a large part of what we call politics is only the facade—a facade of catchwords, slogans, pretenses, nuances, innuendos, and downright lies. The real movements go on behind the facade. If there comes a time when all the students of a university really want to walk out, that university will shut down. If there comes a time when the black people in the ghettos really organize themselves, things will change. I believe with Martin Buber that the reality is in fact more basically social, even though the political always tries to get more power and domination than it needs. In 1954 the Supreme Court struck down the "separate but equal" clause of the Interstate Commerce Act. We have learned to our great cost that this decision was necessary but not sufficient, that it has to become a social reality in every neighborhood, and it is not just law enforcement alone that is going to do that. At the time of the Northern Student Movement and SNCC and the freedom rides, young people were beginning to take part in real social action and not just political demonstrations. There is a danger today that even these young people are being politicized, but I believe that they will not lose sight entirely of the fact that concrete reality is found first of all in actual social living. This reality of our actual human and social life takes awhile to manifest itself. But it is there beneath the surface, awaiting the day when social suffering will transform itself into unmistakable social movement. If you lose sight of the concrete and everything becomes tactics, then you also lose sight of the actual goal you are working toward. Whether it is a labor union confronting management or the troops confronting the young people at the Pentagon, you never entirely remove the human factor. The dangerous consequence of equating politics *tout court* with reality is the depersonalization which turns that situation over to the smoothest and best politician. On the other hand, if you say that politics has nothing to do with persons, people, social reality, and community, then you have indeed made it into what it usually is—the Frankenstein's monster that marches to doom of its own accord. Then the politically most "realistic" people become the people who, like the Gadarene swine, are heading over the cliff to destruction—domestic, social, and international.

This recognition of the human factor in the confrontations of our age can lead us to a new and deepened appreciation of Gandhi's *satyagraha*. This "soul-force," or "truth-force," should not be understood as a universal metaphysical, political, or ethical theory but as *an image of man,* an image of the relations between man and man and between men and society. The effectiveness of *satyagraha* did not lie primarily in Gandhi's theories but in his embodiment of it and in his leadership of others, including his insistence that *satyagraha* practiced without the proper spirit is really *duragraha,* or the force of evil. The truest understanding of Gandhi's nonviolence can only be attained, therefore, through pointing to Gandhi himself as an image of man.

Gandhi was very clear in his teachings that *satyagraha* is not a technique to be applied in miscellaneous acts but a way of life that has to arise out of the deepest human attitudes. Gandhi saw *ahimsa* not only as nonkilling but also as boundless love that "crosses all boundaries and frontiers" and envelops the whole world. "A little true non-violence acts in a silent, subtle, unseen way and leavens the whole society." He knew too that the taking of life is sometimes benevolent compared to slow torture, starvation, exploitation, wanton humiliation and oppression, and the killing of the self-respect of the weak and the poor. *Ahimsa* demands bravery and fearlessness. If the only choice is between violence and cowardice, then violence is preferable. If we do not know how to defend ourselves by the force of nonviolence, we must do so by fighting. But the force of nonviolence is no method that can be taught, like judo or karate. It is the quality of the life that takes place between man and man: "The very first step in non-violence is that we cultivate in our daily life, as between ourselves, truthfulness, humility, tolerance, loving-kindness. One who hooks his fortunes to *ahimsa,* the law of love, daily lessens the circle of destruction and to that extent promotes life and love."*

Gandhi's *satyagraha* cannot be applied to all situations regardless of who is applying it. It is a direction of movement within the interhuman, the social, and the political which brings men

---

* *The Gandhi Sutras: The Basic Teachings of Mahatma Gandhi,* arranged by D. S. Savna (New York: Adair Publishing Co., 1940), pp. 31, 36, 54, 58–60, 63, 66, 68.

away from the vicious circle of violence and toward cooperation and mutual respect. *Satyagraha* is not possible, said Gandhi, unless others have assurance of safety. The only way to conduct campaigns of noncooperation, Gandhi asserted, is if the crowds behave like disciplined soldiers so that the opponents might feel as safe as in their own home "by reason of our living creed of non-violence." "Civil disobedience is sometimes a peremptory demand of love," said Gandhi, but he denied that it was any more dangerous than the encircling violence from the soul-destroying heat of which it was the only escape. "The danger lies only . . . in the outbreak of violence side by side with Civil Disobedience."*

The nature and extent of the power of violence in the world today is such that we cannot assure the safety of those whom we resist or guarantee that violence will not break out side by side with civil disobedience. We cannot conclude from this that Martin Luther King should have given up his nonviolent civil disobedience because of the violence on the part of both blacks and police. But we can conclude that nonviolence must be wed to a situational ethic as a direction of movement insofar as the resources of those involved and the situation itself make possible. Only insofar as *satyagraha* is permeated by the life of dialogue and concretely embodied in the meeting between man and man will it be able to fulfill the claims that Gandhi made for it. *The revelation in genuine dialogue of the hidden human image is ultimately stronger than all violence.* This is the trust that is expressed in Kenneth Patchen's profound and beautiful poem, "The Climate of War":

> Therefore the constant powers do not lessen;
> Nor is the property of the spirit scattered
> On the cold hill of these events.
> Through what is heavy into what is only light,
> Man accumulates his original mastery
> —Which is to be one with that gentle substance
> Out of which the flowers take breath.

* *Ibid.*, pp. 132, 161.

That which is given in birth
Is taken to purer beginnings.
The combats of this world
Rise only upward, since death
Is not man's creature, but God's . . .
And he can gain nothing by manipulating
That which is already hidden in himself.
The sources of nature are not concerned
In peoples, or in battlefields, nor are they mindful
Of the intensity with which man extinguishes his kind.
He who can give light to the hidden
May alone speak of victories.
He who can come to his own formulation
Shall be found to assume mastery
Over the roads which lead
On the whole human event.
The hour of love and dignity and peace
Is surely not dead.
With more splendor than these sombre lives
The gates within us
Open on the brilliant gardens of the sun.
Then do these inscrutable soldiers rise upward,
Nourished and flowering
On the battleslopes of the Unseen. For Victory,
Unlike the sponsored madness in these undertakings,
Is not diminished by what is mortal; but on its peaks
Grows until the dark caverns are alight
With the ordained radiance of all mankind.

MARTIN LUTHER KING:
An American Gandhi and a Modern Job

Martin Luther King, Jr., the man who brought Gandhi's non-violent resistance to the social and racial conflict in America and who, like Gandhi, became a living symbol of the fight for the human in man, was assassinated like Gandhi, in the midst of the very tensions to which he had tried to bring a word of justice and peace. Since his assassination, King has been compared not only with Gandhi but with Christ, and some have spoken of him as "the first citizen of the world." The world has, indeed, mourned the loss of one of its greatest sons, a man whose way of fighting confirmed even the enemy that he fought against and rightly earned him the Nobel Peace Prize. We mourn him and we bear witness to him. Whether we are ourselves religious or not, we cannot fail to pay honor to the man who, like Gandhi, proclaimed the inseparability of the religious and the social revolution.

Martin Luther King first became known to the world through his leadership of the Montgomery bus boycott in 1956. This boycott began because one Negro woman of integrity and courage, without any premeditation or political strategy, refused to move to the back of the bus, as the unconstitutional laws of Alabama required Negroes to do. It continued and gained momentum as Martin Luther King, only twenty-nine years old at the time, took over the helm and held it steadfast in love and in prayer. Even when his own house was bombed and his wife and child nearly killed, he dispelled the angry crowd of Negroes before his house with the declaration that *their* way was to be love not hate, nonviolence not violence. Yet, again like Gandhi, not nonresistance, but nonviolent resistance, a struggle in which the means were as important as the end, in which the end informed the means.

A few years ago on my way to a lecture I was to give on "Man and the Space Age" I heard that J. Edgar Hoover, the director of the Federal Bureau of Investigation, had just called Martin Luther King "the most notorious liar in the United States." I found this a depressing commentary on our progress in the space age, but I was given new hope the next day by the reply that Martin Luther King made to this charge. He did not defend himself; he did not give way before the attack. He said instead that J. Edgar Hoover, in charge of handling one of the most difficult activities in the United States, was obviously feeling the strain. Martin Luther King had to make another very painful decision the day after the Alabama state police had charged the crowd with tear gas and clubs and then the thousand ministers and other people who had come down to Alabama to march again from Selma. At this time there was a court injunction against the march to Montgomery, and Martin Luther King had to decide whether to break the law for the first time in his nonviolent campaign. He decided that the people assembled there had to march, but when they arrived at the bridge and the troopers were lined up to block their way, he accepted that limit and knelt there and prayed.

In *Stride toward Freedom,* the story of King's successful campaign for the desegregation of buses in Montgomery, Alabama, and throughout the South, King criticizes those black ministers who remained aloof from the area of social responsibility out of a sense that religion concerns only the other world, and he puts forward as an alternative a religion true to its nature precisely because it is concerned about man's social conditions. "Any religion that professes to be concerned with the souls of men and is not concerned with the slums that damn them, the economic conditions that strangle them, and the social conditions that cripple them is a dry-as-dust religion." In this attitude toward religion King coincided with that modern Job of whom Buber spoke when he said: "Even when this man knows peace in the sense that God comes near him again, this peace is not incompatible with the fight for social justice." He also embodied the Modern Job in his unwillingness to accept segregation and in his insistence that a peace and harmony defined merely as the absence of tension is a pseudopeace, a negative peace based on the black's acceptance of his state of subordination. True peace, in contrast, is the presence of justice: "The tension we see in Montgomery today is the necessary tension that comes when the oppressed rise up and start to move forward toward a permanent, positive peace."*

Recognizing with Reinhold Niebuhr man's potential for evil as well as good, the complexity of man's social involvement, and the glaring reality of collective evil, King nonetheless upheld true pacifism as "a courageous confrontation of evil by the power of love." Nonviolence to King stood for the Both/And of the Modern Job rather than the Either/Or of the Modern Promethean. Nonviolence "does not seek to defeat or humiliate the opponent, but to win his friendship and understanding." Its goal is the "creation of the beloved community." The love about which nonviolence centers is not affectionate emotion but "understanding, redemptive good will." Agape, to King, "is love seeking to preserve and create community. It is insistence on community even when one seeks to break it. *Agape* is a willingness to sacrifice in the interests of mutuality. *Agape* is a willingness to go to any length to restore community." Personality, to King, can only be fulfilled in the context of community. To meet hate with love closes the gap in broken community. To meet love with hate is to become depersonalized oneself and to intensify the cleavage in broken community. But there can be no split

---

* Martin Luther King, Jr., *Stride toward Freedom: The Montgomery Story* (New York: Ballantine Books, 1960), pp. 28 f., 31 f.

here between love and the demands of justice. "When I am commanded to love, I am commanded to restore community, to resist injustice, and to meet the needs of my brothers." Nonviolent resistance, to King, is the narrow bridge between acquiescence and violence. "With non-violent resistance, no individual or group need submit to any wrong, nor need anyone resort to violence in order to right a wrong." The black man "must convince the white man that all he seeks is justice, *for both himself and the white man.*"*

Our best defense against Communism, says King in *Strength to Love*, is not anti-Communism but positive action "to remove those conditions of poverty, insecurity, injustice, and racial discrimination which are the fertile soil in which the seed of Communism grows and develops." King does not fall into the Modern Promethean's error that by destroying the alien other, one automatically establishes the good. Our fate is not in the hands of the "enemy" but of ourselves; for all men, like Job, are given with their creation a ground on which to stand and from which to act.

> Always man must do something. "Stand upon thy feet," says God to Ezekiel, "and I will speak unto you." Man is no helpless invalid left in a valley of total depravity until God pulls him out. Man is rather an upstanding human being.†

In *Why We Can't Wait* the *rebellion* of the Modern Job comes through clear and strong. In his famous letter from the Birmingham jail, King expresses his disappointment in the white moderate and liberal who prefers the negative peace of absence of tension to the positive peace of the presence of justice and "who paternalistically believes he can set the timetable for another man's freedom." "We who engage in non-violent direct action are not the creators of tension," King points out. "We merely bring to the surface the hidden tension that is already alive" so that it can be seen and dealt with. But again like the Modern

---

* *Ibid.*, pp. 78–85, 174, 176.
† Martin Luther King, Jr., *Strength to Love* (New York: Harper & Row, 1963), pp. 100, 123.

Job, the rebellion is not for the sake of any one person or group but for the sake of the brotherhood of all men. "Segregation, to use the terminology of the Jewish philosopher Martin Buber, substitutes an 'I-it' relationship for an 'I-thou' relationship and ends up relegating persons to the status of things." To stand, as King did, for the I-thou relationship is to stand for the other as well as oneself, for the dialogue between man and man: "Eventually," King writes, "the civil-rights movement will have contributed infinitely more to the nation than the eradication of racial injustice. It will have enlarged the concept of brotherhood to a vision of total interrelatedness."*

In his discussions of Black Power and white racism in *Where Do We Go from Here: Chaos or Community?* King forcefully illustrates the contrast we have made between the all-or-nothing rebellion of the Modern Promethean and the trust-and-contending rebellion of the Modern Job. Pointing out that every period of progress is succeeded by one of counterrevolution, King ascribes black extremism to the unjustified pessimism and despair which feels that no progress has been made and that ignores the fact that "A final victory is an accumulation of many short-term encounters." In the face of those who pronounced nonviolent direct action dead for the tenth time, King points out that nonviolent direct action has proved itself to be the most effective generator of change that the movement has seen, whereas Black Power has so far proved to be a slogan without a program and with an uncertain following. While asserting that riots are indefensible and sympathizing with the whites who feel menaced by them, King insists that the white person recognize that the main culpability lies with municipal, state, and national governments from whom reforms must be demanded if the white (and black) citizens are to be protected. "Negroes hold only one key to the double lock of peaceful change. The other is in the hands of the white community." Although King was not in favor of the Black Power slogan, he recognized that it arose as a psychological reaction to the indoctrination that created the per-

* Martin Luther King, Jr., *Why We Can't Wait* (New York: New American Library, Signet Books, 1964), pp. 84 f., 82, 152.

fect slave whose selfhood was forfeit to his unconditional submission. As Job witnessed to himself and stood his ground, so
King called "the Negro to a new sense of manhood, . . . a deep
feeling of racial pride and . . . an audacious appreciation of his
heritage." The black man "must stand up amid a system that still
oppresses him and develop an unassailable and majestic sense of
his own value."*

Particularly striking is King's recognition of what we have
ourselves so often asserted: that the heroic gestures of the Modern Promethean, in this case of the Black Power sloganeers,
mask the despair of all-or-nothing:

> Beneath all the satisfaction of a gratifying slogan, Black Power is
> a nihilistic philosophy born out of the conviction that the Negro
> can't win. It is, at bottom, the view that American society is so
> hopelessly corrupt and enmeshed in evil that there is no possibil-
> ity of salvation from within. . . . This thinking carries the seeds of
> its own doom.†

The ultimate contradiction of the Black Power Movement is that
it rejects the one thing that keeps the fire of revolutions burning:
the flame of hope. Revolution may be born of despair, but it
cannot be sustained by despair. To respond to the prison of
segregation and discrimination with bitterness, cynicism, self-
pity, or despair is to invite black suicide, black paranoia, black
nihilism, or black resignation. The black cannot achieve political
power in isolation or economic power through separatism. The
determined refusal to be stopped will eventually open the door
to fulfillment, and this will come through alliances with reliable
white allies such as those who have died heroically at the side of
the blacks or have risked economic and political peril to support
the black cause.

There is a great deal the white man can do through his own
efforts to master his paralyzing fears, but if the fear in the white
community is to be mitigated, it will need the help of the black

* Martin Luther King, Jr., *Where Do We Go from Here: Chaos or Community?* (New York: Harper & Row, 1967), pp. 12 f., 18, 21 f., 40 f.
† *Ibid.*, p. 44.

spirit of nonviolence. Willing like Job to stand alone even against his friends, King repeatedly stated: "If every Negro in the United States turns to violence, I will choose to be that lone voice preaching that this is the wrong way." If a new image of man is to emerge from the hidden human image, mankind must begin to turn away from the long and desolate night of violence, and a new power infused with love and justice must appear. Such a power will bring to the surface that kind of tension that is healthy and necessary for growth. "Society needs nonviolent gadflies to bring its tensions into the open and force its citizens to confront the ugliness of their prejudices and the tragedy of their racism." Through such gadflies the liberal will finally "see that the oppressed person who agitates for his rights is not the creator of tension" but merely brings out the hidden tension that is already alive.*

Recognizing that power is not evil in itself but is the ability to achieve purpose, King deplores the common tendency to contrast the concepts of love and justice as polar opposites so that love becomes the resignation of power, power the denial of love. The major crisis of our time is this collision of immoral power with powerless morality.

> What is needed is a realization that power without love is reckless and abusive and that love without power is sentimental and anemic. Power at its best is love implementing the demands of justice. Justice at its best is love correcting everything that stands against love.†

This statement is almost identical with Martin Buber's 1926 poem, "Power and Love."

1

> Our hope is too new and too old—
> I do not know what would remain to us
> Were love not transfigured power
> And power not straying love.

* *Ibid.*, pp. 46–49, 51 f., 60 f., 63 f., 66, 90 f.
† *Ibid.*, p. 37.

2

Do not protest: "Let love alone rule!"
Can you prove it true?
But resolve: Every morning
I shall concern myself anew about the boundary
Between the love-deed-Yes and the power-deed-No
And pressing forward honor reality.

3

We cannot avoid
Using power,
Cannot escape the compulsion
To afflict the world,
So let us, cautious in diction
And mighty in contradiction,
Love powerfully. *

To be afraid to stand up for justice is to be dead already. To take a stand for what is right, though the whole world criticize and misunderstand you, is to be a majority of one with God. For, says King, you are never alone.

In 1963 it seemed as if King had reached a high point of influence with the famous March on Washington and his great speech to a hundred thousand people, "I have a dream!" Within two years after this march, many of those who were concerned about civil rights in America became equally concerned about the disastrous war in Vietnam. In the fall of 1966, King had to make a difficult decision, and he made it unhesitatingly. At that point he declared that the fight for civil rights could not be divorced from the demand for peace in Vietnam. The immediate and all too realistic link was the fact that college students were being exempted from the draft and that the American Negro, as a result, was bearing a disproportionate share of the fighting in

* Martin Buber, *A Believing Humanism: Gleanings*, trans. with an Introduction and Explanatory Comments by Maurice Friedman (New York: Simon & Schuster Paperbacks, 1969), p. 45.

Vietnam. Relatively few American Negroes have had the education or have the financial resources necessary for entering college, and for many young Negroes even volunteering in the
Army seemed better than eking out a subsistence living on the
margin of unemployment and welfare. The more basic reason,
for King, however, was the impossibility of separating into wa-
tertight compartments the fight against injustice at home and the
fight against injustice abroad. Immediately a number of the
leaders of various branches of the black movement in the United
States disclaimed King's action. None attempted to impeach his
sincerity or his patriotism, but all stated that this was not "good
strategy" in the fight for civil rights.

It was at this point that my admiration for King reached its
highest peak. Here was a man prepared to bear witness for the
right as he saw it even at the expense of "strategy." Here was a
social actionist and political leader ready to sacrifice influence
and prestige rather than give in to an argument of expediency.
Knowing that King had on occasion quoted Martin Buber in his
speeches, I was strongly tempted at this time to send him my
translation of two short pieces in Martin Buber's then unpublished book, *A Believing Humanism.* As the American Martin
Luther King was the disciple of Gandhi on the path of nonviolent resistance, so Gandhi in his turn was deeply influenced by
an American of a century ago—Henry Thoreau. Writing on the
centennial of Thoreau's death, Buber testified that reading
Thoreau's classic tract on "Civil Disobedience" had had a strong
impact on him in his youth, but that it was only much later that
he understood why.

> It was the concrete, the personal, the "here and now" in the
> writing that won my heart for it. Thoreau did not formulate a
> general principle as such; he set forth and grounded his attitude
> in a particular historical-biographical situation. He spoke to his
> reader in the realm of this situation common to them so that the
> reader not only learned why Thoreau at that time acted as he
> acted, but also—provided that this reader was only honest and
> unbiased—that he himself, the reader, must have acted, should

the occasion present itself, in just such a way if he was seriously concerned about making his human existence real.*

In writing these words, Buber, like Thoreau, was not just concerned with one of the many cases in which powerless truth struggles against a power inimical to truth. For Buber as for Thoreau, it was "a question of the wholly concrete indication of the point at which time and again this struggle becomes the duty of man *as man.*" What Buber said of Thoreau must be said in still greater measure of Gandhi and of Martin Luther King. Because each of them spoke as concretely as he did from his historical situation, he expressed in the right manner what is valid for all human history.

This is what I felt impelled—though alas not to the point of doing so!—to send to Martin Luther King. I also wanted to send him the longer companion piece in which Buber applied the question of "civil disobedience" to the international situation today. Civil disobedience, if it is to be legitimate, must be obedience to a higher authority than the one that we here and now obey. But there is no general way of demonstrating the legitimacy of this higher authority or of setting the limit to what we have to give to Caesar. Not at all times and places but only in the particular situation, in the here and now, can this question be answered.

In our situation, however, it is easier to answer than ever before, for man is today on the point of letting the determination of his fate slip out of his hands. The all-embracing preparations and mutually outstripping bellicose surprises on all sides in the "cold war" may reach such a point of automation as to transform the human cosmos "into a chaos beyond which we can no longer think." If, as Buber thinks, the rulers of the hour cannot wake up before it is too late, command a halt to the machinery, and learn to talk *to* instead of *past* one another, then who will come to the rescue while there is still time but the "disobedient," those who personally set their faces against the power that has gone astray?

* *Ibid.,* "On 'Civil Disobedience,' " p. 191.

"Must not a planetary front of such civil disobedients stand ready, not for battle like other fronts, but for saving dialogue? But who are these if not those who hear the voice that addresses them from the situation—the situation of the human crisis—and obey it?"*

Who can doubt that Martin Luther King was not just the representative of the Afro-Americans in their fight against racism and social inequality but a man who stood ready for saving dialogue, a man who heard and obeyed the voice of the concrete situation, a man who discovered in the situation, both national and international, not just what affected his race but the wholly concrete indication of his duty *as man*? It was with great pride that I marched with four hundred thousand others in New York City April 15, 1967, in a protest against the war in Vietnam led by Martin Luther King.

The decisions which Martin Luther King had to make in the last months and weeks of his life may have been the most difficult and painful of all. During these months the extremists in the Black Power Movement no longer looked to King as their leader nor to nonviolence as their spirit and their method. In the face of the riots that broke out in one after another of the Negro ghettos in the great American cities, in the face of threats and increasing danger of planned and spontaneous violence, King was placed before a cruel dilemma. If he tried to keep in the forefront of the Civil Rights Movement, would he have to countenance or at least go along with the violence he had so long opposed? If he failed to make common cause with the new forces in this movement, would he be forced into inaction as his only protection against allowing his influence to increase the possibility of violence? Here too, in the face of an ever more polarized situation, King stood firm and walked the way of the Modern Job. He increased his activity, if anything, joining in the strike in Memphis, and planning his great "Poor People's Campaign." Yet he refused to depart from the spirit and principles that had guided

* *Ibid.,* "More on 'Civil Disobedience,'" pp. 192 f.

his social witness in the dozen years since he had assumed leadership.

The speech which Martin Luther King gave in Memphis the night before his assassination is a great witness of a Modern Job—and a modern Moses:

> When people get caught up with what is right and sacrifice for it, there is no stopping point short of victory.
>
> We would go before the dogs in Birmingham singing, "Ain't going to· let nobody turn me around." Then they got out fire hoses. But there's a certain kind of fire no water can put out.
>
> . . . We have got to give ourselves to this struggle till the end. . . . Either we go up together or we go down together. Let us develop a kind of dangerous unselfishness.
>
> Thank God for allowing me to be here. A few years ago I was stabbed in Harlem while autographing my book *Stride toward Freedom*. The tip of the blade touched my aorta, my main artery. If I had merely sneezed, I would have died. . . . If I had, I wouldn't have been around in 1960 when students all over sat down in counters and stood up for the best in America, or in 1961 when we took a freedom ride, or in 1962 when blacks in Georgia put their backs up, or in 1963 when Birmingham showed the nation something, or in Selma, or in Washington to tell the nation that I have a dream.
>
> My plane was protected and guarded all night on the way to Memphis. Then in Memphis the threats were out as to what would happen to me from my white brothers. But it doesn't matter what happens to me now. I have been to the mountaintop, I have looked over and seen the Promised Land. I may not get there with you. But we as a people will get to the Promised Land. So I'm happy tonight. I'm not worried about anything. I'm not fearing any man. My eyes have seen the coming of the glory of the Lord.*

These words were spoken in an ever-rising crescendo ending on a high point of joy, intensity, and victory that even the brutal murder of the next day could not undo!

---

* These partial quotations are based on my notes from a private tape recording of King's speech, April 3, 1968.

The weekend before King's assassination I was giving a seminar in a large Midwestern city in the United States. In the course of the seminar we came to a discussion of the almost certain danger of still more terrible riots occurring in the American cities the following summer and of the massive preparations of the police forces of those cities to meet those riots. I had not followed closely what had been happening in Memphis where King was marching with the strikers and was taken by surprise when one leading citizen after another accused him in connection with the police violence against Negroes that had occurred. Finally I saw a dark-skinned girl who had just come in raise her hand, and I called on her, expecting that she at least would do King justice. "By his very presence there he is inciting violence!" she exclaimed. (She was not, as I had imagined, part Negro, but an American Arab who had been sent to interview me by the local Christian radio station.) "That is unfair!" I replied. "If there is any man who stands for something, it is Martin Luther King. If a small group has used his activities as a cover for violence, that cannot be laid at his door, nor can he be expected to cease his activity because of it." My belief in King was borne out by the facts that I later learned—that only a small group had incited violence, and King had resolutely opposed it. Five days later when the news of King's assassination reached me, I wondered what those faithful churchgoing people in the Protestant church at which I had held the seminar would be thinking. Would their words come back to them with shame? Or would they see precisely this event as a justification for what they said? The possibility of his being murdered was nothing new to King. He and his wife and his co-workers in the Southern Christian Leadership Conference lived with that possibility every time he made an appearance anywhere. But are we going to say then that when a man stands his ground, without flinching and without hatred, he must be held responsible for the fact that precisely such conduct calls forth the murderous hatred and violence of the weak and the cowardly?

The assassination of Martin Luther King is also a murder of

man as man. It is an eclipse of the human image that so much else has obscured and tarnished in our day. Yet Martin Luther King's presence will remain with us—not just as an American Gandhi, or even a Modern Job, but as himself in his unique personal witness. He will remain for us an image of what—in this time of great confrontations and little dialogue—it means to be human.

THE COMMUNITY OF
OTHERNESS AND
THE COVENANT OF PEACE

The "hidden image of man" may suggest to some that our concern is man as an individual. It is not. The image of man exists *between* man and man, it exists in *community*, or it fails to exist, i.e., it is obscured between man and man and still more in those agglomerates that we call our cities. Even if we talk about "real personal growth," it does not just mean individual freedom, either in its roots, its means, its goal, or its effect. That is because the goal is not that of *having* experience or consciousness expansion per se but becoming unique in response to the call of the world. This becoming may entail experience and consciousness expansion; it will certainly entail risk. But experience, expansion, and risk do not automatically lead to this goal. It depends upon how they are used and how they are related to.

Nor is the question one of the rights of the individual versus the rights of the community, but of the person's being open to growth *and* accepting the conditions and limitations of growth as an organic member of the community who must stand on the ground of his personal uniqueness and demand such freedom for growth as the situation at any time allows while at the same time recognizing that his growth does not take place through relationship to himself. He has to confirm others in their uniqueness and in their need. He has to confirm the common ground of communal existence as a meaning larger than that of the individual but inclusive of it. The communal existence here does not equal harmony or obedience to authority, but building together—each from where he is and from what he is—what I have called the "community of otherness."* Communal responsibility in the same way begins and must begin with the individual. It is only possible through overcoming false individualism, through recognizing the interhuman and social corollaries of one's own growth, and through one's stake and trust in the community.

But the communal responsibility is also that of the community. It has to encourage the maximum growth of the individuals and the small groups within it, and this, of course, applies very much to the communes which are springing up everywhere today. The community must set limits where necessary, but, if it is a real community, if it has real communal concern, it can never just cut off the person and cease to be responsible for him. It cannot offer only a conditional confirmation. This again is what I mean by the "community of otherness."

Venture and risk are a part of all life. Risk is implied in the very notion both of personal growth and communal authenticity. Today, however, the venturing on all fronts in order to break out of the unlived life that has confined us greatly multiplies the risk. There is no formula that helps us, no Either/Or of risk or no risk which is of any value. Our problem is to draw the demarcation line responsibly and ever anew: This much risk this group, this community, this family can take and no more in this hour, this situation. This is not at all the same as that self-protection engaged in by the community in casting out the person who raises anxieties or threatens its happy harmony.

The center of a community is not itself. Perhaps this is something which young people in their search for communes have to learn most of all. The center of a commune must be a living center to which all the members are dedicated. They must build

* Maurice Friedman, *Touchstones of Reality: Existential Trust and the Community of Peace* (New York: Dutton Paperbacks, 1974). This chapter is based on the combination of two themes treated separately in *Touchstones of Reality*.

together in a common concern. We must get beyond the parties
and ideologies and be ready to meet one another as persons, as
groups.

When I say a community should have a common concern or
common center, I do not mean a community of affinity that has a
common formula, a common creed. Nor do I mean that everyone
does the same thing and certainly not that they do it from the
same point of view. What I do mean, though, is that what makes
real community is people finding themselves in a common situation—a situation which they approach in different ways, yet
which calls each of them out. The commune which simply meets
each night to inspect its communal navel will be no better off
than the person who withdraws each night to gaze at his private
navel. This is again the whole paradox of immediacy. We want
it, we long for it, but if we aim at it directly, we do not get it. It
comes again and again as a by-product. The very existence in
community is already a common concern, a caring for one another.
In addition, there is the house, the land, the vigilantes marching
in, the courts making trouble about taxes. But just because a
number of people are lonely and say, "Wouldn't it be good to be
communal?" does not mean that it will add up to a commune.
The will to overcome alienation will not in itself overcome it.

A quarter of a century ago I described our time in words that
seem to me far truer today than when I wrote them:

> The common man of today lives in growing fear and insecurity;
> for he does not really believe that the leaders of the nations will
> be able to find those means of unity which will stave off the
> destruction that each country is preparing for its neighbor. The
> leaders themselves are in the clutch of a fear and a distrust which
> are more powerful than all the rational arguments which show
> the need of finding peaceful settlements of our international prob-
> lems. Thus we are caught in a vicious circle. Unsatisfactory polit-
> ical, economic, and social conditions create insecurity which in
> turn prevents that cooperation and trust which might make possi-
> ble the solution of those problems. . . . Those creative forces in
> man which might use the discoveries of science to build a new

and joyous world are paralyzed by that fear which makes man feel helpless before the political and industrial juggernaut which he has himself built up.*

We live in an era in which the social cement that held society together has been dissolved and the most ordinary social confidence is no longer present. We could not imagine, in advance, that people would systematically turn other persons into cakes of soap or irradiate people in such a way that they would die on the spot *or* slowly and horribly over a great many years. Yet now that this has happened, reality creates possibility, and the unthinkable is no longer unthinkable. In *To Deny Our Nothingness* I have spoken of a "Dialogue with the Absurd," implying that it is sometimes possible, without making the absurd anything other than absurd, to enter into dialogue with it, to find meaning in this dialogue. But this "Dialogue with the Absurd" does not in any way mean that the inconceivable horror which it has been our fate to witness and live through is anything other than just that. Any view which enables us to be comfortable with the destruction and endless suffering of countless of our contemporaries is surely a deception.

Wherever men meet in a spirit of common concern, ready to encounter each other beyond their terminologies, the lived reality of "the community of otherness" can come into being. No group is able to confirm all otherness. That is beyond human capacity. But the test of a fellowship is the otherness that it can confirm, which should not begin by going out to gather other people in but by understanding from within the actual people present. If you explain to someone that he is really not a member of the group because he does not fit your conception of the group, you have read him out of existence as far as this moment and this situation are concerned. Trust and openness are the same. It is our lack of trust, our existential mistrust, that makes us feel that we have to have the security of like-minded groups,

---

* Quoted in Friedman, *Touchstones of Reality*, pp. 80 f.; not previously published.

groups based on generalized affinity rather than on the concreteness of open meeting with the real otherness that is present in every group, down to a pair of friends or a husband and wife.

The "community of otherness" implies a relationship that takes place *between* persons and cannot be counted on as a social technique at our disposal. Our whole notion of action—that we use *this* means to *that* end—is a plain violation of the concrete reality, which is that we do not know what the consequences are going to be of almost any action that we do. We must have social planning and social action, but we cannot string together events in such fashion that they become links in a chain of cause and effect or moves in a chess game. We think that we know what will happen because we imagine it happens *through* us. Yet we do not even know our own resources, much less the situation that will confront us. If we are so well "prepared" that we carry the situation off the way we expected, we may be sure that we have not really been present, that we have not heard the real address of the situation. We have to founder and flounder before we can discover what is asked of us. What we have said of encounter groups is true of social planning in general: We can plan the *structure* within which social events will take place, but we cannot plan the events themselves.

This is something John Friedmann has understood clearly in placing "the life of dialogue" at the heart of his book *Retracking America*, and he has understood it within the context of the "community of otherness." Through his experience as director of urban planning at the University of California at Los Angeles, Friedmann has recognized that genuine dialogue begins with the acceptance of "otherness" as a basis for meaningful communication, and that this means in turn the acceptance of the reality of conflict and of the possibility of overcoming conflict "by a mutual desire to continue in the life of dialogue." "Dialogue presumes a relation of shared interests and commitments," "of reciprocity and mutual obligation," "a relationship that unfolds in real time." "Transactive planning is carried on the ground swell of dialogue," writes Friedmann.

> In mutual learning, planner and client each learns from the other —the planner from the client's personal knowledge, the client from the planner's technical expertise. In this process, the knowledge of both undergoes a major change. A common image of the situation evolves through dialogue; a new understanding of the possibilities for change is discovered. And in accord with this new knowledge, the client will be predisposed to act. *

It is particularly in a large and wealthy society like America that Friedmann sees the possibility of building a community of otherness, for it "is quite capable of accommodating a multiplicity of life styles and the simultaneous pursuit of many different interests." Planning for the community of otherness means openness to surprise. Friedmann argues for "the recognition and acceptance of a class of actions that, rather than being goal-oriented, is *exploratory* in nature." Such "non-directed actions" are "increasingly important in a society where we can know relatively little about the probable consequences of actions, except in certain restricted areas of behavior." This open-ended approach leads Friedmann to the recognition of the historically limited validity of social theories in contrast to the claim of general validity made in the scientific method:

> The return of theory to practice in the fullness of historical situations, with none of the variables held constant as in a laboratory, will either confirm or deny the theory's practical value in these specific situations. It will not say anything about the potential applicability of the theory in other situations that, however similar in some respects, will have different overall contexts.†

This distinction is almost identical with the one that I make between testing "touchstones of reality" and scientific testing:

* John Friedmann, *Retracking America: A Theory of Transactive Planning* (Garden City, N.Y.: Doubleday Anchor Books, 1973), p. 185.
† *Ibid.*, p. 235.

However true our touchstone, it will cease to be true if we do not make it real again by testing it in each new situation. This testing is nothing more nor less than bringing our life-stance into the moment of present reality. In contrast to the scientist who is only interested in particulars insofar as they yield generalizations, we can derive valid insights from the unique situations in which we find ourselves without having to claim that they apply to all situations. We take these insights with us into other situations and test the limits of their validity. Sometimes we find that these insights do hold for a particular situation and sometimes that they do not or that they have to be modified. Yet that does not mean that they cannot be valid insights for other situations. *

Calling for networks of communication links relating clusters of task-oriented working groups, or cells, Friedmann envisages a spirit of mutual trust, self-criticism, and collective evaluation within these cells that make each separately and the network in general into communities of otherness. He recognizes that modern man's capacity for dialogue is stunted, that, as I put it, "much of our sharing is pseudosharing because we lift it to a plane of objective discourse" and abstract what the other says from the personal and existential ground from which he says it. Because our relations are determined by roles and utility, we hear without listening and speak without responding. "Extremely skillful in exchanging functional bits of information," writes Friedmann, modern man "fails in assessing the underlying meanings because he assumes, incorrectly, that information has a reality independent of the persons through whom it becomes available and to whom it is addressed." But this failure of the life of dialogue may be overcome, Friedmann holds, through the mutual participation of small, irreducible cells of a learning society, cells which can easily be formed anywhere at any time.

Task-oriented working groups may be spontaneously created in a variety of environments—in factories, offices, neighborhoods, clubs, schools, and universities. Their actions will have an experimental character; the ingenuity of working group members

* Friedman, *Touchstones of Reality*, pp. 24 f.

will lead to innovations and discoveries. The life of dialogue will be encouraged, simply because it is the most natural way to approach a problem solution that asks of every member a commitment to the total effort and, above all, to the group's continued existence so long as the challenge of a task remains. The group has no means of survival but for the strength of its internal dialogue.*

Friedmann believes that there is an even chance of a learning society coming into existence in America, though it would entail "social innovations on a scale unheard of until now." "But so long as the root remains healthy . . . and life is celebrated in dialogue," he concludes, "even the topmost branches will be vigorous and bear new shoots."

We live in a time in which we find ourselves painfully trying to rebuild real communities within the larger social bodies. One of the dangers, of course, is the temptation to betray the "community of otherness" by designating one's own commune or cell "the blessed community" and consigning everything else to total meaninglessness, if not to the profane. Everything is the "real world," including the "godforsaken" part of it. But our responsibility has much to do with our humble awareness of the factual limitations of our resources in any actual situation. One of the serious aspects of a moral way of life is the, repeated, ever-renewed decision as to where to draw the line of responsibility in each unique situation.

Reconciliation depends upon each of us doing his share to build the "community of otherness." Reality is not given in me alone or in some part of reality with which I identify myself. Among primitive tribes, the members of other tribes were often not even considered human beings. Even the civilized Greeks saw the rest of the non-Greek world as "barbarians" and therefore by nature unequal to them and properly forced into permanent slavery when conquered. On the coast of Africa there are still great castles in which for four hundred years the Portuguese, the Dutch, and the English vied with one another as to

* Friedmann, *Retracking America*, pp. 240 f.

who could get the most profit out of shipping fifty million slaves to America for sale there. The ravaging of the American frontier and of the whaling industry, similarly, shows that a good deal of what has characterized modern man, long before the Nazi exterminations, has been a lack of respect for the otherness of creation, including the nonhuman.

The respect for the otherness of the other does not mean that I love everyone or even that I have the resources to meet everyone in genuine dialogue. But it does mean that just everything that confronts me demands my attention and response—whether of love or hate, agreement or opposition, confirmation or merely letting be. There is a growing tendency today, on both sides of the generation gap, on both extremes of the political spectrum, and on both sides of every militant social and racial confrontation, to regard some people as totally irrelevant because they are not "where it is at." The "community of otherness" stands in uncompromising opposition to this tendency. I have freedom, but I am not the whole of reality, and I find my existence in going out to meet what is not myself.

We live in an age of compounded crises, an age of hot and cold war and the constant threat of total annihilation by the weapons that we ourselves have perfected. It is an age more and more bereft of authentic human existence, and even the image of such existence increasingly deserts us.

War, cold war, threatened war, future war, has become the very atmosphere in which we live, a total element so pervasive and so enveloping as to numb our very sensibility to the abyss which promises to engulf us. In the eighteenth century Immanuel Kant searched for "eternal peace" in terms of the rationality, the dignity, and the universal humanity of man. In our day it is faith in these very things that has broken down. The search for a simple universality has gotten us nowhere, and we are as far as ever from overcoming nationalism. New nations keep coming up all the time in the Middle East and Africa, and these nations are not going to be satisfied always to have a lesser share in the "universal" order.

The greatest task of contemporary man is not to build "enlightened" utopias but to build peace in the context in which he finds himself. The true peacemakers are those who take upon themselves, in the most concrete manner conceivable, the task of discovering what can be done in each situation of tension and struggle by way of facing the real conflicts and working toward genuine reconciliation.

"A peace without truth is a false peace," said Rabbi Mendel of Kotzk. What "truth" means here is made clear by the Talmudic statement the Hasidic master partly quoted: Controversies for the sake of heaven endure. This is completely contrary to Aristotelian logic with its assumption that a statement and its opposite cannot both be true. If controversies take place for the sake of heaven, then *both* sides will endure. It does not mean that eventually one will be proved right and the other wrong. The knowledge that the other also witnesses for his "touchstone of reality" from where he stands can enable us to confirm the other in his truth even while opposing him. We do not have to liberate the world from those who have different witnesses from us. The converse of this also holds, namely, that each must hold his ground and witness for his truth even while at the same time affirming the ground and the truth of the other. This imaginative task of comprehending a relationship from the other side as well as one's own is essential to the goal of overcoming war, for every war justifies itself by turning the enemy into a Manichaean figure of pure evil.

If the present crises lead us to succumb to the merely political, we shall have reinforced the mistrust between nations that makes them deal with each other not in social or human terms but in terms of political abstractions and catchwords. "Our work is for education," one of the leaders of an organized protest against atomic bombs said to me. If this is so, then this work cannot afford to be purely political, purely external. It must start from some organic base. It must build on social reality and find its roots in the community already there. It must be concerned about real communication with the people whom it approaches.

For the distinction between propaganda and education does not lie in whether one is a Communist or a pacifist but in whether one approaches another wishing to impose one's truth on him or whether one cares enough for him to enter into dialogue with him, see the situation from his point of view, and communicate what truth one has to communicate to him within that dialogue. Sometimes that dialogue can only mean standing one's ground in opposition to him, witnessing for what one believes in the face of his hostile rejection of it. Yet it can never mean being unconcerned for how he sees it or careless of the validity of his standing where he does. We must confirm him even as we oppose him, not in his "error" but in his right to oppose us, in his existence as a human being whom we value even in opposing.

For the "covenant of peace,"* both the means and the end are the building of true community—the community of otherness. It is not requisite upon a community to forego all action for the sake of the lone dissenter. But much depends upon whether it takes the action as a real community or just as a majority which is for the moment able to override the minority. The reality of community is polyphonic, it is many-voiced. In real community the voice of the minority is heard because real community creates an atmosphere of trust which enables this minority to make its witness. I have been in very few groups in my life, including the finest, where real community has not been violated day after day by a few "weighty" persons imposing their will upon the less sure in the name of what *should* be done.

The true opposite of this imposition is that trust through which the "other voice" is elicited of the person who will speak only in an atmosphere that weights every voice equally no matter how hesitant or how much in the minority it may be. From 1939 until his death in 1965 Martin Buber continued to insist that Jews live *with* the Arabs in Palestine and later Israel and not just *next* to them and to warn that the way must be like the

* For a full-scale discussion of the "covenant of peace"—both its relationship to the biblical covenant and its implications for nonviolence—and peace—see Friedman, *Touchstones of Reality*, Chaps. 7 and 15.

goal—*Zion bmishpat* ("Zion with justice")—that the humanity of our existence begins just where we become responsible to the concrete situation by saying: "We shall do no more injustice than we must to live," and by drawing the "demarcation line" in each hour anew in fear and trembling. The covenant of peace—between man and man, between community and community, and between nation and nation—means dialogue.

Dialogue means the meeting with the other person, the other group, the other people—a meeting that confirms the other yet does not deny oneself and the ground on which one stands. The choice is not *between* oneself and the other, nor is there some objective ground to which one can rise above the opposing sides, the conflicting claims. Rather genuine dialogue is at once a confirmation of community *and* of otherness, and the acceptance of the fact that one cannot rise above that situation. "In a genuine dialogue," writes Buber, "each of the partners, even when he stands in opposition to the other, heeds, affirms, and confirms his opponent as an existing other. Only so can conflict certainly not be eliminated from the world, but be humanly arbitrated and led towards its overcoming."

During three years of work as chairman of the American Friends of Ichud (the Israeli association for Israel-Arab rapprochement led by Judah Magnes and Martin Buber), I was again and again surprised to encounter among men of goodwill, including men working for reconciliation of the conflict, either an attitude which simply did not take into account the real problems to be reconciled, one that saw these problems from one point of view only, or one that proceeded from some pseudo-objective, quasi-universal point of view above the conflict. Every conflict has at least two sides. Even if one of the two sides is "dead wrong" in its opinion or stand, it represents something real that cannot be done away with, namely, its existence itself. In that sense it literally has a different point of view which must be recognized quite apart from the question of the rightness or wrongness of the position it takes. All too often, the word *reconciliation* becomes associated with a sentimental goodwill that looks away from the very conflict that is to be reconciled or assumes that with this or that action or approach a tragic situation can be transformed into a harmonious one. Genuine reconciliation must begin with a fully realistic and fully honest recognition of real differences and points of conflict, and it must move from this recognition to the task of discovering the standpoint from which some real meeting may take place, a meeting which will include *both* of the conflicting points of view and will seek new and creative ways of reconciling them.

The covenant of peace is neither technique nor formula and still less is it a universal principle which needs only be applied by deduction to the particular situation. It takes its start from the concrete situation, including all of its tensions—tensions which we can never hope or even desire to remove entirely since they belong to the very heart of the community of otherness. The covenant of peace is no ideal that one holds above the situation, but a patient and never-finished working toward some points of mutual contact, mutual understanding, and mutual trust. It builds community by way of the mutual confirmation of otherness, and when this community shipwrecks, as it again and again tends to do, it takes up the task anew. The covenant of peace means a movement *in the direction* of the community of otherness, such movement as each new hour allows.

The community of otherness grows out of conflict within mutual cooperation, mutual understanding, and ultimately mutual trust. But in bedrock situations even a negative protest may be a positive step toward dialogue if it is done in the spirit of dialogue by men who embody that spirit. The covenant of peace implies a "fellowship of reconciliation"; yet it is precisely here that we have fallen short. We have tended to turn "reconciliation" into a platform to expound, a program to put over, and have not recognized the cruel opposition and the real otherness that underlie conflict. We have been loath to admit that there are tragic conflicts in which no way toward reconciliation is at present possible. We have been insufficiently tough-minded in our attitude toward love, turning it into an abstract love for mankind or a feeling within ourselves rather than a meeting between us and others. We cannot really love unless we first know the other, and we cannot know him until we have entered into relationship with him.

Only a real listening—a listening witness—can plumb the abyss of that universal existential mistrust that stands in the way of genuine dialogue and peace. The Peace Movement has not adequately recognized the power of violence in our day and that its roots are not just in human nature in general or in the stupidity of men but in the special malaise of modern man—his lack of a meaningful personal and social direction, his lack of an image of man, his loss of community, his basic loss of trust in himself and others and in the world in which he lives, his fear of real confrontation with otherness, his tendency to cling to the shores of institutionalized injustice and discrimination rather than set out upon the open seas of creating new and more meaningful structures within which the "wretched of the earth," the dispossessed and the systematically ignored, can find their voice too. The true heart of the covenant of peace is the community of otherness.

PART VIII

REVEALING
THE HIDDEN
HUMAN
IMAGE

THE MODERN
PROMETHEAN
AND THE
MODERN JOB

If this is the era of the "eclipse of God," it is even more that of the eclipse of man. In forms more terrible than the Four Horsemen of the Apocalypse, the eclipse of man has come riding into our century. Auschwitz, Hiroshima, Vietnam—each of these names symbolizes not only the destruction of man but his degradation. It is only in our era that millions of men have been systematically exterminated like insects and others condemned to the slower death of radiation, napalm, and starvation.

The totalitarianism of the Italian Fascists and the Nazis and of Stalinist Russia has been followed by subtler but in the end perhaps hardly less insidious forms of collectivism. What we call "brainwashing" when it is carried out by our enemies, we call "persuasion" when it is done by ourselves. The very scientists who are busy imposing upon us the image of man as pigeon, rat, or, still lower, flatworm, indefinitely malleable through the injection of the proper chemicals, or as a cybernetic feedback machine capable of being smoothly adjusted to society, are the ones who are receiving the large government and military grants for the furtherance of the manipulation of man!

There is a quite different possibility which we have pointed to. Instead of using every latest scientific concept as a new form of positivism and scientism to nail things down with, we can use science as a form of openness, as a way of asking questions of the world. For that is what science is. Despite the prestige of science, or rather because of it, we have to use our scientific analogies carefully. We ought to know where they are analogous and where they are not. Much of modern science, while it by no means destroys the system that went before, has at least got rid of the dogmatism of the eighteenth century, the dogmatism of universal laws. It has gotten rid of it in favor of hypotheses, questions that we ask and answers that we get. In other words, modern science points to the possibility of a new openness. Even if we cannot image our world, we can live with the uncanniness, the absurdity of an unimageable world.

Psychotherapy is one of the great breakthroughs of our time. It has told us a great deal about man. Yet it has often tended to offer us *constructs* of men and the false security of man turned into an object where the scientist who looks at this "object" does not see that he himself as a subject, *as a whole person seen from within*, must enter into his knowing of man. We cannot know what man is from the safe position merely of the Freudian analytical or the Skinnerian behaviorist observer. What really matters is not that one be without a method and structure of therapy, but the ever-renewed decision as to which is the more basic, the structure that you have set up or the unique event. If the structure is the more basic, then you will have to do as John Dewey said and smooth down the uniqueness of events, get rid of their vividness, and play down their colorfulness so that you can extract from them "data"—that which enables them to be put into abstract categories which in turn can serve as the basis of a generalization. But when you are dealing with a human being, are you really going to do that or are you as a therapist going instead *to listen to this person before you*, to enter into relationship with him in such fashion that your knowing of this person is in the first instance a *mutual* knowing, a knowing *in* relationship? Even if this knowing is not fully mutual in the sense that the patient can experience the relationship from the side of the therapist, this does not prevent it from being a gen-

.uine knowing, a genuine partnership, a genuine "healing through meeting." Into this knowing enter also the things that you know more objectively from the theories of your school and other schools, from case histories, and from your own past therapeutic experience.

Moral action often issues into social action, but it does not simply mean social action. It implies, too, a particular attitude—that a person is not relieved of his personal moral responsibility even while engaging in social action. In 1919, after the terrible years of war and the German revolution, Martin Buber wrote an essay called "What Is to Be Done?" If by "What is to be done?" he said, you mean "What is one to do?" the answer is "Nothing." *One* is to do nothing. But if you mean "What am I to do?" then the answer is "Do not withhold yourself." Moral action refers to actual involvement, actual engagement in a situation.

The situation addresses and claims us, but it cannot itself supply our response. The answer to the claim of the situation is the product of the *meeting* between us and the situation, including the human image that we bring to it—our readiness to respond in personal wholeness to what calls us out. Our image of the human may be confirmed through our response to *this* situation, but it may also be modified by it. The human image embraces the differences *and* the uniqueness of the situation, but some encounters affect the ground tone of our being and with it our image of the human. We must be open to what each new person, each new event that we encounter says to us about man *as man*—what man is, what man can become, what man ought to become. Man is not a given, a finished product. Man constantly shapes himself. This shaping has a great deal to do with the images of man that we make our own by responding to them from the ground of our uniqueness.

If we look deeply into violence, as we have tried to do, we discover that violence is connected with some of the deepest things that make us human beings. Therefore, we cannot remove violence at will. We have to give positive direction to what becomes violence if it is frustrated or suppressed. When you frustrate men enough and apply fear enough, violence is going to erupt. "Nonviolence" is often wrongly confused with nonresistance to evil. It is resistance, as both Gandhi and Martin Luther King emphasized, but if it becomes merely a technique, then it is less than it claims to be. Martin Luther King helped to reveal the hidden human image precisely because he was not merely an engineer shifting various gears on an automobile or tractor called "nonviolence." Though there is, indeed, a power of violence—violence which shows not only an ugly and brutal but an impersonal face—perhaps there is no "power of nonviolence." Perhaps the power lies in the hidden human image which reveals itself in these situations. Only this power makes visible the real resources, that is, the people who are not simply triggered off, people who are not startled by the socially unexpected happening, people who can respond and act in the situation. After a year in England a worker in nonviolent action suggested that one effective step toward social change might be to have an intensive training team live together. It is very important, not just that each person know his or her job, but how "social-change agents" live together and build relationships among and between them.

The cruelest problem for a young man who has to decide whether or not to become a conscientious objector and perhaps also whether or not to refuse to do alternative service, is that he has no way of knowing at the age of eighteen whether this is a decision of his whole self. He has not tested his ideals and thoughts. He cannot know how he will hold up if he is sentenced to a five-year stretch in prison. We are accustomed to demand that persons who take moral stands do so in a heroic way, all in shining armor like Lohengrin. But a young man in our society who has to make a decision in which he is not likely to be confirmed probably will not be able to do so as a whole person and will experience a great deal of anguish and self-doubt in the process. To be able to stand one's ground and witness is something one has to grow to. Yet young men at the age of eighteen or nineteen are faced by the moral decision that may be the most terrible one of their lives. Albert Schweitzer, because of his sacrifice and because of his greatness, became an image of man for people all over the world —even though today we would not accept his patronizing attitude toward the black men with whom he worked. Mahatma Gandhi was not just a great religious and political leader. He was for the whole world an image of man—an embodiment of "soul-force" that made "nonviolent resistance" not just a technique but a way of life. If the black man in the ghetto should be faced by a situation that demanded his response and action, as in the case of a riot, what image of man would guide him? Would it be Martin Luther King, who deeply stirred a great many people, even those who did not believe in his tactics? Or would it be Malcolm X, who stirred his fellow blacks in quite a different way? The way a man responds to a situation does not depend just on the party he belongs to or the particular political or economic theories he espouses, but also on the image of man that draws him. For many people, especially many young people, Che Guevara is the image of the intellectual rebel, the fighter for Third World wars of liberation. The image of man for other rebels is Albert Camus, who rallied as a fighter, who took part in the French *Résistance*, but who also lived the life of dialogue and refused to turn causes into mere ideologies.

Some years ago a real force and presence at Pendle Hill, the Quaker center for study and dialogue, was a Quaker who taught the social action course and who wrote a pamphlet entitled *Visible Witness*, in which he said that it is not enough to make a witness if it does not show. The hidden human image is revealed, indeed, in action. But I often wondered whether this "change agent" recognized the extent to which *he* was a part of his witness? When people saw this old man walking in the rain, picketing against atomic bomb plants or marching for peace or civil rights, it was what he *was* as well as what he did—the two indissoluble—which was the visible witness. If there is a connection between the image of man and moral and

social action, it is that of the visible witness, and what it means
to make a witness visible.

When I was a young man, I tried conscientiously and in all
sincerity to decide my attitude to all war. Now I realize that in
asking young people whether they oppose *all* war, the draft
boards are asking them to be Platonists. How can they know
how they would act in *any* situation? The real conscientious
opposition to war begins in your world with *your* war—the Second World War, Korea, Vietnam, or whatever. That may lead
you to a larger and deeper attitude, to be sure, but the old
distinction that I made between someone who is a pacifist in an
absolute and general sense and someone concerned only with a
particular war and therefore merely a political objector, I now
hold to be oversimple. I believe that there can be conscientious
objection to a single war or to any single situation. We cannot
create justice in the abstract; we cannot have peace in the abstract. We have to learn in each new situation where we shall
take our stand and say, "Here and no farther."

The confirmation which we receive in moral action is often
only the conviction that this is what is asked of us in this situation, strengthened perhaps by those images of man that we have
responded to and come into dialogue with—Socrates living and
dying for his dialectic, Jesus walking the lonesome valley that we
too have to walk, the Buddha being a lamp unto himself. It is
the confirmation that can come to any man who stands his
ground, finds his way, and responds with as much depth of
commitment as he can to the situation and the people who claim
him. It has nothing to do with moral perfection or being certain
that one is "in the right" and the other "in the wrong." The
sphere in which the image of man is created and sustained is the
sphere of the between. An image of man is a way of openness, a
way of responding, a way of being in relationship. We are
greatly helped on our road by the revelations of the hidden
human image in the lives of those who have gone before—those
who stood their ground, who witnessed for something, who
spoke a word which reaches us in our situation and speaks to our

condition. We walk in fellowship with them, responding to them with our lives and our actions—out of a concern as deep as the human, as real as the situation that faces us, as whole as we are able to be.

Danilo Dolci said that when he first heard about people burning draft files, it seemed an original thing to do. But later when he heard about more and more people burning draft files, he questioned whether taking the response to one unique situation and imitating it in another is really meaningful. Revolution as a way of life starts anew with each new situation. It takes courage to enter the situation and falter and not always be the master. But how could you be "master of the situation" without leaving the other persons out of account? The great American image of "mastery" as strength, and hesitation as weakness, is really an image of monologue, of leaving out the other person's point of view. The human image is reborn not in our mastery but in our bewilderment, our anguish, our self-doubt, in our losing ourself in the situation or relationship and letting ourself be changed. Ultimately, images of man are relational, and they cannot be known outside of the dialogue between man and man, between person and situation. To bring all that we are, including our anxiety about our adequacy, into the situation or relationship and allow it to be reborn—that is the true revealing of the hidden human image.

In the age of the antihero, the man who stands for something must witness for it with his death. The murder of the social hero has often been depicted in literature—Kyo and Katov in Malraux's novel *Man's Fate*, Pietro Spina in Ignazio Silone's *Seed Beneath the Snow*, Tom Joad and Jim Casey in Steinbeck's *The Grapes of Wrath*, and the permanent disappearance underground of the black hero of Ralph Ellison's *The Invisible Man*. Life has more than kept pace with literature. The assassination a half century ago of Maurice Jaurès in France and the brutal murders of Gustav Landauer, Rosa Luxembourg, Karl Liebknecht, and Walther Rathenau in Germany have been paralleled in our days by the assassination of Trotsky in Mexico, of Gandhi in India, of Malcolm X, Medgar Evers, Martin Luther King, John F. Kennedy, and Robert Kennedy in the United States.

The degradation of man is both fruit and root of the degeneration of the life between man and man. Cain's question "Am I my brother's keeper?" might be formulated, "Am I the keeper of the human image?" For it is in open immediacy between man and man that the human image is ever again created and confirmed, and it is in the closing up and choking off of that immediacy that it is tarnished and destroyed. As terrible as the extermination of the six million Jews and a million Gypsies by the Nazis was the Nazis' systematic attempt totally to dehumanize their victims before they herded them into the gas chambers. But there are other, less conscious ways in which the life between man and man is destroyed. One is that crisis of motives that prevents us from taking either our own or others' motives at face value and reduces much of the transaction between men to a game of mutual unmasking and seeing through, whether in terms of psychological, social, economic, political, or ideological hidden causes, which, once unearthed, are taken to be the true and complete explanation of all our actions. If *one* television show is dedicated to finding out "What's My Line?" untold millions of interpersonal relations are focused on the question "What's *your* line?" "What is it that you really want out of me and why?"

A corollary and even more potent source of social and existential mistrust is the widespread tendency to polarize the concrete reality of our situation into a set of catchwords, a life-destroying, life-denying Either/Or that demands one be *for* the Establishment or *against*, *for* the Free World or *against*, *for* Black Power or *against*, *for* the state of Israel or *against*, *for* America or *against*, *for* the New Left or *against*. Our life together has become so politicized that abstract slogans are taken for concrete reality and qualifications of these slogans for equivocation. The Modern Promethean shows himself today in sloganeering, polarization and politicization, in both the violent *and* nonviolent when they are dogmatic, when what they use is concealed vio-

lence, when what they do, in fact, is either to preserve the violence of the *status quo* or to build a new violence into the
situation in their reaction against the *status quo*.
For Chaucer in *The Canterbury Tales* and for Archibald Mac-
Leish in *J. B.*, Job is a symbol of patience, humility, and blind
faith. For Herman Melville in *Moby Dick*, the Book of Job is a
symbol of the terror of man before nature and before the problem of evil. For Thomas Hardy in *Jude the Obscure*, Job is a
symbol of the Modern Exile, of the terrible curse of the day of
his birth, which stands at the beginning of the biblical poem but
at the end of Hardy's novel. For Dostoevsky in *The Brothers
Karamazov*, Job is consciously split into two opposite symbols:
For Ivan Karamazov, Job stands for rebellion against the injustice of creation; for Father Zossima, he stands for humble love
and trust.

For me, in contrast, Job is neither the man of blind faith nor
the rebel blindly striking out. He is the man who brings his
contending within his dialogue with God. Job experiences the
renewal and deepening of trust only after the realization of the
bitterest exile and the expression of the bitterest rebellion. My
Job is not the Job of the Prologue who says, "The Lord gives, the
Lord takes away. Blessed be the name of the Lord," but the Job
of the poem itself who begins by cursing the day of his birth. He
is the man who loses all ground beneath his feet, who walks
through the abyss of absurdity and despair, and who uses that
very groundlessness as the ground on which to contend: "It is all
one. I despise my life. Therefore, I say He mocks at the calamity
of the guiltless." Even in recognizing that he is in God's hand
("He may slay me. I await it."), Job insists that he will argue his
ways before God and comforts himself with the thought that
hypocrites like his friends, who cannot face the dreadful reality
of God, cannot come before God's face. My Job is an image of
the renewal of trust after exile, but he is equally an image of the
impossibility of such renewal had Job not had the courage to
trust and contend, the two together.

If I speak of the existential trust that is present in the Modern

Job, the trust that is possible in the Dialogue with the Absurd, that is not to be interpreted as another world view, something which can be used to shut out the reality of the otherness which is going to be grotesque and absurd in great measure. We must avoid both the sentimental optimism which tries to reassert the lost order because it thinks it would be horrible if we did not have it and the sentimental pessimism which spends its time bewailing that the world is not the way that we would have it, rational and clear. There is a meaning which *can* be confirmed insofar as each of us individually and as a community and as a people has revealed the hidden human image in his or her situation. To limit ourselves to *this* meaning does not mean despair, nihilism, or the abyss. It means that we can live without a *Weltanschauung*, or world view.

I have been chided for calling Martin Luther King a Modern Job. Job in the Bible was with himself, perhaps with God too, I was told, but he never got out, like Martin Luther King, to meet life "out there." Job had a lot of "hang-ups" which he did not work through until the end of the story, whereas Martin Luther King must have worked through his hang-ups before he was able to go out and act. This point of view arises in the first instance because one thinks of man's relationship with God as quite unconnected with his relationship to existence. In the second instance it psychologizes even the relationship to God into man's working through his own inner problems. Martin Luther King was a black man in a new age who helped it become a new age, and the problem for him, as for Job, was the problem of existential trust—of trust in existence itself. Job cursed, not God, but the day of his birth. Modern man does not have Job's biblical trust. Yet there may be sufficient trust that an atheist like Camus and his hero Dr. Rieux can continue to enter into Dialogue with the Absurd and find meaning. And where do we find the absurd but in our existence itself, in the modern crisis of values, in the situation of the breakdown of dialogue, the growth of mistrust on every level—social, political, international, and existential? Our real existence, that is where we have to wrestle with the problem and not in some theological question as to whether in addition to all this there exists some metaphysical absolute. It does not matter if a man is an atheist like Camus so long as he is open to what faces him and goes out to meet it. Reality is met in the meeting itself—even in situations like the plague, the Nazi occupation of France, Hiroshima, Biafra, Vietnam, Bangladesh, and Auschwitz, in which man and the image of man have been all but destroyed.

The Modern Promethean, unlike the ancient one, does not rebel on the ground of order, on the ground of immortality, or on the ground of foresight, as we find it in Aeschylus' *Prometheus Bound*. Rather he rebels against all order. He rebels not only because he wants to recapture the creative freedom of man which has been alienated to the transcendent, but also because of the desperation which makes him believe that he stands in an all-or-nothing situation. He desperately defies the inhuman world, which he sees as indifferent to man, or the inhuman social and political order, which he sees as crushing man. As Captain Ahab in Melville's *Moby Dick* believes he must destroy the White Whale or it will destroy him, so the social and political rebel believes he has to destroy his enemy or be destroyed by him, whether that enemy is seen as a ruling class, the government in power, another nation, or a coalition of nations. Underneath his romantic rebellion lies a philosophy of despair. For our human existence, in the simplest terms, is an existence which places us over against the reality that comes to meet us, whether this be nature or other men or other countries, and we cannot remove this facing quality of our existence. If we cannot remove it, must we submit to whatever we meet? No. It is possible to hold our ground before it. But to do this there has to be that existential trust which the Modern Promethean does not have. Existential trust does not mean the belief that values already exist "out there." But it does mean an openness to finding values in genuine dialogue, even in the Dialogue with the Absurd.

The path from the Modern Promethean to the Modern Job is one that we are forced to take by the very situation in which we find ourselves. Eighteenth-century man could hope for a peace based on a universal human nature and a universal society patterned on the harmony of a Newtonian world order. Nineteenth-century man could reject this universal harmony in favor of the competitive struggle of each nation against the other, rationalized perhaps, in Nietzschean fashion, as the creation of higher values through the dialectical conflict of each people's "will to power." In the last half-century this view has been increasingly supplanted by that of the Modern Promethean, who sees the competing "world power" as an alien and hostile reality, like Ahab's White Whale, a reality that must be destroyed if one's own civilization and culture is to flourish. Now, however, we are in a situation in which it is no longer possible to think of the destruction of the other civilization as the road to creativity and freedom for one's own. The danger of unimaginable destruction and annihilation that today threatens all nations alike has established, writes Reinhold Niebuhr, a sense of community "across the chasm of a great ideological and power conflict."

If this community is rightly called a "community of fear,"* it is, nonetheless, the starting point from which the Modern Job may enter into dialogue with the absurd, affirming the existence of the other even while contending with him. The only alternative to ideology is not another and better ideology but (what Camus repeatedly called for) the willingness to talk even with those who are not "like-minded," those who do not share our rationales and our world views. We cannot minimize the otherness of the civilizations that oppose us, an otherness which may often seem to us alien and absurd. Yet we must affirm and contend, like the Modern Job, trusting that meaning can come in wrestling with the absurd and recognizing that it is only here that meaning can be found.

The all-embracing, all-suffocating "cold war" and its cancerous outgrowth, the war in Indochina, lend a special, dreadful rele-

---

* Harrison Brown and James Real, *Community of Fear*, Foreword by Reinhold Niebuhr (Santa Barbara, Calif.: Center for the Study of Democratic Institutions, 1960).

vance to the Modern Job. We live in an era which makes it increasingly meaningless for any nation to declare that it is perfectly willing to make peace *entirely on its own terms.* It is not just that this is contradictory to ordinary common sense; it has to do with the situation in which we find ourselves. We cannot make the world "safe for democracy" any more than the Communist nations can make it safe for Communism. Each nation and each bloc of nations finds itself facing an enemy it must often oppose but cannot eliminate. If this is so, then the greater strength, the greater nobility, the greater heroism, and the greater courage would be to emulate Martin Luther King; that is, to hold our ground when we meet other countries and cultures, yet to confirm them even in opposing.

We are so used to the stereotype of the unreconciled rebel that we interpret the ending of the Book of Job to mean that he was no rebel at all. Yet the strongest rebellion is that which is able to hold its ground *and* confirm the other. Only this double action prevents that transformation of rebellion into new tyranny against which Camus warns. The Modern Promethean's fight against what oppresses him—that fight which surely must have been in the hearts of many of those in Selma after the brutalities of the first day of the march and of other fighters for justice and equality on countless occasions since then—is part of us too; we cannot ignore it. Yet we have to bring it into the larger framework of the Modern Job. In the Modern Job, exile and rebellion become a way of man—a way for individuals but also, in this hour of confrontations, a way for races and for peoples.

Rebel we must if we do not simply want to settle down into alienation or if we do not simply want to deepen the alienation of which we become aware. We must rebel in order to exist, and, what is more, we all must go through the rebellion of the Modern Promethean, the rebellion of the Either/Or, of all or nothing. We cannot expect all our rebellions to be strong and courageous ones. But the heroic, desperate, despairing rebellion of those who can mostly succeed only in destroying and cannot deal with the existence that comes to meet them is less courageous, less mature than the rebellion of those who, even in the face of absurdity, can still hold their ground and contend. The rebellion of the Modern Job points the way toward the ever-new revelation of the hidden human image.

Black Power, New Politics, women's liberation, civil disobedience—all these can be either the rebellion of the Modern Promethean or that of the Modern Job. Whether the balance lies toward the one or toward the other is more important for our society and for the persons and groups that make it up than what particular slogan triumphs or what particular cause is inscribed on the banner of the social actionist. "We cannot escape history," says Camus. "We are in it up to our necks." But we can fight within it for that part which is man's, attacking all the ideologies that claim the day. In this time of abstractions, this "vast conspiracy of silence" which threatens to destroy the living dialogue of mankind, someone is needed to give a meaning to everyday life. This is the Modern Job, the rebel to whom I point.

It is not just the Modern Job that I celebrate, but the Modern Rebel out of which he develops. I celebrate this Rebel because of what he is and because of what he can become. I celebrate him in his anguish, his honesty, in his refusal to give up his rebellion, and I hope for him that he may learn to find a ground of his own from which he can go forth to meet others openly, responding out of his own uniqueness to the unique demand of the situation as he hears it. I celebrate him in his witness for his comrades and his leaders, and I hope that he may grow to the strength where he can stand alone when necessary. I trust in his courage to persevere through the dark times ahead—affirming where he can affirm and withstanding where he must withstand. I wish for him a clear-sighted trust beyond idealistic enthusiasm and disillusioned bitterness, awaiting the time when new possibilities of personal and social witness and of effective social action open up.

My hope for the Modern Rebel is also a tribute to all the many comrades who have grown from strength to strength and have kept fresh in their hearts their own images of authentic personal and social existence, moving in this direction each time their breath returned to them after being knocked down. From the gropings and contradictions of the Modern Rebel there may yet emerge a new trust in existence, a new image of what it can mean to be human in a time of the eclipse of man.

INDEX